Water and the Chinese Culture

高京燕　韩福乐　李慧敏　周艳芳　于　敏　王晓燕　译

·北京·

内 容 提 要

空气和水乃人类生存绵延之必需。限于科技水平与认知能力，先民对无色无味的空气描述和作为并不多。与其他民族一样，自古以来，中华民族关于水的故事数不胜数，大禹治水、精卫填海、哪吒闹海等。

老子在《道德经》第八章写道："上善若水。水善利万物而不争，处众人之所恶，故几于道。……夫唯不争，故无尤。"老子赞扬水，因之与善同类，以示弱、利他的原则存于世；以不争而得理想心境。"知者乐水，仁者乐山。知者动，仁者静……"这是儒家学派的创立者孔子传世的名言。知者，即智者，指那些思维敏捷、反应迅速的人能够因势利导，迅速适应世界的变化，故与水同质，柔和、多变；仁者稳定厚重，故如山般。孔子眼中，水可以为善也可以为恶。

中国人爱水、赞水、怕水，也开动智力利用水。水可以用来表达思想，儒道墨家，老子、孔子、管子、墨子都拿水来说事传道，农业、政治、战争和工程的发展也都和水息息相关，文学、艺术和民俗中也无法脱离水的痕迹。本书作者阅古观今，打破学科界限，收集中华大地自南至北、从东到西形成的丰富而独特的中华水文化。本书共十三章，除第一章绪论外，分别以水与中华文明、水与农业、水与政治、水与战争、水与工程、水与儒家、水与道家、水与管子、水与墨家、水与文学、水与艺术、水与民俗为题，试图描绘中华水文化的巨幅画卷。我们看到中国人与水相亲，也与水相恶；从口头相传到文字和实物记录，中华水文化塑造了中国人独特的气质，折射了中国人的精神，是中华文明独特的组成部分。

图书在版编目（CIP）数据

中华水文化 = Water and the Chinese Culture : 英文 / 高京燕等译. -- 北京 : 中国水利水电出版社, 2021.7
ISBN 978-7-5226-0475-6

Ⅰ.①中… Ⅱ.①高… Ⅲ.①水－文化－中国－英文 Ⅳ.①K928.4

中国版本图书馆CIP数据核字(2022)第024609号

书 名	**Water and the Chinese Culture**
作 者	高京燕　韩福乐　李慧敏　周艳芳　于　敏　王晓燕　译
出版发行	中国水利水电出版社 （北京市海淀区玉渊潭南路1号D座　100038） 网址：www.waterpub.com.cn E - mail：sales@mwr.gov.cn 电话：（010）68545888（营销中心）
经 售	北京科水图书销售有限公司 电话：（010）68545874、63202643 全国各地新华书店和相关出版物销售网点
排 版	北京时代澄宇科技有限公司
印 刷	清淞永业（天津）印刷有限公司
规 格	184mm×260mm　16开本　22印张　560千字
版 次	2021年7月第1版　2021年7月第1次印刷
定 价	**90.00元**

凡购买我社图书，如有缺页、倒页、脱页的，本社营销中心负责调换
版权所有·侵权必究

译者序

国家级精品在线课程《中华水文化》配套教材的英译本经过华北水利水电大学几位译者的共同努力，终于奉献给广大读者了。

《中华水文化》在华北水利水电大学国家级教学名师毕雪燕教授及其团队成员：杨华轲、罗玲谊、陈超、刘明、张建松和朱伟利几位老师的共同努力下编纂而成。以该书为依托的《中华水文化》课程在中国大学慕课运行短短几个学期就受到了热烈的欢迎，每学期的学习人数高达15000余人，来自各行各业的学习者积极参与并就书中内容进行热烈讨论，无论是从大禹治水中感受伟大的精神，还是从道家思想中明白"上善若水"的真谛，古老却又焕发着勃勃青春的中华水文化都滋养了数以万计的水文化学习者。

中文版《中华水文化》是国家级精品课程《中华水文化》配套教材。近期，又荣获了一系列新的荣誉：它被列为河南省高等教育重大项目——黄河流域水文化遗产保护和利用现状研究（2018—YYZD-22）、河南省"十四五"普通高等教育规划教材（重点立项）共同研究成果，也是河南省教育教学改革项目——黄河文化多维度融入高校课程体系育人模式教学探索与实践研究成果（2019SJGLX289）、河南省哲学社会科学规划项目——新时代中国特色社会主义视域下的道家核心思想创新性转化研究（2019BZX010）。

《中华水文化》英译本由华北水利水电大学国际交流与合作处牵头组织翻译，用作海外孔子学院读物、来华留学生学历教育和中资水利水电企业员工培训辅助教材等。所有参与翻译的译者无不竭尽全力、精益求精，力图向读者传递出中华水文化的博大精深及无穷奥妙，向世界阐释推介具有中国特色、体现中国精神、蕴藏中国智慧的优秀文化。主要参加翻译的人员如下：高京燕、韩福乐、李慧敏、周艳芳、于敏、王晓燕、Philippe Gourbesville（法）和Cody Allen Turner（美）。此外，还有不少同事和相关专业人士为翻译工作提供了各种各样的方便和帮助，我们对他们所予的支持、所做的工作和提供的帮助表示衷心的感谢。

我们同时也要感谢毕雪燕教授的团队，没有他们精彩的论著，就不可能有机会在这里将中华水文化用英语娓娓道出，将中华民族的智慧传播到世界的舞台！更多地还要感谢中国水利水电出版社的编辑老师，是你们让中华水文化的各种精妙跃然纸上！

因原文以水为线索，串联起古往今来的水历史、水故事、水经典、水哲理等，涵盖面广，融合了大量中华文化内涵，涉及较多文言文、传统文化概念等，本书适合对中华文化有一定了解基础的读者，或对中华文化怀有兴趣的读者。译者在翻译的过程中面临诸多挑战，我们力求忠实原文，尽可能选用适合海内外读者阅读习惯的语言形式，尽可能从海内外读者的视角重现中国古代人民的智慧和想法，帮助读者从人类赖以生存的基础自然资源——水的角度，理解中华文化内涵，传播中华文化正能量。但鉴于译者水平所限，加之时间仓促，偏颇之处在所难免，恳请各位读者斧正。

Preface

The English translation of the textbook accompanying the national quality online course "Water and the Chinese Culture" is finally available to the public after the joint efforts of several translators from North China University of Water Resources and Hydropower(NCWU).

The book *Water and the Chinese Culture* was compiled by Prof. Bi Xueyan, the national renowned teacher of NCWU, and her team members including Yang Huake, Luo Lingyi, Chen Chao, Liu Ming, Zhang Jiansong and Zhu Weili. With the book as backbone, *Water and the Chinese Culture* MOOC has received great popularity since its launch a few semesters ago. For each semester, the number of learners reached 15,000 covering all walks of life. The ancient but vibrant Chinese culture related to water has nourished tens of thousands of the learners from the great spirit of Yu's flood control to the essence of Taoism that "Great Virtue is Like Water".

Recently, the book *Water and the Chinese Culture* has further won a series of awards. It was listed as the Higher Education Major Project of Henan Province-research on the protection and utilization of the Yellow River Basin water culture heritage, "14th Five-Year Plan" Regular Higher Education Programming Teaching Material of Henan Province, Teaching Reform Project of Henan Province, as well as Philosophy and Social Sciences Programming Project of Henan Province.

The English version of *Water and the Chinese Culture* was translated under the lead of NCWU International Office, to provide students at Confucius Institute, foreign students in China and overseas staff of Chinese hydro-power enterprises with reading materials. All the translators devoted themselves to the translation for precision and perfection, tried to unfold the extensive and profound charm of the Chinese culture from the perspective of water. The translators include Gao Jingyan, Han Fule, Li Huimin, Zhou Yanfang, Yu Min, Wang Xiaoyan and Cody Allen Turner (American). In addition, colleagues and professionals have also provided supports. Thanks for their assistance!

We'd like to thank the team of Prof. Bi Xueyan, without whose works we never have the opportunity to narrate the Chinese stories related to water in English. Besides, more thanks shall be given to the editors of China Water & Power Press for their efforts on the delicate publication.

Since the original text was themed with water, telling the Chinese history, stories, classics, and philosophies relevant to water, there involved an abundance of classical Chinese and traditional cultural concepts, for which translators confronted many challenges during the translation. Thus, the book is more appropriate to those with a basic understanding or interest of the Chinese culture. We, translators, took the principle of being faithful to the original and tried the best to express in the ways conforming to the audience's reading habits. But because of the limited competences and time constraint, it is inevitable to that some errors or biases remain within the current document. We are eager to receive your corrections!

Contents

Chapter One   **Introduction** ·· 1

    Section I   Defining Water Culture ··· 1
    Section II   Water Culture Plays an Important Role ··························· 2

Chapter Two   **Water and the Chinese Civilization** ·· 5

    Section I   The Yellow River: the Cradle of the Chinese Civilization ············ 5
    Section II   Water and the Yellow River Civilization ······························ 19
    Section III   The Yangtze River—Another River Breeding the Chinese Civilization ··· 29
    Section IV   The Rise and Fall of the Yangtze River Culture ················ 38
    Section V   Yu and Flood Control Stories ··· 42
    Section VI   Yu and the Chinese Civilization ·· 48

Chapter Three   **Water and Agriculture** ·· 54

    Section I   Water and Farmland Infrastructure ···································· 54
    Section II   Water and Water Conservancy Tools for Agricultural Use ············ 69
    Section III   Water and Customs Related to Agricultural Production ············ 77

Chapter Four   **Water and Politics** ·· 83

    Section I   Water Management and Governance of China ················ 83
    Section II   Wise Rulers' Governance of Water and National Prosperity ············ 87
    Section III   Virtuous Officials' Management of Water and National Prosperity ·· 95
    Section IV   Water, Country and People ··· 109
    Section V   Water and the Construction of the Ancient Cities ············ 113

Chapter Five   **Water and Wars** ··· 124

    Section I   Fight for Water ·· 124
    Section II   Water-aided War ··· 133

    Section Ⅲ   Water as Soldiers ·· 141

Chapter Six   Water and Water Conservancy Projects ··············· 150

    Section Ⅰ   Irrigation Projects ·· 150
    Section Ⅱ   Canal Projects ··· 166
    Section Ⅲ   Embankment Projects ·· 178
    Section Ⅳ   Water Diversion Projects ··· 198

Chapter Seven   Water and Confucianism ··· 213

    Section Ⅰ   The Wise Delight in Water ··· 213
    Section Ⅱ   Comparing Water to People's Virtue ······························ 217
    Section Ⅲ   Comparing Water to Country Governance ······················ 220
    Section Ⅳ   Unity of Man and Nature ·· 223

Chapter Eight   Water and Taoism ··· 226

    Section Ⅰ   The Highest Good is Like that of Water ························ 226
    Section Ⅱ   Models with Virtue of Water ·· 229
    Section Ⅲ   Actionless Administration ··· 231
    Section Ⅳ   The Enlightenment of Actionless Administration ············ 232
    Section Ⅴ   The Soft Triumphs over the Hard ·································· 234

Chapter Nine   Water and Guanzi's Ideology ··· 239

    Section Ⅰ   Water is the Origin of the World ··································· 239
    Section Ⅱ   Water and Self-cultivation as well as Statecraft ············· 240
    Section Ⅲ   Water and Governance ··· 242
    Section Ⅳ   Water and Choice of Residential Environment ··············· 246

Chapter Ten   Water and Mohist Ideology ··· 248

    Section Ⅰ   Manners of Yu and Universal Love ································ 248
    Section Ⅱ   Self-cultivation through Clarifying Morality by Water ···· 250
    Section Ⅲ   Water and Non-attack ··· 252

Chapter Eleven   Water and Literature ··· 254

    Section Ⅰ   Water and Poetry ·· 254
    Section Ⅱ   Water and Lyrics ··· 262
    Section Ⅲ   Water and Fu ··· 268
    Section Ⅳ   Water and Essay ·· 272
    Section Ⅴ   Water and Novel ·· 276

Chapter Twelve　Water and Art ·· 285

 Section Ⅰ　Water and Painting ·· 285
 Section Ⅱ　Water and Music ··· 290
 Section Ⅲ　Water and Dance ··· 297

Chapter Thirteen　Water and Folkways ·· 304

 Section Ⅰ　Water, Birth and Wedding Customs ························· 304
 Section Ⅱ　Water and Funeral Customs ··································· 309
 Section Ⅲ　Praying for Water ··· 312
 Section Ⅳ　Suppression of Water Monsters ······························ 321
 Section Ⅴ　Water and Festival Activities of the Han People ········ 327
 Section Ⅵ　Water-related Festivals and the Ethnic Groups ·········· 337

Chapter One Introduction

Section I Defining Water Culture

Culture is one of the inclusive concepts that have attracted the great interest of many intellectuals worldwide. Critics have exhausted themselves by approaching it from a wide variety of perspectives and given as many as over one hundred distinctive definitions. Readers are at a loss to find one all-agreed definition. Some define culture as the arts and other manifestations of intellectual achievements collectively, which differs from economy, politics, and other sectors. Others define it as the sum of the customary beliefs, social forms and other activities practiced by a particular people or a social group. It creates, maintains and develops the inner spirit of a particular social group.

We could see that culture, in a general sense, is the sum of material and intellectual achievements. In a narrow sense, it merely refers to the intellectual achievements made by humans, like language, literature, arts and ideology. In this book, when we talk about culture, we borrow its general sense and take it as the sum of material and intellectual products.

Water culture is part of culture. It refers to the cultural phenomena, customs, values, and principles generated when humans live with water. Water culture is an issue that is both old and new. We say water culture is ancient because it has been an integral part of human life since the birth of humans. We say water culture is a new concept because it is in the late 1980s that Chinese intellectuals coined the term and initiated the systematic study of it. Water culture also includes two parts, that is, the material and intellectual aspects. Water is an integral part of human life, and it is related to our ways of thinking, literature and art. In this book, we will examine water in its relation to other sectors, such as water and the Chinese civilization, water and agriculture, water and politics, water and war, water and engineering, water and philosophy, water and literature, water and art, water and folk customs, etc.

Section II Water Culture Plays an Important Role

Till now, the Earth is the only planet in the universe where life has been found. Without water, there would be no life on the earth. Water breeds humans and it has been an integral part of human life. We could offer enough evidence to show that the human history has been a history of getting to know the importance of water, admitting to the power of water, governing water and developing water resources. In other words, the Chinese people have pushed their civilization forward while combating floods and droughts.

1. Water Breeds the Ancient Civilizations

Each region breeds a civilization with its own characteristics. Throughout the world history, the birthplaces of the early civilizations were all close to the rivers. The four ancient civilizations emerged and developed in regions situated at 30–40 degrees north latitude. For example, the ancient Egyptian civilization was founded along the Nile, the ancient Indus Valley civilization was built along the Indus River, the ancient Babylonian civilization was in the areas of the Tigris and Euphrates, and the Chinese civilization was found along the middle and lower reaches of the Yellow River. The four oldest civilizations occurred in this geographical area, like pearls dotting a belt around the earth. In addition, without water, the marine civilization and the grassland civilization would not develop.

2. Water Culture is an Important Part of Culture

Living with water, the Chinese people have not only accumulated enormous material wealth, but also made great intellectual achievements. The long-term water management activities have formulated the Chinese spirit. Water culture is an indispensable part of the culture which had been formed and developed by the Chinese ancestors while having lived in nature and combated natural disasters for thousands of years.

Water culture has grown with agriculture alongside the construction of water conservancy projects. Over 2,000 years ago, the ancient Chinese observed the changing patterns of the natural world, the climate, the turning of the seasons, precipitation, and astronomy. They measured and divided the sun's annual motion in the ecliptic plane into twenty-four equal parts and created the twenty-four solar terms that provided a schedule for agricultural activities in ancient China. Even till this day, their discoveries still guide the lives and traditions of hundreds of millions of Chinese people. Many folk customs were formed around the twenty-four terms. China had put in use many water conservancy projects. A rich and colourful engineering culture has grown out of the construction and operation of these projects. Inspired by water, the ancient Chinese sages brought with them a lot of philosophical thoughts. For example, Laozi quoted water more than one time to highlight his perception. He wrote, "The best of men is like water as water benefits all things and does not compete with them" and "water is the weakest object but it can win over the strongest objects". Confucius likened morality to water, putting forward to the idea that "the wise delights in water and the virtuous delights in mountains". He promoted the state of equilibrium and harmony and believed that one could better himself and live a happier life when indulged into the mountains and water. The philosophers were not the only ones who resorted to water for their expressions. Numerous writers also alluded to water to state their emotions or ideas. Li Yu was a famous poet and a dethroned emperor of South Tang Dynasty during the Five Dynasties period (907-979). In his captivity by the new emperor who built the Song Dynasty, Li Yu used water to allude to his endless sorrow in his famous poem, "To the Tune of Yu Mei Ren", "How much sorrow do I have? It is like the spring flood of a long river flowing east!" Wang Bo, one of the greatest poets in the early Tang Dynasty wrote in "A Tribute to King Teng's Tower", "A solitary wild duck flies alongside the multi-coloured sunset clouds, and the autumn water is merged with the boundless sky into one hue." Besides those poetic lines describing water, the ancient Chinese scholars also included water in a large number of four-character phrases or popular sayings. To list some among many, in a popular phrase "di shui zhi en, yong quan xiang bao", "shui" means "water" and "quan" refers "spring", which can be explained as "Little help brings great returns." Another well-known saying, "Shui ke zai zhou, yi ke fu zhou" means "Water either can carry or capsize a boat", an often-quoted analogy to remind the rulers of the terrible consequence of neglecting the well-being of the common people. All in all, these phrases show that water does matter a lot to the Chinese culture, as it does to other cultures. Mastering the essence of an excellent culture, one can unconsciously improve oneself in his or her deeds, thoughts, and taste in life. The charm of culture lies in this. Similarly, learning water culture will benefit us a lot.

3. Water Culture Boosts One's Cultural Confidence

In his report to the 19th National Congress of the Communist Party of China, President Xi Jinping proposed that China strengthens cultural confidence to promote the prosperity of culture with socialist characteristics. Without full confidence in the Chinese culture, a rich and prosperous culture, the Chinese nation will not be able to rejuvenate itself. China will develop a creative socialist culture with Chinese characteristics. Then, what is cultural confidence? Cultural confidence lies in full confidence in the vitality of the culture and requires the positive cultural practice of a nation and a political party to realize its values. Culture reflects the spiritual pursuits of a nation and has always been the driving force for the Chinese people to seek greatness and strength.

A nation that has no confidence in its culture cannot stand steady in the world. The unique culture is the backbone of each nation. To build cultural confidence, people need to have a better understanding of the culture. A document issued by the Chinese government in 2017 called on students of all levels to learn traditional Chinese culture. Only by getting to know their own culture, could the Chinese people build the confidence in their nation. And the familiarity with the national culture will help the Chinese people realize their pursuit of peace and prosperity. In addition, culture is also a global language, with which the Chinese people could communicate with the world. The more one knows about each other, the more understandings one will give to people of other nations. Water culture, as one branch of culture, plays the similar role. As of now, more than 100 Confucius Institutes and over 1,000 Confucius classrooms have been built in more than 100 nations and regions, making it more convenient for the Chinese people to share their culture with the world.

4. Water Culture Helps Cultivating a Sound Personality

Culture can help shape one's spirit and taste. Learning water culture would also help one shape a sound, noble personality. For example, when seeing the water dripping from the pipes, some might turn a blind eye while some will turn the tap off because they couldn't bear to see water wasted. Some would even go far to praise the dripping water for it drips continuously and one day it might wear through the rock. People differ greatly with different values.

As for saving water, some people believe that they can afford the expenses no matter how high water price is and they would love to use water as they please. In contrast, some will save water as they can because they are worried about the exhaustion of water in the future of the earth. For them, to save water is not a matter of expenses but a matter of life or death. The awareness of saving water can be improved when humans are taught to know the worldwide shortage of water. The world examined related to water is also part of water culture.

5. Water Shortage and Water Pollution

Currently, such issues like water shortage and water pollution are getting increasingly serious. In 2018, Wang Xinlu, a member of the National Committee of the Chinese People's Political Consultative Conference said, "At present, the development of water resources cannot keep up with the fast-escalating demands in life and economic activities in China. Fresh water resource per capita in China is 2,100 m^3, accounting for 28% of the world average. Water quality in nearly one third of China's seven major rivers is worrying. Among 4,778 groundwater monitoring points in China, the proportion of poor and extremely poor water quality is close to 60%. On average, more than 1,700 water pollution incidents occur every year, threatening the safety of drinking water of nearly 300 million people."

Water shortage and water pollution coexist in a way, which is threatening human lives. To cherish water is a way to protect nature and humans. Therefore, to adopt a scientific attitude towards water, to protect water and live in harmony with water is what humans should do.

Chapter Two Water and the Chinese Civilization

Section I The Yellow River: the Cradle of the Chinese Civilization

The ancient Chinese created the splendid Chinese civilization. As early as 5,000 years ago, the Chinese ancestors had already inhabited the middle and lower reaches of the Yellow River, the Yangtze River and along the Liaohe River. Archaeological documents show that the Chinese civilization is featured with unity, diversity, plurality, inclusiveness and continuity.

The early civilizations were bred near the rivers. The ancient Egyptian civilization was founded along the Nile, the ancient Indus Valley civilization was built along the Indus River and the ancient Babylonian civilization grew in the areas of the Tigris and Euphrates. In ancient China, the Yellow River and the Yangtze River bred the Chinese civilization. Among the four oldest civilizations, the Chinese civilization is the only one that has continued to this day.

Since the ancient times, the Yellow River had been regarded as the mother river of the Chinese nation. It's a "holy river" in the minds of the Chinese descendants. The Yellow River provided water, the source of life, to the Chinese people who inhabited along the river and nourished them for generations. Besides, it is a cultural sign that has been rooted in the blood of the Chinese people. It has forged the soul, the spirit, and the character of the Chinese nation.

1. The Yellow River

The 5,464 km (about 3,395 miles) Yellow River is the second longest in China and the fifth longest river in the world. Originating in Bayan Har Mountains in north-western Qinghai Province, the Yellow River runs through nine provinces and autonomous regions on its way to the Bohai Sea. Glancing from a bird's-eye view, the river has numerous bends and the trunk stream, taking the shape of the Chinese character "几" that winds through a large part of China. Its total drainage area is about 750,000 km². There are countless branches and tributaries feeding it through its course. The trunk stream of the Yellow River consists of the upper, middle and lower reaches.

Water and the Chinese Culture

Figure 2-1 The Zigzag Yellow River

(1) The Upper Reaches

The upper reaches of the Yellow River constitute a segment starting from its source in the Bayan Har Mountains and ending at Hekou Town, Togtoh County, in Inner Mongolia Autonomous Region. This segment has a total length of about 3,471.6 km, with a total drainage area of about 428,000 km^2, accounting for 53.8% of the total. Heyuan is called "Maqu" by the local people in which "Ma" means "peacock" in Tibetan while "Qu" "the river". Then "Maqu" means "Peacock River". The Yellow River flows through the junction of the Tibetan Plateau and the Loess Plateau, where Longyang Gorge was found. On one side of Longyang Gorge, one can see the rugged mountains, and on the other side one can see the continuous wilderness. Because of its geographical functions, the Yellow River skirts around mountains and becomes interchangeably narrow or wide, forming gorges of various shapes and width, including the longest Laga Gorge, the narrowest Yehu Gorge and the steepest Longyang Gorge.

The length of the section from Xiaheyan to Hekou Town is 990 km. It is a wide and shallow alluvial river. Here one can have a glimpse of the fertile Ningxia Plain and Inner Mongolia Hetao Plain.

(2) The Middle Reaches

In the upper section of the middle reaches of the Yellow River there are mainly mountains and plateaus whereas the lower part of the middle reaches are mainly plains and hills. The middle reaches of the Yellow River start from Hekou Town and end in Taohuayu of Zhengzhou City, Henan Province. The Yellow River takes a sudden turn southward and speeds its way for as long as 725 km to Yumenkou with a drop of 607 m. The turbulent River splits the Loess Plateau into two parts, forming a river course running through the canyon dividing Shanxi Province and Shaanxi Province. So the valley here is called Jin-Shaan Valley (Jin is short for Shanxi while Shaan for Shaanxi). On both sides of Jin-Shaan Valley are Loess Plateau with loose soil and severe soil erosion. However, there are as many as 56 tributaries that are longer than 100 km. The drainage area of the valley is about 110,000 km^2, accounting for 15% of the whole drainage area. The tributaries in the Yellow River Basin contribute 900 million tons of mud and sand to the trunk stream every year, accounting for 56% of the silts annually discharged into the river (Fig. 2-2).

Figure 2-2 The Yellow River Has the World-largest Sediment Load Concentration

Emerging out of Jin-Shaan Valley, the river suddenly gets wider, starting to run slow and steady. From Yumenkou to Tongguan, the river course is 125 km long and its drop is 52 m, and the average width of the valley is 8.5 km. In this section, the river course has wide shoals with an area of up to 600 km^2. The surface of the shoal is 0.5-2.0 m above the water surface. Due to the drastic change resulting from scouring and silting and frequent moving of the trunk stream in this section, the river course has moved frequently. Therefore, there is a popular saying there, "on the east of the river for 30 years and then on the west for 30 years". When the river flows through Jin-Shaan Valley, it has many moraine currents. The famous Hukou Waterfall is the only waterfall along the trunk stream (Fig. 2-3).

The Yellow River flows 356 km eastward through Tongguan to Taohuayu of Zhengzhou City, Henan Province, with a drop of 231 m. The Loess gorge of 113 km above Sanmenxia (Sanmen Valley) has a wider course. From Sanmenxia to Mengjin, the river runs between Zhongtiao Hill and Xiaoshan Hill. It is the last valley before the Yellow River empties into the Bohai Sea. As the valley is situated in both Henan and Shanxi Province, so it is called Jin-Yu Valley. The Luohe River and the Qinhe River are the major tributaries in Sanmenxia-Taohuayu section. With the two rivers, this section saw more rainstorms than in other sections along the Yellow River. The

Figure 2-3 Hukou Waterfall, the Only Waterfall in the Trunk Stream of the Yellow River

rainstorms lead to floods in the lower reaches of the Yellow River(Fig. 2-4). Mengjin County is where the Yellow River runs from the mountainous area to the plain. This section is adjacent to Mangshan Hill in the south and Qingfengling in the north and dikes are built in some sections.

Figure 2-4 Flood in the Yellow River

The middle reaches flow through the Loess Plateau where, with the loose and easily eroded soil, the concentrated rainfall and the easily damaged natural vegetation, soil and water loss is particularly serious during the flood seasons in summer and autumn. Loads of silt are carried into the Yellow River from its tributaries and down to the lower reaches. The accumulations of these sediments led to the elevation of the river bed, forming a "hanging river".

(3) The Lower Reaches

The lower reaches of the Yellow River extend from Taohuayu to Haikou, with a drainage area of about 23,000 km^2, accounting for only 3% of the total drainage area. The gradient is steep in the upper part and gentle in the lower part. The lower reaches run through the North China Plain and is mostly controlled by dikes. The river runs relatively slow in the lower reaches and the accumulation of a large amount of sediment is constantly uplifted, the riverbed is 3 m to 5 m higher than the surface of the floodplain. Some river sections, such as Caogang of Fengqiu County, Henan Province, are 10 m higher than the ground, making it a world-famous "hanging river above the ground" and the watershed of the Huaihe River and the Haihe River.

The current course of the lower reaches is wide in the upper part and narrow in the lower part. The section from Taohuayu to Dongbatou in Lankao County of Henan Province is still the river course of Ming and Qing Dynasties and some dikes have a history of 300–500 years. The Dongbatou-Taochengpu section changed its course after the Yellow River burst in 1855. Then the River ran wild for twenty years before the dike was built. The old course of the Daqinghe River starts from Taochengpu.

The Yellow River is very unruly in the lower reaches and there have been frequent devastating floods and course changes. Over a history of about 4,000 years, the levees burst and overflew for more than 1,500 times. The flood affected the areas extending north to the Haihe River and south to the Huaihe River, which has had a great impact on the Huanghuaihai Plain. The river produces nearly 1.6 billion of sediment every year, of which 1.2 billion tons flow into the sea, and the remaining 400 million in the lower reaches, forming an alluvial plain. This has greatly influenced the Chinese civilization. On one hand, it brought disaster; on the other hand, it also connected the alluvial plains into the vast North China Plain (Fig. 2-5).

Figure 2-5　North China Plain

The Yellow River estuary is located between Bohai Bay and Laizhou Bay. In this coastal area the river is not turbulent but flat with the tidal range being about one meter. It has the weak tide and much sand, which is a continental estuary with frequent course swing. Since the early modern times, a large amount of sediment was transported to the estuary area and most of it was deposited in the coastal area, forming the Yellow River Estuary Delta. The delta has the fertile land. With the deposition, extension and swing of the Yellow River Estuary, the flow of the river changes accordingly. In history, the river course below Lijin had been changed frequently. Since 1949, its course has been changed artificially for three times, and the length of the river course in the estuary has also changed constantly. In the 1990s, the river estuary into the sea is a new channel formed by gradual deposition after artificial diversion through Qingshuigou in 1976. In the past 100 years, the river has been reclaimed to form a large area of new land.

The Yellow River Basin starts from Bayan Har Mountains in the west, reaches Yinshan Mountain in the north, reaches Qinling Mountain in the south, and finally empties into the Bohai Sea in the east. The Yellow River Basin originates from the plateau and mountainous areas and flows through the plain. This Basin is high in the west and low in the east, with great differences in elevation, forming three steps from west to east and from high to low. Due to the complex changes of topography, the Yellow River is characterized with silts, frequent course changes and floods, which makes it one of the famous rivers in the world.

2. The Yellow River Basin Offers Proper Natural Conditions for Crops Growth

The climate in the Yellow River Basin is mild and humid with four distinct seasons. The temperature and precipitation are conducive to the growth of crops. With many mountains, there is a great height difference between its east and west, and the geomorphology of each area differs greatly. Located in the middle latitude zone, the basin is affected by the atmospheric and monsoon circulation. Therefore, there are great changes in the annual and seasonal changes of climate. Overall, the basin climate has the following main characteristics.

(1) Sufficient Illumination and Strong Solar Radiation

With annual sunshine hours generally reaching 2,000 -3,300 hours, there is abundant sunshine in the Yellow River Basin; its annual sunshine percentage is mostly between 50% and 75%, which is second only to the Qaidam Basin, and generally doubles that of the Yangtze River Basin.

The total solar radiation in the Yellow River Basin is in the middle level in China. Compared with that in southwest China, the total amount of solar radiation is lower, but it is generally higher than that in eastern China.

(2) Climate Diversity: Distinct Seasons and Vast Temperature Variations

The seasons in the Yellow River Basin differ greatly. For example, it is winter all year round in the headwater area, Jiuzhi County of Qinghai Province while from Jiuzhi to Lanzhou in the middle and upper reaches of the Weihe River, it has a long winter and no summer because there is autumn immediately after spring. Winters can last up to six or seven months and summers as short as one or two months from Lanzhou to Longmen. It is cold in winter and hot in summer with four distinct seasons in the rest of the basin.

The great temperature difference is a predominant feature in the Yellow River Basin. Overall, with the change of topography, it is gradually getting warmer from west to east. The minimum temperature in the basin occurs in the source region, with an annual average temperature of 12–14℃; the high-temperature area occurs at the lower reaches in Shandong Province. The maximum temperature in the basin appears in Yichuan County, Luoyang, Henan Province.

The daily temperature range with the Yellow River Basin is also relatively large, especially in the high latitude area of the middle and upper reaches. The daily temperature range of each season in the entire year is about 13–16.5 ℃, which is in the high or sub-high value area in China.

(3) Precipitation with Concentrated and Uneven Distribution and Its Great Variance between Years

The annual average precipitation in most areas of the Yellow River Basin is between 200 mm and 650 mm, and it is more than 650 mm in the southern and lower region of the middle and upper reaches. Greatly affected by topography, the precipitation can be as high as 700–1,000 mm in the northern slope of Qinling Mountains while the precipitation is less than 150 mm in some areas of north-western Ningxia and Inner Mongolia. The precipitation is unevenly distributed and the ratio of precipitation difference between north and south is greater than 5, not found in other rivers in China.

The whole basin is dry in spring and winter, and rainy in summer and autumn. The rainy season is from June to September, accounting for about 70% of the annual precipitation; in which the most abundant being in July and August, accounting for more than 40% of the whole year. The annual variation of precipitation in the basin varies greatly. The ratio of maximum to minimum precipitation is about 1.7–7.5, and the rainfall distribution is uneven. The uneven distribution of precipitation leads to different characteristics in the agricultural production of the Yellow River Basin.

(4) Low Humidity and High Evaporation

The middle and upper reaches of the Yellow River are areas with low humidity in China. For example, the average water vapor pressure in Wubao and regions in its west is less than 800 Pa and the relative humidity is below 60%. Especially in the areas in Ningxia, Inner Mongolia and the western areas to Longyang Valley, the annual average water vapor pressure is less than 600 Pa, and the relative humidity from Lanzhou to Shizuishan is less than 50%.

The Yellow River Basin has a strong evaporation capacity, with annual evaporation of

1,100 mm. The largest annual evaporation area in China turns out to be in Gansu, Ningxia, the central and upper western regions of Inner Mongolia, that is, the areas in the upper reaches of the Yellow River. The maximum annual evaporation can exceed 2,500 mm.

(5) Hailing or Sandy Days and Frequent Dust Storms

Hail is one major disaster in the Yellow River Basin. Statistics show that the annual number of hailing days in Lanzhou, Inner Mongolia and part of the upper reaches of the Yellow River, is usually more than 2 days; this figure will reach up to 15-25 days in the upper western areas to Maqu and the areas in the upper reaches of the Datong River, where the frequency of hail ranks first both in the Yellow River Basin and in the entire country.

Sandstorm and sand blowing are mainly caused by strong wind, and are closely related to geological and vegetation conditions in the local (or nearby) areas. According to statistics, in Ningxia, Inner Mongolia and northern Shaanxi, the average number of strong windy days is 30. There are Tengger Desert, Ulan Buh Desert and (known as Mao Wusu Desert or Ordos Desert) in the region. The annual number of days with dust storm is more than 10 and the number of days with sand blowing is more than 20. In some years, the maximum number of sandstorm days is between 30 and 50, and the sand blowing days are more than 50. In addition, in the upper reaches of the Fenhe River and along the Yellow River in the lower part of Xiaolangdi, Henan Province, there is also an area where the annual sandstorm or sand blowing days exceed 20 days. This is mainly related to the vast coverage of sandy land in the Yellow River.

(6) Short Frost-free Period

The first frost date occurs differently in different areas of the Yellow River Basin. The frost date starts earlier in the west and the north than in the east and south. Besides, it occurs earlier in the mountainous areas than that in the plains, rivers, valleys, and deserts of the same latitude. For instance, the first frost date in this area occurs roughly in the last ten days of August in the upper reaches while the first frost date happens in general in the first ten days of October in the middle and lower reaches of the Yellow River. As for the other areas, the frost date mainly starts in September. On the contrary, the last frost date occurs earlier in late March in the plain of the lower reaches while it ends generally in the middle of August in its upper reaches. And the last frost date occurs generally between April and August.

Therefore, the Yellow River Basin has a relatively short frost-free period. Even in the plain of its lower reaches, the frost-free days are only up to 200. The frost date lasts all year round in the upper reaches of Jiuzhi and the areas above, and the frost-free period lasts between 20 and 200 days in the rest of the basin.

Since the ancient times, humans chose to live close to water. Water was a key factor affecting the settlements of the primitive tribes for it was related to the fertility of soil. The Yellow River as an important river in North China had been a proper choice for the Chinese ancestors to settle down. This has been recorded in *The Book of Songs*, [1]A wise man named Gong Liu built a city in a vast plain near the springs and rivers. Then, this place had been turned into a center where many people flooded into. It is a typical example to show how the ancient people built the capital in a place close to water. In the ancient times, the climate in the Yellow River Basin was mild with proper amount of rainfall and heat. The average annual precipitation was 500−600 mm. Abundant water and superior climate conditions are conducive to plant growth. According to *Guanzi*[2], "All cities, big or small, if built on a high place, should not be at the foot of a mountain; if built in a low land, they should be near a river." Those built in highlands should not be close to dry areas and should have access to sufficient water resources; those built in lowlands should not be close to waterlogging and marshes so as to avoid floods. This is the principle according to which the ancient people chose their settlements. Zuo Qiuming noted in *Guoyu*[3], that Huangdi or the Yellow Emperor[4] and his tribes seeded down near the Jishui River while the Yan Emperor[5] led his people to live near the Jiangshui River. One could see from their stories that the ancient Chinese tended to live near water.

The Yellow River Basin has a variety of landforms like plateau, plain and basin. It has the fertile plain and basin. Taking the Fenwei Basin as an example, it includes Taiyuan Basin in Central Shanxi Province, Yuncheng-Linfen Basin in southern Shanxi Province and Guanzhong Basin in Shaanxi Province. These basins are rich in groundwater, mountain springs and rivers. They have the fertile land and a rich variety of produce. They are known as "米粮川" ("a fertile flat land rich with grain").

The Yellow River flows through the Loess Plateau (Fig. 2−6), which is relatively flat and Sandy (Fig. 2−7). The soil here is loose, fertile, and easy to cultivate, which provides favourable conditions for the development of the primitive agriculture. In many places of the Yellow River Basin, the gradient is relatively steep (Fig. 2−8). If a water inlet is built, water itself would flow into the land on its own. In the age when harvest was determined by the weather, irrigatable fields were no doubt a treasure. At present, some areas in the lower reaches of the Yellow River, such as Hebei, Henan, Anhui, Shandong and Jiangsu, have been the main wheat producing areas in China (Fig. 2−9). Henan in particular has been a major grain producing province in China, and agriculture has been the pillar of its economy. The Yellow River has nurtured the people in the upper, middle, and lower reaches of the whole basin for generations.

---

[1] A collection of Poems forms *The Book of Songs*, or *Shijing* (《诗经》). It is the oldest existing collection of Chinese poetry, comprising 305 works dating from the 11th to 7th centuries B. C..

[2] *Guanzi* (《管子》), an ancient Chinese political and philosophical text. It is named and usually attributed to the 7th century B. C. philosopher and statesman Guanzi(wikipedia).

[3] *Guoyu* (《国语》), an ancient Chinese text that consists of a collection of speeches attributed to rulers and other men from the Spring and Autumn period(771−476B. C.) (wikipedia).

[4] Huangdi (黄帝), one of the legendary Chinese sovereigns among the mytho-historical Three Sovereigns and Five Emperors (2698−2598B. C. E., mythical).

[5] Yandi (炎帝), a legendary Chinese ruler.

Figure 2-6 The Yellow River Flows through the Loess Plateau

Figure 2-7 The Sandy and Fertile Land at the Loess Plateau

Figure 2-8 The Steep Slopes at the Loess Plateau

Figure 2-9 The Lower Reaches of the Yellow River
are the Main Wheat Producing Areas

3. The Geographical Environment in the Yellow River Basin is Suitable for Human Habitation

Archaeological documents show that the Yellow River Basin is the earliest birthplace of Chinese architecture. *The Book of Changes*① records, "上古穴居而野处" meaning "the primitive lived in caves". The existing ancient books and the myths in ancient times also offer evidence that the primitive in the Yellow River Valley lived in caves. Some experts estimated that they started to live in caves as early as 700,000 years ago. The caves they dwelt in were mainly natural ones. When the caves could not meet human needs for the comfort, the primitives began to dig the caves themselves. In the clan society, people in the Yellow River Basin mainly lived in man-made caves. This is closely related to the unique geographical environment of the Yellow River Basin.

The Yellow River has many tributaries in its middle and lower reaches. The hills and basins in these areas made it possible to develop agriculture and provided the favourable conditions for the ancestors to live in. Yangshao Culture is the representative of the Neolithic culture in the middle reaches of the Yellow River. It occurred about 5,000 - 7,000 years ago and was distributed in areas between Gansu and Henan Provinces. The Loess Plateau covers much of Gansu, Shaanxi, Shanxi and other areas. The region is overlain by a mantle of fine-grained, wind-deposited, yellowish alluvium. Architecture in this loess-clad region is unique to its topography. The soil

---

① *The Book of Changes* or *I'ching*《易经》, an ancient Chinese divination text and the oldest of the Chinese classics.

layers here are thick (Fig. 2-10), some of which are as deep as one or two hundred meters, resulting in poor water permeability. In addition, the lack of rainfall on the Loess Plateau makes it possible for cave dwellings.

Figure 2-10　The Loess Layers

　　Due to the low productivity in ancient times, it was common for the local people to dig caves or built earth houses on the cliff of the mountains. The Chinese ancestors dug holes and built the unique cave dwellings which are environment-friendly (Fig. 2-11). People lived in the loess layers. Even till now, those types of caves are also a unique residential building in the northwest of China. Cave dwellings are also an ancient residential form on the Loess Plateau in China. The history of cave dwellings can be traced back to more than 4,000 years ago. They can be seen in Shanxi, Shaanxi, Henan, Hebei, Inner Mongolia, Gansu and Ningxia.

　　Cave dwellings are dug on the hillside, which can not only save raw materials but also keep warm with thick roofs and walls made with the thick loess layers. The cave dwellings are warm in winters and cool in summers. One could dig a hole anywhere and live in it in the Loess Plateau with a depth of 100 - 200 m! It is the unique natural environment of the Yellow River Basin that made those cave dwellings possible. Therefore, the Yellow River Basin has given a home for people to live in and has bred the Chinese nation. That's why it is known as the mother river of the Chinese nation.

　　The geographical conditions of the upper, middle, and lower reaches of the Yellow River Basin differ immensely. When the Chinese ancestors built the residential buildings, they usually would take its geography into consideration. A courtyard (Siheyuan) is the most representative in the Central Plains in northern China, while a cave dwelling is popular in the Loess Plateau. There are many plank houses in Longxi mountainous area, flat roofed mud houses in Hetao Plain, flowing

Figure 2-11　Cave Dwellings

yurts in grassland, and stone blockhouses in Gannan Plateau. In the Yellow River regions where Han culture prevailed, an overwhelming number of people used to live in Siheyuan or cave dwellings.

Loess cave dwellings are mainly built in the loess landform areas of Shaanxi, Shanxi, Henan and Gansu Provinces. The Yellow River runs through the Loess Plateau, where a great number of tributaries flow into it. The continuous erosion of water made valleys everywhere. As a result, the forests are rarely seen. Where could people live under such circumstances? Adapted to nature, the local people built cave dwellings. The cave dwellings are easy to be constructed, cost-saving, warm in winters and cool in summers, well insulated, earthquake resistant and durable.

According to the surface shapes, there are mainly three types of cave dwellings: cliff caves (Fig. 2-12), pit caves (Fig. 2-13), etc. The cliff caves are formed through digging horizontally on the Loess cliff, while the pit caves are made through digging a regular concave space vertically down from the loess ground, and then horizontally dug holes in the four pit walls, which are also called "sinking caves". The proverb that goes "there is no one in the village, but smoke rises from the flat ground" is a vivid portrayal of the life in the sinking caves. Cliff caves are the most typical in northern Shaanxi, and pit caves are mainly built in southern Shanxi Province. Cliff caves and pit caves can only be built when there is the Loess cliff or deep soil layers, so the cave dwellings in a village are often scattered. Cliff caves are mostly distributed along the mountains and ditches in accordance with the local geographical conditions. Courtyards pertaining to pit caves are of different sizes and are arranged in constellation form, which is a unique residential landscape in the Loess Plateau area. In some places, due to the unique topography, there are two kinds of cave dwellings at the same time. For example, Liangjiazhuang village of Shaanxi Province has more than

170 pit kiln yards and over 50 households of cliff cave yards. In addition to the deep soil layers, cave dwellings must be built near the wells, springs or streams, making it convenient for farming and living. Gu caves are a kind of independent caves made of adobes or sun-dried mud bricks, brick and stone walls. They have arch ceilings with doors and windows in the front. The most famous of all is Pingyao in Shanxi Province. The ancient Pingyao city architecture is a typical representative of Gu cave dwellings. As a result, Pingyao has become a famous historical and cultural city. In 1997, the architecture was included in the world cultural heritage lists.

Figure 2-12　Cliff Caves

Figure 2-13　Pit Caves

Section II Water and the Yellow River Civilization

The Yellow River is not only the mother river of the Chinese people, but also played a very important role in the formation of the Chinese civilization. With a civilized history of 5,000 years in China, the Yellow River Basin had been the political, economic, and cultural centre of China for more than 3,000 years. It bred Yangshao culture, Majiayao culture, Dawenkou culture, Longshan culture and other splendid ancient civilizations.

1. The Early Founders of the Chinese Civilization

First, let's look at the early founders of the Chinese civilization. China originated in the Yellow River Basin, with its cultural founders mainly living in the middle and lower reaches of the Yellow River. The legendary Three Sovereigns and Five Emperors ("三皇五帝") performed their duties as tribal leaders in this area. Archaeological discoveries reveal that the time when the five legendary leaders ruled corresponds to the period of "Longshan culture". During this period, the clan tribes in the Yellow River Basin began to shift from the period of the matrilineal commune to that of the patrilineal commune.

A famous book entitled as *Ancient Documents* (《尚书》) records that the three Sovereigns were Suiren, Fuxi and Shennong while the five Emperors refers to Huangdi, Zhuanxu, Diku, Yao and Shun. "Suiren" was honoured as the head of the three rulers (Fig. 2-14). About hundreds of thousands of years ago, in the Paleolithic age, Suiren made fire by drilling wood and taught people to cook food, ending to the history of those ancestral Chinese eating uncooked meat. It is said that he usually lived in Shangqiu, a south-eastern city in the south of Henan Province. Fuxi (Fig. 2-15) tied ropes into nets, hunting birds and fishing. It is said that he was married with Nuwa, his sister. Their offspring's lived in the middle and lower reaches of the Yellow River.

Figure 2-14 Suiren

Figure 2-15 Fuxi

A ruler of the prehistoric China called Shennong (Fig. 2-16) has been honoured as a God-king of Chinese medicine and agriculture. Legend has it that he tasted herbs in order to discover their medicinal qualities, invented some important farming tools (Fig. 2-17), and taught people to practice agriculture. Leisi is a plough-like farming tool used in the ancient times. Why does the first group of farming tools include Leisi, a digging tool, but not a water wheel? This is because there was not enough rain in the Yellow River Basin and Shennong invented agricultural tools to be used in dry lands. It is agreed that the invention of Leisi initiated the early farming culture in China. As one of the earliest agricultural countries in the world, crops planted at that time included millet, wheat and others which were crops mainly growing in dry lands, and directly related to the dry climate and insufficient rainfall there. China is the first country to plant millet around the world, the evidence of which can be found in Banpo ruins in Xi'an. Millet (Fig. 2-18) is popular in North China even now (Fig. 2-19).

Figure 2-16 Shennong

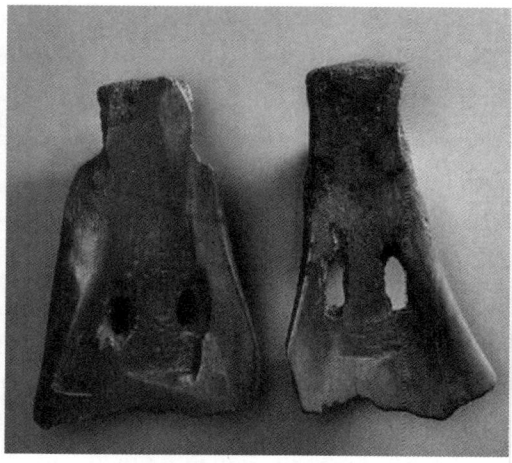

Figure 2-17 Leisi, a Plough-like Farm Tool Used in Ancient China

Figure 2-18 Millet Unearthed at the Banpo Ruins

Figure 2-19 Millet

Huangdi, or the Yellow Emperor (Fig. 2-20) is the first of the five emperors, named Xuanyuan. He was a famous tribal leader in the current Central Plains. Later generations in this area honoured Huangdi as their ancestor. Yao, Shun (Fig. 2-21) and Yu were descendants of Huangdi's clan. Now, Xinzheng City of Henan Province, Xuanyuan or Huangdi's hometown is considered to be the root of all the Chinese descendants.

Figure 2-20　Huangdi (the Yellow Emperor)

Figure 2-21　Yao and Shun

Legend says that Huangdi led his people to build houses, make clothes and dig wells, make ships and carts laying a foundation for the clothing, food, housing, and transportation of future generations. With his support, his wife Leizu first practised silk reeling skill, taught their people to make clothes with silk.

In terms of politics, Huangdi unified the Chinese tribes and clans. His deeds of conquering the eastern Yi tribe were also closely related to water. The battle of Zhulu between Huangdi and Chiyou's tribes is a major historical event, which played a crucial part in establishing Huangdi's reputation as an able ruler. It is said that during the early stage of the war they encountered severe storms, posing a great threat to Huangdi's tribe and settling them at a disadvantage. They had been defeated many times, and it was not until the sky cleared up and the heavy rain stopped that Huangdi's tribe started to win. Huangdi's tribe finally won the war and unified the Yan and Huang tribes.

Zhuanxu and Diku (Fig. 2-22) were Huangdi's descendants. They called their tribes "Hua" or "Xia" tribes. "Hua Xia" refers to the later Han people that made up 90% of the Chinese people. At that time, the Chinese mainly lived in the Central Plains. The Central Plains is roughly the middle part of ancient China and China means the middle part or the centre of world. According to historical records, Huangdi built his capital in Xinzheng, Henan Province. There are many relics recording his activities. Every March the Chinese people worldwide hold a ceremony to worship their ancestors.

Figure 2-22 Zhuanxu and Diku

2. The Yellow River Culture

(1) Yellow—A Sign of Culture

The Chinese people worship the colour of yellow, and the Chinese civilization is a yellow civilization. This might be attributed to the fact that the Chinese ancestors lived on the Loess Plateau near the Yellow River. In the early stage of the human society, the "five elements" hypothesis was popular. The five elements are gold, wood, water, fire and earth, which correspond to five colours, white, green, black, red and yellow. Of all these colours, yellow was the main colour and located in the centre. In the early stage of the Chinese civilization, the Central Plains was the centre of the four directions, and the Yellow Emperor, as the clan leader, first succeeded in realizing the unification of the Central Plains. The Yellow River (Fig. 2-23) culture has become a birthplace of the Chinese civilization, and yellow a symbol of culture. The Yellow River is yellow from all the angles. For example, many food with which people are familiar are yellow such as wheat (Fig. 2-24), soybeans, millet, pears, apricots, etc. Yellow is also a colour that represents the supreme power. Therefore, the derived "emperor" (皇帝, "皇" 同 "黄") became the appellation of the supreme ruler, "yellow" became the symbol of imperial power, and became one of the distinctive symbols of traditional Chinese culture.

Figure 2-23 The Yellow River   Figure 2-24 Wheat

(2) The Dragon Totem

Chinese worship of the dragon totem (Fig. 2-25) can be traced back to 7,000 years ago. The totem is the manifestation of the religious belief in the primitive society. Ancient Chinese believed that they were the dragon's descendants. Legend has it that dragons lived in water. So the choice of

Figure 2-25 The Chinese Dragon

the dragon totem must be related to water.

The dragon is a legendary animal with a scaly and long body, and a pair of horns projecting from the forehead. It can walk, fly, swim, make clouds and rain. It mainly lives in the water. In the ancient times, China was punctuated with marshes. With low productivity and underdeveloped tools humans were often attacked by beasts, so the dragon must be used as a totem to fright off the wild beasts and pray for the blessing of the gods.

Xu Shen, in *Origin of the Chinese Characters* (《说文解字》, *Shuo Wen Jie Zi*), described "dragon" as "an animal that could transform its length, give out light, fly into the sky in spring and summer and live in deep water in autumn and winter." Wen Yiduo, a famous Chinese scholar, analysed in his *Legends of Dragons and Phoenixes* that the idea that the Chinese were addressed as "the dragon's descendants" originated from the dragon totem and stories popular during Huangdi's reign.

After defeating Yandi (the Yellow Emperor) and Chiyou's tribes and unifying the Central Plains, Huangdi (the Yellow Emperor) asked people to decide the totem for their tribe. Legend says that dragons helped Haungdi fight Chiyou and unify the Central Plains and people worshiped them for their great strength. So Huangdi's tribe took dragons as their totem.

3. He tu (the Yellow River Map) and Luo shu (Inscription of the Luoshui River)

(1) An Overview

In a general sense, He tu and Luo shu are concepts that refer to the diversified objects rather than a specific one. Legends have that He tu and Luo shu were shown in the mythical animals in the form of patterns and these patterns inspired the sages to form ideas and control the flood. They were signs of auspice. In a narrow sense, He tu and Luo shu refer to the map of numbers made of black and white dots. Thus, He tu and Luo shu have rich and diversified connotations. It has had a gradual and complex evolution process.

References of He tu and Luo shu could be found in many ancient documents. In *The Analects*, a collection of Confucius and his disciples' words, thoughts and behaviours, Confucius said, "When the phoenix comes, the charts would appear in the Yellow River and the charts would foresee the appearance of the sages. But now I have no hope of seeing the sages appear." Kong Anguo (156B-74B.C., a famous scholar during the Western Han Dynasty) explained, "The appearance of the phoenix and the Yellow River Map are signs of the appearance of the sages. Now there are no such signs of auspice. Confucius couldn't help regret that he had no chance to see the sages in his life." Mozi wrote, "A red bird carried a jade and landed in Kingdom Zhou. The bird said, 'Heaven orders your king to overthrow Yin Dynasty. Now you can see the Yellow River Map.'" Guanzi said, "legends have that when sages appeared, the dragon that carried the map would be seen in the Yellow River, the inscription would be seen on the turtle's back, the mythical beast would roam on the land. Our time is not the time when these three auspicious things would appear."

According to the ancient Chinese classics, the appearance of He tu and Luo shu indicated that the emperors or rulers would embark on a great journey in their career. Along with them, there were the phoenix, the dragon, the turtle, and Cheng huang the divine animal. These indicated that the rulers were ordained by Heaven. Those signs forebode the reign of the wise rulers. Politics had a lot to do with the celestial changes.

There were several mythological stories about He tu and Luo shu. *The Book of Changes* records, "The Yellow River provided the Map and the Luoshui River presented the inscription." Later scholars added that when Fuxi ruled the land, a dragon-like horse leaped out of the Yellow River, carrying the map on its back. A turtle appeared from the Luoshui River, a branch of the Yellow River, with the inscription on its back. Based on the inscription, Da Yu(Yu the Great) controlled the great flood and made a governance system of 9 states (river islands). During the Western Zhou Dynasty, King Wen of Zhou performed *The Book of Changes*, deriving the trigrams from the river map. *The Book of Changes* is a collection of ancient Chinese thoughts. He tu and Luo shu was regarded as a very important document.

In 1987, Xingyi tomb was unearthed in Xishuipo, Puyang City, Henan Province. It has a history of about 6,500 years old. The four hexagrams of the River Map and 28 constellations were discovered in the tomb. Of the same year, the tortoise belly jade piece unearthed in Hanshan, Anhui Province, presented the charts of Luo shu. These evidence authenticated what Shao Yong and other scholars believed—He tu and Luo shu were ancient star maps. It also explains human recognition of the movements and changes of the universe in the ancient times. Ancient people held that all things are composed of images, numbers and reasons which correspond to of heaven, earth, and man in *The Book of Changes*. Here we can see the unity of heaven, earth, and man. It contains the ancient and simple dialectical philosophical ideas from which *The Book of Changes* is also derived from it. The following illustration would show that He tu and Luo shu has a lot to do with eight trigrams (Fig. 2-26).

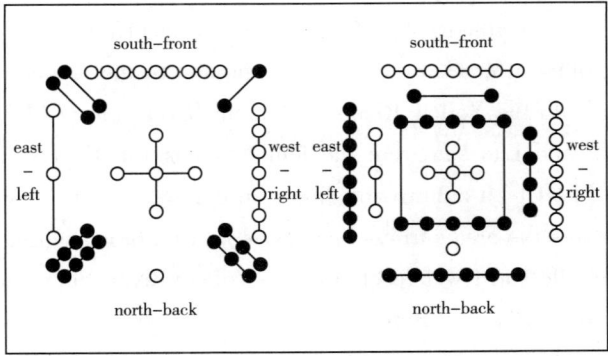

Figure 2-26 He tu and Luo shu

(2) The Yellow River and the Luoshui River Culture

Scholars hold different opinions about the exact meaning of He tu and Luo shu. As part of the Central Plains culture, it is of great significance to the formation and development of the Yellow River civilization. He tu and Luo shu first appeared in the Yellow River and Luoshui River, which shows that it has a close relationship with water. Records of the classical literature show that dragon-like horses and turtles were springing out from the Yellow River and the Luo River, its tributary. Four hexagrams of He tu and Luo shu were found in Puyang, Henan province and Hanshan, Anhui Province respectively. These two provinces are in the Yellow River Basin. Thus, as a cultural phenomenon, He tu and Luo shu are closely related to the water culture of the Yellow River Basin.

As a cultural symbol, He tu and Luo shu are closely related to the myths in Central Plains. There are many mythological stories about He tu and Luo shu in the Central Plains of China. Those stories around He tu and Luo shu mainly describe the miraculous occurrences when the emperors or kings offered sacrifices to Heaven. They were regarded as the evidence of the emperor's reign as Heaven's will. According to *Notes on Water Classics*, "Huangdi visited Luoyang in the East, built the altar and sank the wall, received the River Map from the dragon in He tu and got the Luo shu from the tortoise in the Luo River." Starting from Haungdi, the great rulers would go to the Yellow River and Luoshui River to offer their sacrifices. They wished to consolidate their political power by doing this. He tu and Luo shu recorded the rise and fall of their power. Yao, Shun, Yu and Tang also held ceremonies to accept He tu and Luo shu and show their respect and thanks to heaven. The throne of Yao was given to Shun and Shun gave it to Yu, and Yu offered sacrifices to the Yellow River and the Luoshui River. It is recorded that Yu was awarded with He tu and Luo shu. During Yu's reign, there was the turtle floating in the Luoshui River, carrying the "Luo shu" on its back. This shows that Yu's management of the flood was the mandate of Heaven and his victory was destined. Besides, Yu's water managing activities were endowed with a magical colour. With the help of the dragon and the turtle, as well as the manifestations of Yu's divine power, he completed a variety of difficult and dangerous projects and finally achieved the success of flood control.

Zhang Zhenli, a famous mythologist in China, believes that He tu and Luo shu are the source of the Central Plains culture. He relates He tu and Luo shu to the myths and legends, and seeks the regional connection with the Yellow River-the Luohui River culture (He-Luo culture) from its distribution area. He tu and Luo shu were the foundation of the He-Luo culture. Together with other regional cultures like Qi-Lu culture and Jing-Chu culture, it is an important regional culture. In a narrow sense, it covers the area surrounding Luoyang. In a broad sense, it refers to the Central Plains culture in the middle and lower reaches of the Yellow River. So, we take He-Luo culture as an equivalent to the Central Plains culture.

The He-Luo river culture originated in the primitive times, which played an important role in the formation of the Chinese civilization. The mysterious He tu and Luo shu are closely related to water. As the root of the He-Luo river culture and the core of Central Plains culture, it can be said that it is the meta symbol of the Chinese culture.

Both He tu and Luo shu and the He-Luo river culture were born and developed in the Yellow River Basin. Water culture in China has been constantly enriched and diversified.

4. The Origin of the Chinese Surname Culture

The origin of Chinese surnames can be traced back to Fuxi and Nuwa's time, which was closely related to the evolution of clan structure and marriage at that time. The Chinese surnames originating from the Central Plains were related to Fuxi, Yandi, Huangdi, Shun and other Chinese ancestors. At the beginning of the formation of surnames, there were differences among surnames. "Surname" is a symbol used to distinguish clans and tribes in the clan society. Each clan had its own surname. For example, Huangdi's tribe is surnamed as "Ji", Yandi's tribe "Jiang", while Taihao had the surname "Feng". After Huangdi's tribe defeated Yandi and Chiyou's tribes and unified the nation, the three tribes took "Ji" as their surname. Therefore, the "Ji" family was not only taken as the Ji family's ancestral surname, and it was also regarded as the shared surname of all the Chinese descendants.

Since Fuxi, Nuwa, Huangdi, Yandi and other clans mainly lived in the Central Plains of the Yellow River Basin in the ancient times, Chinese surnames originated in the middle and lower reaches of the Yellow River, mainly in Henan, the core area of Central Plains culture. In the latest ranking list of 100 surnames, 78 originated this area. Therefore, the middle and lower reaches of the Yellow River are the birthplaces of surnames (Fig. 2-27). As the root of surname culture, it has constructed a huge family name system in China, maintained the 5,000 years national system

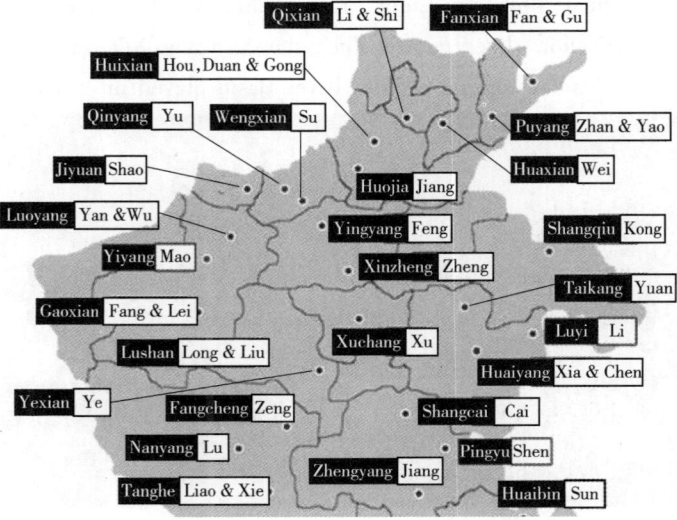

Figure 2-27 The Roots of Henan Surnames

of China, formed a strong national cohesion, united Chinese people at home and abroad, and showed the strong centripetal force of the Chinese nation.

The Yellow River has a long history and culture and produced the early human civilization of the Chinese nation. Human beings have bred and lived here, and Chinese surnames are mostly produced here. As a part of Chinese culture, surname culture represents a kind of cultural identity, which is of great significance to promote the solidarity and revival of the nation.

5. The Capitals of Many Dynasties

In the 5,000-year history of the Chinese civilization, the middle and lower reaches of the Yellow River had served as China's political, economic, and cultural centre for more than 2,000 years. Xia, the first dynasty in Chinese history, was founded in the Yellow River Basin. From the Xia Dynasty (21st century, B.C.) to the Northern Song Dynasty (960-1127), the capitals were mostly built in the Yellow River Basin. Anyang, Xi'an, Luoyang and Kaifeng, four among the seven ancient capitals in China's history, were located in the Yellow River Basin or along both sides of the Yellow River. From the Western Zhou Dynasty to the Sui and Tang Dynasties, Xi'an had been the capital of 13 dynasties. Luoyang had been the capital of 9 dynasties. Since the beginning of the Eastern Zhou Dynasty, Luoyang had been established as the capital successively by the Eastern Han Dynasty, the kingdom of Wei, the Western Jin Dynasty, the Northern Wei Dynasty, the Sui Dynasty, the Tang Dynasty, the Later Liang Dynasty, the Later Tang Dynasty, and the Later Jin Dynasty. Kaifeng has a history of more than 4,000 years. In history, the state of Wei in the Warring States period, Later Liang, Later Jin, Later Han and Later Zhou in the Five Dynasties, the Northern Song Dynasty and the Jin Dynasty all built their capitals there.

Among the eight ancient capitals in China (Fig. 2-28), five of them were located in the middle and lower reaches of the Yellow River, namely Zhengzhou, Anyang, Xi'an, Luoyang and Kaifeng. This could be attributed to the leading role the Yellow River Basin played in economic development. With

Figure 2-28 Eight Ancient Capitals of China (from left to right): Xi'an, Nanjing, Beijing, Hangzhou, Zhengzhou, Anyang, Kaifeng, Luoyang

the unique and favourable geography and climate, the people who had settled down here actively developed agriculture and economy, which laid the foundation for its being a political centre.

The numerous ancient cultural sites in the Yellow River Basin are incomparable in terms of number and systemization, which fully proves the important role it played in initiating Chinese civilization. In the long history of civilizations, the Yellow River has been the symbol of the Chinese nation and the cradle of Chinese civilization, having made great contributions to the formation of Chinese civilization. It can be said that, because of the nourishment of the Yellow River, the middle and lower reaches of the Yellow River have established themselves as the birthplace of the Chinese nation, the birthplace of Chinese civilization, the highest highland of agricultural civilization, the birthplace of scriptures, the root of surname culture, and the capital of many dynasties.

For Chinese, the Yellow River is not only a river, but also the symbol of the Chinese nation, and it is admired as the mother river of the Chinese nation. It plays an important role in the historical process of the Chinese nation. The Yellow River has been witnessing the Chinese nation's unremitting, indomitable, courageous, and enterprising efforts in its course.

Section III The Yangtze River—Another River Breeding the Chinese Civilization

Before 1973, the Yellow River Basin had been regarded as the single birthplace of the Chinese civilization while the Yangtze River culture had been deemed as a barbarian one. The ancient civilization born in the Yangtze River Valley had not yet been known to the world. In 1973, Hemudu culture (Fig. 2-29) was discovered when people were building a water conservancy project in Yuyao, Zhejiang Province. This finding set to rewrite the history of the Chinese civilization.

Figure 2-29 Hemudu Ruins

Since then, both the Yangtze River and the Yellow River have been recognized as the origin of the Chinese civilization. To quote some lines from a popular Chinese song, "There is a river in the remote East. It is the Yangtze River; another river is in the remote East and it is the Yellow River. There is a group of people living in the remote East. They are all the dragon's descendants", suggesting the collective unconsciousness of the Chinese people—the two rivers are regarded as the sources of the Chinese civilization.

With abundant water, fertile land and other favourable natural conditions, the primitive people inhabited and reproduced in the Yellow River Basin and the Yangtze River Basin. Two cultural regions were formed along the Yellow River and the Yangtze River. The northern culture developed around the Yellow River and the southern culture around the Yangtze River. Numerous archaeological findings show that with a history of more than 7,000 years, China has taken the two rivers as the cradle of the Chinese civilization.

Hemudu culture, as an ancient and varied Neolithic culture in the south of the lower reaches of the Yangtze River Basin, represents another aspect of the ancient Chinese civilization, which is different from the Yangshao culture in the Central Plains of the middle and lower reaches of the Yellow River.

1. Hemudu Culture

Hemudu ruins was first excavated in 1973. Its name came from its location in Hemudu village, Yuyao County, Zhejiang Province. Hemudu culture mainly appeared in Ningshao plain and Zhoushan Archipelago. It is the site of a village in a matriarchal clan commune in the Neolithic age, which reflects the activities of the clan society in the lower reaches of the Yangtze River about 7,000 years ago and contains rich water culture.

(1) Rice Culture

Before the discovery of rice at the Hemudu ruins, it was believed that rice was introduced into China from India and Japan rather than a local product. However, archaeologists found layers of rice in Hemudu ruins (Fig. 2-30). This is one of the earliest crops discovered in China, which proves that China is one of the earliest around the world to cultivate rice. The "rice culture" in the Yangtze River civilization affected the East Asian civilization and, one could argue, the world civilization.

Rice is a paddy crop. The reason why rice can be planted in the Yangtze River Basin is because of the geography, climate, and farming tools there. First, the Yangtze River Basin has the favourable natural conditions for rice farming. The total length of the trunk stream of the Yangtze River is more than 6,300 km, ranking the third longest in the world after the Nile River and the Amazon River, and the longest one in China. The Yangtze River flows from the west to the east and is rich in water resources with numerous tributaries. The Yangtze River Basin is in the unique North Latitude 30°, where most of the early civilizations emerged. In the west of the Yangtze River

Chapter Two Water and the Chinese Civilization

Figure 2-30 Rice Layers at Hemudu Ruins

Basin mountains rose and the Qinghai-Tibetan Plateau blocked the warm and humid southeast monsoon from the Pacific Ocean in the East, making it a region with abundant rainfall, which provided unique conditions for agricultural production in the paddy fields. Hemudu is located in the lower reaches of the Yangtze River in the Wuyue region, where the climate is mild, the soil fertile, its water network dense, and the rainfall abundant, which provides good conditions for rice planting.

Moreover, the development of the primitive agriculture depended on advanced farming tools. Rice planting in Hemudu relied largely on an advanced tool, Gu lei or Bone lei (Fig. 2-31). More than 3,000 pieces of bone artifacts unearthed from the Hemudu cultural ruins are major farming tools used by the primitive, among which the most distinctive is the Bone lei. The Bone lei used by the ancestors of Hemudu is different from the Lei invented by Shennong. Lei in the Yellow River Basin is a tool of ploughing used in the dry land

Figure 2-31 Lei: A Bone-made Farming Tool

while Bone lei of Hemudu is smooth, and some of its edges are incomplete due to long-term wear and tear, ending up a tool with two or three forks. It was the major tool Hemudu people used in agriculture. It is lighter and more dexterous than stone tools, and more smooth, not easy to be mudded, and suitable for people to use in the rice paddies of south of the Yangtze River. It is not only a ploughing tool, but also can be used for digging. It is useful in cultivating low-lying and swampy land, which greatly reduces the intensity of labor. For example, people could dig small ditches to drain water or divert water for irrigation. Bone lei, an advanced farming tool, made it possible for Hemudu people to plant rice.

(2) Stilt-style Architecture

Adapting to nature, the primitive built houses featured with stilt-style architecture through imitating "nest dwellings" (Fig. 2-32). Wooden or bamboo pillars bore the weight of the houses. The traditional pattern of stilt-style architecture has two or more floors with the ground floor for sheltering animals and the second or above for living and storing cereals, as often seen in the south of the lower reaches of the Yangtze River in China. This kind of building was usually built near the water systems, and it could reduce the tedious work of digging the foundation and defended against the attacks of wild animals and enemies. The stilt-style architecture is a typical design in areas near ponds, lakes, or rivers. Another feature of this type of houses is that it has a larger floor area despite its relatively small space. It improved people's living standard and was the crystallization of the wisdom of the primitive.

Figure 2-32 Stilt-style Architecture

There is a large number of river systems in the Yangtze River which led to higher humidity in the Yangtze River. People lifted the house to a higher level for the purposes of avoiding moisture, better ventilation, and heat dissipation. To the eastern part of Hemudu ruins is a lake. To build the stilt-style houses here was a wise decision. The hardworking and intelligent Hemudu people first built stilt style buildings, which could avoid moisture, dissipate heat, ventilate well, and help avoid the threats of insects, wild animals and floods. The stilt-style architecture has been one of the important architectural forms in the south of the Yangtze River since the Neolithic age. The houses in Hemudu ruins are the earliest stilt-style architecture found in China till now, and the wooden tenon and mortise components were applied, which laid the foundation for the traditional wooden architecture in China. Nowadays, in the middle and lower reaches of the Yangtze River, this unique style of residential houses is still in use. Such dwellings are mainly found in the mountainous areas of Guangxi, Hunan, Hubei, Sichuan, Yunnan and Guizhou, and most of them are dwellings of ethnic people.

(3) The Well

Well (Fig. 2-33) is mainly used for groundwater exploitation, which is rarely seen in the urban areas currently, but it is still used in some rural areas in China. Throughout human history, people have chosen to live by water, and human civilization has always been closely connected with rivers. The development of human society has been inseparable from the rivers. The primitive mainly used the surface water for their use, but living by the water could brought many problems and made life inconvenient. Gradually, humans dug wells to exploit the groundwater. This made lives easier because of the improved quality of drinking water and expanded the living space. So we can see that the digging of wells could have a significant impact on the development of human society.

Figure 2-33 The Well

The remains of the well in Hemudu is important because it shows that our ancestors began to drink groundwater 7,000 years ago, which made them free from the total dependence on surface water.

At the Hemudu ruins, archaeologists found the remains of a shallow well with wooden structure (Fig. 2-34). The well is in a shallow circular pit with a square wellhead and a side length of about 2 m. Inside the well, the ancients planted dozens of wooden pillars on the four walls. A long log is put on the top end of the pillars, which forms the framework of the wellhead. This is the earliest well remains known in China, and it is also the oldest well remains with shaft supporting structure found so far. More than 7,000 years ago, it was hard work for people to build wells like that. It is amazing to see that there are pavilions sheltering the wells. With the pavilions the sand and rain couldn't contaminate water in the well.

Figure 2-34　Well Ruins in Hemudu Village

　　The use of wells proves that as early as 7,000 years ago, Hemudu people began to settle down to live a settled and stable life. They began to take care of drinking water hygiene and pursuing a high-quality life. Archaeologists believe that the Hemudu people first built the wells and used groundwater in their life, which was 3,000 years earlier than that in the Tigris and Euraphrades River Basin. And the latest archaeological discovery in 2018 showed that a well built nearly 9,000 years ago was found in Xiping County, Henan Province, which is even 2,000 years earlier than the wells used by Hemudu people.

　　The Hemudu Culture Ruins fully reveal the development of culture in the southern Yangtze River Basin in the middle of Neolithic age. It shows that as early as 7,000 years ago, our ancestors had begun to live and work on this fertile land and made great contributions to the formation and development of this multicultural country.

　　In addition to Hemudu culture, there are other ancient cultures such as Liangzhu culture, Sanxingdui culture, Qujialing culture and so on. They all existed in the Yangtze River Basin. The number and density of cultural sites in the Yangtze River Basin top the world. That's why the Yangtze River Basin is also taken as the birthplace of the Chinese nation now. It represents another aspect of the ancient Chinese civilization. The Yangtze River civilization and the Yellow River civilization interacted and integrated with each other in ancient China for a long time, and eventually formed a pluralistic Chinese civilization system.

2. Personality Traits and the Yangtze River Basin

From the psychological perspective, personality is closely related to the environment where one lives. Each person differs in personality. Different natural and social environments and different cultures would shape different people differently. Naturally, regional culture would exert an influence upon people living in that area. China's vast territory, diverse climate and geography have influenced the formation of its people's personalities. For example, people in the northwest tend to be bold and unconstrained; people in the northeast are straightforward and people in the south of the Yangtze River are sensitive while people are supposed to be modest and prudent in the Central Plains and simple and plain in the southwest of China.

Personalities might be determined by geographical, material conditions and regional culture as well. Resorting to the ancient documents we would find that many ancient people believed that living in different regions people would foster different personalities. About 2,000 years ago, *Annals of Han Dynasty* recorded the living environment has impacts upon the way people speak; for example, people in some regions generally speak with a soft voice while people in certain areas speak harshly. *Guanzi* also wrote, "The rivers in Kingdom Qi are running wildly and recklessly, so its people are crude and impetuous; the river in Kingdom Chu are clear and slowly moving so its people are alert and resourceful." In the preface to *Annals of Lingxian County*, the editors wrote, "People who live in the plains are simple, honest and unsophisticated." These documents show the ancient Chinese had studied how geographical conditions impact personalities in certain regions.

The Yangtze River Basin has covered a wide area. Thus, its physical and geographical conditions differ greatly in its upper, middle and lower reaches. Accordingly, Ba-Shu culture, Jing-Chu culture and Wu-Yue culture take on characteristics of their own. With different natural environment, culture and economy, people living in the Yangtze River Basin differ greatly from those living in the Yellow River Basin. People in the Yellow River Basin are most likely loyal, simple, conservative, hard-working, patient and perseverant because people used to believe that the Yellow River flows slowly, and the slope of the plateau along its banks are gentle. However, the Yangtze River is characterized by large drop in elevation and swift flow. The flowing area in the upper reaches has numerous cliffs while its middle and lower reaches are vast and open, and the mountains and deep gorges along the river are steep and straight. The great difference in different regions formulate people's characters accordingly. People living in the Yangtze River Basin are flexible, resourceful, changeable and adaptable.

As the Yangtze River passes through a large part of China with landforms differing greatly in geography, history and culture, so people from different regions also differ greatly in their personalities.

The Ba-Shu civilization in the upper reaches of the Yangtze River, the ancient Dujiangyan water project and the Chengdu Plain made Kingdom Shu(mainly Sichuan Province) a fertile and prosperous land for thousands of years. People in this land are confident, easy-going, open, and smart.

In the middle reaches of the Yangtze River, Qu Yuan and Song Yu, two famous figures during the Spring and Autumn Period pioneered the romantic spirit of Chinese literature; Laozi [①] admired nature and discussed Taoism by using water as an analogy; Zhuangzi's[②] pursuit of spiritual realm by "following nature" had a far-reaching influence on Jing-Chu culture in this region. Therefore, people in the middle reaches of the Yangtze River were romantic and passionate. As a result, many literati emerged, leaving numerous poems that described the beautiful lakes and sighed over the ups and downs of life. At the same time, Jing-Chu culture, featured with self-improvement, openness, integration, innovation, and untiring spiritual pursuit has had a great impact on the formation of the local people's character.

The Yangtze River Delta in the lower reaches of the Yangtze River is "a land of fish and rice". With advanced economy and people have been living a relatively stable life. The formation of people's character had been deeply influenced by Wu-Yue culture. Wu-Yue culture happened in an area between mountains and the sea, and people there had to struggle for a living in such natural condition. They were adventurous, simple, brave, and having an enterprising spirit. The embodiment of those spirits can be seen in merchants from Yiwu, Zhejiang Province who do their business all over the world. After the Tang and Song Dynasties, the tranquil and elegant gardens in the south of the Yangtze River provided good environment for the local scholars to read, to write poetry, to play musical instruments or to do paintings. Under such circumstances, the unique Jiangnan culture was formed. After thousands of years of historical development and cultural integration, people in the south of the Yangtze River turn to be delicate in personality with profound learning seen in a scholar and shrewdness usually seen in a businessman.

Experts have summed up that people living in the Yellow River Basin are generally hard-working and persevering. There are lots of popular stories describing their diligence. An elderly man named Yugong wanted to remove the mountains that blocked their way to the outside world and so he was determined to remove the mountains despite his old age. He worked hard and eventually moved the gods who helped him remove the mountains. The hardworking, self-reliant, Dazhai people (Fig. 2-35) fought bravely against the harsh natural environment, and improved the sterile land, and turned the steep mountains and slopes full of rocks into "sponge fields" with high and stable yields, becoming a model to fight against harsh nature.

It is worth noting that most of the typical cases of reform and opening up and economic system reform first took place in the Yangtze River Basin. For example, in December 1978, 18 farmers in Xiaogang Village, Fengyang County, Anhui Province, signed a contract with the village so that they had the right to manage and harvest the land independently only paying a certain sum to the village

---

① An ancient Chinese philosopher and writer, the author of *Tao Te Ching*, the founder of Philosophical Taoism (wikipedia).
② Another Taoist, author of *Zhuang Zi*, an influenfical text of Taoism from the late Warring States Period (476-221B.C.).

Figure 2-35   Farmers in Dazhai Village, Shanxi Province

committee (Fig. 2-36), which initiated China's rural reform. The rural and urban economic reform addressed as "Wenzhou model" and "Southern Jiangsu model" took place in the Yangtze River Basin.

Figure 2-36   A Musuem to Remember the Start of the Contracted Responsibility System

In history, many political reformers were born in south of the Yangtze River while many conservatives were northerners. For example, both Wang Anshi and Sima Guang were important officials in the Song Dynasty, but their political views were quite different. Wang Anshi was a southerner from Fuzhou, Jiangxi Province, and Sima Guang was a northerner, a native of Xia County, Shanxi Province. To lift the court out of the political crisis, Wang Anshi enforced the reform of developing production, enriching the country and strengthening the army, but Sima Guang was opposed to it. Sima Guang wrote in a paper dedicated to Emperor Shenzong of the Song Dynasty: "People from Fujian Province are narrow-minded while people from Kingdom Chu love changes. How can people be honest and generous when the imperial court is filled with narrow-minded people?" Sima Guang criticized the southerners as being "narrow-minded" and "unsteady". His remarks also showed that deep in the heart of the southerners they are quick and decisive. The so-called "honest and generous" is descriptive of those abiding by the rules.

The Spring and Autumn Period and the Warring States Period (770-221B.C.) saw the scene of the contention of a hundred schools of thought and the cultural and intellectual expansion in China. The intellectual society of this era displayed their opinions on the methods of government, war, diplomacy and the relation between humans and nature, etc. Confucius and Mencius of Confucianism highly praised ethics and political practice. Their thoughts represented the Chinese culture in the Yellow River Basin. Laozi and Zhuangzi (369-286 B.C.), representative of Taoism, worshiped nature, explored the relationship between man and nature and advocated a life free from all occupations and achieved transcendence. Their philosophy occupies an important part in the Jing-Chu culture in the Yangtze River Basin.

All in all, in the Yellow River Basin and the Yangtze River Basin, people in different areas show different personality in different regions due to the influence of the natural, social, and cultural sectors.

Section IV   The Rise and Fall of the Yangtze River Culture

1. Why the Yangtze River Civilization Lagged behind Temporarily

The continuous archaeological excavations reveal that the Yellow River and the Yangtze River are both the cradle of the Chinese civilization and China is an ancient country with a civilized history of more than 7,000 years. The evolution of civilization is affected by the natural environment and more importantly, the influence of human activities.

Although the Yangtze River Basin bred the splendid Chinese civilization, it developed slowly and lagged in Xia, Shang and Zhou Dynasties and the following 2,000 years, compared with the Yellow River civilization. The reasons for the formation of this situation are as follows. Since the Chinese civilization started with farming culture, the early Chinese civilization was built based on farming economy. In the Yellow River Basin, the soil is loose, the terrain is flat, and the rain and heat are conducive to the cultivation of crops. However, the topography of the Yangtze River Basin is quite complex. The plains in the middle reaches are in the basin, and the Jiangsu-Anhui plains in the lower reaches are narrow and long. The steep mountains and continuous hills made it difficult for people to live and communicate with each other. It was difficult to cultivate thorny barren hills with simple tools and to build water conservancy projects. At the same time, due to abundant rainfall, during the long frost-free period, weeds grew too fast. During the farming seasons, background agricultural technology and the physical situations directly affected the development of economy and culture. However, productive force in agriculture during the corresponding period reached a higher level in the Yellow River Basin, which made the Yellow River Basin the political, economic, and cultural centre of China. In this case, the Yangtze River culture lagged behind the Yellow River Basin.

Moreover, Confucianism, the mainstream of traditional Chinese culture, is rooted in the north. Historically, China's political and cultural centres were mostly in the north. In the long-term development of the Chinese civilization, the Yellow River Basin civilization is superior to other civilizations.

2. The Revival of the Yangtze River Culture

However, the backwardness of the Yangtze River culture was only temporary. During the Warring States Period, after iron tools were widely used, the advantages in geography in south of the Yangtze River gradually came into play. Its economy caught up with and eventually surpassed that of the Yellow River Basin. The Chu culture in the middle reaches of the Yangtze River merged with the barbarian culture and formed a distinctive one. For example, during the Spring and Autumn Period, its technology in making bronze wares developed and formed the unique Chu style. During the Warring States Period, the style of Chu Ci represented by Qu Yuan's *Li Sao* broke away from the sentence pattern constraints represented in *The Book of Songs*, mainly a northern classic. It opened up new stylistic forms and created a precedent for the future romantic writings. During the Three Kingdoms Period, the Yangtze River civilization represented in Kingdom Wu and Shu, southern forces, achieved the same level with the Yellow River civilization represented in Kingdom Wei, a northern power.

(1) The Cultural Centre First Shifted from the North to the South during the Eastern Jin Dynasty

China saw the shifts of the cultural centre to the south form the north three times and boosted the rejuvenation of the Yangtze River culture. The first shift took place during the Eastern Jin Dynasty. In 317 A. D. , Sima Rui, the imperial clan of the Western Jin Dynasty, moved the capital from Luoyang to Jianye (now Nanjing), known as the Eastern Jin Dynasty. Many famous families moved to the south and the Yellow River cultural circle began to expand to the Yangtze River Basin. At that time, the northern tribes frequently harassed and plundered in the northern border, resulting in continuous wars. The agricultural activities in the Yellow River Basin that used to be the major producing areas of agricultural products were greatly disturbed. As a result, China's agricultural areas had to be expanded southwards, gradually to the middle and lower reaches of the

Yangtze River and the south-eastern coastal areas. With the shift of the agricultural production centre, the geography and superior natural conditions of the Yangtze River Basin had gradually had advantages in the development of agricultural economy.

With the expansion of the farming area to the south, the Central Plains culture moved southward, gradually integrating with the local culture and the grassland culture in the frontier ethnic people. The blending of diversified cultures had created a pluralistic cultural era. During this period, China's philosophy, literature, art, history, science and technology and other fields prospered. A group of brilliant scholars appeared in the Yangtze River Basin. In terms of literature, Tao Yuanming, an innovative poet, created the "Pastoral Poetry School". In calligraphy, Wang Xizhi was one of the most influential calligraphers. He combined the styles of various calligraphers and made innovations to form his own style. Gu Kaizhi, a great painter, was very proficient in portraying Buddha statues, mountains, and rivers. People called him "a master of three arts"—painting, calligraphy and poetry. Gu Kaizhi's paintings were vivid and true to the soul of the objects. He laid a solid foundation for the development of Chinese paintings. Among many of his works, *Zhuoqin* (Yaoqin, an ancient Chinese musical instrument) and *Luoshen Fu* (Ode to Goddess Luo) are his representative works, manifesting his unique style. In terms of music and dancing art, music from the western regions like "Qiuci music", "Shule music", "kangguo music" and other musical forms were introduced into the Central Plains, while the foreign music such as Tianzhu music, Funan music, and Gaoli music were also very popular. In this period, dance was featured with a pluralistic colour, and the most famous dances were *Big face* and *City Dance*.

The well-known Legend of Butterfly Lovers also took place in the Eastern Jin Dynasty. When Jin Dynasty moved its centre to the south, scholars and civilians followed the royal family southwards, which formed the first large-scale migration of Han people and first multi-ethnic integration in China's history, which greatly affected the political pattern of Han and Jin Dynasties. The literati class surnamed as Wang, Xie, Sima, Yin, He, Xu, Cao, Jiang, etc., performed the leading role in terms of economy and politics. One of the Seven Sages of Bamboo Groves, Ruan Ji's descendants and the landlord class including the families of Zhou, He, Gu, Ji, Kong, Dai, Yuan, Yu, Gan, Ge of Jiangnan area (south of the Yangtze River), mostly settled in Kuaiji (currently Shaoxing, Zhejiang Province) and made it a metropolis at that time.

(2) The Second Shift of the Cultural Centre—after the An-Shi Rebellion

The second shift started after the An-Shi Rebellion which took place in the middle and late Tang Dynasty. After the rebellion, internal and external troubles mushroomed. For example, the separatism of the vassal towns, the invasion of other ethnicities, the autocracy of eunuchs, the rivalry between Niu and Li families, etc. Years' war had done great damage to the Central Plains, while the Yangtze River Basin had maintained a relatively stable and peaceful situation. Therefore, the rulers had to reign mainly in the south, which caused a large number of northern people to move to the south and had greatly stimulated the development of the Yangtze River culture. At that time, the northerners in China mastered advanced production technology and farming tools. As the northern people moved southwards, they brought what was needed for the economic development of the south.

After nearly 200 years' development, the economy in the Yangtze River Basin had far surpassed that of the north. The middle and lower reaches of the Yangtze River rapidly became the major supply of grain, cloth and other important materials for the capital and the borders. The popular saying "when Jiangsu and Hangzhou have their harvests, there would be no lack of grain in China" is a true portrayal of the society at that time. At the same time, the political and cultural status of the southern literati had also been improved. By the end of the Northern Song Dynasty, among the powerful officials who oversaw the important offices, the number of the southern literati had exceeded that of their northern counterparts. For example, the famous "Three Sus"(a famous poet Su Shi, his father Su Xun and his younger brother Su Zhe) were all from Meishan, Sichuan Province. Su Shi, a famous literary giant, once served as Minister of War and Minister of Rites. Important officials and scholars like Ouyang Xiu and Wang Anshi were from Jiangxi Province(also a province in the south of the Yangtze River). All these could show that with the economic, political and cultural centre moving to the south, the culture of the Yangtze River Basin had also been greatly developed in this period.

(3) The Third Shift of the Cultural Centre—after the Jingkang Event in the Northern Song Dynasty

The third southward shift took place after the Jingkang Event. In 1126, the soldiers of Kingdom Jin, a northern tribe, went south and took captive two emperors, Emperor Hui and Qin of the Northern Song Dynasty. Their invasion ended the reign of Northern Song Dynasty, which was known as "the Jingkang Event". The cultural development of the Yellow River had been seriously hindered once again. Moving to the south, the Song Dynasty established the Southern Song Dynasty regime in its new capital, Lin'an (now Hangzhou). Then China's political and economic centre moved to the south, which once again promoted the development of the Yangtze River culture. After that, in terms of economy, the Yangtze River Basin had got the advantage over the Yellow River Basin. In order to adjust the pattern of "administration centre in the north and economic centre in the south", the government concerned carried out the North-South Grand Canal Project whose construction had been intermittently carried out from the Sui and Tang Dynasties to the Song and Yuan Dynasties.

During this period, due to its advanced economy, the Yangtze River Basin served as a pillar for the northern political and military centre. The evidence could be found in the old Beijing proverb "the Forbidden City benefited greatly from the Grand Canal". In the Yuan, Ming and Qing Dynasties, Beijing's material supplies were mainly "from the southern and the eastern provinces" and goods and other objects were transported from the south and east to the capital through the

Grand Canal. The revenues from the south and the east supported the rule of the Yuan, Ming and Qing Dynasties. The Yangtze River Basin contributed a lot to the national economy and the development of the feudal dynasties.

After the completion of the transfer of the economic and cultural centre from northwest to southeast, the Yangtze River Basin had also seen the expansion from the lower reaches to the middle reaches. This can be seen from a proverb popular during the Southern Song Dynasty, "If farmers in Jiangsu, Hunan and Hubei Provinces had a good harvest, the world would be prosperous". But in the later Ming and Qing Dynasties, the proverb changed to "when Hunan, Hubei and Guangdong Provinces had a good harvest, the whole world would be prosperous". From the Southern Song Dynasty to the Ming and Qing Dynasties, the most important grain base in China gradually expanded from the Yangtze River Delta to the total middle reaches of the Yangtze River, because it had more fertile land and abundant water and heat resources.

Economy in the Yangtze River Basin had been thriving. In terms of culture, scholars in the Yangtze River region had emerged in large numbers, leading the literary world to prosperity. For example, the official scholars like Wen Tianxiang and Lu You were from Jiangxi and Zhejiang Provinces respectively. Their poems as well as their patriotic spirit had been praised continuously.

In the process of the southward shift of the Chinese cultural centre, the Yangtze River Basin had formed a unique regional culture. For example, Ba-Shu culture in the upper reaches, Jing-Chu culture in the middle reaches and Wu-Yue culture in the lower reaches. These different regional cultures have become an integral part of the Yangtze River civilization, and jointly constructed a profound and diverse Yangtze River civilization system.

Section V Yu and Flood Control Stories

Yu's flood control activities had been one of the greatest feats in the history of the Chinese civilization. The mythological story about Yu's flood control activities reflects how the ancient Chinese thought about the origin of the universe. The story originated from the possible happening—the frequent overflowing of the Yellow River in prehistoric times. Myth is the reflection of social reality in ancient times, and it is the transformation of our ancestors' life. The flood control stories recorded in books like *Mencius* and *Shangshu* (*The Book of the Old Times*) are vivid portrayals of the origin of human beings in China.

In the mythological period of "Three Sovereigns and Five Emperors", following the Huangdi, Zhuanxu and Diku, three tribal leaders with both political integrity and ability appeared in the Yellow River Basin. They were known as Yao, Shun and Yu. They lived in the ancient society of 5,000-6,000 years ago, and their main contribution was to carry out large-scale water control activities in the middle and lower reaches of the Yellow River.

1. Background—Gonggong and Gun's Flood Control Activities

During Yao and Shun's reign, the Central Plains was devastated by flood. That was a time when the Central Plains were frequently plagued by floods. People had to leave their homelands for a living. This was caused by the overflowing of the Yellow River. The records in *Shangshu*, show that people were harmed by the torrential flood at that time. The flood seemed to be high enough to reach the sky. People were sighing and begging, "Who could tame the flood and save us?" Yao the wise ruler was determined to control the flood. To this end, he began to look for talented people to manage water. Since then, the ancestors of the Chinese nation launched a heroic struggle against the flood.

According to *Bamboo Annals*, "In the 19th year of Emperor Yao's reign, he ordered Gonggong to control the waters." Gonggong was the water god in ancient mythology. Gonggong "leveled hills and filled marshes to stop floods" and intended to block the waters by building dikes and dams. This method of stopping the floods turned into a phrase, "Blocking water with soil"(shui lai tu yan). But Gonggong failed to block the waters. Instead, the floods were getting worse. Gonggong was punished for his ineffectiveness and exiled to the state of You. That is in today's Beijing, Tianjin and Hebei Province.

Figure 2-37　Gun Taking Soil to Manage Water

Gonggong failed in his mission and King Yao assigned Gun to handle the problem. Gun was involved in the arduous and thorny water controlling activities. He had no experience to follow. But he didn't learn from Gonggong's failure. Gun continued to adopt the method of blocking water with soil(Fig. 2-37). Nine years passed, the situation had become even worse with the river overflowing everywhere. Gun failed to get the flood under control, and he was killed by the king. The underdeveloped technology, the method and other factors led to Gun's failure in his work. Despite his failure, Gun won the admiration of the Chinese people.

2. Yu's Control of Floods

According to the myth about Yu, Yu was a tribal leader. He regulated the waters in areas covering Shanxi, Henan, Hebei and Shandong. These areas were in the middle and lower reaches of the Yellow River. But the stories about Yu's flood control activities were spread to the whole country (Fig. 2-38). Yu's deeds not only benefited his clans and tribes, but also had an impact on the development of flood control technology in the future.

After Gun's death, his son Yu was appointed to take his father's position. Yu didn't bear the grudges against the king for his father's death. He valued the interests of the public. He learns from the people with great humility. He carefully summarized the experiences of curbing the waters from his predecessors. He adopted a new way of dredging waterways and conducting the rivers to the sea. It meant that they would allow the water to flow instead of blocking it. Based on this he conducted the waters into the sea. After 13 years of intensive and diligent labour Yu and his workers had finally eliminated the onslaught of flooding.

Figure 2-38 Yu's Flood Control Activities

Yu's control of the waters mainly included three aspects.

First, he chiselled the mountain to guide the waters through. To be exact, he chiselled Longmen Hill. From a legendary story in Luoyang, "Carps Jumping over Longmen", we could infer that Longmen was in today's Luoyang, Henan Province. *Records of Grand History* (or *Shiji*) and *Water Classics* have stories about splitting Yinque. A Ming Dynasty travelogue entitled as *A Journal of Travelling* in Yinque wrote that Yinque was "commonly known as Longmen". Scholars of the past dynasties believe that Longmen is the Longmen Hill (Fig. 2-39) at the junction of Shaanxi and Shanxi today, and Yinque (Fig. 2-40) is a place near the Longmen Grottoes in Luoyang today. Many documents reveal that the myths of Yu's flood control was spread in the Central Plains, which formed a huge cluster of myths and was spread to the surrounding areas. That's why Yu's stories were spread in the lower reaches of the Yellow River, such as Shaanxi and Shanxi Provinces.

Figure 2-39   Longmen Hill

Figure 2-40   Yinque

The popularity of Yu's flood control myth was the result of the flood control activities. The myth of "Yu Chiseling Longmen Hill" is an important part of Yu's flood control myths. Experts believe that the earthquake or rainstorm at that time may have caused massive landslides in the two places, blocking the way of the flood. This might be related to the geological changes at that time.

With the help of manual laborers, Yu used fire and water to remove the mud and stone that blocked the flowing water. He widened the waterways in Longmen and Yinque so that the flood could flow through. The myth of "Yu chiseling Longmen Hill" was closely related to the development of well drilling technology. With this technology, people could get water to develop agriculture, build villages and perform large-scale farming activities, thus forming many tribal alliances. We can see that Yu's work not only controlled the floods that ravaged the land, but also promoted farming technology.

Second, Yu conducted many rivers into the sea. Yu led the people to dredge the tail reaches of the Yellow River. The tail reaches were the estuaries where the rivers flew into the sea. Yu guided the floods from the large number of tributaries in the upper reaches to enter the sea through many courses so as to avoid the flooding of the Yellow River. These tributaries ran through the lower reaches of the Yellow River where there was the plain from Hebei to Shandong. The middle and lower reaches of the Yellow River flew through the loess area where silt was flushed into the river. The Yellow River often overflowed in the eastern plain in summer and autumn before Yu's time. Yu led his people to investigate the mountains and rivers in the middle and lower reaches. After that, he decided to dredge the rivers and canals systematically to conduct the flood. Yu's flood control activities changed the old course of many tributaries and formed the present course through his management of the Yellow River. His work had played an important role in the formation of many lakes, rivers, and water systems in the Yellow River Basin.

Third, Yu dug as many "Gou xu" as possible. "Gou xu" means the "waterways" dug in the fields and here it refers to the construction of large-scale farmland infrastructure. Water conservancy projects were lifelines for the rise of agriculture. To develop agriculture, Yu had to develop water conservancy projects. Yu adopted scientific methods to control floods. He also worked hard to construct water conservancy and irrigation projects. Yu not only made a success in flood control, but also greatly promoted the development of agricultural production. In the ancient society, water conservancy projects were something of paramount importance for agriculture. Yu saw the close relations between water conservancy projects and agricultural development and worked to build the projects while harnessing flood. The *Analects of Confucius* records, "Yu didn't care for the Imperial Palace, but spent most of his time in building water conservancy projects and conducting waterways." After Yu dredged the flood into the sea, he soon substituted the flood control work for the construction of water conservancy projects in the farmland. The waterways dug in the farmland could drain the water from the fields, remove the water logging, open up fertile fields and greatly increase the land area, which provided a sound material basis for the development of agriculture. *Mencius* records that Yu not only controlled the flood of the Yellow River, but also dredged and drained the water systems along Taihang Mountain in the North Bank of the Yellow River. Yu's work not only subdued the floods of the Yellow River, but also promoted the farming technology and boosted the development of water conservancy projects, agriculture, and animal husbandry.

In this way, Yu's mission in flood control had a social implication. It is recorded in history that

"Yu becomes the ruler of the world by bowing to the crops". Here "bowing to the crops" means attaching much importance to agricultural production. Yu led people to dig rivers and canals and develop irrigation technology, which provided favourable conditions for the development of agriculture. Yu's flood control greatly promoted the development of agricultural civilization and started the civilized history of rural society in China.

3. Stories about Yu's Control of Floods

Yu's flood control activities went beyond the Yellow River Basin and spread to part of the Huaihe River and the Haihe River basins. Even in Sichuan, Zhejiang and other regions, there were stories about Yu's control of the floods. Yu's stories mainly took place in the middle and lower reaches of the Yellow River, especially in southern Shanxi Province and western Henan Province. As a representative of flood control heroes in the ancient times, Yu was remembered as a legendary hero in the Central Plains. We are shown that Yu's flood control acts were a huge, complex, and systematic project. All these made his job an arduous one.

Considering backward productivity, levels of science and technology, means of transportation, the difficulties and obstacles Yu faced with were beyond our imagination. First, Yu spent 13 years being committed to his work. This could show how difficult his task was. *Records of Grand History* said that Yu "worked hard and lived away from his home for 13 years but had no time to visit his family." *Mencius* wrote, "In the eighth year, Yu passed through his gate three times and did not enter his home." We could get from these documents that Yu had no time to take care of his wife and children to control the flood. Moreover, it reflected the difficulties and his confidence in controlling the flood. Secondly, Yu worked in a vast area. Yu's footprints were found all over the country. *Zhuangzi* wrote, "In the past, Yu blocked the flood, conducting the rivers and passing through the vast areas where the minor ethnicities ruled. He also worked in three hundred famous mountains." According to the statistics, there are more than 50 relics in China related to Yu. For example, the temples named as Yu Temple are many across the country. It shows these might be the places where Yu once performed his work. Where he might appear, there are high mountains, thorny places, dangerous beaches and roads. Without advanced production tools and technologies, Yu had to make arduous efforts in overcoming obstacles, cutting mountains, cultivating land, digging wells and canals, and dredging waterways, etc. All these show that Yu's flood control project was extremely great. Therefore, people worshipped Yu and called him "Yu the Great", "Da Yu", or "Yu the God". Moreover, under the extremely harsh natural conditions, Yu worked hard in the flood-stricken areas. It is said that Yu didn't have one single good nail left. He even suffered from severe rheumatoid arthritis, numbness of limbs and difficulty in walking. There are many records about how he suffered due to harsh work. He was rather languid, and bruises were seen all over his body. He walked with a limp, etc. All these established an image of Yu who was hard-working and sacrificed himself for the people.

Through his hard work, taking advantage of the situation, scientific methods as well as the people-oriented concept, Yu overcame many difficulties and finally made the success in his flood control work. Yu's achievements laid the foundation for the Chinese civilization and was a milestone in the history of the Chinese civilization.

Section VI Yu and the Chinese Civilization

Why do we call Yu "Da Yu" (Dayu, Yu the Great)? As the great ancestor of the Chinese nation, Yu (Fig. 2-41) had two great achievements, one was to control the flood and the other was to establish a country. His water control activities laid the foundation for the establishment of the country which consolidated and developed the water control project, making the sporadic primitive tribal alliances gradually united as a multi-ethnic country. Yu was not only a hero of flood control, but also the founder of the Chinese nation.

Figure 2-41 Yu

1. The Birth of the First Slavery State

Scholars at home and abroad attributed the birth of the Chinese civilization to the large-scale water control activities. Why? China is an ancient nation based on agriculture while agriculture is very dependent on water. This dependence directly leads to the large-scale development of "levelling the land and controlling the water" activities in China.

China as a civilized society began in the Xia Dynasty, a slavery society which was built by Qi, Yu's son. The establishment of Xia Dynasty indicates that the class society has replaced the primitive society, and the civilized age has replaced the barbaric age.

The Xia Dynasty (from the 21st century B.C. to the 16th century B.C.) is the first hereditary dynasty recorded in Chinese history books. It is generally believed that Xia Dynasty was a country with many tribal alliances or complex chiefdom. The cultural relics left in Xia Dynasty, like ritual vessels made of bronze and jade could be dated from the late Neolithic Age to the early Bronze Age. These could help trace when Xia Dynasty ruled.

According to the historical records, Yu's son inherited the throne, which changed the abdication system (Shanrang system) that had been long practiced in China for nearly 4,000 years. The hereditary system started. Since then, "one family ruling the nation" system started. The eleven tribes of Xia nationality had blood relations with Xia Hou, the ruling family. They were politically and economically related. The land they ruled roughly constituted the core territory of Xia Dynasty. It covered an area from the west of Henan Province, and the south of Shanxi Province to the junction of Henan Province, Shandong Province, and Hebei Province in the East. It also included areas extending to the north of Hubei Province and the south of Hebei Province in the north. The geographical centres are Yanshi, Dengfeng, Xinmi and Yuzhou (currently four regions in Henan Province). Examining the myths related to Yu, flood control activities took place along the Yellow River in the Central Plains, which became the birthplace of Xia tribe's prosperity. Based on archaeological excavations from 2002 to 2020, a large-scale city site with an area of 300,000 m^2 has been found in Wangchenggang site of Dengfeng by an archaeological group, which is the largest city site of Longshan culture in Henan Province. Some important remains such as sacrificial pits, jade objects and white pottery were found there. Archaeologists have carried out a series of archaeological excavations at Wangchenggang site in Dengfeng, Henan Province as well as their research in areas around Mount Song and southern Shanxi Province in the past three decades. They've achieved a lot in exploring Xia culture. According to the project of dating Xia, Shang and Zhou Dynasties, Xia Dynasty existed from 2070 B.C. to 1600 B.C., that is, from the 21st century B.C. to the 17th century B.C., great progress has been made in the study of Xia culture. These findings offered evidence for the myths of Yu's flood control practice in areas around Mount Song, Yinluo and Yu County and the myths that Yu built a capital in Yangcheng, Dengfeng City and Qi of Xia Dynasty built a capital in Yu County (Yangdi). The myth of Yu's flood control practice, stories about his family members and other activities were also recorded in the documents. The remains of Taishi Mountain, Shaoshi Mountain, Qi's mother's Temple, Kaimu temple, Qi's mother's tomb and other relics in Mount Song area have also been proof of Yu's existence.

First, material base determines the superstructure. Yu's successful governance of floods played a key role in the establishment of the Xia Dynasty. The state organization must be established on a certain material basis. As the first country in China's history, Xia Dynasty's emergence must also have certain material conditions. Due to Yu and other rulers' unremitting work, the floods were relieved, which greatly promoted the recovery and development of agricultural production. Stable agricultural production helped improve the mode of production and the development of productive forces. The development of productive forces inevitably promoted the corresponding changes in the relations of production and productive forces would be adapted to the level of productivity. The success of Yu's flood control provided a strong material base for the change of production relations, which in turn promoted the establishment of Xia Dynasty.

Then, during the process of taming the flood, Yu won the support of tribal leaders, able men, sages as well as the support of people from all walks of life. The increasingly centralized leading power laid a solid social foundation for the formation of the state. *Records of Grand History* writes that "Yu, Yi and Houji, were ordered by the ruler, to control the flood." *Xunzi* recorded that "Yu worked hard for the people and he had Yi, Gaotao and Hengge as his assistants." Yu was assisted by many able men and sages. In addition, Yu was supported by people of all walks of life. According to *Records of Grand History*, all classes participated in the water control activities. As a result, the alliance of the great sages and the people were strengthened in the whole process of governing the flood.

Finally, Yu's success in flood control laid an ideological foundation for the birth of the country. In the process of flood control, Yu convinced people by practice and virtue. He led the people to fight together in the front line of flood control. He worked hard and shared weal and woe with the people. Yu's dedication, selflessness and his people-oriented spirit were respected by people. By harnessing the water, people could develop agricultural production activities; at the same time, people also realized the importance of the leadership of wise leaders, and they aspired for a unified centralized society to achieve their goals.

2. The Formation of the Earliest Chinese Territory

When dealing with flood, Yu travelled across the country to get to know the topography and geomorphology of various places. He again "classified the world into nine states", namely, Jizhou, Xuzhou, Yanzhou, Qingzhou, Yangzhou, Jingzhou, Liangzhou, Yongzhou and Yuzhou (from *Classics of Mountains and Seas*). This formed the earliest territory of China. Therefore, we often use "Jiuzhou" (or nine states) to refer to China.

When containing flood control, Yu and his tribe gradually integrated with other tribes and expanded their territory. The coordination and cooperation among the tribes were deepened, which made a united tribal alliance in the Central Plains. This alliance took the Huaxia (Han) people as the centre, integrating with other ethnic groups in a common area. It showed the expansion of national territory. Jiuzhou was the territory under the reign of Xia Dynasty.

According to the documents, the hundred-official system had been formed under Yao, Shun and Yu's reign. Yu sent nine governors to rule the nine states. And he took Xiayi as the centre of his communes. That is, their organization changed from blood relationship to geographical relationship, which was one sign of the formation of the state.

Yu's achievements were recorded in various historical documents. For example, Sima Qian noted in

Records of Grand History, "Yu divided the country into nine states and dredged nine rivers".

3. The Development of Science and Technology

Water control is a very complex systematic project. Without the assistance of advanced technology, hard work alone didn't necessarily lead to the completion of the project.

With the assistance of many scientific and technological inventions, Yu had successfully completed his work. He followed scientific laws, adopting proper methods in flood control. *Shangshu* or *The Book of the Old Times* and other classics recorded that Yu conducted water through the hills, dug the canals, and cultivated the farmland. Yu not only tamed the floods, the construction of water conservancy projects also promoted the agricultural production. His way of containing the floods continuously inspired the later generations.

Xia Dynasty was founded in the Central Plains. The emergence of the country represents the most advanced level of productivity at that time, and the basic national policy of building a country based on agriculture had been established. Yu was not only a hero fighting against flood, but also an able ruler who made agriculture the basis of his country. To feed his people, Yu adopted migration as a measure. There are records saying "Yu asked Houji to feed the people who were short of food. When they were short of food, he transferred the grain from the rich areas to the food deficient areas. And Yu moved people in the food deficient areas to where there was the fertile land. People settled down and lived a peaceful and steady life. Then the vassal states were well governed." Through the flow of the population, the pressure on food had been relieved and the people's living problems had been solved.

Records of Grand History wrote that Yu used his own body length as a yardstick to make a unified measuring tool, the ruler. It was said that when Yu was surveying the river, he had a ruler in his left hand and a standard rope in his right hand and he drew a circle with a compass, and he used ropes to measure the length. The rulers(gui ju) and the standard ropes(zhun sheng) we're talking about today derived from Yu's practice.

Shangshu said that Yu surveyed the terrain, cut down trees along the mountains, took the trees as the marks and recorded the survey data so as to determine the trend of the mountains and rivers. He had to compare data he collected and made counts. That is to say, Yu's engineering and technical activities to control floods had driven the germination of the surveying methods and primitive mathematics.

4. Yu's Unremitting Spirit of Regulating the Rivers

Sumerians, the early inhabitants living in the Mesopotamian Plain wrote about flood in their literary works, "rampant flood, no one can fight against it, it can shake the sky and the earth... The crops are ripe, and the rampant floods drown them." These poetic lines expressed people's fear of flood and presented Sumerians' pessimistic view towards the terrible consequences natural disasters brought about.

The biblical story, Noah's Ark (Fig. 2-42) tells that Noah, following God's instructions, built a large ark so that his family and the land creatures in the world could escape from the deluge. Humans were helpless when facing the flood. That Yu led people to fight against the flood successfully presented the other possibility. Even if people knew the natural disasters were powerful enough to damage them, they would fight bravely when there was no choice. They could be damaged, but they would not be defeated.

Figure 2-42　Noah's Ark

The spirit and virtue embodied in Yu's flood control practice had a profound impact on traditional Chinese culture. It was one of the great events that had shaped the character of the Chinese nation.

Yu was a model the descendants could follow. During his practice, he was devoted to his work, prioritized the national interests, put people's interests in his mind, adopted the scientific methods and so on (Fig. 2-43). His spirit has continued and will continue to inspire the later comers and become part of the Chinese civilization.

First, Yu's perseverance and courage were long praised in China. When flood was ravaging people's lives and properties, Yu was ordered to deal with the flood. He started his work immediately after his marriage. He devoted himself to his work and spent 13 years away from home. With hard work, Yu was exhausted and had a heavily sunbathed face. Callouses covered his hands and feet. He worked with people on the front line. Yu put his country and people above everything else. His unremitting spirit, his country-and-people oriented concepts were inherited by the Chinese people.

Second, Yu attached much importance to agriculture, valued the well-being of the people. He made policies which provided food and meat to the hungry people, allocated and supplied food to

Figure 2-43 Yu's Water Governance Concepts

people in the food-insufficient areas. Thus, he won the support and love of his people. When flood was recessing, Yu adopted a series of measures to develop agriculture. For example, he constructed water projects, irrigated the dry farmland, and encouraged people to extend arable land. Despite all his great work and his position, Yu lived a simple life. He preferred simple food and plain clothes. He was an example of self-discipline. All these showed that he put people's well-being in mind. He was a practitioner of governing by virtue.

Moreover, Yu fully demonstrated the spirit of scientific innovation in his practice. Yu learned from Gun's failure in flood control and explored and summarized the laws and methods of flood control. He adopted the water control strategy based on dredging and conducting the flood instead of filling and blocking water with soil. He conformed to the natural law to solve the problem. This is the spirit of adopting the proper method that is adapted to the situation. At the same time, in the process of harnessing water, he dared to invent and create a measuring tool, ruler, which created ancient surveying and gave birth to primitive mathematics. Yu went beyond the limited situation and dared to be the first to carry out innovative flood control activities.

Yu's flood control practice shows the ancient Chinese conducted great work in fighting against natural disasters. It shows their courage, perseverance and wisdom Chinese people had. Various studies have proved that Yu's flood control practice is a major event related to the survival and development of the nation. Later generations regarded Yu as a national hero. Yu's stories reflect the harsh environment Chinese people were faced with 4,000 years ago. The myth of Yu's flood control practice is of great value in both literature and science. It is not only the core of Chinese water culture, but also the source and a symbol of the Chinese civilization.

Chapter Three Water and Agriculture

Water is the life blood of agricultural development and the indispensable primary condition of agricultural production. Reliable water supply has always been the most important support and guarantee of agricultural production. Statistics show that 75% of China's grains were produced in irrigated land, and the water resources consumed by agricultural irrigation account for 60% to 70% of the total consumption of water resources. Water conservancy projects and water resources are the lifeline of agriculture. Without water conservancy, there will be no agriculture.

As the saying goes, "The people are the foundation of the country and food is the first necessity of the people." As a large agricultural country, China has been putting water conservancy in a crucial position since the ancient times. The rise and fall of agricultural production, the prosperity and poverty of the country, and social stability and turmoil are closely related to the rise and fall of water conservancy. To ensure the stability of their political power, the rulers of all previous dynasties put water conservancy as one priority. Previously we mentioned that Yu's flood control practice boosted the construction of water conservancy projects and the development of traditional agriculture. Agriculture was closely linked with water. The history of water conservancy is, to a large extent, a history of the construction of water conservancy projects in farmland.

The close relationship between water and agriculture makes agriculture become an integral part of water culture and form a unique "agricultural water culture" in China. It is reflected in farmland construction, water conservancy tools and production customs. Spreading this distinctive agricultural water culture is not only conducive to the construction and publicity of water culture, but also can promote the public awareness of water-saving, loving and protecting water resources and facilitate the construction of a water-saving society.

Section I Water and Farmland Infrastructure

Crops couldn't grow without water. Therefore, people must take water into consideration no matter where they construct farmland infrastructure and what terrains and what climate they are in. The relationship between water and farmland construction is so close that water culture had been bred in the birth of farmland.

Chapter Three Water and Agriculture

About 10,000 years ago, Chinese history entered the Neolithic Age. Before that, the primitives were in the food collecting era. They gradually learned the method of artificial cultivation of crops and invented primitive agriculture. But in those days, weather was the decisive factor for harvests and the amount of annual precipitation largely determined the harvests.

At the end of the primitive society, China entered the period of the canal agriculture period (Xia Dynasty, Shang Dynasty, Western Zhou Dynasty, the Spring and Autumn Period). The ancient people dug field ditches to allow the irrigated water to flow into the farmland. It was a transitional period from primitive agriculture to intensive and meticulous farming. It is said that when Yu controlled the flood, Yu tried his best to develop the canals. In addition, according to the records of *Guoyu*, Yu dredged the rivers through the canals; at the same time, he drained off water in the farmland and achieved the goal of developing agriculture. Archaeologists later found a ditch of 2-3 m wide and 1 m deep in the second-phase of Meishan type cultural ruins in Luoyang (Fig. 3-1), which proved the existence of canals in the Xia Dynasty.

Figure 3-1 A Circular Trench at the Second-phase of Meishan-typed Cultural Ruins

During the Shang Dynasty, the canals were clearly reflected in the Chinese characters. At that time, the farmland was divided neatly according to a certain amount of farmland area. In bone inscriptions (Jiaguwen) that presented oracles, there were pictographs reflecting the neat fields. Some characters were divided into four blocks, like the shape of 田, and some were divided into six squares ⊞, while some were divided into eight ⊞, nine ⊞ or twelve squares ⊞. There is a word 𐎖 for a Chinese character "田". Judging from its original form, it means "田", or "川" (chuan or river) reflecting the running ditches closely surrounding the field. Words are the reflection of objective facts, and the characters for "Tian", like "田", "⊞" or "𐎖" show that in the Shang Dynasty, the web-like canal system was arranged in the divided farmland (Fig. 3-2).

All in all, from what was mentioned we could see that the canal system (Gou xu system) is a well-

Water and the Chinese Culture

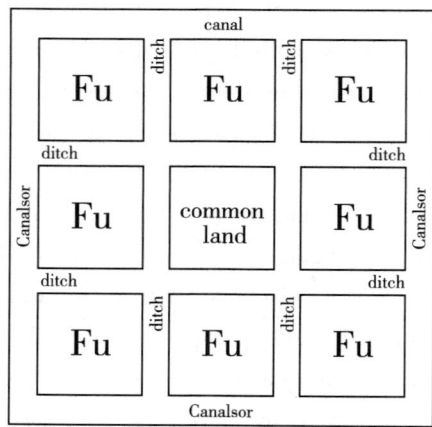

Figure 3-2　Canals in the Farmland①

organized network system composed of five levels of canals. The five-level canals that crisscrossed were getting increasingly wider and deeper, and flew into the rivers. The combination of the canal system and the road system forms the image of the "井" styled field with crisscrossing fields.

The canal agriculture is a unique agricultural form. It not only differs from the primitive agriculture relying on weather, but also varies from the later irrigation agriculture. The canals function to "guide water into the field and discharge water to the river". They not only prevented the damaging of floods, but also kept the soil moisture.

But the canal agriculture couldn't provide water to the fields in dry seasons. During the Spring and Autumn Period and the Warring States Period, with the continuous expansion of cultivated land, the original way of drawing water from the small natural pools to irrigate farmland no longer met the needs. Farmers had to build water conservancy projects for irrigation. That led to the appearance of irrigation agriculture. During the reign of King Zhuang of Chu, Sun Shu'ao, an able Minister of the Kingdom of Chu (equivalent to the prime minister), built the earliest water storage and irrigation project (Quebei, see Fig. 3-3, Fig. 3-4) in Chinese History near Anfeng City (now Shouxian County, Anhui Province). This greatly increased grain production in Anfeng City and quickly made it an important economic area of the State of Chu.

In the early years of the Warring States Period, Marquis Wen of State of Wei ordered Li Kui to preside over the reform. In the reform, the original land ownership system was reformed and a new irrigation canal system was built. Among them, the twelve canals that diverted water from the Zhanghe River was the most representative water conservancy project.

In the 25th year of Marquis Wei's reign (422 B.C.), Ximen Bao was appointed head of Ye (a place in Anyang City, Henan Province). On the one hand, he severely punished the village heads and witches who cheated and victimized the people, disenchanted the evil activities of worshiping

---

① The land was divided into nine squares, the surrounding eight parts named Fu, which respectively belonged to eight separate households, and the central one named common land, which should be farmed by the eight together.

Figure 3-3　A Scenary at Today's Quebei

Figure 3-4　Forests and Villages on the Mountain

the river god; on the other hand, he mobilized the people to dig 12 canals and conducted water into the fields. The barren land on both sides of the Zhanghe River were quickly turned into fertile farmland. The water conservancy project benefited the local people till Han Dynasty.

In the Kingdom of Qin, King Zhao appointed Li Bing, a water conservancy expert, as the governor of Shu County, and asked him to preside over the construction of the famous Dujiangyan water conservancy project, making the Chengdu Plain a land of abundance where people could control water and never suffered from famine. When the First Emperor of Qin ruled, Zheng Gong, an engineer of the Kingdom of Han, was ordered to construct Zhengguo Canal in the Guanzhong area (currently, several cities surrounding Xi'an, Shaannxi Province). The completion of this project changed the barren land in Weibei Plain into fertile farmlands, which laid the foundation for Qin's annexation of the six other kingdoms.

Starting from the Qin and Han Dynasties, the rulers of all dynasties had been keen on the construction of water conservancy projects. Based on the specific water resources and their geographical situations, diversified farmland infrastructure had mushroomed. Farmland forms with distinct regional characteristics came into being.

1. Hani People's Terraced Fields

It was from the Sui and Tang Dynasties that the Hani people started to build terraced fields and grow rice when they moved to Ailao Mountain area. Their ancestors built terraced fields by taking advantage of the local geographical features that seemed to be cut by swords and axes in Ailao Mountain area. Affected by the Indian Ocean wind in the south and the great differences in altitudes, Ailao Mountain area preserved dense old forests in the relatively cold mountains, covered with clouds and fog all the year round, and thus breasting abundant rainfall. At the same time, the water vapor that evaporated from the rivers and lakes was transformed into fog and rain that continuously fell into the hot and dry valley throughout the year. The rain fell and formed numerous pools and streams in the forests and in the mountains. The natural reservoirs provided a reliable guarantee for Hani terraced agriculture in Ailao Mountain area. Therefore, no matter how high it was in Ailao Mountain area, there would be enough water to irrigate the field.

The Hani people usually built terraced fields in the gentle slopes with high temperature and high humidity at an altitude of 800–1,300 m, which is suitable for the growth of rice. If the slope is gentle and the land large, then the large tracts of fields could be reclaimed; if the slope is steep, the small patches of fields would be reclaimed. They would reclaim land in every possible spot, even the small parts between the stones. Therefore, the terraced fields were built in layers with different sizes. Some fields are merely as small as bathtubs and some are a few acres. There are tens of thousands of acres on one slope. They extend along the slope. Looking from the foot of the hill, the terraced fields seem to have reach the sky. And between the terraced fields the narrow paths are built so that farmers could walk and work conveniently.

After more than 1,300 years' development as well as painstaking efforts of generations of Hani people, the Hani terraced fields in Yuanyang County have reached 3,000 levels and 170,000 mu (roughly, 11,339 hectares), which is the largest in the world.

As for the relationship between water culture and the terraced fields, some people say that the core of Hani culture is embodied in terrace culture that cannot develop without water.

Water is an indispensable element of Hani terraces. Hani terraces are not built all the way to the top of the mountain, where the primordial forest grow. Hani people believed that many personified mountain gods lived in the mountainous forests. These mountain gods had infinite power. These gods could tell the good from the evil. The gods of each mountain protected the good people and punished those who defiled gods and did wrong. Considering that mountain gods were sacred in people's minds, the sacrificial activity of taking a tree as a god gradually evolved into the annual "Angmatu" festival. The villagers organized themselves to protect the trees in the forest. From an ecological point of view, this kind of protection is certainly beneficial. These primitive forests played an important role in conserving water. Without them, the terraces couldn't be kept. Without terraces, the terrace culture would have lost their roots.

To reclaim terraced fields, the surface of the fields should be levelled first. And the industrious Hani people said, "If the field is uneven, it doesn't matter. Water will help you." As we all know, water flows to the lower place. If there is more water in one place, it means that the field surface is lower. If there is less water in one place, it means that the place is at higher elevation. Therefore, Hani people judged the height of field surface according to the amount of water.

To solve the irrigation problem in terraced fields, the Hani people dug ditches above the terraces to collect spring water. On the ditches and ridges, you will see a wooden trough lying across the junction at the ditch and the terraced fields. The wooden trough is usually made of hard wood such as the chest tree and black fruit tree. It has the same flat bottom but differs in width. When water

Figure 3-5 Wooden Trough Used to Divert Irrigating Water

overreaches the groove, it will automatically overflow to the lower terrace. The wooden trough is used to divert irrigating water(Fig. 3-5). This shows an unwritten village regulation formed by the Hani people after long-term practices in terrace agriculture. Based on the irrigation area of a mountain spring or ditch, the owners of the terraces negotiate the amount of water consumption and allocate water resources proper to the size of terraces. Thus, we can see that these wooden troughs placed at the junction of the ditch and the fields are used to divert water into the terraces and regulate the amount of water used.

The wisdom of the Hani people in using water doesn't end with this. When the ditches are dug, if there are big rocks they couldn't bypass, they would burn dry wood on the rocks and pour them with cold water while the stones are burnt hot and red. The stones would be exploded into pieces due to the principle that objects would expand with heat and contract while cold. Water flowing through the villages, the Hani people make use of this to build some living facilities such as water mills and water wheels. They not only make full use of the kinetic energy of water, but also effectively reduce the erosion of ditches and terraces by the currents. Every village on the mountain has a common composting pond where villagers store the faecal sewage of livestock. After fermentation, it becomes ecological farm manure. When it comes to spring ploughing, the pond mouth is dug and the water flows into it. The fertilizer flows with water into the field. Pouring water and fertilizers into the field together is time saving and labour saving; and it is also highly effective and eco-friendly. Cows, horses, pigs and sheep are usually grazed in the mountains, and livestock manure is also piled up on the mountains. In June and July of each year, the heavy rain washes them down and flows into ditches and fields to meet the growth needs of rice.

The villagers don't have tap water. People wash in the pond and the used water flows down the mountain to the terraces below. There was no waste. This is the most natural and low-cost way of water utilization, and it is also something that the Hani people were used to. Hani people's lives are closely related to terraces and water. For example, according to the local customs when a child is born the family should hold a "naming ceremony". If a boy is born, another boy of 7 or 8 years old will be found to perform farming with a small hoe in the square in a courtyard that symbolizes the terrace; if the child is a girl, another girl of 7 or 8 years old will be found to perform the act of collecting the spiral shells or capturing rice field eels in the square symbolizing the "terrace". In a local village, most of the laborers working in the fields are women. Children help their mothers when they are young, so they live in harmony with water (Fig. 3-6).

Figure 3-6 The Hani Children

Yuanyang terraces have distinct ecological characteristics. Standing in the Hani villages and looking up to the top of the mountain, you will see the exuberant forest. Looking down at the foot of the mountain, you will see the vigorous terraces. At the foot of the mountain, you will see the flowing river. This model is praised as a forest-village-terrace-river isomorphic ecosystem. This is the best proof that man can live with nature in a harmonious and sustainable way. For thousands of years, this ecosystem has been full of vitality. Yuanyang terrace is neither a simple natural landscape nor a simple cultural landscape. It integrates countless wisdom and painstaking efforts. It is a human creation that shows unity of nature and man. It is also the foundation of material and spiritual life of the Hani people. In Yuanyang Hani terraced agriculture, water closely connects forests, villages, terraces, and rivers, and plays an indispensable role in the cycle of ecological system of terrace agriculture. At the same time, water has been integrated into the production and life of Hani people in many aspects. It has influenced the Hani people imperceptibly. The concept of harmonious unity between man and nature in Yuanyang terrace is the direction of the development of ecological civilization of rural water conservancy in China.

2. Xinghua Duotian (Piled Farmlands)

In Xinghua City, central Jiangsu Province, there is a unique kind of farmland—Duotian. The farmland presents a beautiful scenery. There you can see the farmland that is piled higher than the water surface is surrounded by streams; lotus is growing in the streams, fish and shrimp are swimming freely while vegetables and melons are planted in the farmlands. Local people have dug the river mud in the low-lying marsh areas, the mud is piled high and reclaimed farmland is put on the piled mounds. Islands-like farmlands of different sizes and shapes are scattered and surrounded by canals of different width. That's why Xinghua is known as the "hometown of thousands of islands" (Fig. 3-7).

There are three kinds of views about how Duotian was first built. One is that "Yu created farmland". It is said that when Shun was the ruler, news reached him

Figure 3-7　Xinghua Duotian—Hometown of Thousands of Islands

that Yu succeeded in flood control. Shun summoned Yu to see him quickly. Receiving the order, Yu was eager to share the good news with Shun, so he started his journey to see the ruler in such a hurry that he even had muds on his legs. When he passed a bay on the east coast, Yu felt the gentle wind and saw the water grass was overgrown. So he turned to his followers, saying, "How fertile the land here is. It would be great if water receded, and people could reclaim farmland here. While he said, he wiped the mud off his legs and the mud fell into the sea. Magically, the mud grew into numerous earthen mounds." Seeing that, Yu was very happy. Yu immediately led the people near the sea to build dikes to stop water, grow melons and vegetables on the mounds. That's how Duotian came into being.

Some are of the opinion that the origin of Duotian was related to Yue Fei, a famous patriotic general of the Southern Song Dynasty. Yue Fei stationed his military camps in Xinghua when leading his army to fight against the northern nomadic tribes who invaded the Central Plains and marched southwards. Yue's army piled many mounds in the wild. Later, during the reign of Emperor Hongwu of the Ming Dynasty, many immigrants came to Xinghua to reclaim the wasteland. They found the mounds left by Yue Fei's army and cultivated vegetables there. The soil was of high quality, so the vegetables grew well. Inspired, people piled earth high and grew vegetables in the wasteland. They had a good harvest. As years went on, Duotian of different shapes and sizes were formed.

Some proposed the "Fengtian theory". Xinghua's cultural department thinks that Duotian might derive from the ancient "Jiatian". The ancestors who lived in this area may have put wooden trellis in the swamp, covered them with soil and aquatic plants. Therefore, it is believed that the earliest Duotian might float on the surface of the water so as not to be submerged.

Some scholars inferred that Duotian was most likely formed in the Ming and Qing Dynasties. A project was put into practice that clean and clear water was stored to brush the silt off. Consequently, the highest flood levels of Hongze Lake and Gaoyou Lake in the northwest of Xinghua City were 16.9 m and 9.64 m respectively, which were higher than the highest position in Xinghua City. In the flood season, water from the rivers and lakes quickly flowed and converged in the lower Xinghua area. Flood occurred frequently in Xinghua area. The local people tried every possible means to fight against flood. They chose a slightly higher plot, dug soil to increase height, formed soiled mounds, and then planted crops on the mounds to form Duotian.

To protect life and property, Duotian is much higher than the surrounding areas. Looking from a distance, these higher-than-usual-plots are like islands rising from the water. The construction of Duotian continued until the founding of the People's Republic of China. According to the statistics of the 1960s, Duotian is generally higher than it is now, and the highest one is 5-6 m above the water surface. With such a height, when flood hit, the local people could be free of their worry. The surrounding slopes are all planted with crops. People not only grow vegetables and crops on the flat top of Duotian, but also on the slopes. These could feed the whole family in disaster-stricken years.

Besides flood prevention, Duotian has other functions. Duotian has loose soil and nutrients rich in inorganic matter like calcium, iron, manganese, and other trace elements. In addition, it is surrounded by water, with sufficient light, good ventilation, easy irrigation, and cultivation, which is very suitable for the growth of a large variety of fruits and vegetables. The production of vegetables is superb both in quality and yield. In the 1950s, the yield of rapeseed per unit area in Duotian of Xinghua was the highest in China. Moreover, the unique geographical features of farmland surrounded with water makes it rich in freshwater fish and shrimps. Therefore, Duotian Lake area is known as "the freshwater products museum".

Since its formation, Duotian has made a beautiful landscape (Fig. 3-8). Three of the "Twelve Beautiful Sceneries of Zhaoyang" are with Duotian. Now every spring rapeseed clot Duotian with millions of golden flowers. The flowers on Duotian and their reflections in the water are fluttering and dancing in the breeze like a boundless yellow carpet. Taking a boat, wandering in a zigzag way among Duotian, one could indulgenced in the beauty of nature. The professional or amateur photographers, near or far, come to this sea of rapeseed flowers to record the beautiful moment.

Chapter Three   Water and Agriculture

Figure 3-8   Scenery of Duotian

3. Mulberry-Dike-Fishpond in the Pearl River Delta

In the Pearl River Delta, the interlocking water systems and the low-lying lands lead to frequent floods. To develop agriculture here, the local people were faced with problems like flood control, waterlogging drainage and reduction. The low-lying areas in the Pearl River Delta were easy to become marshes, seriously threateneing agricultural activities, especially rice planting. People found the measures to reduce the losses caused by floods after long-term experiences and experiments. They dug the low-lying waterlogged lands into ponds, piling soil into dikes where water was stored and fish was raised. Then mulberries were planted on the dikes or in the higher areas near the ponds (Fig. 3-9).

Figure 3-9   Fishponds with Mulberries on the Bank

Water and the Chinese Culture

Historical records show that as early as the Han Dynasty, in Zhuya (today's Hainan Island), the south of Guangdong Province, and some areas near Guangzhou, women had already planted and picked mulberries, silkworms, fed the silkworms and woven silk. During the Jian'an period of the Han Dynasty, when an official travelled to Nanhai (now a place near Guangzhou), he saw mulberries growing on the high dikes while fish swam in the pond. This could show that local farmers already planted mulberries in the higher dikes.

In the Tang Dynasty, Guangzhou had become a trading port. Merchants and foreigners from all over the world came to Guangzhou to do business, especially to buy silk. Agriculture developed very fast. At that time, in the Pearl River Delta and its surrounding areas, rice would be ripe twice in a year and those who fed silkworms would harvest cocoons five times in a year. In the Tang and Song Dynasties, China's economic centre gradually shifted from the north to the south. At the end of the Northern Song Dynasty, a large number of northern scholars migrated to the south and settled down in the Pearl River Delta. They built large numbers of water conservancy projects and reclaimed land there.

Since the Northern Song Dynasty, dikes had been built on both sides of the rivers in the Pearl River Delta, thus forming the basic pattern of farmland and water conservancy projects. Especially during the period of Emperor Hui in the Northern Song Dynasty, farmlands surrounded by mulberries fields were built in the Pearl River Delta, extending to areas in Nanhai County and Shunde County. According to A History of Luoge, dikes were built in the northwest of Nanhai County in the Song Dynasty. The dikes first built was in Luoge of the Beijiang River, which was 86.60 km long, guarding 400 hectares of farmland. Later, there were numerous large-scale mulberry-surrounded farmlands (Fig. 3-10), protecting over 1,000 hectares.

Figure 3-10　Mulberry-Dike-Fishpond

In the early Ming Dynasty, sericulture in the Pearl River delta developed not only in Nanhai, Shunde, Zhongshan, Xinhui and Panyu along the West River and North River, but also in Dongguan and Zengcheng along the East River and Qingyuan along the North River. In Pingbu Village of Shunde County, people harvesed silkworms and wheat in April, and sold grain and spinned silk at the end of summer. Residents of Xiqiao in Nanhai County made a living by trading tea, mulberry and silk. There were 4,751 mulberry trees in eight counties of Guangzhou. The main areas producing silk and mulberry trees in the Pearl River Delta were in Jiujiang of Nanhai County, and Longshan and Longjiang in Shunde County.

In the late Ming Dynasty, with the increase of raw silk trade in Guangzhou, sericulture in the Pearl River Delta region began to develop rapidly, which promoted the emergence of a new way of water conservancy and water and soil resources utilization, namely Mulberry-Dike-Fishpond.

In the Qing Dynasty, due to the promotion of sericulture commodity economy, many low-lying fields were changed into fishponds. People dug ponds and piled soil into farmlands in Jiujiang of Nanhai County and Longshan and Longjiang of Shunde County. After the Opium War, sericulture developed at an unprecedented speed. In the original ponds area, large mulberry fields and large ponds were made. The local people planted mulberry trees instead of grain in the fields. The atmosphere of digging fields and building ponds expanded to neighboring villages and nearby areas, reaching its heyday in history.

Mulberry-Dike-Fishpond, the new form of sericulture, was first recorded in *New Accounts of Guangdong* in the Qing Dynasty. The book introduces that Mulberry-Dike-Fishpond means that mulberry trees are planted on the dikes, fish raised in ponds and mulberry leaves used to feed silkworms while silkworm excrement are to feed fish and pond mud used as fertilizers for mulberries. The proper combination of mulberry planting, silkworm rearing, and fish feeding forms a virtuous circle in which mulberry, silkworm, fish and mud depend on each other (Fig. 3-11). There are other records to describe mulberry fields and fishponds. There is a saying in Sangtang District that goes "silkworms are strong, fish is fat, mulberries are flourishing, ponds rich in fertilizers and cocoons are fruiting", fully explaining the relation among mulberry, silkworm and fish.

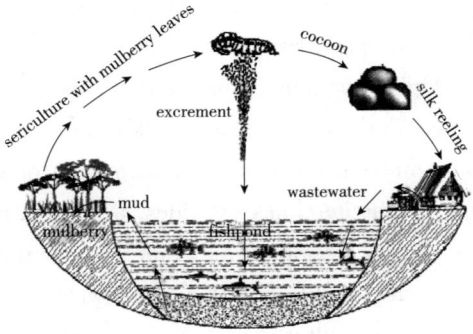

Figure 3-11 The Circular Diagram of Mulberry-Dike-Fishpond

Mulberry-dikes & Fishpond is a kind of agricultural production and water conservancy project. It makes full use of the land and freshwater resources in the Pearl River Delta by digging deep ponds, raising fish there and planting mulberries on the dikes. In the middle and late Ming Dynasty, the area ratio of mulberry fields to fishponds was three to seven or four to six. In the late Qing Dynasty, people applied a more appropriate proportion of mulberry fields to fishponds based on the relationship between mulberry leaves, silkworm excrement, fish feed and sediment that fish in per mu of pond(roughly 667 m^2) needs. Due to the long-term rain erosion and muds piling on the dikes, the pond surface gradually increased, and the dike surface correspondingly decreased. Therefore, the ratio of pond to dike was six to four or seven to three or "seven ponds and three dikes". At present, the ratio is four to six, that is to say, about 40% of the low-lying land is dug as fishpond. Then, the excavated mud in ponds is applied to the dikes. Fish and shrimps are raised in the ponds, and mulberry or other crops planted on the dikes. The fishponds are not only dug for fish, but also for storing waterlogging in polder fields, which plays the role of draining and reducing water logging, and can provide irrigation water so as to reduce loss when drought hits.

With mulberry fields and fishponds people can not only maximize the use of polder fields, but also fully use water resources and turn water damage into water benefit. At the same time, it can also flexibly adapt to the dual needs for crops planting and household handicraft production. In addition to mulberry trees, rice, fruit trees, sugarcane, flowers, and grass can also be planted. Therefore, there are rice fields, fruits fields, sugarcane fields, flower fields, etc.

As for fruit trees, longan, litchis, banana, and orange trees are planted; in terms of flowers, there are jasmine, rose, chrysanthemum and orchid trees etc. In addition, there are cabbage, lettuce, broccoli, tomato and other vegetables, soybean, corn, peanut, sweet potato and other food crops, as well as elephant grass, water lily and other land and aquatic plants. In terms of animals, in addition to silkworms, there are silver carp, bighead carp, grass carp and mud carp. At the same time, there is the mixed breeding of carp, crucian carp, bream, green and other omnivorous fish, as well as shrimp, eel, aquatic fish, California perch and other high-quality aquatic products, and chickens, ducks, pigs and other poultry and livestock. According to the statistics about migratory birds, insects, plankton, and microorganisms living in the ponds, there are hundreds of diversified species of organisms in the field and pond system.

We have understood the typical pattern of mulberry fields and fishponds, that is, planting mulberry on the dikes, raising fish in the ponds, rearing silkworms with mulberry leaves and feeding fish with silkworm excrement, achieving the organic combination of mulberry planting, silkworm rearing, fish raising and other production links. Besides, there are other production forms, like interplanting elephant grass, soybean, vegetables, and flowers in mulberry fields, raising chickens and rabbits in mulberry forests and ducks in water. And water hyacinth, water peanut, green duckweed and other aquatic plants are cultured on the water surface, and pigs are raised by using water lilies and elephant grass, to realize the three-dimensional production of agriculture, fishery and animal husbandry. If the biogas production with pig manure, chicken manure and cocoon water is added, as well as the processing of silkworm, cocoon making, silk reeling, silk spinning and dyeing and other products, this Mulberry-Dike-Fishpond system can be called a multi-form and multi-link comprehensive production mode combining agriculture, fishery, animal husbandry, industry and trade.

This Mulberry-Dike-Fishpond model could be first traced back to orchards-based fishponds. People dug the ponds to raise fish and fruits trees that were planted on the dikes. The layout of fishponds plus orchard appeared after the rise of raising fish in ponds in the early Ming Dynasty. In the low-lying areas, which were unsuitable for the growth of fruit trees, people piled soil to build foundations to raise the low areas. Fruit trees were planted on the foundations and fish was raised in the sunken water pools. Farmers could harvest both fruits and fish. During the Wanli Period of the Ming Dynasty (1573-1620), farmers in Jiujiang area of Nanhai County dug deep in the low-lying waterlogged land or easily flooded farmland and turned them into ponds for fish farming. The excavated soil was put around the ponds as the foundations where litchi, citrus, longyan and other fruit trees were planted.

The Mulberry-Dike-Fishpond model in the Pearl River Delta emerged in the late Ming Dynasty. This model combines fish farming and silkworm rearing to form a more reasonable recycling system. This is what fruit-field-fishpond model lacks. According to historical records, where the Mulberry-Dike-Fishpond model that developed rapidly in the late Ming Dynasty was mainly located in some areas of Nanhai County and Shunde County, Guangdong Province. In the early Qing Dynasty, due to the increasing demand of international trade for silk, the profits from mulberry planting and silkworm rearing greatly exceeded that of fruits. The continuous development of sericulture led to the rapid decline of fruit-field-fish-pond model. Historic records wrote that farmers turned to sericulture and fish farming from fruits trees planting. In many areas, the fruit-field-fish-pond model had been changed to the specialized Mulberry-Dike-Fishpond one. For example, in Jiujiang of Nanhai County, sericulture had not been widely developed during the Jiajing Period of the Ming Dynasty(1522-1566). Women's daily labor was mainly spinning and weaving, and lonyan was growing everywhere, a fruit-field-fish-pond model was naturally their choice. Later, this model had gradually evolved into the Mulberry-Dike-Fishpond one, which could better solve the problem of waterlogging in low-lying areas. The development of fruit trees planting to mulberry planting had laid a foundation for the export of pond fish and silk in the Pearl River Delta.

Similarly, this was a highly intensive ecological agriculture in the south of the Yangtze River in the Ming Dynasty. After the Ming Dynasty, the sericulture industry in Hangjiahu area of the south of the Yangtze River developed. To adapt to the characteristics of mulberry trees, such as "growing in dry, fertile, sunny, and open land rather than wet, barren and sheltered fields", the low-lying areas were dug deep and made into ponds and the silt from the ponds was used to build high dikes. In this way, farmers had made farms with dry fields, paddy fields, ponds, and farmlands of various heights. Various agricultural activities were carried out according to local conditions, forming the unique landscape of fish farming in ponds, rice planting in fields and mulberry planting in dry lands.

The common production mode between the ecological agriculture in the south of the Yangtze River in Ming Dynasty and the Mulberry-Dike-Fishpond in the Pearl River Delta was the ecological process with the combination of mulberry planting, silkworm rearing and fish culture, forming a virtuous cycle of feeding silkworm with mulberry leaves, feeding fish with silkworm excrement and cultivating mulberry with ponds mud (fish manure). From the ecological point of view, the waste generated in each production process is the raw materials needed in the next production process that can be recycled, which is consistent with the food chain law among organisms. The balance of food chain in artificial ecology involves not only land and water resources, but also plants and animals, as well as agriculture and handicraft industry. In the whole process of ecological production, there is no need to utilize the energy and nutrients outside the system. This production mode of high-efficient agriculture and handicraft industry has completely realized the goal of ecological agriculture, which is emphasized in contemporary ecological agriculture, that is, "ecologically self-sustaining, low input and economically viable".

The Mulberry-Dike-Fishpond model has produced huge economic benefits. According to *New Accounts of Guangdong*, "One mu (667 m^2) of mulberry fields could produce 250 kg of leaves. Then one can have 2 kg of silk after silkworms eat the leaves. One family of eight members could be well fed if they have 10 mu mulberry fields." "One takes fish to the market and brings money back." "One boatload of raw silk could be exchanged for a boatload of silver." *Records of Longjiang* wrote that during Emperor Daoguang's reign in the Qing Dynasty, people in Shunde had enough to eat because the local people planted mulberries, reared silkworms, pigs and fish. Farmers could make more profits with mulberries and fish than with crops. The huge gains brought by the Mulberry-Dike-Fishpond model made the Pearl River Delta gradually a land of abundance in the tide of commodity economy.

The Mulberry-Dike-Fishpond model is one of the important achievements in developing traditional water conservancy and agricultural technology in China. It shows that Chinese culture encourages people to find resources and forces to develop from within rather than expand from without. This concept is rooted in the China's agricultural civilization. It is conservative and does not encourage expansion. The same is true of the attitude towards land and natural resources. It does not advocate excessive and unchecked development of land and natural resources, but encourages intensive farming and management on the basis of developed land and natural resources, so as to improve the output of per unit land area.

The water culture in this agricultural model is reflected in its ecological awareness. The water cycle, together with other cycles, constitutes a positive trend, which can better maintain the ecological balance, achieve water, soil, and water conservation, and stabilize the natural ecological structure and function well.

Affected by the Mulberry-Dike-Fishpond, the rich and colourful food culture, clothing culture, folk culture, architectural culture and religious culture boomed. The biodiversity of this model has laid a rich material foundation for the diversity of food culture. People make a variety of edible animals and plants into a variety of exquisite food. Pond fish can be cooked into dozens of delicacies. "Best cuisine in Guangzhou, the best cooking from Fengcheng" portrays a picture of the local food culture in this Mulberry-Dyke-Fishpond district. In addition, the popularity of Xiangyun silk, the fashionable clothing (Fig. 3 – 12) and its manufacturing technology reflects the unique fashion culture.

Figure 3-12　Xiangyun Silk

Shunde Ancestral Hall, Nanhai Temple, and many ancestral temples were built to worship the ancestors and deal with family affairs or to worship various gods such as silkworm God, land God, Kitchen God, Great Emperor Zhenwu, Mazu, etc. Various folk literature and religious activities such as dragon boat race were held to celebrate or pray for a bumper harvest. And the layout of villages with bridges and rivers shows its featured architectural culture which embodies the cultural diversity in the Mulberry-Dyke-Fishpond district.

Section II　Water and Water Conservancy Tools for Agricultural Use

Water conservancy tools for agricultural use refer to the tools, machinery, instruments and equipments used in the process of agricultural production. Every agricultural water conservancy tool condenses human wisdom and creativity and is an important carrier of water culture. The water conservancy tools for agriculture use represent the water culture of different times.

Well is the product of human civilization. The survey, digging, construction technology and well extraction integrate the science and technology of hydrogeology, machinery or construction

Figure 3-13 Boyi

materials. In *Prince of Huainan* (Huainanzi) of the Han Dynasty, Boyi (Fig. 3-13), a famous figure who once assisted the emperors, Yu and Qi, invented the technology of shaft sinking. Legend has it that when Boyi dug out the well, the dragon and the immortals fled for they thought there was a great change in the world. The legendary tale shows how seriously the ancestors took the well digging matter.

Archaeological excavation shows that about 5,000 years ago, there were water wells with a depth of 6-7 m and a diameter of 2 m. During the Warring States Period, there were wells specially used for agricultural irrigation. A water well for farmers was discovered in Litangzhuang, a village of Xinzheng, Henan Province. A well ring made with tiles was built on the inner wall of the upper well. The blocks were overlapped and connected by a tenon and a button. When sinking a well, with the increase of the well depth, the tiled well rings are put in layer by layer. After the well is dug, the well ring is formed. In the Han Dynasty, people not only used a lot of well water for domestic use, but also for irrigation. The lining materials of shaft in Han Dynasty were abundant, and there were ceramic shaft linings and brick shaft linings. To facilitate the irrigation, agricultural water conservancy tools such as Jiegao and windlass were set up at the wellhead to draw water, excavate diversion channels and lead water to the farmland that needed irrigation.

1. Jiegao

Jiegao (Fig. 3-14) is a labour-saving tool to get water for farming. The early records of Jiegao can be found in a dialogue between Yanyuan and Shijin in *Zhuangzi* written by Zhuang Zhou in the Warring States Period. The picture of Jiegao on the stone relief of Wuliang temple in the Han Dynasty is the oldest one so far.

From the pictures of Jiegao drawn in ancient documents, we can see that the structure of Jiegao is equivalent to an ordinary lever. The middle of the long cross bar of Jiegao is supported by vertical wood or suspended by rope. One end of the cross bar relates to a bucket by a straight bar, and the other end a big stone.

According to the legend, the inventor of Jiegao was Yiyin, the famous Prime Minister of the Shang Dynasty and also known as the ancestor of Chinese cooking (Fig. 3-15). In the early years of King Tang's reign, a severe drought hit and Yiyin taught the people to dig wells to fight against drought. In the process of drawing water from wells to irrigate the fields, he used the newly invented tool, Jiegao.

Chapter Three Water and Agriculture

Figure 3-14 Jiegao

Figure 3-15 Yiyin

During the Spring and Autumn Period and the Warring States Period, Lu, Wei, Zheng and other economically developed countries had commonly begun to use Jiegao. According to the records in *Tracing the Origins*, Deng Xi, a senior official of Lu and the Kingdom of Zheng, happened to see five farmers "entering the well to get water with urns on their backs and could only irrigate a small tract of leek field all day long" in the state of Wei. Getting out of his carriage, Deng Xi introduced Jiegao to the farmers and told them that if they used Jiegao to irrigate the leeks, they wouldn't feel tired even after a day's work. However, these farmers in the Wei State replied that it was not that they did not hear of that machine, but they thought the machine might make their work efficient and it surely would also have disadvantages, so they were not willing to use it. This proves that Jiegao had already been known to the local people for a long time.

Zhuangzi's story "Holding the Pot to Irrigate the Orchard" (Fig. 3-16) illustrates this situation once again. Zi Gong, one of Confucius students, was travelling in the State of Chu in the south. When he passed the south bank of the Hanshui River, he saw an elderly man using a pot to get water from the well to water the orchard. The farmer dug a narrow path beside the well so that he could get close to the water level of the well. In this way, he went down, got his pot filled, then held the pot in his arms along the ramp up and poured the orchard. After that, he would go down the path to the well to get water again. Obviously, this method of irrigating would take him a lot of efforts but had little effect. Zi Gong introduced Jiegao to the man and told him he could save much labour and did his work more efficiently if he applied the tool. To his surprise, the elderly man didn't accept his advice. He thought that using the tools would lead people to form the mentality of making gains by trickery. If one wanted to maintain a simple and natural state of mind, he shouldn't take advantage of the tools to save his labour. So even though he knew that there was such a tool as Jiegao, he wouldn't use it at all.

Figure 3-16 Holding the Pot to Irrigate the Orchard

Through this story, Zhuang Zi was meant to advocate the return to simplicity. But we could see that in the Spring and Autumn Period, Jiegao as a convenient and efficient farming tool had been widely used for irrigation.

2. Windlasses

It is convenient to get water with the use of Jiegao, but it limited its use only in the shallow wells or open ditches. If the well for irrigation were too deep, Jiegao would not be practical because the ropes were not long enough to reach the well water. The ancient Chinese upgraded the water drawing tool and invented the windlass which was installed on the wellhead (Fig. 3-17).

The windlass is a kind of water lifting device commonly used by the Han people and mainly popular in northern China. Windlass is composed of windlass head, bracket, well rope, water bucket and other parts. It is a well water pumping and lifting device made according to the principle of wheel and axle.

Figure 3-17 The Windlass

Windlass is a water drawing tool that had evolved from the lever. Its main feature is to change the one-way force to the cyclic force. People erect a derrick on the wellhead, which is equipped with a shaft that can be swung by a handle. A rope is wound on the shaft, and a bucket is tied on one end of the rope. When drawing water, the person who takes the water shakes the crank of the windlass, and the windlass head that rotates with the crank winds the well rope to pull the bucket out of the wellhead, which is convenient and labour-saving. Because of its practicability, the windlass can still be seen in some rural areas nowadays.

According to *An Introduction to the Ancient Inventions* (*Wuyuan*), a book written by Luo Xin of Ming Dynasty, the windlass was first invented by Shi Yi. Shi Yi was a famous historian when King Wu of Zhou Dynasty ruled. He was known as one of the "four sages of the early Zhou Dynasty" and the other three were Zhou Gong of Ji Dan, Jiang Ziya and Zhao Gong of Ji Shi. It shows that as early as 1100 B.C., the working people of the Han nationality may have invented the windlass.

During the Spring and Autumn Period, the windlass was widely used. In the 1970s, archaeologists found two wooden windlasses in an ancient mine in Tonglushan, Daye, Hubei Province. It was estimated that they were used during the Spring and Autumn and Warring States Periods. In *Essential Technique for People's Welfare* (Qi Min Yao Shu), an ancient Chinese agricultural encyclopaedia that was written by Jia Sixie of the Northern Wei Dynasty, the windlass was widely used in farmland irrigation at that time. In the Five Dynasties Period, Li Jing, the ruler of the Southern Tang Dynasty included the windlass in his poem. Then, both Wang Zhen's *Agricultural Book of Yuan Dynasty* and *Technological Encyclopaedia* of Ming Dynasty included the pictures of the windlass. Wang Zhen's *Agricultural Book* also introduces a kind of double windlasses, also known as twin windlasses, which is said to be able to continuously draw water. It can still be seen in some rural areas of Henan Province in the 1950s.

3. Waterwheels

Compared with Jiegao and the windlass, the two agricultural water conservancy tools, the waterwheel appeared in a relatively later period. Waterwheel is an agricultural equipment which can continuously draw water from the rivers and lakes. It is mainly used for lifting water to the higher fields and drain off water from the low fields. Waterwheel plays an important role in traditional Chinese agriculture. Especially in the southern rice growing areas, the waterwheel is a necessity for the farmers.

It is documented that the waterwheel was first used in the Han Dynasty. At that time, it was called as Fanche (a cart that could roll over). According to *Records of the Later Han Dynasty*, Bi Lan, the inventor of Fanche, was a eunuch in the late Eastern Han Dynasty. During the reign of Emperor Ling of Han Dynasty, Bi Lan and nine other eunuchs were called "Ten Chang Shi" (ten close attendants) who made the court in disorder. Later, he got killed by Yuan Shao. At that time, Bi Lan didn't mean to use the waterwheel for irrigating the farmland but used it as a tool to flatter the emperor. He used the waterwheel to draw water from the low place to the high to spray water to the roads where the emperor passed through.

In Three Kingdoms Period, there was an inventor named Ma Jun in State of Wei, who improved Fanche for irrigation and drainage of the farmland. The improved Fanche is composed of trough, scraper, chain, gear and other parts. The chain is initially driven by manpower to rotate circularly.

The scraper installed on the chain scrapes water into the trough, and the water rises along the trough and flows into the field. Because the upper and lower parts of the pavement board are connected by a section of keel plate leaves with wooden pins, which is similar to the skeleton of a dragon, so people call it "keel waterwheel" (Fig. 3-18). The lifting height of the keel water wheel truck is generally 1-2 m, and the water output is determined by the size of the slot and the speed of the gear. Because of the exquisite structure of the keel waterwheel, it could continuously lift water, and its operation can save labor; even children could operate it, so it had rapidly been made popular.

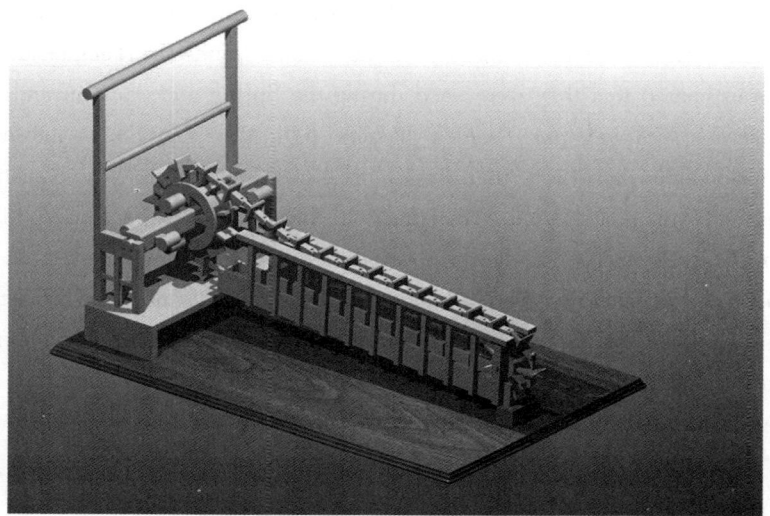

Figure 3-18 Keel Waterwheels

The man-powered keel waterwheel is mostly operated by foot or hand. There are detailed records about the keel waterwheel in Wang Zhen's *An Agricultural Book* in the Yuan Dynasty and Wanyan Linqing's *Illustrations of River Tools and Instruments* in the Qing Dynasty. *An Agricultural Book* includes the introduction to the waterwheel which is completely the same as the previous water wheel. Its power machinery is installed by the fast-flowing river. People first set up a large wooden frame, in the centre of which a rotating shaft is erected. The rotating shaft has been connected with two large horizontal wheels. The underlying wheel is a waterwheel, which is equipped with plate blades, so as to make the waterwheel rotate with the flowing water that drives the tool.

The upper horizontal wheel is a big gear, which connects with the vertical gear on the upper end shaft of the waterwheel. When the waterwheel is installed in a deep ditch dug near the bank of the river, the running water impacts the waterwheel to rotate. The horizontal gear drives the vertical gear on the shaft of the waterwheel and then the waterwheel to rotate, bringing water from the river to the bank and then to the farmland. Later, due to the development of wheel and axle and the progress of mechanical manufacturing technology, people invented a new type of keel waterwheel with power storage, wind and waterpower, which was widely used across the country.

As early as the Tang Dynasty, the appearance of the high turn bobbin wheel had promoted the development of the waterwheel. Liu Yuxi, a famous poet and stateman of the Tang Dynasty, and Chen Tingzhang, a scholar of the Tang Dynasty, both vividly described the function of the high turn tube waterwheel in their "On a Water Drawing Machinery" and "Ode to the Waterwheel" (Fig. 3-19). According to Wang Zhen in his *An Agricultural Book*, the structure of the high turn bobbin waterwheel is introduced. It shows that with the use of the high turn tube waterwheel, water can be raised to a higher level to irrigate the high farmland.

In the Ming and Qing Dynasties, the traditional waterwheel was further improved, and large waterwheels appeared. Lanzhou waterwheel (Fig. 3-20) is a typical representative of large waterwheels. Lanzhou Yellow River waterwheel is also called "crane", "Fanche", "irrigation waterwheel" and "tiger waterwheel". It has been nearly 500 years since Duan Xu invented the Yellow River waterwheel suitable for local use during Emperor Jiajing's reign in the Ming Dynasty.

Figure 3-19 The High Turn Bobbin Waterwheel

Figure 3-20 Lanzhou Waterwheel

Lanzhou waterwheel is a kind of water conservancy facility which makes use of the natural flow of the Yellow River. The diameter of the spoke of the waterwheel is up to 16.5 m. There is a scraper at the end of the spoke, and a rectangular bucket is installed between the scrapers. The waterwheel stands on the south bank of the Yellow River, which is propelled by the natural flow in the high flow season, while in the low flow season, the dam is used to divert and gather water, and the water flows by itself through the small channels between the weirs. When the current impulses the wheel blade plate naturally, the waterwheel is pushed to rotate, and the water bucket scoops up the river water and lifts the water about 20 m. After turning to the headspace, the water is poured into the wooden trough and continuously flows into the farmland for irrigation. This kind of water conservancy facilities, which can automatically lift water to irrigate farmland by turning the waterwheel, is an ancient "tap water" project.

Compared with the southern waterwheel, Lanzhou waterwheel has two characteristics. First, its wheels are very tall, and some wheels can reach 30 m in diameter; second, the materials to make waterwheels are well selected. The wood used to make Lanzhou waterwheel is local elm, sophora or willow, and the selection of materials for different parts is stressed. For example, the spindle must be made of hard and dense elms and willows that could bear water immersion for hundreds even upto one thousand years. The spokes and braces should be the best of the whole pine tree with fewer scars and no cracks. The outer chord must be a good poplar board. All wedges must be smooth and have no cracks. Therefore, the production and installation of a large waterwheel takes about three months.

Since its birth, Lanzhou waterwheel has gradually integrated into the cultural life of the local people. During the reign of Emperor Qianlong of Qing Dynasty, there was a Lanzhou man named Jiang Defu, who missed the scenery of his hometown and wrote twelve poems "Remembrance of Lanzhou". His second poem is to remember the waterwheel by depicting the summer landscape. The poet first wrote about the beautiful landscape of the Yellow River in midsummer, and finally returned to the cool riverside at night. The rolling waterwheel caused the poetic feeling, which was full of twists and turns.

The waterwheel is a favourite subject for the artists. In the late Qing Dynasty, Ma Wu, a folk painter in Lanzhou, painted a panoramic view of the golden city (Fig. 3-21), in which there were two waterwheels. These two waterwheels might be the first included into the painting. Now, the production technology of Lanzhou Yellow River waterwheel has been listed as one of China's

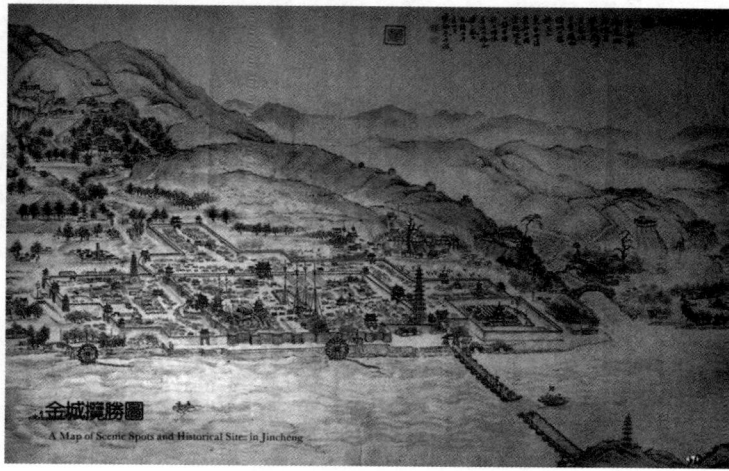

Figure 3-21　A Panoramic View of Lanzhou, the Golden City

intangible cultural heritage and has become an important part of Lanzhou regional culture.

Section III Water and Customs Related to Agricultural Production

For thousands of years, Chinese people have accumulated rich experience in agricultural production. These experiences have affected the agricultural practice and have been passed down from generation to generation, and eventually been turned into customs. Due to the different geographical environment, climate conditions and eating habits, various agricultural production customs have been created. Water culture has been among these customs.

1. Customs Related to Agricultural Production in the North

The northern farmers have long practised intensive farming, believing that "If you invest your time, money and concern into the land, you will make great profits from it. If you invest no efforts, you will get no good harvest." The northern farmers have been long practicing "deep ploughing and fine harrowing".

Farmers habitually pay special attention to soil moisture when ploughing (Fig. 3 – 22). The so-called "moisture degree" refers to the moisture content in the soil suitable for seed germination. There are two ways to measure soil moisture. The first method is that the farmers walked, observed the furrow, and evaluated the soil moisture while ploughing. As for the other method to measure soil moisture, the farmer would first grasp a handful of soil tightly from the plowed land and see whether it can be made into a mud ball. If the mud ball can be made but breaks into pieces when thrown to the ground, they'll say that the soil has proper moisture.

Figure 3-22 Ploughing

But if it remains as a mud ball, it is called "soil moisture deficiency". If it remains a mud ball while thrown to the ground, or it couldn't be made into a mud ball in one's hands, it shows the soil doesn't have proper moisture. After checking soil moisture, farmers would arrange the following work. From the perspective of modern agronomy, proper soil moisture would ensure the crops grow sturdily. Otherwise, it would lead to failure of good harvests.

Farmers would adjust the soil moisture while ploughing the fields. The way farmers plough the fields would help the soil achieve the proper moisture level.

Harrowing is also an important part of farming. The popular sayings related to agricultural activities describe the importance of harrowing, "ploughing deeper and harrowing more, the crops would grow well", and "more ploughing is not better than more harrowing". Harrowing can crush the soil in the fields, flatten the fields and conserve the soil moisture. The early sowing lands especially need more harrowing. And after every rainfall, farmers would rake the ground. Only when the farmers stand on the rake while harrowing the field to a relatively level degree and they would go as steady as a boat and won't feel bumpy, can the harrowing work be considered complete.

After the ploughing the farmers would do the harrowing work. Harrowing is meant to flatten the field. According to different field conditions the farmers would decide how many times the fields need harrowing. Generally, the field needs to be harrowed twice. If the field doesn't have proper soil moisture, either being too dry or too wet, it should be raked several times to get proper soil moisture.

Farmland irrigation is an essential part of agricultural production in northern China. In the past, irrigation of the land was basically dependent on the rain or snow. Farmers looked forward to proper weather for their farming activities. What they were most afraid of was drought and flood. Therefore, in a dry year, farmers would work hard to divert water from the nearby river to irrigate their fields. And even those far away from the river would dig the wells to irrigate their fields. In northern China, it is common to drill the wells in the field when drought hits (Fig. 3-23). Before drilling a well, farmers would ask an expert to select the site, which is called "checking the water vein". A slightly higher stacking platform is padded around the wellhead, which can not only prevent rainwater from entering, but also facilitate the speed of watering the fields. Such a platform is called "well platform". A small pool is opened on one side of the wellhead to keep the water that will flow into the irrigated field. This pool is called "well pool". The channel leading from the well to the field is called "waterway".

Figure 3-23　Drilling the Well　　　　Figure 3-24　A Pit to Store Water

In the hilly areas, farmers often dig pits (Fig. 3-24) to store water so as to irrigate the farmland. The "water pool" is actually a dry well dug by farmers. It looks like a pottery urn. It is generally three or six meters deep and has a diameter of two or three meters. It has an opening and a lid and is set beside the field used to store rainwater. It can only be used to irrigate the land to meet an urgent need when dry season occurs.

In the past, people often competed or chanted to relieve fatigue and activate the atmosphere. For example, in some parts of Henan Province, when people irrigate the farmland with waterwheels (Fig. 3-25), the people who use waterwheels usually work in shifts, with 3 to 6 people in each shift. Although there was no watch for measuring time, people were gifted in inventing ways to count time. They wound the rope around the head of the waterwheel. When the rope finished turning with the head of the waterwheel, they would change to the next shift. So the last shift is called "offline". Each group would show their strength before they are "off the line". They were shouting, pedaling and running with enthusiasm. At this time, if a person showed poor physical strength and couldn't keep up, he would be called "a hanging black fish" by his companions.

Figure 3-25 Irrigating the Farmland with Waterwheels

Normally, a water pool would be used by several families. In dry seasons farmers would fight for water due to limited storage. If the farmers along the river encountered severe drought, they often needed three or four levels of waterwheels to carry water. In this way, they could not only improve efficiency, but also attract a large number of laborers. However, when the multi-level waterwheels were used to carry water for irrigation, each level of waterwheels dare not lag behind. If the lower level waterwheels were backward and failed to supply enough water, they would be drained by the higher-level waterwheels; if the higher-level waterwheels rotated slowly, the water carried by the lower-level waterwheels would submerge the small faucet of the higher-level waterwheels, so that the farmers in control would feel heavier and heavier when they stepped on the waterwheels. Therefore, in order to keep up, people at all levels of waterwheels were desperately stepping on their tools. Many were hurt, and some were so tired that they even vomited blood on the spot.

In some parts of the north, when people use the windlass to carry water to irrigate the field, it will usually take 3 or 4 people to operate the tool. If there are four workers, they would often be divided into two groups. The two groups will hold a contest and see which will go faster. At the climax of the contest, only the whirring of the pulley and the clang of the bucket were heard. While the farmers were working, one could only hear the clanking of the windlass operator because the workers were busy with their task. Only upon the completion of the work, could they have time to meditate on the tight work and burst into laughter.

2. Customes Related to Agricultural Production in the South

Compared with the north, the southern water culture is more abundant. Take the solar term Xiaoman as an example. The southern agricultural proverbs give Xiaoman a new meaning, using "man" to describe the abundance of rain. If abundant water is not stored in Xiaoman, the field might not have enough water for irrigating the crops and might be dry enough to crack, seriously affecting the harvest of a year. Xiaoman season is the time of giving fertilizers to early rice fields and transplanting the rice seedlings in the south of the Yangtze River. Therefore, in dry years, people will take precautions and use waterwheels to irrigate paddy fields.

In the south of the Yangtze River, to use waterwheels used to be a big event in the village. There is a saying in the local agricultural proverb that says "On the day of grain buds, farmers drive three carts". Namely, three carts are silk carts, oil carts, and field carts. As a rule, the waterwheel should start to be used at this season. Before that, the farmers would hold a grand and interesting "water grabbing" ceremony in the village. This kind of ceremony used to be very popular in Haining of Zhejiang Province. Generally, the village head gathered all the families, made appointments and preparations. At next dawn, people lighted torches near the base of the waterwheel, picked up the prepared wheat cakes and wheat balls, and had a good meal at the side of the waterwheel. When the village head gave orders with drums and gongs, they knocked on their farm tools to cooperate. Then, people set foot on the waterwheels installed on the riverside beforhand and began to pick up water. As many as dozens of waterwheels started to work and to irrigate the farmland. The scene is very spectacular. On a merry atmosphere, the running river was introduced into the field channels, and soon the water in the river bank was drained. This festive and lively water grabbing ceremony is no longer hard work in the field. It has been changed into an interesting entertainment.

There used to be a custom of offering sacrifices to god of waterwheels in Jiaxing, Zhejiang Province. Just like the water robbing ceremony, it was another way for farmers to show their attention to waterwheels. According to the local folklore, the "god of chariot" is a white dragon. Every Xiaoman, farmers would put fish and incense on the base of the waterwheel to worship "god of chariot". They would also put a cup of clear water in their offerings. When the sacrifices were held, nobody was allowed to touch the cup of clear water and would be poured it into the field which is a means to wish abundant water. This ceremony fully shows that farmers attached great importance to water conservancy and irrigation.

In addition to Xiaoman, Mangzhong is also a popular solar term among the southern farmers.

Farmers would often pray for good weather conditions and a good harvest during this season. In the south of Anhui Province, people would hold a Rice Planting Festival around the day of Grain in Ear in order to pray for a good harvest in autumn (Fig. 3-26). When the rice planting in the village is finished, the influential farmers in the village will choose a day to celebrate. In the morning of the ceremony, an altar was set up on the beach or in front of the village. From inside the temple, people invited the black and red Taiwei to mount the altar. Flags were put around the altar, and the words "good weather, peace and prosperity of the country, and bumper harvest" were written on the flags. Incense tables were placed in front of the altar for villagers to worship.

Figure 3-26 Rice Planting Festival

Farmers in Shexian of Anhui Province planted rice in the paddy fields, they would hold a special banquet to pay homage to God and Goddess of fields. They would burn three incense sticks on the ridge, then kneel and sing prayer songs.

Some would even invite the monks in the village temples to help them. Some would parade along the paddy fields with the black and red Taiwei. Villagers were holding banners to open the way, with black and red Taiwei sitting on the sedan chairs carried by four or eight people, followed by the band. In this way, with the sound of gongs, drums, and firecrackers, black and red Taiwei toured the farmland of the village and then returned to the front of the temple. This was the end of the ceremony. In some other places such as Wang Village and Yu Village of Jixi, farmers surnamed Wang would lift up the portrait of their ancestor Wang Hua to tour the field at the Rice Planting Festival. This was called "Lord Wang Inspecting the Rice".

On the day of Rice Planting Festival, people in southern Anhui often use newly harvested to make bread and new rice for their meals. Skilful women also steam flour products in the shape of five grains, birds, fruits, vegetables, etc. as a tribute to their ancestors. On the same day, the neighbours also exchange their food. The rice planting baozi made by the leftbehind wives of Hui merchants also has twelve pleats to show the wives' missing of their husbands. In Xin'an, Qimen County, Huizhou City, on the day of Rice Planting Festival, every household steams rice cakes, makes rice rolls and grinds tofu to send them to relatives and friends. Some villages also set up a colourful stage to invite opera troupes to sing and pray for good weather and a bumper harvest.

In addition to the fields crops, fishery in the south also contains the content of water culture. For example, the fishermen are very particular about fishing methods. There are many ways of fishing. In some places, the fishermen would first use a wooden basin to knock on the water surface and make a loud sound. When the turtle in the water is frightened, it will hide in the soil and flood out a string of bubbles. Fishermen follow the bubbles to catch them. It is commonly known as "fishing by knocking on the basin". There are also people carrying "lanterns" at night, carrying fish covers made of bamboo. When fish see the light, they will swim to the bright place. Fishermen take advantage of the opportunity to catch the fish with a fish cover.

In contrast, the way of using ospreys to fish (Fig. 3-27) can better reflect the state of the unity of man and nature. In Fangcheng, Nanyang City of Henan Province, the fishing boat is commonly known as "Yidan boat". This kind of boat is made up of two buckets. Each bucket has three interconnected cabins, which are used to place nets to catch fish and shrimp. A boat usually carries three or four ospreys. When fishing, the fisherman holds a pole to support the boat, and the osprey stands at the bow. When they arrive at the fishing area, the fishermen drive the osprey into the water to catch fish. To release the osprey once is called "a battle". There will be "two battles" in half a day with a short break in the middle of their work. Ending the work is called "ending the battles". While fishing, in order to prevent the osprey from eating too many fishes, before driving them into the river, the fishermen would first feed them with water, and then tie their necks with a rope. The osprey will not be fed until the fishing is over.

Figure 3-27 Ospreys Fishing

Chapter Four Water and Politics

Section I Water Management and Governance of China

People take food as the paramount necessity which grows in water or soil. In China, a farming society with a long history, agriculture is not only closely related to the national economy and people's livelihood, but also related to the rise and fall of the country. A bumper or poor harvest in agriculture mainly depends on whether there is favourable weather or the rivers could supply abundant water. Thus, water is firmly linked to politics through the intermediary of agriculture.

1. The Fortune of a Nation is Determined by the Construction and Maintenance of Water Conservancy Projects

Guanzi once said, "The key for the sage's governance of the world lies in his management of water." The Chinese civilization has seen a history of the management of the rivers. The development of water conservancy projects would often bring prosperity to many industries. When the water conservancy projects were in disrepair, it would cause floods and consequently lower people's livelihood, lead to wars, social unrest and even the downfall of the dynasties.

Yu's success in flood control laid a political foundation for the formation of the first slavery state. During the Spring and Autumn Period and the Warring States Period, the construction of water conservancy projects played an important role in enhancing national strength. Guanzi (Fig. 4-1) built water conservancy projects in the lower reaches of the Yellow River, which was one of the dominant driving forces for Duke Huan of State Qi to seek hegemony. Ximen Bao's governance of Ye City and the construction of 12 canals made State Wei a rich and powerful nation. State of Qin built a canal that irrigated 40,000 hectares of farmland. Since then, the Guanzhong area was free from the bad harvest. Moreover, with this, State Qin was made a rich and powerful nation that eventually defeated the other six states and

Figure 4-1 Guanzi

achieved the unification of the whole nation. Liu Bang borrowed Guanzi's ideas, unified the whole country and built the Han Dynasty. Liu Xiu of the Eastern Han Dynasty took a well irrigated area near the Qinshui River as the base and unified the whole country. The excavation of the Grand Canal provided a powerful material condition for the prosperity of the Sui and Tang Dynasties. The water transport of the Northern Song Dynasty extending in all direction brought about the prosperity of the feudal culture. The solid levees over the Yellow River and the navigation of the Grand Canal from Beijing to Hangzhou guaranteed the unification and prosperity of the Yuan, Ming and Qing Dynasties.

The prosperity of a country depends upon the construction and maintenance of water conservancy projects. The key to develop water conservancy projects is to develop river transport. China's history saw repeatedly that water shortage caused extreme poverty in people which then led to the decline or disintegration of a nation. The history of the peasants' uprising in China shows that most of these uprisings took place when there was political corruption, disrepair of water conservancy projects and frequent occurrences of floods and droughts. To list among some, Chen Sheng and Wu Guang led the uprising in the late Qin Dynasty, the Lulin and Red Eyebrow uprising in the late Western Han Dynasty, and many other peasants' uprisings had to do with floods in late Tang, Song, Yuan and Ming Dynasties. One of the main reasons for the outbreak of these peasant uprisings is the poor maintenance of water conservancy projects, and people suffered from floods and droughts. Peasants' thatches collapsed and they were driven away from their houses. The hungry people who begged for food from the passengers on the roads were seen everywhere.

Water could be governed when the country was in prosperity while rivers would be out of control when the country was in turbulence. Water conservancy activities are generally carried out in a certain economic and social environment. A clean, stable, and prosperous society can provide a good environment for the development of water conservancy projects. During the Qin, Han, Sui, Tang, Song, Yuan, Ming and Qing Dynasties, with national unity, social stability and political cleanliness, water conservancy projects were built at a fast speed. During the Five Dynasties and Ten States Period, Wei, Jin, Southern and Northern Dynasties, feudal separatism and frequent wars led to the decline of water-related projects. Qian Zhengying, a famous water conservancy expert and academician of the Chinese Academy of Engineering, once said, "Before the founding of the people's Republic of China, China experienced three times of reunification and peace, stimulating the construction of water conservancy projects and population growth for three times. The first time was during the Qin and Han Dynasties. As a result of the establishment of a unified political power, it was possible to break through the Sichuan defence and remove the dangers, which created conditions for the unified management of rivers. The Yellow River Basin was greatly developed, and the population of the whole country increased from about 20 million to more than 50 million. The second time was in the late Tang Dynasty. The Yangtze River regions and the south-eastern coastal areas were developed on a large scale, and the Grand Canal running through the north and south was built. The population of the whole country increased to nearly 100 million. The third time was during Yuan, Ming and Qing Dynasties, when water conservancy projects developed nationwide, with a population of 410 million by 1840."

2. Water and Governance of China

In ancient China, water and national politics were closely linked. The long-term stability of a nation depends on whether it could effectively deal with the social crisis including disasters like flood and drought. The operation of irrigation and agricultural system greatly affected the founding and stability of the centralized empire. The political system in China had to make constant responses and adjustments to the changing environment. Therefore, politics in China had been deeply branded with the characteristics of Chinese water culture.

First, when the ancient rulers chose the political centre, the river had been the important factors that they would take into consideration. The ancient capital city usually served as the political, economic, and cultural centre. In the agricultural society, an agriculture-developed area was naturally the economic centre. Therefore, normally the economic centre was located near the rivers where water conservancy projects would be built so that floods or droughts could be alleviated or prevented. For example, the seven famous ancient capitals of China, including Anyang, Xi'an, Luoyang, Kaifeng, Beijing, Nanjing and Hangzhou, were all built near the rivers. These cities not only have had a solid economic foundation, but also could benefit from water transportation. Boats were used to transport people and materials. At the same time, in the ancient times, mountains were usually connected with rivers. High mountains and deep waters were natural resources for military defence, which was an important guarantee for the stability of the political power.

Second, the close relationship between Chinese politics and rivers can also be seen from the administrative divisions of ancient China and names for the ancient or modern places. China's complex geographical, climatic, and hydrological conditions determined that the rulers could not govern their land in a unified way, so the political thought of regional governance had been applied in China. One of the preconditions of local governance was to divide regions. So you can see the division and naming of the administrative regions in China were closely related to rivers.

In the ancient times, the world was divided into nine states. *Lu Buwei's Spring and Autumn Annals* records that Yuzhou, Jizhou, Gunzhou and Xuzhou, four of nine states were divided by the water systems. This tradition of the administrative division has been maintained to this day. Heilongjiang Province is named because the Heilongjiang River flows through the province; Zhejiang Province is named after the Qiantangjiang River (the ancient name for the Qiantangjiang River was the Zhejiang River); the Xiangjiang River in Hunan Province winds down from the south to the northeast and runs through the territory of Hunan Province, so Hunan is called "Xiang" for short; the Ganjiang River runs through Jiangxi Province from the north to the south, so Jiangxi "Gan" for short. In addition, the Chinese often use rivers as the mark of the geographical boundaries. For example, Jiangnan (south to the river), Jiangbei (north to the river), Jiangzuo (left to the river) and Jiangyou (right to the river) are named according to the Yangtze River while the Yellow River is the dividing line between Henan (south to the river) and Hebei (north to the river). The cities like Jiyuan, Jinan and Jining are named because they are located near the Jishui River.

With underdeveloped transportation and insufficient information, it is easily understood and accepted by people that the ancient Chinese rulers used rivers as the basis of the administrative divisions and the names of the regions. The geographical and climatic characteristics of the different regions were often reflected in the names for the regions. This made easier the regional governance according to local conditions.

Third, constructing water conservancy projects, seeking advantages and shunning from disadvantages had become an important part of the Chinese rulers' political life. The large-scale water conservancy programs helped the formation and consolidation of a centralized state in ancient China. Karl Marx discussed the political relationship between water conservancy programs and the Oriental society in "The British Rule in India". He pointed out that as the public works that guaranteed national security and prosperity of the Oriental society, water conservancy programs played a very important role in its productive mode and political activities. Marx believed, "This prime necessity of an economical and common use of water, which, in the Occident, drove private enterprise to voluntary association, as in Flanders and Italy, necessitated, in the Orient where civilization was too low and the territorial extent too vast to call into life voluntary association, the interference of the centralizing power of Government. Hence an economical function devolved upon all Asiatic Governments, the function of providing public works." The American scholar Calvin Weiteff, in his book *Oriental Despotism*, proposed that the centralizing power of the Chinese government had been related its productive relations in its major river basins. With its distinctive geographical, climatic, and hydrological conditions, China had to rely on artificial irrigation rather than rain for its crop fields. Thus, water works had to be built to overcome the shortage of water supply. Such projects required large-scale collaboration, which in turn required discipline, subordination, and a strong leadership. To manage these projects effectively, it was necessary to establish an organized network across the country or at least in the important populated centres of the country. As a result, those who controlled these networks were well prepared to exercise the highest political power. As a result, the political science related to water conservancy, autocratic monarchy and oriental despotism came into being. From the perspective of China's water environment, Weiteff discussed the great influence of water environment on China's political system. When Yu worked for thirteen years to contain floods, different tribes had a unified goal, consistent orders, and sustainable constructions. This contributed to Yu's success and won him fame and power. Flood control activities, like a catalyst in chemical reactions, promoted the birth of the country. Finally, Yu's son Qi inherited his power and established the first slavery state in China. Since then, all unified dynasties would build water conservancy programs and develop agricultural production to stabilize politics and promote national development.

Section II Wise Rulers' Governance of Water and National Prosperity

Throughout the Chinese history, all the wise rulers of the past paid attention to water control, and every able ruler would take water conservancy as the key point of his governance. The prosperous dynasties all benefited from the rulers' attention to water conservancy and to the construction of water related programs. Emperor Shihuang of the Qin Dynasty attached great importance to water works and ushered in the national unification. During the reign of Emperor Wu of the Han Dynasty, the water conservancy industry developed rapidly and laid the foundation for the economic prosperity and political stability of this period. All of these led to the unprecedented prosperity in the Western Han Dynasty. Emperor Taizu of the Ming Dynasty improved agriculture by building water conservancy projects. Emperor Kangxi and Qianlong attached great importance to the construction of water conservancy projects and took part in the practice of water control which promoted the economic development of the Qing Dynasty and ushered in the prosperity during Kangxi and Qianlong's reign.

1. Emperor Qin Shihuang's Water Governance Policies and the Unification Process

As the first emperor in China's history, Qin Shihuang's deeds in building the Great Wall and unifying the whole country were well known. However, few people know that water conservancy works were important in Qin's unification process. Urged by Qin Shihuang, Zhengguoqu Canal and Lingqu Canal were built.

The State of Qin developed from a small and desolate country to one of the five great powers in the Spring and Autumn Period, and then to the first of the seven great powers in the Warring States Period. Finally, it swept the other six states and ruled the whole country. There are various reasons to explain Qin's success. Undoubtedly, Qin's power was closely related to the construction of water conservancy projects. For example, when King Zhao of Qin, the great grandfather of Qin Shihuang, ruled the nation, a governor of Shu, Li Bing built the Dujiangyan Dam (Fig. 4-2), which turned flood caused by the Minjiang River into irrigating water, making the Chengdu Plain become the "land of abundance" where flood and drought wouldn't deprive the people of the good harvest and become the granary of the State of Qin. This greatly enhanced the national strength of Qin.

After he ascended the throne, Emperor Qin Shihuang worked to achieve national reunification. To meet the huge consumption of food and materials caused by the war, Qin Shihuang attached great importance to the development of water conservancy in the Guanzhong area, and built the Zhengguoqu Canal, which took the Jingshui River as the source and crossed the Weibei Plain, so as

Figure 4-2   The Dujiangyan Dam

to create a granary in Guanzhong area. Guanzhong Plain was the political, economic and military centre of the State of Qin. It is in the Weihe River Basin and the land was fertile, but it lacked water and the grain yield was not high. Therefore, an urgent need for the State of Qin was to develop water conservancy projects in Guanzhong area and increase grain production. State Han, Qin's eastern neighbour, sent Zheng Guo, a hydraulic engineer, to the State of Qin to lobby Qin Shihuang to build a water conservancy project to connect Jingshui with Luoshui. In this way, a large area of land in the northern part of Guanzhong Plain could be irrigated. The ruler of State of Han originally wanted to see Qin spend a large amount of human, material, and financial resources on the construction of this large-scale water conservancy project, thus unable to launch a war of annexation, so as to protect itself. However, this plan coincided with Qin Shihuang's ideal of developing agricultural economy through constructing water conservancy works. He could enrich the country and strengthen the army, unifying the whole country. Due to the joint efforts of Zheng Guo and thousands of workers, the canal was finally built several years later. After the completion of the project, more than 40,000 hectares of saline alkali land in the north of Guanzhong could be irrigated with the Jingshui River, and a good harvest was made. From then on, Guanzhong became a fertile field. As a result, the State of Qin became rich and powerful, annexing various vassal States and unified the country. In order to commemorate Zheng Guo for his achievements, the people in Guanzhong area named this canal "Zhengguoqu Canal".

After defeating the other six states, Qin Shihuang sent a troop of 500,000 soldiers to the South of the Five Ridges. However, high mountains dangerous rivers and heavy miasma made their journey very difficult, plus insufficient supplies, the Qin army was defeated again and again. In order to get through the road from the Central Plains to the South of the Five Ridges, Emperor Shihuang ordered Shi Lu to dig the canal connecting the Xiangjiang River (a branch of the Yangtze River) with the Lijiang River (a branch of the Pearl River). In the 33rd year of Qin shihuang's reign(214 B.C.), a canal was established. It was first named as a Qin-digging canal, and later called as Lingqu. It was also known as Xing'an canal because it was located in Xing'an territory of

Guangxi. With the benefit of water transportation, the Qin army swept the South of Five Ridges in one fling. From then on, the South of Five Ridges was included in the territory of the great Qin Empire, which promoted the national integration, social and economic development.

2. Emperor Wu's Governance of Water and National Prosperity

Liu Che, Emperor Wu of Han Dynasty (56 – 87B. C.), was one of the greatest emperors in Chinese history. He implemented a series of political and economic measures and devoted himself to consolidating the frontier and expanding the territory, which made the Western Han Dynasty a country of unprecedented prosperity. His reign saw the rapid development of water conservancy works in China's history. Emperor Wu attached great importance to water conservancy. During his reign three water related programs were completed. First, dug the water channels in Guanzhong so that grain could be transported to the capital city (Xi'an); second, built groups of irrigation projects in Guanzhong; third, Emperor Wu led the generals and soldiers to participate in the closure of Huzi breach where the Yellow River burst its banks and flooded the vast areas.

(1) Dig the Water Channels in the Guanzhong Area to Transport Grain to the Capital City

In the Western Han Dynasty, although the Guanzhong area was a place of abundance, it had the risk of food shortage with its limited land, a large population, and the large-scale wars against Xiongnu, a northern nomadic tribe. Therefore, it was a necessity to transport grain from the east of Xiaoshan to Xi'an, the capital city (currently Shaanxi Province). Starting from the east of Xianyang, the Weihe River was too tortuous. To build a channel between the capital city and Tongguan so the supplies could be transported, Emperor Wu of Han Dynasty accepted the suggestion of Zheng Dang, the official in charge of the agricultural affairs and gave orders to Xu Bobiao, a hydraulic engineer. Leading tens of thousands of laborers, Xu spent three years in building the canal. The canal was more than 300 Li (150 kilometers) long. With this canal, it would take three months to transport grain from Tongguan to Chang'an (Xi'an) which would originally take six months and cost more. Moreover, the canal could be used to irrigate over 10,000 hectares of farmland. This man-made canal continued to be used until the Tang Dynasty and was the lifeline of Chang'an for its supplies.

(2) Build Irrigation Engineering Projects in the Guanzhong Area

During Emperor Wu's reign, the officials had unprecedented passion about the construction of the water conservancy projects. The Longshou Canal was the first project built along the Luohe River. More than 10,000 farmers were recruited to dredge the channel from Chengcheng County to Dali County (both in Shaanxi Province). After more than 10 years of construction, the project had been completed. Then the canal could be used to irrigate more than 10,000 hectares of saline alkali land in the east of Chongquan County (Shaanxi Province). However, because the well canal was not lined at that time, it collapsed seriously after water was supplied, so it was out of use. But the project did show the high level of surveying and construction technology more than 2,000 years ago. Several canals like Liufu Canal and Baiqu Canal were built during this period. These projects promoted the rapid economic development of Guanzhong area, making it a famous economic zone in China at that time. Emperor Wu issued an imperial edict, requiring the local governments to construct water conservancy projects, organize people to dig ditches and build ponds to store water, to prepare for the coming drought. This edict effectively promoted the development of water conservancy construction in the Han Dynasty.

(3) Emperor Wu Directed a Closure of Breach at the Yellow River

In the third year of Yuanguang (132 B.C.), the Yellow River burst at Huzi in Puyang City (now Henan Province). The river surged southward, submerging the large areas in the present eastern Henan Province, east and south of Shandong Province, north of Anhui Province and north of Jiangsu Province. Flood plagued and lasted over 20 years. In the second year of Yuanfeng (109 B.C.), Emperor Wu ascended Mount Tai and passed through the flood stricken areas. Seeing the torrential flood and the displaced people struggling on the death line, he was very sad. So he sent ministers Jiren and Guo Chang to recruit tens of thousands of soldiers and civilians to block the flood. Emperor Wu himself came to the scene to command the closure. He held a ceremony of offering sacrifices to the river god, "sinking the white horses and jade in the river". Then he ordered the civil and military officials and his entourage to carry firewood to block the running water. It was spring, the local people warmed themselves and cooked by burning firewood, so firewood was very scarce. Emperor Wu ordered to cut down the bamboo in Qi garden, sinking bamboo poles into the bottom of the river and building a dam with the earth. Rows of bamboo sticks were hit into the earth and then filled with earth, rock and firewood. The progress of the project was very difficult. Emperor Wu wrote two impromptu poems which showed his deep worries about the flood. Here are two verses by Emperor Wu entitled as *Songs at Huzi* (Fig. 4-3).

Song at Huzi Dike 1:
Huzi dike was breached and there is no way to deal with it.
The floods drowned the towns and villages!
The beautiful countryside is not peaceful, and people fail to block the flood.
The Juye plain is submerged in the water and fish is jumping in the water-covered farmland.
The village in winter presents a pathetic sight.
The river god is so cruel that he doesn't come to help,
The government and the people are discontented with the cruelty of the river god!
The floods in the Huaihe River recesse slowly.
Song at Huzi Dike 2:

This poem describes how the laborers blocked the flood. The laborers worked in the turbulent

Figure 4-3 A Stone Tablet on the Ruins of Huzi Dike

currents. They used firewood, reeds, or bamboo sticks to block water. But they didn't have enough firewood to fill the gap. That was because the local people burnt the firewood for warmth. The bamboo sticks were obtained to be made into rows and sunk into the bottom of the river. The water was successfully blocked. The officials took the chance to tell the local people the importance of blocking the water.

3. Emperor Taizu's Governance of Water and Economy in the Early Ming Dynasty

Zhu Yuanzhang, Emperor Taizu of the Ming Dynasty, was one of the few emperors who built China into a cultural and military power in the Chinese history. Born in a poor family, he took part in the peasant uprising at the end of the Yuan Dynasty that ended the rule of the Yuan Dynasty in China. He pacified Sichuan, Guangxi, Gansu, Yunnan and other places, and unified China. After the establishment of the Ming Dynasty, he took a series of measures to restore and develop the production activities. Consequently, economy of the Ming Dynasty developed.

When Zhu Yuanzhang established the Ming Dynasty, famine, and pestilence as well as years of wars struck the society and economy hard. The people lived a desperate life. Seeing the economy collapsed completely and the people were in dire needs, Zhu Yuanzhang carried out a policy of rest and recuperation to restore the vitality of economy, releasing slaves and reclaiming wasteland. The implementation of these measures increased the labor force and achieved remarkable results in the reclamation of wasteland. By the end of his reign, the total farmland of the country doubled compared to that of the end of Yuan Dynasty. The development of a large number of lands required the improvement of agricultural production conditions and the increase of grain yields. Therefore, to build water conservancy projects was a necessity.

At the beginning of his accession to the throne, Emperor Taizu ordered that local officials should promptly report any suggestions on water conservancy proposed by the common people, otherwise they would be punished. Besides, he sent the officials to supervise the construction of

Water and the Chinese Culture

water conservancy projects. In 1394, Emperor Taizu issued a special edict to the Ministry of Work, requiring that all the ponds and lakes in the whole country that could store and discharge water to prevent flood should be repaired and built one by one according to its terrain. Under the supervision of Emperor Taizu, remarkable achievements had been made in the construction of water conservancy projects all over the country. During his 28 years' reign, 40,987 ponds, 4,162 rivers and 5,048 dikes were built, which led to the unprecedented development of water conservancy projects.

Water conservancy projects guaranteed the rapid recovery and development of economy in the early Ming Dynasty. The grain outputs and revenues were twice as much as that in the Yuan Dynasty. According to *History of Ming Dynasty*, even if every state and county had to transport a large share of their grain to the capital, there was still a large amount of grain stored in local granaries. This record indirectly reflected Taizu's governance of water conservancy projects effectively improved economy.

4. Emperor Kangxi's Governance and the Prosperous Period during the Qing Dynasty

Emperor Kangxi(1654-1722) was the second emperor of the Qing Dynasty after the armies of the northern nomadic tribe crossed the pass and ruled China. Emperor Kangxi devoted great efforts to building water conservancy projects. Since his accession to power, he attached great importance to the governance of the Yellow River and transportation of grain from the south to the north. The Yellow River affairs and water transport were issues related to water conservancy.

In view of the serious situation that the Yellow River overflowed frequently and the Huaihe River and the Beijing-Hangzhou Grand Canal were both in the state of disrepair, Emperor Kangxi appointed Jin Fu, an able minister, as governor of the Yellow River to carry out the comprehensive management of the Yellow River, Huaihe River and Yunhe River. In the later years of Kangxi's reign, a large number of migrant workers were mobilized to excavate a new channel with a length of more than 200 Li (100 km), so that the overflowing Hun River was diverted and discharged. From then on, the flood no longer affected the local area, and agricultural production on both sides of the bank was restored. To commemorate the success of water control, he renamed the Hunhe River as "the Yongding River".

Kangxi was very practical in water control and paid special attention to investigation and research. In addition to providing guiding policies for water control, he also personally studied water conservancy theory and carried out the extensive field investigation. From 1684 to 1707, he went southwards and made six surveys of the river, focusing on the Yellow River channel, Hongze Lake, the upper and lower canals from Suqian to Huai'an in Northern Jiangsu Province. The longest ship survey lasted more than 20 days, with a voyage of thousands of miles. Wherever he went, he made a careful inspection. According to his investigation, he put forward the management strategy of taking both upstream and downstream into consideration, which effectively promoted the development of water control works. Later, his remarks on governance of water were collected and made into a book, *Emperor Kangxi's Plan on Harnessing Water in China*. This is one classic reference book that centred upon governance of water.

Kangxi attached importance to the use of technology and was proficient in hydraulic survey. In the spring of the 38th year of Kangxi's reign (1699), he made a tour to the Li Canal in northern Jiangsu Province. He himself operated instruments and measured that the water level of Baoyingqing lake canal was over 1.3 feet, higher than that of the nearby lakes. He immediately instructed the accompanying officials in charge of river governance to speed up the construction of the stone dikes.

Emperor Kangxi not only paid attention to water conservancy projects, but he was also very strict with the officials in charge of water governance. Those officials who built high quality projects would be praised while the opposite would be punished. Once Emperor Kangxi was very angry about one official and severely reprimanded and punished him. Kangxi made clear the rewards and punishments to the water control officials, and his measures were very beneficial to the water control cause.

In Chinese history, many emperors were concerned about water conservancy construction during their tenure of office, but few of them were able to practice and put forward the theory of water control. It was rare and commendable that Emperor Kangxi achieved all those requirements. He made contributions to the development of China's water conservancy, in turn promoted the economic development of the Qing Dynasty, and ushered in the "prosperous era during Kangxi and Qianlong's" reign.

5. Emperor Qianlong's Water Control Practice and the Consolidated Governance of a Multi-ethnic Country

Emperor Qianlong (1736 – 1796) was Emperor Kangxi's grandson. He was another brilliant ruler in China. As the longest lived emperor of the Qing Dynasty, Emperor Qianlong lived through almost the entire eighteenth century. During his long reign, he took water control as the foundation of his governance. He was opposed to the idea that a good harvest was determined by nature and when disaster hit humans were rather passive and had nothing to do with it except for relying on charity. He advocated that water conservancy projects should be built to relieve people of disasters. He stated repeatedly that governing a nation, a ruler should work to help his people live a better-off life. To achieve the goal, water conservancy projects had to be built because they will guarantee a good harvest and sufficient grain storage.

During Emperor Qianlong's reign, floods and droughts alternatively struck across the country, which made people a wretched life. Emperor Qianlong ordered his ministers to take a prevention-based policy, building water conservancy projects. He ordered the governors of all provinces not to neglect water related issues and repair the dilapidated or damaged water conservancy facilities even when there were no threats of floods or droughts. Since water conservancy facilities were in disrepair for a long time, he asked the local officials to take the construction of water conservancy as a long-term and regular task.

To master the first-hand information, Emperor Qianlong attached great importance to field research. He sent many ministers to investigate the actual situation of waterways in various important water conservancy construction sites in the country. He also sent ministers such as Zhao Dian, Minister of the Ministry of Household Affairs, to inspect the Weihe River, the Beijing-Hangzhou Grand Canal, the Jinsha River and other water systems. He ordered Sun Jiagan, governor of Zhili, to plan of building water conservancy works, initiating the large-scale water control activities. Then, based on the achievements of the previous dynasties, Emperor Qianlong used a lot of manpower, material and financial resources to dredge and regulate the Huaiyang canal and the Huaihe River channel. In more than 30 years, he visited the areas in the south of the Yangtze River six times (Fig. 4-4). Every time he went there, he would visit the Hongze Lake Basin to inspect the river defence works. Emperor Qianlong issued hundreds of flood control orders, inspected the regulations project of the Yellow River and the Huaihe River five times. He and his government instructed people to clean up the West Lake in Hangzhou. Urged by the emperor, the local officials from Henan, Anhui, Yunnan, Guizhou and other provinces started to dredge rivers, strengthen dikes, build ponds, ditches, dams and other large water conservancy projects. For example, the Yellow River levee that extended 170 km from Nanyang to Shangqiu in Henan Province was newly built. The canals built were dredged into proper places and the embankment was built. In addition, during his reign, he built a 121 km long canal to block the flood and boost the development of agriculture. These water conservancy projects played an important role in flood control and agricultural production.

Figure 4-4 Part of the Long Scroll about Emperor Qianlong's Visit at the South of the Yangtze River, in the Qing Dynasty

The flood control capacity of the Yongding River was greatly improved after many flood control activities in Yongding River area.

Dealing with water issues, Emperor Qianlong deeply realized the importance of having talents in water conservancy, so he paid more attention to training and selecting the relevant talents. He noted that the officials who served in water conservancy sector or those familiar with water control business could be given priority in promotion. For example, Wanyan Wei, General Inspector in Zhejiang, was promoted as governor of Jiangnan River course because he was familiar with Zhejiang seawall affairs and presided over the construction of Jinshan seawall. With the emperor's encouragement, more and more officials were keen on water conservancy issues, which promoted the development of water conservancy in China in Qing Dynasty.

Section III Virtuous Officials' Management of Water and National Prosperity

To build the large-scale water conservancy programs is to mobilize the whole nation's strength to control water. The construction of the local water conservancy projects that meet the needs of the local people is one function of the local government. At the same time, the daily maintenance and management of water conservancy projects such as maintenance of the riverbanks and canals also need the local governments to shoulder the responsibility. In the Chinese history, many able officials attached much importance to the water conservancy construction because this might serve as the driving force to bring prosperity to their governed places. They were Sun Shuao, Ximen Bao, Ma Zhen, Fan Zhongyan, Lin Zexu, etc.

1. Ximen Bao and the Twelve Canals of the Zhanghe River

Ximen Bao (dates of birth and death unknown), was a native in the State of Wei in the Warring States Period. He was a famous politician and water conservancy expert in China's history. In 422 B.C., Duke of Wen in State of Wei appointed Ximen Bao as governor of Ye. Ye was an important place in the State of Wei, It was near the Zhanghe River, so it had frequent floods. The local people believed that there was a river god wanted to punish them by floods. If they offered sacrifices to the river god, they would be pardoned. So, each year young girls would be thrown into the river and become the river god's brides. Those girls got drowned in the river. In this way, the local people believed that they could be relieved of flood. Ximen Bao banned the superstitious activity. He called on the local people to build twelve canals from which they would draw water and could irrigate their farmland. The head of these twelve canals (Fig. 4-5) was built over the Zhanghe River which was nine kilometers from Ye. Ximen Bao built a total of 12 low weirs over a 6 km river course. On the south bank of each of the 12 upstream weirs, one water intake was

Figure 4-5 the Twelve Canals of Water Diversion from the Zhanghe River

opened and a gate was set for control. Every intake connected with a channel and a total of 12 water diversion channels were used to irrigate nearly over 6,667 hectares of farmland on the south bank of the Zhanghe River. The Zhanghe River was full of silt that could be used to fertilize the fields and increase the yields. Consequently, Ye was turned into an abundant place. At the end of the Eastern Han Dynasty, Cao Cao led his army and occupied Ye. He repaired the original twelve weirs and renamed them as Tianping weir and made into one single head of the canals. The irrigation area was expanded. After Sui and Tang Dynasties, irrigation districts were formed surrounding the Zhanghe River and the Huanhe River. In the Tang Dynasty, Tianping canal was rebuilt, and branches were opened to irrigate more than 6,667 hectares of farmland. In the Qing Dynasty and the Republic of China, they were restored and utilized. In 1959, Yuecheng Reservoir was built over the Zhanghe River. Based on the old project, Anyang City excavated the main canal of Zhangnan and built a large irrigation area, that is, south Zhanghe River irrigation area with the designed irrigation area of 80,000 hectares, replacing the ancient irrigation canal.

The twelve-canal diversion project from Zhangzhou was the earliest large-scale water diversion and irrigation project in the history of China. From the overall layout of the project, it presented how advanced science and technology was at that time. The intake gate works were all built with stones, and the gate could both store and release water. It can be used to irrigate and fertilize the fields in case of drought, and drainage and flood control in case of flood. This kind of ingenious engineering construction has been praised by later generations. Even today one can see the remains of Ye canal and gate in Gaoxue village of Anyang City.

After Ximen Bao's death, the people in Ye built a temple for him in the place where he managed the water, and stone tablets were set up for him in the Song, Ming and Qing Dynasties. Sima Qian in *Records of Grand History* praised him as a sage.

2. Jia Rang's Three Strategies for River Management

Jia Rang (date of birth and death unknown) was a government counsellor in the late Western Han Dynasty.

In the early years of Emperor Ai of Han Dynasty (5-6 B.C.), floods occurred frequently in the Yellow River. The count called on local officials to recommend talents with river management experiences. In the 7th year B. C., Jia Rang provided three alternative schemes for river regulations, known as "three river management strategies" in history. The three river harnessing strategies took "widening the river and discharging the flood" as the core idea. The best policy advocated changing the course of the flood into the river. The middle policy proposed building canals to divert water, and the lowest policy was to repair the old dikes. It was after studying the history of river regulations and surveying Dongjun in the lower reaches of the Yellow River that Jia Rang proposed his ideas.

Jia Rang pointed out that the best way to solve the problem of the Yellow River was to change the course of the Yellow River. He suggested that the levee of the Yellow River in Zhehai Pavilion (now southwest of Huaxian County, Henan Province) was dug open so that the river would flow northeast into the sea. With the Taihang Mountain blocking in the west, and the Golden Levee as a barrier in the east, the Yellow River would not overflow. A new river course was formed within a month. Without doubt, the newly formed river course meant a huge number of people had to be resettled and relevant social problems followed.

The middle policy was to dig more branch canals in the lower reaches of the Yellow River and these branches were used to irrigate and drain water from the farmland. That is, in Zhehai Pavilion area, along the eastern side of today's Beijing-Guangzhou Railway, a dike was built to guide the Yellow River into the Zhanghe River. Then, the embankment of the Yellow River from Qikou to Zhehai Pavilion would be reinforced with stones and several water gates would be built on the dikes. At the same time, a number of water gates were opened on the eastern dike of the newly built canal. In this way, between the Yellow River trunk road and the new canal, there were many diversion canals. When droughts hit, the eastern gate could be open and water could be used for irrigation; when disaster struck, the gate in the west would be opened to discharge water.

The least satisfactory strategy was to continue the existing measures, constantly heightening and consolidating the riverbank. Jia Rang believed if the first two measures were not adopted, merely heightening and consolidating the levees didn't work well and would continue the costs. Over Jia Rang's proposal of measures, there were controversial opinions. Some scholars thought his three policies were rather inclusive and the following measures could be included. Some scholars didn't approve of the third measure while some believed that the first two were not feasible.

Jia Rang's "three river management strategies" were the earliest comprehensive and systematic river management documents in China. He not only put forward measures to combat the disasters caused by the Yellow River, but also included the control measures in terms of irrigation, silting, alkali control and navigation. It was he who for the first time put forward the concepts of "compensation for the waste of time" and "compensation for the migrants". Jia Rang's measures were the first comprehensive plan to increase benefits and eliminate threats and disasters in the history of the governance of the Yellow River in China. The ancient people took him as the model of the future generations. Up to now, many of his thoughts and methods are still applicable.

3. Ma Zhen and the Jianhu Lake

Ma Zhen (88-141) directed the building of one of the largest irrigation projects in ancient China, Jianhu Lake in 140 when Emperor Shun of the Eastern Han Dynasty ruled. He was then the prefect of Kuaiji (now Shaoxing City, Zhejiang Province). This project contributed to the development of agriculture in Shaoxing for nearly a thousand years. Jianhu was the first recorded water conservancy project in the south of the Yangtze River and Ma Zhen was regarded as the founder of water conservancy project in the south of the Yangtze River.

Jianhu Lake (Fig. 4-6) is the famous mirror lake under the pen of Li Bai, a great poet of Tang Dynasty. Li Bai wrote in "A Dreaming Visit at Tianmu Mountain", "Taking this legend, I would like to dream-travelling to Wu and Yue,/Flying over the Mirror Lake in a night with moonlight shed./ My shadow is woven by the moonlight mirrored from the lake,/In a second I am flying to the Shanxi Stream as fate." He depicted the magnificent scenery of Kuaiji Plain in eastern Zhejiang Province. In the Eastern Han Dynasty, Kuaiji Plain was full of marshes because it was adjacent to the sea in the north and mountains in the south. Whenever the flood struck, the plain was submerged in the water. But in dry season there was no enough water for irrigation. In addition, Hangzhou Bay sometimes had a raging tide upstream, and farmland was often flooded by the sea, which resulted in failure of harvest. Under such an environment, people there lived in poverty and starvation.

Figure 4-6 Jianhu Lake

After a detailed investigation, Ma Zhen gave a design of Jianhu project. That is, to heighten and thicken the lake dike built in the past dynasties, and build a new dike to connect it into a length of 63.5 km. This dike was centred on Kuaiji County and was divided into two sections. The east section started from Wuyun Gate to Cao'e River and had a length of 36 km while the west section started from Changxi Gate to Puyang River and had a length of 27.5 km. This man-made dike intercepted 36 streams in Kuaiji and Shanyin Counties, forming a large Lake, long and narrow, with a circumference of 155 km and a width of 2.5 km. This was the Jianhu Lake, also named as the Long Lake and the Mirror Lake. Because the terrain in the east was slightly higher than in the west, Ma Zhen built a 6-mile long road in the middle of the lake as a dike, which divided Jianhu into two parts, the East Lake and the West Lake. Because the water surface was more than ten meters higher than the farmland near the dike and the farmland was more than ten meters higher than the sea level of Hangzhou Bay, the situation of gravity irrigation had been formed. With a complete set of facilities such as sluice, weir and culvert, Jianhu Lake could be used for both irrigation and drainage. During the dry seasons, the drainage facilities would be used to allow the lake to irrigate the field. When the mountains torrents rushed down, the drainage facilities were closed to store the flood in the lake. When there wasn't enough space in the Jianhu Lake, the discharge gate would be opened to discharge water into Hangzhou Bay.

According to historical records, after the completion of the Jianhu Lake, the entire northern plain of Kuaiji Mountain was free from flood. About 9,000 hectares of land to the west of Cao'e River was covered with thousands of rice land. Book of the Song Dynasty described the fertile land in this area was superior to that in Guanzhong. Besides the good harvests in thousands of miles of Kuaiji Plain free from drought and flood, the 400 km Jianhu Lake was also rich in fish and lotus roots. According to historical records, Wang Shipeng of the Song Dynasty praised, "Beauty in Hangzhou lies in the West Lake, which was as important as one's eyebrows to a human. The Jianhu Lake in Kingdom of Yue was like one's intestines and stomach." In this way, Shaoxing(Kuaiji) Plain had become increasingly prosperous and had become a famous land of fish and rice.

4. Fan Zhongyan's Construction of the Hanhai Weir and Treatment of the Taihu Lake

Fan Zhongyan (989-1052) was a native of Suzhou, Jiangsu Province. He was a statesman, a writer and a scholar-reformer of the Northern Song Dynasty. He spent his early years in poverty and grew to be an erudite scholar proficient in classics, and a brilliant poet. What was worth mentioning was that Fan Zhongyan also made great achievements in building water conservancy projects and successfully combat disasters like floods and droughts.

In 1023, Fan Zhongyan was appointed supervisor of salt wareshouse at Xixi of Taizhou (now the west of Taicheng, Dongtai City). There he witnessed severe damage the sea tides did to the local people. The local seawall had collapsed due to lack of repair for a long time. The waves not only left the salt fields and the stoves for processing salt exposed and unguarded but also threatened the farmland and residential buildings. When big tides occurred, the sea water would besiege Taizhou City, leaving thousands of residents displaced. Fan Zhongyan submitted the statements to his superiors, pointing out the importance of the dikes for protecting the properties of the local people and suggesting that the imperial court should rebuild a solid dike along the coast of Tongzhou, Taizhou, Chuzhou and Haizhou (from Lianyungang to the North Bank of the Yangtze River estuary). Under the conditions at that time, to build a project according to Fan Zhongyan's proposal was risky, difficult, costly and highly demanding. His proposal was approved of by the court. Fan Zhonghua was appointed as the General Commander of the water transport project.

The construction of the long dike began in the autumn of 1023, and more than 40,000 people from Tongzhou, Taizhou, Chuzhou and Haizhou were mobilized to do the work. But they soon met with difficulties. A big tide swallowed up more than 100 migrant workers at the seaside, which shocked the emperor. However, Fan Zhongyan was fearless in the face of danger and insisted on guarding the weir. He and his colleague, Teng Zongliang, rushed to the front line of the project, regardless of the risk of being swept away by the waves. The imperial court sent envoys to investigate. The construction was suspended. Later, the imperial court sent Hu Lingyi, an envoy in charge of transport, to inspect the construction site and decide whether to continue the project. Hu Lingyi supported Fan Zhongyan. In the fourth year of Tiansheng, Fan Zhongyan had to return home for his mother died. He had to observe a regular memorial period as an official. However, he was still caring about the long dike protecting people from the sea. He left a letter to Zhang Lun, stating the benefits of building the dike. Zhang Lun submitted it to the imperial court and asked for supervising the project by himself. His request was approved of. Then he was appointed to be a governor of Taizhou. In the autumn of 1027, the fifth year of Tiansheng, the project continued. After nearly four years of hard work, the 143 Li (72 km) long dike along the coast was finally completed in the spring of 1028, which was across the Yellow Sea beach. From then on, the submerged area had been turned into fertile farmland, and more than 2,000 refugees returned to their hometown. Consequently, agriculture and salt industry developed steadily, and the court gained increasing profits from the salt industry. In order to express their gratitude, the local people named the weir along the seacoast as "Fan Gong Dike". Many people in Xinghua County, Taizhou City, the centre of the disaster-stricken area, chose Fan as their surname. From 1054 to 1056, Shen Qi, the magistrate of Haimen County, built another 70-Li (35 km) dike to connect with the weir built by Fan Zhongyan and Zhang Lun. Later, these dikes were all called "Fan Gong Dike" ("Gong" is a word showing people's gratitude for Fan) (Fig. 4-7). In this way, the Song Dynasty built a long dike to defend people and the properties against the sea in the coastal areas of Tongzhou, Taizhou and Chuzhou, which was one of the great projects in the history of seawall in China.

In September, 1034, Fan Zhongyan was transferred to his hometown and served as the chief executive of Suzhou. Suzhou happened to be stricken by flood which didn't decline even after autumn was gone. The farmland was submerged in water and there was no hope of a good harvest.

Figure 4-7　Fan Gong Dike in Funing County, Jiangsu Province

Tens of thousands of farmers were facing the threat of starvation. Fan Zhongyan submitted to the imperial court to dredge the five rivers so as to guide the water from Taihu Lake into the sea. He came to the site in person to supervise the repair of the project and paid the laborers for their work. Under his leadership and through the joint efforts of Suzhou people, five rivers in Suzhou were finally dredged. The canals were built, and water was guided into the sea, which not only relieved the flood, but also benefited the descendants. In addition, his work played an important role in developing agriculture in areas like Suzhou, Changzhou, Huzhou and Xiuzhou around Taihu Lake.

In the following 10 years, Fan Zhongyan was undergoing the rise and fall as a government official. He even was appointed as a general and went far to the northern frontier, fighting against the northern nomadic tribes. But what haunted him was his concern over the management of Tailu Lake. He studied the ancient system of polder fields in the south of the Yangtze River and summed up the experience of harnessing the Taihu Lake. Based on his governing practice of Taihu Lake, he put forward the integrated water control principle, that is, the combination of building dikes, dredging rivers and setting sluice gates. He combined water control and farmland management and solved the contradictions between water storage and discharge and between tides blockage and waterlogging drainage. Fan Zhongyan's measures were adopted in the water conservancy construction of polder areas in the later dynasties.

5. Su Shi's Governance of the West Lake

Su Shi (1037-1101) was born in Meizhou (now Meishan City, Sichuan Province) in the Song Dynasty. He was a famous writer, calligrapher, and painter in the Northern Song Dynasty. He was one of the "eight great masters of Tang and Song Dynasties" in the history of Chinese literature. In most of his life Su Shi had been sent out of the capital for local office services. As a local official, he did a lot to benefit the local people. He directed the construction of urban water conservancy in

Xuzhou, Hangzhou, Yingzhou, Huizhou, Guangzhou, Qiongzhou and other cities.

Su Shi twice served as an official in Hangzhou. During his term of office, he presided over the water conservancy construction of Hangzhou for many times. The more important ones included the rehabilitation of six wells, the dredging of Maoshanhe River and Yanqiaohe River, and the regulation of the West Lake.

(1) Rebuild Six Wells

Hangzhou was close to the sea and the underground water was sour and salty. Six wells were dug in Tang Dynasty to solve the problem of drinking water for residents. However, due to the long-term failure of dredging, the "six wells" were almost abandoned. When Su Shi took the post of general judge in Hangzhou, he saw that the residents had problems with drinking water. Then Su Shi and the Prefect organized the local people to clean up the six wells and solve the drinking water problem for the residents.

(2) Dredge the Maoshanhe River and Yanqiaohe River

Maoshanhe River and Yanqiaohe River were two major rivers in Hangzhou City, which connected the Grand Canal in the north and finally flew into Qiantangjiang River. When the Qiantangjaing River joined the Grand Canal, a large amount of sediment carried by the Qiantangjiang River would be discharged into the Grand Canal and pile. Su Shi dredged the Qiantangjiang River cleaned up the silt and built a gate on the tributary connecting the two rivers, so that it would first flow into the Maoshan River. After the tides abated and water was clear, the gate would be opened, and the clear water was discharged into the Yanqiao River. In this way, the main channel in the city would not be blocked. Since then, the river tides no longer entered Hangzhou City, and the urban area was free from the harm of silts.

(3) Renovate the West Lake

Today, the West Lake (Fig. 4-8) is known as "paradise on earth". However, the West Lake in Su Shi's time was overgrown with weeds and filled with muds. When Su Shi first worked as a judge of Hangzhou, nearly one-third of the West Lake was covered with aquatic plants. But when Su Shi was the governor of Hangzhou and worked as a local official there the second time, more than half of the lake was blocked. He dredged the West Lake and built weirs and gates to store or discharge water. In the dredging process, watergrass sludge from the lake was collected and piled up in the lake to build a long dike 30 miles from the north to the south, which formed the famous "Su dike". Six bridges were built on the levee. Both sides of the embankment were planted with hibiscus and willows, which eventually made a convenient path for enjoying the scenery of the lake. In order to make it possible to dredge the West Lake frequently and timely in the future, Su Shi set up a special institute called "Lake Dredging Department", which was responsible for regulating and dredging of the West Lake. At the same time, he hired people to plant lotus roots in the lake and profits from selling the lotus roots would be used for the annual maintenance costs. Three stone pagodas were set up, and the lake surface within the stone tower was not allowed to reclaim as the farmland. The original site of the three towers has also evolved into the famous scenic spot, Three Pools Mirroring the Moon. It can be said that why the West Lake today is reputed as "paradise on earth" could be greatly contributed to Su Shi's work.

Figure 4-8　The West Lake

Su Shi wrote *On Yu's Methods of Dredging the Rivers*, which was considered as a classic article on management of water. Su Shi proposed that the basic principles for water management were to understand "the situation of water" as well as "interpersonal relationship". Only on the basis of "the situation of water", could people guide the water and turn threats into benefits. In the process of water control, Su Shi believed that people shouldn't neglect the long-term benefits and merely give attention to the present gains.

6. Jia Lu's Management of the Yellow River

Jia Lu was a native of Gaoping County(now Gaoping County, Shaanxi Province). In 1351 (the Yuan Dynasty), Jia Lu, the Minister of the Ministry of construction, was appointed as Director General of River Management. He led 170,000 soldiers and civilians to block the flood and regulate the river. They restored the Yellow River into its old course and made it merge with the Huaihe River and flew into the sea together. Jia Lu's management of the Yellow River was an important chapter in the history of management of the Yellow River in China.

The Yellow River was the cradle of the Chinese civilization, but the frequent floods, especially caused by many diversions, had also posed threats to the Chinese people. The Yuan Dynasty saw the most serious flood-stricken period. According to *Chronicles of the Yuan Dynasty*, the Yellow River burst its banks and overflowed 14 times in less than 100 years. In summer of 1344, the most disastrous flood occurred, hitting severely. Continuous rainfall led to the rise of the water level of the Yellow River, leaving the Baimao dike and the Jin dike all burst. The flood lasted for seven years, laying thousands of miles of land in southwestern Shandong Province waste and the people in dire poverty. At the same time, the river intruded into the Huitong River and the situation was getting worse. In 1345, the Yellow River burst again in Jiyin(the south of the Jishui River, now Caozhou, Shandong Province), and the situation worsened. In February of 1348, the imperial court issued an edict to set up a Water Conservancy Bureau in Yuncheng, with Jia Lu as the chief inspector in charge of water control.

Quoting from *Records of Yuan Dynasty* and other books, three features could be summarized about Jia Lu's containment of the flood. First, a relatively short construction period. The river regulation project started in April. In July, more than 280-li (140 km) of river course was built. In August, the river could be guided into the newly excavated river channel where boats could float in September. In November, dikes were built, and all the works were completed. The river returned to its original course and flowed southward to the Huaihe River. The two rivers merged and went to the sea together. The whole project lasted only 190 days. And the main project was carried out in flood season. This worsened the situation of his work. Second, it was a huge project. All in all, Jia Lu led the workers to dredge more than 280-li (140 km) original course of the Yellow River. The 19-li (9.5 km) dam across the river and 36-li (18 km) dikes were built on both sides of the Yellow River. In order to block the breach in a place, three layers of dikes extending over 10 km were built. Third, during the river regulating process, outstanding innovations in engineering technology had been made. In the process of embankment construction, bamboo was used as the frame; dirt, reed ropes and grass bundles were used to fill the gap. In this way, the embankment was consolidated. In addition, when the breach was blocked, Jia Lu completed the closure by sinking the ships into the river. He put 27 large ships at the entrance, connected them with ropes and bamboo poles to form a big ark, which was fixed by iron anchors upstream. Then he arranged people to nail pegs on the dikes on both sides of the river. The pegs were tied with the thick and long bamboo poles. The other end of the poles was connected with the ships so that the ships could not flow with the river. The ships were loaded with scattered grass and small stones. Two boatmen who were excellent swimmers stood at both ends of each ship, each with a big axe in hand. Then, with the drum sound on the shore as the signal, the boatman chiselled the ships at the same time. After a while, the ships were made leaked and sunken where the river burst. After that, the high fascine section was added on the ships immediately, and then the large fascine was rolled up and pressed down. Many ships sank into the river in the same way. After all the ships sank to the bottom of the water, three layers of straw fascine were added behind the ships. Finally, a fascine of seven meters high was put to block the burst. As water potential was heavy, the closure of the mouth meant great danger. And it was even more difficult when the closure was almost completed. The river burst again and sank the fascine. Despite the difficulty, Jia Lu remained calm, ordered more than ten thousand workers to continue their work. Finally, in November, the burst was closed. The river that was out of control for seven years was regulated and returned to its past course. Jia Lu sank the ships loaded with stones and made them the dams. In this innovative way, he made a success in regulating the river. With the absence of modern machinery, such a practice showed his creative spirit.

When Jia Lu ruled the river, the peasant uprisings broke out and would soon bring the rule of the Yuan Dynasty to an end. This huge project of governing the river was costly and demanding. Workers did heavy labour under harsh conditions and were paid little. Jia Lu's work had drawn controversies. Cao Yuke in the Ming Dynasty and Hu Wei in the Qing Dynasty disapproved of his project. Jin Fu, a water conservancy expert in Qing Dynasty, gave praise to Jia Lu's ability to harass the flood but thought its implementation was politically unwise. Pan Jixun, an outstanding water conservancy expert in Ming Dynasty, affirmed Jia Lu's contribution to river management. It is agreed that Jia Lu was great in organizing such a large-scale river regulation activity and successfully blocking the floods. The technology he applied and his courage were far beyond the imagination of his contemporaries. He combined the methods of dredging and plugging, he attached importance to the layout of the project, the deployment and technology. His practice provided valuable information to the development of river regulations in China. To quote a poem written on the walls of Jia Lu's residence:

Jia Lu ruled the Yellow River,
Praises more, Criticisms more.
A hundred years later,
Truth out, and praises would last.

7. Pan Jixun's Management of the Yellow River

Pan Jixun (1521–1595) was born in Wucheng (today's Huzhou, Zhejiang Province). He served as General Governor of River Management four times (the highest official in charge of river regulations in the Ming Dynasty) and took charge of the management of the Yellow River for 27 years. He was one of the longest serving ministers in river regulations in the Ming Dynasty. He wrote a brilliant chapter in the history of the Yellow River regulation.

1565 saw Pan Jixun's first management of the Yellow River. In July of that year, the Yellow River burst in Peixian County, Jiangsu Province. The Grand Canal in Pei County section had been silted up for more than 100 km, causing unprecedented disasters. Pan Jixun suggested that new rivers should be dug upstream to guide water into other areas and the clogging areas downstream should be dredged. The result of Pan's river regulation scheme led to the digging of 70 km new rivers and the repair of 26 km old rivers. More than 100 km dams were built and 15 km stone embankments were completed. His project was a great success. In 1569 and 1570, the Yellow

River burst in Peixian County and Pizhou. The 50 km canal was silted up and was turned into the flat land. In August 1570, Pan Jixun was ordered by the imperial court to control the water. He led the workers to consolidate and repair the dikes, blocked the bursts and dug more channels. In addition, he believed that the fundamental solution lied in "building the dikes to restrain the flow of water in nearby places and building remote dikes to prevent the breach". With his work, the bursts were all closed and flood was eliminated. After that, he directed the workers to build higher dikes, dredged the clogging areas and reused the old dikes. With his work, the river course that was used to transport the grain was restored.

In 1578, Pan Jixun was appointed for the third time to oversee the river affairs. Pan Jixun noticed that loaded with the accumulated sand, the regulation of the Yellow River had to be different from that of other rivers. Based on his previous practice, on-the-spot investigations and the unique features of the Yellow River, Pan Jixun proposed to regulate the Yellow River by digging up more rivers and to wash the sand off with water. First, he suggested that they should build dikes to prevent floods. Pan led people to build the secondary levees, dredge the trunk of the river and block its tributaries, fix the river channel, and increase the scouring force of the current. Yao dikes (outside the secondary dike, used to fight floods) were built to block the water potential and use the flood to wash the main channel. They built the lattice dikes between Yao dikes and the secondary dikes. As the Yellow River was full of sand and met with frequent floods, even when there was a broken bank, the water flow would stop. When flood was gone and water reclined, sand piled up and formed a plain which was higher than the river. Although the water level was high in the flood made plain, it would not break the dike, which played the role of silting the beach and scouring the channel. Second, the Gaojiayan dike on the East Bank of Hongze Lake was reinforced to clear the Yellow River. The Yellow River and the Huaihe River merged and formed a strong scouring force, which was conducive to discharge sediments into the sea. In this way, the sea was opened despite that it was not dredged; the river was not dug but the sand in it was washed off and it was getting deep and clear. That was Pan's measure of using water to wash sand off and regulate water with water.

In 1588, Pan Jixun started to manage the river the fourth time. In view of the fact that the levee built last time had reduced its flood control function due to "the ravages of vehicles and horses, and the erosion of wind and rain", Pan Jixun paid more attention to the construction of dikes. He thought that there was no once-and-for-all method for controlling the river. He put forward the measures of silting the beach and consolidating the dike by using the law of scouring and silting of the Yellow River itself. In Henan, Shandong and other places, he renovated and strengthened the existing 810 km long dikes, secondary dikes and dams. He also built long remote dikes, secondary dikes and lattice dikes on both sides of the Yellow River. He also built weirs and dredged the rivers. His work played a great role in restoring the smooth flow of the canal and developing agriculture.

Pan Jixun managed the Yellow River four times in his life. He started his first management of the Yellow River at the age of 45. When he stopped his work, he was already 73 years old. He was all the time concerned with the Yellow River management. Even after his retirement, he cared about how the rivers were controlled. Pan Jixun's theory and practice about river regulations were collected in his work, *A List of River Defence*. The book contained a detailed picture of river regulations, edicts on river regulations and important statements son river risk prevention. It is a precious record of Chinese experience in managing the Yellow River and a major achievement in water conservancy science in China.

8. Lin Zexu's Practice in Water Management

Lin Zexu (1785-1850) was a native of Houguan(now Fuzhou), Fujian Province. His name was associated with the anti-opium movement in China. Few people know that he was a successful official who managed water affairs. In his rise and fall as a government official for 40 years, he took priority of the construction of water conservancy projects and developing agriculture. From the Haihe River in the north to the Pearl River in the south, from the Taihu Lake Basin in the southeast to the Ili Area in Xinjiang in the northwest, he left his footprints in water control activities. Devoting himself to the study of the works and documents on water control written prior to his time, he submitted *Opinions on Water Management in Areas near the Capital* and many relevant memorials to the throne. Few officials could match Lin Zexu in terms of the expenses, energy and time devoted to water governance in history.

In the summer of 1841 in the Qing Dynasty, Lin Zexu was removed from his office and was deployed to Yili, Xinjiang. The overflowing Yellow River just besieged Kaifeng, a major city in Henan Province. A minister named Wang Ding recommended Lin Zexu to control flood despite Emperor Daoguang's objections. His recommendation was finally agreed to by the emperor. Lin Zexu was sent to do the relief work. He spent 41 days traveling from Yangzhou to Kaifeng. Regardless of the fatigue after the long journey, he immediately arrived at where flood hit severely. It was autumn and flood was just gone. As soon as Lin Zexu took office, he started his work. He organized laborers, collected the materials and consulted experienced river workers for advice. They decided that they would build dams to close the opening of the river and in the meantime, they dug a river to force the Yellow River to return to its original course. In 1842, their work was completed. After that, Lin Zexu wrote in his poem to state his political belief, "If you are determined to work for the country and the people, you wouldn't care about your own fate." Wang Ding, who oversaw blocking the Yellow River in Kaifeng, praised Lin's work and petitioned to Emperor Daoguang to forgive Lin Zexu for his offences and exempted him from exile. But Emperor Daoguang refused. At the emperor's decision, Wang Ding couldn't help his tears. The officials and the laborers who worked with Lin couldn't accept the result and were filled with indignation. Lin didn't allow him to indulge in complaints but to persuade them that there was no need for caring about the post so much. He said that fortune and misfortune happened interchangeably. He asked those who admired him not to shed tears for his exile. He left calmly and resolutely and embarked on his journey to Xinjiang, then a barren place.

Lin Zexu and his party travelled westward day and night, passing Luoyang, Xi'an, Liupanshan, the Yellow River, the Hexi Corridor and the Gobi Desert and finally arrived in Yili in early November in 1842. He had been in Xinjiang for less than three years, but he had made great contributions there. He built water conservancy projects, reclaimed farmland and constructed the canals to guide water. Under his direction, they dug a 120 km long Yi River canal. It started in June 1844 and took 4 months to complete the project. This project helped reclaim a large area of wasteland in the east of Ili City and the local people had a good harvest that year. The canal is still flowing today. The people of Ili never forget Lin Zexu. They call it "Lin Gong Canal" even now. In 1844, still under Daoguang's reign, Lin Zexu took his two sons to the south of Xinjiang to carry out the work of farming. Within a year, they cultivated 45,985 hectares of farmland. They travelled 30,000 km. In Iralik, he helped the local people dig the ditches, work to make snow water flow through the desert and irrigate the farmland. In the Turpan Basin, Lin Zexu vigorously promoted building Karez (Fig. 4-9), which turned the barren land into fertile soil. In memory of Lin Zexu, the local people changed the name of Karez as "Lin Gong Well". They admired him and set up steles to show their adoration.

Figure 4-9　Karez

Section IV Water, Country and People

Good governance and proper use of water can bring national prosperity. On the contrary, poor governance would shake the foundation of the country, bring the downfall of the regime and make people suffer severely.

1. Water and Political Instability

Either in feudal times or in modern society, whether the government can effectively deal with the social crisis including floods and droughts is related to people's confidence and trust in the government. In feudal society, influenced by the traditional concept of the unity of man and nature, great disasters were often associated with the rulers' immorality, which was regarded as a warning from heaven. If disaster relief projects couldn't work, people would lose confidence in the rulers and this would affect the stability of the country.

At the end of the Yuan Dynasty, there were increasingly sharp class conflicts and clashes between nationalities. Multiple disasters, such as flood, locusts, hails and earthquake, occurred consecutively. To make things worse, there was also the pandemic. *A Biography for Emperor Shun in History of Yuan* recorded how much people suffered from disasters, hunger and diseases. To quote from it, "the dead bodies were piled in the ditches and parents had to desert their beloved children for they had no food to feed them". Under such circumstances, should the Yellow River that was out of control be harassed? There were controversies over this issue. We mentioned previously that Jia Lu insisted on relieving people from their sufferings by regulating the river. He put forward the measures to manage the Yellow River, "The northern part has to be blocked and the southern part has to be dredged. The Yellow River has to be changed to its original course". However, Cheng Zunze, head of Ministry of Construction, was firmly opposed to Jia Lu's suggestion. He mainly considered from the political point of view, "People in Shandong have been suffering from famine for years and they have no food to eat. If 200,000 hungry people are dissatisfied with the government and if they gather together, it might be a bigger trouble than floods." Despite the objections, with the support of Prime Minister Tuotuo, Emperor Shun appointed Jia Lu to govern the Yellow River. His work would not only eliminate the threats to the people and save the country, but also be able to help facilitate the smooth transport of grain from the south of the Yangtze River into Beijing through the Grand Canal. Jia's water governance project was costly. 150,000 hungry farmers and 20,000 military men were recruited to complete the work. The total amount of money spent was more than 1.845 million ingots. These were heavy expenses. In addition, there were continuous peasants' uprisings in Hunan, Hubei, Henan and Shandong Provinces. Jia Lu's work was the last straw to hit the declining Yuan Dynasty. Poor governance, corruption, the corrupt officials who recruited the laborers but paid nothing to them led to the fall of the Yuan Dynasty. Those officials robbed people of their lands and properties, which aggravated the already heated social conflicts. Seeing this, Han Shantong and Liu Futong called on people to rebel against the ruler of Yuan Dynasty (according to the book, *A Brief Account of the Heroes in the First Several Years of Ming Dynasty*) written by Qian Qianyi.

In addition, the uprising of Li Er and Zhao Jun in Shandong Province was also triggered by Jia Lu's river management project. The tremendous expenses in Jia Lu's governance of the Yellow River led people to abandon their business and led to their complaints. Li Er and his neighbor Zhao Jun conspired to start a rebellion. Li said, "Now the imperial court is devoted to constructing the river works, robbed common people of their property, and led to their poverty. The common people's complaints were left unheeded by the emperor. I heard that there are the rebellion armies rising in Yingshang County, but the imperial armies have nothing to do with it. Now it is the right time for us to win reputation and wealth." Guo Zixing in Anhui also took the heavy expenses and poverty river regulation project that caused as the excuse for the rebellion.

Hunan and Hubei Provinces were the national granaries even in the Qing Dynasty. However, in 1909 and 1910, long-term rainfall caused floods that led to the reduction in the grain yields. Grain prices in Wuhan (Hubei Province) and Changsha (Hunan Province) continued to rise, and there were more than 4 million disaster-hit farmers in the Yangtze River Basin. As a result, the lives of people in Jiangsu and Zhejiang, the once big granary, had also been seriously affected. At the end of 1910, the rice price in Jiangsu and Zhejiang increased by 50%. In 1911, floods occurred in Shandong, Jiangsu, Zhejiang and Liaoning. As a result, the revolutionary party called upon millions of hungry people to rebel against the Qing Dynasty. The Qing government allocated money and food to the victims. At the same time, it began to send troops to suppress the uprising. Yuan Shikai, the leader of the Qing army, and Sun Yat-Sen, the leader of the revolutionary party, reached an agreement, forcing Emperor Xuantong to abdicate and the Qing Dynasty perished. Here we see flood might lead to the collapse of a dynasty.

2. Water Management and People's Burden

The development of water conservancy project is beneficial to the country and the people, but it is costly, so there is the need to consider the affordability of the country and its people. In the heyday of the Qing Dynasty (581-618), the river works consumed almost one third of its total revenues in a bumper year. Therefore, the improper timing of water conservancy project construction would lead to the exhaustion of national strength, increase the burden of the people and intensify social contradictions. The excavation of the Grand Canal in the Sui Dynasty was a typical example. The Sui Dynasty saw the construction of the first large-scale artificial canal in Chinese history. The two emperors, Yang Jian and his son Yang Guang successively dredged the long canals including Guangtong canal, Tongji canal, Shanyangdou canal, to list some. This long canal could transport goods or grain. Among them, the construction of the canals such as Shanyangdou canal and the canal over Jiangnan River played a very important role in the Grand Canal.

The Grand Canal that connected the south and north was built with an unprecedented scale and completed during the Yang regime (581-618). Guangtong canal was excavated in May of the fourth year of Emperor Kaihuang (584). Shanyangdou canal was excavated in April, 587. Tongji canal and Yongji canal were successively excavated in March, 605 and Shanyangdu canal was excavated in the same year. Yongji canal was completed in March, 608. And over Jiangnan River a canal was built in December 610. So far, the north and south canals along the Yangtze River had been completed. Pi Rixiu, a poet of the Tang Dynasty, said in his essay *"Notes on Bianhe River"*, "People of the Sui Dynasty suffered greatly because of the construction of the Canal while People of the Tang Dynasty benefited greatly from it." He not only criticized the heavy taxes imposed by Emperor Yang Guang of the Sui Dynasty on his people in order to dig the Grand Canal, but also saw the great achievements the people of the Sui Dynasty made. At the same time, he also recognized the historical role the Grand Canal played in developing social economy and water transportation.

The North-South Grand Canal, with a total length of more than 1,000 km, was a great pioneering work in the Sui Dynasty. More than 3 million people and soldiers were involved in the canal construction. It was their efforts that made the longest artificial canal possible on the earth. As the initiator of the north-south canal excavation project, the role of Emperor Yang of Sui Dynasty should not be neglected. However, while ordering people to dig the canal, Yang Guang was cruel, arbitrary and eager for quick success and instant benefits; after the completion of the project, he lived an extravagant and reckless life which brought disasters to his people. It had destroyed the normal life of the society. For example, in the first year of Daye, the three major projects of dredging Shanyangdou, digging Tongji canal, and building Luoyang as the eastern capital were carried out at the same time. More than 3 million people were recruited, and all "men aged over 15 and under 50" were included in the recruitment. When the canal was opened to Xuzhou, more than 1.5 million people died after being tortured by the soldiers. "Where there were the villages, there were dead bodies laid everywhere". One would see the miserable situation, "The country collapsed due to the excessive recruitment and hard work and the families lost their wealth". Excessive profligacy, a large number of consumptions of social wealth hurt the emperor's reign. While digging the canal, Yang Guang forced people to build Royal Roads along the river, plant green willows everywhere, and build the palaces, which increased the economic burden on people. When Yang Guang toured Jiangdu by a big dragon boat, he forced more than 500 women, aged 15 or 16, from Wu and Yue States, to pull his large boat. He ordered people to use the coloured silk to pull the boat. Many boats lined and extended for one thousand meters over the river. The emperor, imperial concubines, royal families, courtiers, officials, monks and Taoists, celebrities, sailors, and guards enjoyed the scenery in their boats. The officials offered precious food within 250 km of the state when the boats passed. Such a tyranny finally led to the resistance of the people living along the canal. At the end of the Sui Dynasty, the people's uprisings on both sides of the Grand Canal were a severe punishment on Yang Guang's tyranny. Finally, seven years after the canal was built, Emperor Yang of the Sui Dynasty was killed, and the the Sui Dynasty perished.

3. Water Control and the Corrupted Officials

Water conservancy projects, as the highly costly works that demanded intensive and extensive work, had to be organized and implemented by the country in the society with the individual household as the basic production unit. As the organizer and performer of national works, the officials' responsibility, honesty and governance ability would determine the results of the works. Due to the lack of effective supervision and punishment mechanism, corruption prevailed. Where there were things to do, there were malpractices. The huge investment in water conservancy projects led to corruption. This would hinder the smooth progress of river control, consequently leading to frequent disasters.

In the Qing Dynasty, there was a popular saying, "If the Yellow River burst, thousands of gold would be needed to control it." The funds raised for river management were coveted by the greedy officials, who were willing to engage in river management. When Emperor Yongzheng of the Qing Dynasty (1721–1735) ruled, a governor talked about how the funds for disasters relief were abused in a careless and negligent way. Even if the officials took no bribes and spent all on the projects, only 40% or 50% would be used for the projects. What's more, money would be robbed by officials at all levels. The real cost of river management might be less than 20%. Yongzheng was famous for the strict management of his officials. After him, when Emperor Jiaqing ruled, the corruption and embezzlement worsened.

In 1900, Prime Minister Li Hongzhang of the Qing Dynasty summoned Hoover, who was then employed as a coal mine engineer in Kailuan, China. Hoover later became the 31st president of the United States. Li Hongzhang asked him to inspect the Yellow River. In his report to Li Hongzhang, Hoover analysed in details why the Qing Dynasty government had little effect in harnessing the Yellow River flood. Hoover affirmed the capability of the Chinese river officials, especially their skills in keeping the river under constant maintenance. He stated that what was done by these officials was a passive post-disaster defence measure, which could not eradicate such problems as silts and the suspended operation of the Yellow River caused by the fast flow of the Yellow River. Hoover also put forward, "the officials' corruption and dereliction of duty were the root causes of their poor performance and were also the important reason for the ineffective river management.

Gu Yanwu (1613–1682), a scholar in the late Ming Dynasty, analysed in one of his well-known academic books entitled as *Daily Notes* (*Ri Zhi Lu*), why Yu in the remote past could control water while people failed to do so in China after the Song and Ming Dynasties. Three reasons were proposed. First, the increasing population in the central area of the dynasty would occupy the increasingly larger area and even the river course. So it was not that the river flew into the residential area but vice versa. Second, the governmental river control policy centred upon two things: transporting grain by river to the capital and preventing the vassals in their states from threatening the security of the country. The rulers prioritized the security of the country over economic development, the safety of the people and their properties. Third, those officials of all levels, even those who had something to do with the river management would take every chance to embezzle from the floods. With such thick profits they were willing to see the floods and allow the floods to take place so that they could make profits from the restoration.

In ancient China, the governments of all dynasties had made great efforts on water control projects, but the effects differed. Some benefited the people greatly while some ended in vain.

Section V Water and the Construction of the Ancient Cities

Water has played the important role in building and developing the cities. Since the ancient times, water would be given priority over other things when the cities were built. Historically, water has been closely related to the development of the cities. At the same time, water has affected the development of the urban culture, for example, shaping the image of the cities.

1. Water and the Cities

(1) Water Brought the Emergence of the Cities

Water is important in building the cities. *Guanzi*, an early historical document in China, mentioned the relationship between water resources and selecting the location of the cities, "Capitals are usually built either at the foot of the mountains or near the rivers. If the cities were built above the rivers, they would not be easily affected by drought for they would have sufficient water for use. If the cities were built in places lower than the reaches of the rivers, they should be in faraway places." That is to say, in face with the choice of the urban sites people should have access to water and avoid possible floods. *The Book of Songs* also records the ancestors of the Zhou Dynasty chose the places close to the mountains and rivers for their settlements. To have easy access to water, the ancient people settled their homes near the rivers. It is also common to see that rivers were dug before the cities were built. Urban planning would be in accordance with the directions and twists of the river.

(2) Water Led to the Prosperity of the Cities

The development of water works will bring vitality to the cities. That many cities would appear and thrive along both banks of the rivers could prove it. The Beijing-Hangzhou Grand Canal connected the five water systems, including the Qiantangjiang River, the Yangtze River, the Huaihe River, the Yellow River and the Haihe River, carrying ships from south to north. It had become the major means of transportation between the north and south and created numerous cities along the two banks of the rivers. Linqing, a small village of Shandong Province, for example, was turned into a central city in the Ming and Qing Dynasties due to the busy use of the Grand Canal. A magistrate of Linqing during Kangxi's reign recorded the prosperity there in a poem. Besides the Grand Canal that connected the north and the south, the development of water transportation in the north also promoted the prosperity of the cities along the banks. The Bianhe River was an important hub of material transportation in the Northern Song Dynasty. Materials from the south of the Yantze River and other places were transported by water to Kaifeng and Luoyang. These materials provided rich supplies of goods for people of Kaifeng and Luoyang and promoted the prosperity there. The places near the rivers were turned into the city centres. During the Kaiyuan period of the Tang Dynasty, Wang Wei passed through Xingyang, Henan Province and recorded the prosperity of Xingyang in his poem, indeed, along the canal, Wang Wei saw the vitality of human life and the thriving businesses. The poet drew his inspiration from the fishermen, the chickens and dogs walking on the shores and the hustle and bustle of the human life.

(3) Water Destroyed Cities

In history, water has benefited human beings and brought about the emergence and prosperity of the cities, but it has also brought the decline and disappearance of cities. Without water, the cities will have no vitality to develop. Floods and other disasters buried some cities underground. The Yellow River nurtured the early Chinese civilization and gave birth to numerous cities around its banks, but many cities along the river were also destroyed and buried under the water. For example, Bianjing, the capital of the Northern Song Dynasty, is buried underground in Kaifeng, Henan Province. This once splendid city was inundated by the rising waters of the Yellow River in the Ming Dynasty. Today, the only landmark related to the ancient city that is exposed above the ground is the Iron Tower in the northeast corner of Kaifeng. It has witnessed the prosperity and decline of the Northern Song Dynasty. Another example is Sizhou, a city with a long history. The ancient Sizhou City is located on the North Bank of the Huaihe River in Jiangsu Province, facing Xuyi across the river in the south. Sizhou City was built in the Northern Zhou Dynasty, and its rise was closely related to the Tongji canal excavated in the Sui Dynasty. With the opening of Tongji canal (also known as "Bian canal" or "Bian River" in the Tang and Song Dynasties), Sizhou was in the position of an important transportation hub. Therefore, Sizhou City experienced a long period of prosperity. However, during the reign of Emperor Kangxi of the Qing Dynasty, the lower reaches of the Huaihe River were silted up, and the water level of Hongze Lake was further raised. At the turn of summer and autumn in the 19th year of Kangxi (1680), due to the continuous rainstorm in Sizhou, the water level of Hongze Lake rose sharply and the dam burst, which eventually led to the flooding of Sizhou City. It was submerged in the rising water.

(4) Urbanization Prompted the Continuous Digging and Utilization of the New Water Systems

The natural water system brought about the emergence of the early cities. Urbanization and the changing social environment urged people to constantly consider the planning and construction of new urban water system. For example, with the increasing number of the urban population, to improve people's life, it is necessary to build the water related projects near the city according to the natural conditions so that the urban water systems will be connected with the water system outside the city that will flow into the urban water system. Take Dadu (today's Beijing), the capital of the Yuan Dynasty, as an example. To solve the shortage of the local water resources, the rulers spared no effort developing and constructing a number of water conservancy projects. Among them, the Tonghui River, which Guo Shoujing presided over, introduced Baifu spring from Changping County into Dadu, which is a great feat. In addition, moats were often excavated out of the need of urban defense. For example, the Haohe River in Nantong, one of the most complete ancient moats in Chin, was first built in 958 in order to defend the city.

2. Water and the Ancient Capitals

As the political and economic centre of the country, the capital is a big city with large population. The convenient access to water for many people is an important factor to consider when considering the location of the capital.

Guanzi stated, "The capital of a country should be built either under the mountain or above the wide river. If it was built under the mountain, it should be too high to have access to water, or drought would strike. On the other hand, if it was built near the river, it should be located in a place lower than the river." *Guanzi* emphasized that water source should be considered carefully in terms of the selection of the capital so as to prevent drought and floods. Therefore, in ancient China, water would be considered as an important issue when selecting the sites of the capitals.

(1) Chang'an and the Rise and Fall of Its Water Transport

Chang'an is probably the most famous capital in Chinese history. It has become a symbol of the capitals of all times. People in the Ming and Qing Dynasties even used "Chang'an" to refer to their capital city, Beijing or Dadu, in their poems. Many elements led to Chang'an as a capital and its geographical location is the most important one. As far as the military fortress is concerned, there are Tongguan in its east, Dasanguan in its west, Wuguan in its south and Xiaoguan in its north. The four passes controlled the entry into Chang'an, which made it easy to defend but difficult to attack. Geographically, Chang'an was in a safe area. There were two Chang'an cities in history. The first Chang'an was in the Han Dynasty and located in the northwest of present Xi'an; the second one was in the Sui and Tang Dynasties and located in the centre of Xi'an. It was built by Emperor Wen of the Sui Dynasty. At that time, it was not called Chang'an, but Daxing City.

Why was Chang'an made the capital of the Western Han Dynasty? At that time, Liu Bang, the founder of the dynasty, and his officials intended to build Luoyang as their capital, but Zhang Liang, an important advisor, thought that Chang'an was not easy to have access to with Hangu pass and Xiaoshan Mountain as its natural barriers. Guanzhong Plain that was close to the land of abundance in Bashu (Today's Sichuan Province and Chongqing City) was fertile. With convenient waterway transportation through the Yellow River and the Weishui River, food could be transported to the capital. If there were risings or rebellions outside Chang'an, the soldiers from the capital could act promptly and go fast downstream to the rebellious areas. At Zhang Liang's suggestion, Liu Bang built the capital in Chang'an, a city long known as "surrounded by mountains and rivers" since the ancient times. It was located in the Guanzhong Plain and rich in water resources in the Han Dynasty. There were eight famous rivers such as Jingshui, Weishui, Luoshui, Bashui, Chanshui and Fengshui, as well as 17 lakes such as Hechi, Panchi, Bingchi, Haochi, Chuchi and Michi. With so many rivers, it was known as "the sea on the land". Besides the Western Han Dynasty, starting from 770 B. C., 13 dynasties including the Eastern Zhou Dynasty, the Sui Dynasty and the Tang Dynasty made Chang'an their capital.

Then, why did Chang'an stop being the capital after the late Tang Dynasty? This was also caused by water. The increasingly inconvenient shipping condition added difficulties to water transport. This occurred in the middle and late Tang Dynasty. In the early Tang Dynasty, Chang'an was in affluent Guanzhong Plain that could provide a large share of the supplies needed in the capital. Chang'an also got its supplies from the north, such as Shandong and other areas. Those supplies started from Shandong, through Luoyang and Sanmenxia and then to Chang'an by artificial canals. In Sanmenxia, boats couldn't easily get through. Ox carts had to be used on the rugged mountain roads. It was very dangerous, and the traffic volume was limited. After the An Lushan and Shi Siming rebellion, the economic centre moved from Chang'an to the south, and the Northern Warlords separated the regime, so the grain was provided through the transport of the Yangtze River and Huaihe River, so the role of the canal was reduced, and the canals were blocked and out of use. It was a long way to transport grain from southeast to Chang'an, and it must pass through the Weihe River. At this time, the Weihe River was shallow and had a lot of sediment. Poor shipping conditions, time-consuming and laborious, the grain couldn't be transported in time, resulting in the shortage of food in Chang'an. So the emperor had to stay in Luoyang for food. In Emperor Gaozong's reign during the Tang Dynasty, the scale of the government expanded rapidly, and the population of Chang'an city also increased, so there was lack of food there. As soon as there was a bad harvest in Guanzhong, Li Zhi and Wu Zetian (then the rulers) would take all the civil and military officials to Luoyang just to feed them. Chang'an was still their capital. When the famine years passed, Li Zhi and his family went back to Chang'an, the royal family and their subjects all looked like refugees. The first year of Yongchun (682), some retinues who followed the emperor to Luoyang even starved to death on their way to Luoyang. There were many starving people along the way. When Wu Zetian became Empress, she made a bolder decision, that is, establishing Luoyang as the real capital of the Empire, which was renamed "Shendu", meaning "God-chosen capital". Luoyang then was a city more important than Chang'an. During Wu Zetian's 25-year reign, she lived in Chang'an for merely 2 years and in Luoyang for 23 years. In addition, Xuanzong, Wu

Zetian's grandson, lived in Luoyang for over nine years during his 25-year reign.

The late Tang Dynasty saw the fights over the construction and management of the canals. If the empire could control the canals and maintain the water transport, it could survive and then Chang'an would remain as the capital. As for Luoyang, it was extremely dilapidated at the end of the Tang Dynasty. At its worst, it had less than 100 households and was like a ghost city. In the process of competing for the canal, Bianzhou (now Kaifeng, Henan Province) replaced them as the new capital. In Bianzhou, the Bianhe River would flow into the Yellow River, so this city was a key point of the canal. Controlling it would control the materials transported by water. Finally, Zhu Wen, a warlord, took it as the base, defeated the emperor of the Tang Dynasty and established the late Liang Dynasty. Since then, the canal that stretched from the east to the west, the important artery of China, turned into the south-north artery and this pattern lasted until the Qing Dynasty.

(2) Kaifeng and the Rise and Fall of the River Transport

Kaifeng is known as "the ancient capital of seven dynasties". It rose during the Spring and Autumn Period and the Warring States Period, developed in the Sui and Tang Dynasties, flourished in the Northern Song Dynasty, and declined after the Jin and Yuan Dynasties. The three prosperous periods of Kaifeng saw the development of the canal in the Central Plains. After the Northern Song Dynasty, the abandonment of the canal led to the decline of Kaifeng. We can say that the rise and fall of Kaifeng is closely related to that of the canal.

Urged by Emperor Yang of the Sui Dynasty, Tongji canal (renamed as Guangji canal in the Tang Dynasty and also Bianhe River) was excavated. It was dredged into the Grand Canal with Luoyang as the centre, reaching Zhuojun (today's Beijing) through Yongji canal in the north and Hangzhou in the south. According to relevant documents of the Tang and Song Dynasties, Tongji canal flew eastward from the east of Luoyang to Luokou, Gongxian County, into the Yellow River, from Banzhu (also known as Bancheng Qingkou, now Niukouyu in the northwest of Rongyang county), eastward to Heyin County (now northeast of Rongyang County), southeast to Zhongmou and Bianzhou (Kaifeng), and through Chenliu and Yongqiu (now Qi County), Xiangyi (now Suixian), Ningling, Songzhou (now South of Shangqiu), downstream through Gushu (now east of Shangqiu), Yongcheng, Suxian, Lingbi, to Linhuai County into the Huaihe River. This is the famous Bianhe River in history. It is the main water transportation line between the north and the south of China after the Sui and Tang Dynasties. This waterway further shortened the voyage between the Yellow River and the Huaihe River, and strengthened the connection between Luoyang, the capital city, and the other parts of the country.

For the central government of the Tang Dynasty, the Bianhe River was like a blood vessel, extending from Chang'an and Luoyang to the south of the Yangtze River through Bianzhou. The Tang Dynasty relied on this river to sustain. Bianzhou was the centre of this blood vessel. Through its control of Bianzhou, the rulers of Tang Dynasty controlled the northern and southern transportation routes.

Kaifeng was built as the capital in the Northern Song Dynasty because of the Bianhe River. Located in the plain, Kaifeng couldn't rely on the precipitous place for safety. When there were conflicts between the Song Dynasty and the Kingdom of Liao, it took only a few days for the cavalry of Liao Kingdom to arrive at Kaifeng after quickly crossing the flat North China Plain. Another disadvantage of taking Kaifeng as the capital is that it was not conducive to drainage. Located in the low-lying plain, it was difficult to drain off water and easy to lead to floods. Therefore, in the early Song Dynasty, there was a long and fierce debate within the ruling group over where to build the capital. Emperor Taizu intended to build the capital in Luoyang or Chang'an. However, his brother, King Jin (the later Emperor Taizong of Song Dynasty) and some officials wanted to have Bianzhou as the capital because they advocated a centralized political and military system. If so, there must be enough food and materials to ensure the implementation of this political system. At that time, the economic centre had shifted to the south of the Yangtze River and the capital had to rely upon the south of the Yangtze River for the huge supply of food and materials. Therefore, water transport was the top priority of the country. Kaifeng had the convenience of water transportation, and that was why it was chosen as the capital.

After Kaifeng was established as the capital of the Northern Song Dynasty, the Wuzhang River and Bianhe River were dredged, and the Jinshui River and Huimin River were newly excavated to connect the capital with the other parts of the country through water transport. These four rivers were named as "four canals" in Kaifeng. *Records of the Prosperous Capital City, Kaifeng* described the four canals. The "four canals" were distributed radially near the capital, which could relate to other parts of the country; the grain and materials all over the country are transported to the capital and be sent to the north through the four canals.

Kaifeng in the Northern Song Dynasty surpassed Chang'an and Luoyang in terms of the scale of the city, population, and economy. It was not only the political, economic, and cultural centre in China, but also one of the most prosperous cities in the world. Under Emperor Zhenzong's reign, Kaifeng was an affluent city with a large number of rich people. The shops were decorated with embroidered objects and the colourful buildings were seen everywhere. "That the transactions were over tens of millions is not scarce." The scale of the city was ten times larger than that of the Han and Tang Dynasties. According to *Records of the Prosperous Capital City, Kaifeng*, the number of the urban population reached 1.7 million.

At the end of the Northern Song Dynasty, most of the rivers and lakes between the Yellow River and the Huaihe River were gradually obliterated due to the flood of the Yellow River. In addition, frequent wars and political corruption led to the paralysis of the canal management and the relaxation of the system. During the reign of Emperor Qianlong and Daoguang of the Qing Dynasty, the canal was "almost levelling with the shore, with troops and horses running across it, and on top of some of them were built houses." Others, such as the Wuzhang River and Huimin River, were out of use. Kaifeng, the development of which was closely related to the favourable conditions of water transportation, naturally declined. The Yuan Dynasty established Beijing as the capital. The Grand Canal and maritime transportation were opened, and the political centre and transportation routes were transferred. The two pillars of Kaifeng's development had been destroyed. Therefore, during the Yuan and Ming Dynasties, Kaifeng changed from a city of national significance to a regional political and economic centre.

3. Water and the Prosperous Towns and Cities

Not only the development of the capital, but also the development of many cities and towns are closely related to water. The opening and development of the canal promoted the prosperity of the capital cities and towns along the canal. Huai'an, Yangzhou, Zhenjiang, Wuxi, Suzhou, Hangzhou, Kaifeng, Cangzhou, Linqing, Jining, Tianjin, Beijing and other cities prospered because of water. Many ancient towns also prospered and declined because of water.

Zhuxianzhen, a town that is 20 km away from Kaifeng, is currently an obscure northern town, but in the Song, Ming and Qing Dynasties, it was a prosperous place that saw the boats come and go and the thriving commerce.

Before the Northern Song Dynasty, Zhuxianzhen was merely a residential area. Because of the excavation of the Xicai River and its connection with the Bianhe River, it ushered in its first prosperity. It had turned from a village to a post station and then into a market town. Boats came and went. Large crowds of people came and left. It was made a very prosperous place. In the Jin and Yuan Dynasties, with the decline of Kaifeng as a major city, the change of the canal and the diversion of the Yellow River, Zhuxianzhen also declined. In the Yuan Dynasty, the opening of the Jialu River revived the water transport in Kaifeng, and the commerce along the river soon flourished. After that, Zhuxianzhen became the largest water transport terminal in North China and was once one of the four famous commercial towns in China. Zhuxianzhen reached its peak during Emperor Kangxi's reign. Later, during Emperor Jiaqing and Daoguang's reign of the Qing Dynasty, Zhuxianzhen declined because the Yellow River overflowed the Jialu River. In 1900, the Jialu River was finally filled with sand, and its navigation was completely blocked. In addition, the Beijing-Hankou railway and Longhai railway came into use, and the transportation route was greatly changed, so the water transport at in Zhuxianzhen lost its advantage. At the beginning of the 20th century, Zhuxianzhen was reduced to an extremely dilapidated market town, destroyed by floods, sandstorms, and other factors. Today's Zhuxianzhen is constantly developing, but it is not as prosperous as it used to be.

4. Water and the Urban Culture

The development of many cities is closely related to water. Water would promote and restrict the development of the cities. And water would fashion the cities, marking them with unique cultural symbols.

(1) The Cities Got Names from the Rivers

Cities and water are closely related. Whether in water abundant areas or water deficient areas, one could trace water culture from the name of some cities. For example, some cities are named after the rivers and lakes, such as Lijiang City (Lijiang River) in Yunnan Province, Mudanjiang City (Mudanjiang River) in Heilongjiang Province, Huzhou City (Taihu Lake) in Zhejiang Province, etc. In some other cases, many cities are adjacent to water and their names also contain words related to water. For example, "Ningbo" (a city in Zhejiang Province) reveals its coastal location. In the thirteenth year of Emperor Hongzu's reign (1381, the Ming Dynasty), Shan Zhongyou, a member of Mingzhou prefecture (the ancient name for Ningbo), wrote to the government that Mingzhou had the same name as the Ming Dynasty and asked for a change of the name. He suggested that Mingzhou prefecture should be renamed as "Ningbo", which meant that the peaceful sea would produce no big waves. So the Ming Court issued an imperial edict, naming Mingzhou prefecture as Ningbo. There are more examples. Henan Province used to have rich water resources. So many places were named after these water systems. Kaifeng was called "Bianzhou" in ancient times, because the city was close to the Bianshui River; Luoyang had its name because it was located near the north of the Luoshui River; Puyang had its name during the Warring States Period, because it was located on the northern side of the Pushui River (the tributary of the Yellow River and the Jishui River, which was later silted by the Yellow River); Jiyuan had its name from the Jishui River. In addition, some cities are named because of the local water conservancy projects. Dujiangyan City in Sichuan Province had its name from Dujiangyan Dam and Sanmenxia City in Henan Province was named after the most dangerous gorge in the large section of the Yellow River.

(2) Water and the Spatial Layout of the Cities

Water influences the formation of the urban architecture. The buildings are arranged along the river. The centre of the cities would appear along the rivers and each has the overall pattern with its own characteristics, thus forming a part of the urban culture. The water networks in the south of the Yangtze River crisscross and the layout of the cities had the characteristics unique to their rivers. For example, Pingjiang City in the Southern Song Dynasty, with river system as the urban context, constructed the spatial pattern of "three streets from the east to west and four streets from south to north, the streets in the front of the houses and the rivers behinds the houses". For another example, the ancient Changshu City was designed according to its unique natural landscape, integrating the southeast corner of Yushan Mountain into the ancient city, and the seven streams of Qinchuan at the foot of Yushan Mountain are like the seven strings of the ancient Chinese musical instrument, Qin. These unique landscapes constitute the urban style of the ancient city which integrates the local mountains and rivers. The rich waterways and convenient water transportation in the ancient city have affected the composition of the neighborhoods, resulting in the formation of a distinctive spatial pattern of the urban streets and alleys in the south of the Yangtze River.

Today, some big cities continue to make use of water facilities to build ecological spatial layout. Wuhan is where the ancient Yunmengze was located. Yunmengze was a swamp. The ancient settlements were surrounded by water. The terrain was low, and the drainage was not smooth. And the city had to solve the problems caused by water. The names for many places and buildings in the cities are the witness and epitome of water control activities. Qingchuan Pavilion was built to commemorate Yu's activities in flood control. Zhang Gong Dam not only blocked the flood, but also circled the rudiment of Hankou. Longwang Temple is the watch post of flood fighting, and the Wuhan Flood Control Monument in Jiangtan park marks the city's solidarity and it is a spiritual symbol. There are 166 lakes in Wuhan. Today's urban construction of Wuhan is following "Great Lakes +" pattern to create a unique lakeside space.

In the past 10 years, Wuhan City has built an ecological water network of "Great East Lake" (Donghu Lake) to continuously control the water and clean the East Lake. The data shows that the water quality of Donghu Lake continues to improve, and the overall water quality of Donghu Lake has remained stable in class Ⅲ to Ⅳ in recent years. At present, the third phase of Donghu greenway has been completed. With the Yangtze River going through the city and the Donghu Lake as the centre, Wuhan has built a network of 100 km ecological greenways, making the Donghu Lake an urban ecological "green heart", which is meant for Wuhan citizens to be close to nature. The Donghu Lake greenway (Fig. 4-10) is located in the centre of the city. It is very convenient for people to play and enjoy a green life in places not far away from home. So you see that Wuhan City is arranging its urban space by making great use of the Donghu Lake.

Figure 4-10　　An Autumn View of the Donghu Lake Greenway

(3) Water and the Charm of the City

Different water systems have different characteristics. The gurgling stream makes people feel the softness in hearts while the turbulent torrent might arouse a sense of indifference and cruelty.

The magnificent water endows some cities with a rough and magnificent touch. When it comes to water towns in Jiangsu and Zhejiang Provinces, people often think of small bridges, gently flowing water and the streets paved with bluestone slabs near the river. They think of "the soft dialects", "apricot flowers and misty rain" and "people living close to the river". "Water towns" seem to be synonymous with the poetic Jiangnan City. Water systems differ in their spirits, so the products and scenery of the city are colourful. "Fabulous South, familiar scene. The rising sun dyes the water blazingly red; the spring radiance paints the water azure blue. How can I not miss the South?" The poem *"Memories of Jiangnan"*, written by Bai Juyi, a poet of the Tang Dynasty, is so popular because the beautiful scenery related to water is fascinating. Naturally, the shaping of the urban culture by water goes beyond the region. The north also has beautiful cities because of water. Xinyang, Henan Province, boasts beautiful mountains and rivers, outstanding people, and the natural scenery of Nanwan Lake scenic spot (Fig. 4-11). Xinyang also enjoys the reputation of "a north city in the south of the Yangtze River", "south of the Yangtze River in the north" and "Suzhou in the south of Henan".

Figure 4-11   Nanwan Lake, Xinyang City

Since the ancient times, water is an important source to stimulate people's imagination, and some cities carry a romantic or mysterious colour. Water has gradually promoted the emergence of an urban culture in the increasingly urbanized society. Ancient bridges, pagodas and other historic buildings are often located in the urban riverside area, which are the precious wealth of the city. For example, the West Lake has become a name card of Hangzhou.

Taking the West Lake as the centre, there are many legendary stories: the eternal masterpiece of Liang Shanbo and Zhu Yingtai in Wansong academy, the beautiful legend of broken bridge, Leifeng Pagoda, Xu Xian and a white snake, and Su Xiaoxiao, a famous prostitute of Six Dynasties buried in Mucai Pavilion, who pursues love despite the humiliation. These tragic and romantic love legends and true stories, which took place on the Bank of the West Lake, add gentle and romantic colour to the city. Even the neighbouring buildings are closely related to these touching stories. The Leifeng Pagoda, built in the period of the State of Wu and Yue, is also a romantic tonic for Hangzhou. Leifeng Pagoda is located on Xizhao Mountain on the south bank of the West Lake. At dusk, the setting sun shines on the Pagoda. This is described as "Sunset at Leifeng Pagoda" (Fig. 4-12), becoming one of the famous "ten sceneries of the West Lake". Myths and legends such as the legend of the white snake have made the beautiful Leifeng Pagoda well-known. Bai Juyi built the Bai dike when he was the governor of Hangzhou, and Su Shi built the Su dike in the West Lake when he was in Hangzhou. The relationship between Bai Juyi, Su Shi and the West Lake intensifies the classical culture of the West Lake. Similarly, the modern coastal cities have the distinctive charm, like Shanghai, Xiamen, Beihai, Haikou and so on.

Figure 4-12 Sunset at Leifeng Pagoda

Chapter Five Water and Wars

Section I Fight for Water

Being the source of all lives, water plays an important role in affecting social development, while war is an armed struggle for political purposes after human beings enter the class society, and it is the product of class struggle and intensification of ethnic conflicts. Water and war, due to the nature and function of water, create a natural and inseparable connection. China's 5,000-year history of cultural development has witnessed an interwoven relationship between water and war. The Zhuolu Battle between the *Yellow Emperor* (Huangdi) and *Chiyou*, the first war ever recorded in China, is a well-known case of the comprehensive use of water as a substitute for soldiers and water as an aid to war. Since then, wars in China have been endowed with significance of water culture. The water culture, military culture and war art complement each other, and together they have made magnificent and colourful Chinese war epics and war pictures.

China is endowed with many large rivers, lakes and swaps, and it is also close to the Bohai Sea, Huanghai Sea, East China Sea, South China Sea and Pacific Ocean. The unique terrain is suitable to be developed as water battlefield, and sometimes even the leading one for heroes to fight for supremacy. Hence water war emerged as one of the three main warfare forms together with fand war and chariot war.

When it comes to water wars, many people will think of the Battle of Chibi because of the famous poem written by Su Shi, an outstanding poet in the Song Dynasty, when he visited the ancient battlefield of Chibi. In the poem, he left his sign of life by writing:

"The Great River eastwards flows,
With its waves are gone all those
Gallant heroes of bygone years.
West of the ancient fortress appears
The Red Cliff.
Here General Zhou won his early fame

When the Three Kingdoms were all in flame."[1]

The Battle of Chibi is one of the most famous water wars in ancient China, which promoted the division of ancient China into three Kingdoms, namely Wei, Shu and Wu. The Battle of Chibi is also the first large-scale river battle in Chinese history on the basin of the Yangtze River, marking that China's military and political centre is no longer limited to the basin of the Yellow River. In this war, many strategies were purposely used like causing discord among the enemy, deceiving the enemy by torturing one's own man, coordinating one stratagem with another and fire attack, covering forms of field battle, siege, encountering, fire, retreat and pursuit, providing useful references for the coming generations.

The Battle of Chibi, due to its decisive role in shaping the political situation in ancient China, has inspired many literati, who either visited the old battlefield to reflect on the past, or expressed their thoughts by writing poems or wielding their writing brushes to draw pictures, hence countless poems, calligraphy and paintings chanting the Battle of Chibi were left, adding cultural and literature flavour to the war. Among those masterpieces, *Reflection on the Ancient Red Cliff—To the Tune of Niannujiao* written by Su Shi is the most famous one. Another poem written by Yang Shen in the Ming Dynasty and placed at the beginning of *The Romances of the Three Kingdoms* by Luo Guanzhong, has gained great popularity in modern China since it is be used as the theme song of the famous TV series of *The Romances of the Three Kingdoms* (Fig. 5-1).

Figure 5-1 Su Shi and His Poem "*Reflection on the Ancient Red Cliff—To the Tune of Niannujiao*"

The earliest water battle recorded in Chinese history occurred in the summer of 549 B.C.. In *Zuo Zhuan*, it was recorded that Chu attacked Wu by warships and sailors, but finally came back with no success. This is the earliest water battle in ancient China with clear time records, and also the earliest reliable record of warships and water forces. During the Spring and Autumn Period, in

---

[1] The poem is translated by Mr. Xu Yuanchong.

southern China, the powers of Wu, Yue, Chu and Qi, who faced the East China Sea, have gradually developed and become increasingly stronger. To fight for hegemony in ancient central China, continuous wars erupted among those kingdoms. To achieve success, these kingdoms have begun to build warships and established forces on the water, hence water war started in ancient China.

During the Three Kingdoms Period, the navy fleet of Wu State had sailed on the Bohai Sea, the Huanghai Sea, the East China Sea and the South China Sea. So far, as an important military force, the water army has been active in the war stage, and water wars have been escalated on a larger scale in a wider water area. The Battles of Feishui, Huangtiandang, Poyang Lake, Hukou, Baijiangkou, Tangdao, Yashan, Lianghai, Majiang and Jiawu are all famous examples. In the Ming Dynasty, Zheng He led a huge fleet to visit countries along the Pacific Ocean and the Indian sea for seven times, showing the great military power of the Kingdom and acquiring respect from those countries without actual wars.

The water war has outstanding advantages when fighting against ethnic minorities who are not good at it. In the 31st year of Shaoxing in the Southern Song Dynasty (in 1161), Wanyan Liang, king of the Jin Kingdom, intended to defeat the Southern Song Dynasty with his ambition shown in his poem *"leading a million of soldiers to fight to the bank of Xihu*①*, mighty on my horseback, I will tread on the peak of Wushan mountain*②*"*. Army of the Jin Kingdom easily defeated that of Song on the Huaihe River and reached the north bank of the Yangtze River. In the Battle of Caishi, the Song army defeated the Jin army on the Yangtze River with small-sized warships, blocked the enemy's boat at the mouth of Yanglin River, attacked them with bows, and burned their warships. In this war, the number of the forces of the Southern Song Dynasty were far less than those of the Jin army. The Jin army alleged to have "400,000 soldiers, several times the number of horses", while the Southern Song Dynasty had only "about 8,000 soldiers, and a few hundred of horses". Were the two forces to fight on the land, the result would be no surprise. Advantages in water forces contributed greatly to the victory of the Southern Song Dynasty. After the defeating, Jin army, led by Wanyan Liang, retreated to Guazhou with a purpose to cross the river. Yu Yunwen, the leading general of Song, mobilized warships to confront Jin army on the Zhenjiang River. General Yu ordered the soldiers to skilfully turn the vehicles and boats up and down the middle stream like flying, which greatly shocked and frightened Jin soldiers out of their fighting courage. What's worse, Wanyan Liang was murdered by his subordinates when he forced the troops to cross the river in a very limited time. Subsequently, the Song army won without fighting.

Great differences exist between fighting on water and that on land due to the different natural conditions. First there should be special weapons and equipment for water warfare, such as warships, hooks, shooting poles and firearms. Warships can be roughly divided into two categories: large warships and small ones. Large warships include building warships, Fujian warships and

---

① Xihu Lake was located in Lin'an (Hangzhou now), capital city of the Southern Song Dynasty.
② Wushan Mountain was located on southeast of Xihu Lake and was a place of prosperity in the Southern Song Dynasty.

Guangdong warships, while small warships mainly include fighting warships and walking boats. Secondly, it is necessary to train the water forces so that they can drive warships, master the necessary knowledge of hydrology and astronomy, strictly abide by military discipline, and have proficient swimming skills. Thirdly, it is also the most important that there are dedicated warfare tactics and strategies in water war.

Wei Yuan, a famous thinker, historian and litterateur in the Qing Dynasty, wrote a special historical book called *Shengwuji*, which summarized the essentials of water battle as the following: "if a bigger boat fights with a smaller one, the bigger one wins; if a stronger boat fights with a weaker one, the stronger one wins; the downwind attack wins against the upwind one; the downstream attack wins against the upstream one; in water battles, efforts need to be developed to protect warships from stranding, fire, wind, chiselling and iron locks." Main forms of ancient water war can be summarized as collision and contact. The collision war is that between ships; while the contact war means to getting close to the warship of the enemy and then trying to get aboard their ship to have hand-to-hand fighting. In this case, key factors in the water war leading to the final victory lie in three main elements: Firstly, physical condition like the size and quality of warships can sometimes dictate the results of the battle, which can be well exemplified when the Western Jin Dynasty annihilated the Wu Kingdom. Jin army got the victory by totally relying on the water army and huge warships. This battle was recorded in the biography of Wang Jun, Volume 42 of the *History of the Jin Dynasty*, "Emperor Wu of the Jin Dynasty planned to attack the Wu Kingdom, and ordered Wu Jun to build the warship. Jun built a large-sized ship, which was 120 steps long and 120 steps wide, and can hold more than 2,000 people. Jun also built wooden wall around the ship, established observation towers and opened four doors on the wall. The ship was large enough for people to go swiftly on horseback." When confronted with such a huge warship, the water army of the Wu Kingdom, once dominating in the water battle, was unable to combat with it. Liu Yuxi, a famous poet in the Tang Dynasty, sighed in his poem Xisaishan Mountain: *Reflections on an Ancient Battle*

> "Down from Yizhou, Wang Jun's battleships came tearing,
> Jinling, the Wu's capital, lost its regal bearing.
> With the blocking iron-chains broken and sunk,
> Over the city wall a white flag appeared, wavering."

In the battle, the water army of the Wu Kingdom adopted some defensive measures like setting iron locks on the river surface in an effort to block the enemy's warship, only to find that those passive measures were useless in stopping Jin's large-sized warship, and they had to choose to surrender finally. In the Southern Song Dynasty, the insurgent force led by Zhong Xiang and Yang Yao developed quickly in the Dongting Lake. In the early years of the Southern Song Dynasty, under the call of Zhong Xiang, people from different places had active responses, and the team expanded rapidly to hundreds of thousands of people. The insurgents led by Zhong Xiang soon occupied 19 counties around the Dongting Lake including Dingzhou, Lizhou, Jingnan (Jiangling, Hubei), Tanzhou, Xiazhou (Yichang, Hubei) and Yuezhou (Yueyang, Hunan). After the death of

Zhong Xiang, more than 80 people, including Yang Yao, Yang Hua, Yang Qin, Huang Cheng and Zhou Lun, continued their struggle. Although Yang Yao was only one of the leaders under Zhong Xiang, he has gradually consolidated and developed his own power and became the most important leader after Zhong Xiang because of his resolute struggle, wise leadership, and bravery. Yang Yao called himself "the great sage king of heaven" and established Zhong Yi, Zhong Xiang's youngest son, as the prince. According to the characteristics of the local terrain, he gradually formed a set of strategic guidelines for land farming and water war, and made vehicles and boats suitable for water war on the lake, thus the insurgents fully mastered the initiative of water war on the Dongting Lake, and defeated the official army for many times. Secondly, the final war outcome will also be influenced by natural climate conditions, or facts whether it is downwind or downstream. The wars between the Jin Dynasty and the Wu Kingdom, the Sui Dynasty and Chen Kingdom, and the conquering of Lin'an by army of the Yuan Dynasty were all won by going eastward from the upper reaches of the Yangtze River and then taking Nanjing directly. Thirdly, strategy and tactics are also critical. It mainly includes:

a. **Fire attack**: This is a common tactic in ancient Chinese war. Qi Jiguang, a famous anti-Japanese general in the Ming Dynasty, wrote in his *Collections of Records on Army Drilling* that "among the five kinds of war tactics, fire is the most powerful one; judging from the history of water and land wars, fire attack has won the most of successes". The reason is due to the fact that ancient warships were made of wood, and its canopy, cable, mast, sail, and board were also made of inflammable material. When applying fire attack, one way is to use a long-range weapon to cast to enemy ships combustibles like rockets (arrows tied with combustibles or powder packs), stone throwers, and thunderbolt firecrackers; the other is by means of a fire ship. The operation is to load a warship with combustibles, ignite it , and then rushes it to enemy warships with the help of wind to achieve the purpose of burning down enemy ships. In the Battle of Chibi, the allied army led by Sun Quan and Liu Bei used the latter method to defeat Cao Cao's army.

b. **Blockade**: The defensive side sets up different kinds of obstacles in the watercourse of the enemy fleet to prevent the passage of warships, which includes wooden bars, iron cones, iron ropes, iron chains to lock the river, and the building of floating bridges and mobile lookout; while the attacking side needs to work out different solutions to overcome these obstacles.

c. **Chisel through the bottom of the ship**: In *The Outlaws of the Marsh*[①], Gao Qiu led his army to fight against heroes in Liangshan Marsh. He specially supervised and built a hundred large-sized warships. When they arrived at the water marsh of Liangshan, the three brothers of Ruan family dived into the water and chisel through the bottom of the boats, which soon paralyzed Gao Qiu's fleet and he himself was also captured by Liangshan heroes.

---

① A 14th-century Chinese novel attributed to Shi Nai'an. It was considered one of the Four Great Classical Novels of Chinese Literature. The story set in the closing years of the Northern Song Dynasty, tells of how a group of 108 outlaws gather at Mount Liang (or Liangshan Marsh) to found a sizable army before they are eventually granted amnesty by the government and sent on campaigns to resist foreign invaders (Liao) and suppress rebel forces (Fang La).

When it comes to one specific war, the tactics will be combined, and the change of any condition would likely to lead to a different outcome accordingly.

a. **Fire attack with the help of wind direction**: In water combat, good command of the wind direction can make the war situation develop in the direction beneficial to one's own side. However, if the originally favourable wind direction suddenly changes, dramatic changes will occur, and it will eventually affect the results of the war. The Caishi Battle was a good example of this, which was a battle that the Northern Song Dynasty defeated the Southern Tang Dynasty. After the Song army conquered Caishi, Zhu Lingyun, the general stationed in Hukou, led the army to the East as ordered by Li Yu, the emperor of the Southern Tang Dynasty, tried to smash the pontoon to cut off the back-up force of the Song army, and then planned to go straight to Jinling to rescue the emperor. Near Wankou (now 7.5 km southwest of Anqing), Zhu lingyun met with both water force led by Wang Ming and land troop led by Liu Yu of the Song army. He set fire to the fleet of the Song army when there was a strong southwest wind blowing on the river, and Song army was just at the downwind. The "fire engine" rushed directly at Song army, and terribly terrified them. The Southern Tang fleet under Zhu Lingyun's command was full of energy and high morale. Unexpectedly, the wind direction suddenly reversed, the northeast wind started, and the Southern Tang fleet began to be placed at the downwind. The "fire engine" was pushed back by the wind and rushed directly to the Southern Tang fleet. Unluckily, the fleet is too dense in allocation to be evacuated for a while, and many of them have been gulped by the fire. Zhu Lingyun himself was also killed by the fire, and the 100,000 water troops of the Southern Tang Dynasty were totally annihilated.

Similarly, the same story happened in another battle in Caishi between Jin army and that of the Southern Song Dynasty. When Wanyan Liang first led his fleet to attack Caishi, he took the river wind and his 70-odd warships soon arrived at the east bank of the river. But all of a sudden, the river wind stopped, and the speed of Jin's subsequent warships slowed down. Yu Yunwen seized this fleeting opportunity and ordered the water force stationed at the midstream to fight back. The next day, Wanyan Liang led the army to the mouth of Yanglin River to try to attack Caishi again. The Song army set fire to the Jin army's warships with rockets and thunderbolt firecrackers. A strong wind suddenly blew on the river, and Jin army was just at the downwind. With the help of wind, the fire developed quickly and even the boat of Wanyan Liang was ignited. As a result, more than 300 warships of Jin were half burnt, and the rest were partly damaged, so was the ambition of Wanyan Liang to annex the south of the Yangtze River. Yu Yunwen saved the Southern Song Dynasty and became famous because of this war.

b. **Fire attack with the help of light boat**: The fierce battle between Zhu Yuanzhang[①] and Chen Youlang on the surface of Poyang Lake in the late Yuan Dynasty was a typical example. In April of the 23rd year of Zhizheng era (in 1363), Chen Youlang led the water and land armies,

---

① The Hongwu Emperor (21 October 1328-24 June 1398), was the founding emperor of the Ming Dynasty, reigning from 1368 to 1398.

with the claiming amount of 600,000, to besiege Hongdu. The siege has been performed for a long time without success. Zhu Yuanzhang led 200,000 troops to rescue Hongdu. Eighty-five days after besieging Hongdu, on hearing that Zhu Yuanzhang's reinforcements were on the way, Chen Youliang released the siege of Hongdu, led the Han army eastward to enter the vast Poyang Lake, and planned to destroy Zhu Yuanzhang's reinforcements first, and then took Hongdu.

Anciently known as Pengli, Pengze or Penghu, Poyang Lake, located in the northeast of Hongdu and southeast of Jiangzhou, is naturally shaped like an irregular gourd. A wide water area is located at the south end of the lake with Kanglang Mountain (now known as Kangshan Mountain) situated in it; when going northward, the water surface becomes narrow and crooked. Yingzikou, at the east of Nankang (now known as Xingzi County in Jiangxi Province) is located at the shrinking point of the lake body, and therefore served as a throat for Poyang Lake to flow into the Yangtze River. Dagu Mountain, like a bird's wing, stands at the mouth of the north end of the Poyang Lake, making this area extremely dangerous. Many small islands scatter in the lake, and the water depth is different. When the water level rises, it's possible to operate boats in most part of the lake except that near the shore and the island; however, when the water level falls, the lake is very shallow, and it is difficult to operate large boats.

After leading the water army to arrive at Hukou, Zhu Yuanzhang, the first emperor in the Ming Dynasty, made a few arrangements: He deployed a force to guard Jingjiangkou (now in the northeast of Hukou, on the North Bank of the Yangtze River) and Nanhuzui (now 20 km northeast of Jiujiang, next to the mouth of the Poyang Lake), and transferred troops in Xinzhou to guard Wuyangdu (now the southeast of Nanchang), threatening the Han army. He himself then led the main force into the Poyang Lake to fight with army led by Chen Youliang. The two armies met in water area around Kanglang Mountain. Chen Youliang's army was well staffed and equipped, which was acclaimed that "the boat was big, riding high, and the blades were sharp". Chen linked the huge boats and warships to form an array. The mast was more than 30 meters high, and the flags and shield were stacked as high as a mountain. The fleet spread in a row, stretching for tens of miles, like the Great Wall on the water. While Zhu Yuanzhang's army were mainly equipped with small ships and fishing boats, and their forces were very weak. The sharp contrast terribly shocked and terrified some of the soldiers.

Zhu Yuanzhang adopted the advice of generals, recruited "death squad" in the army, and more than 30 brave generals and 300 excellent fearless sailors signed up. At the beginning of the night, Zhu Yuanzhang's "death squad" took dozens of fishing boats to move toward Chen Youliang's camp. In addition to carrying more than 350 generals, some explosives such as gunpowder and tung oil were also hidden in the boats. After pretending to surrender to Chen Youliang's camp by waving white flags, the death squads seized a good opportunity to set fire to Chen Youliang's army at midnight as planned earlier and attacked the enemy's water fleet. In a moment, the flames grew quickly, and the thick smoke therefore produced spread with the wind, and a sea of fire was suddenly formed on the surface of the lake. The death squads shuttled in the enemy's watercraft array, fighting on their own. Whenever they saw the enemy's ships, they set fire to them, and whenever they saw the enemies, they fought with them bravely until they can kill them eventually. This attack was a great blow to Chen Youliang's watercraft. The final victory of the Poyang Lake war laid a good foundation for Zhu Yuanzhang to unify the south of the Yangtze River and further on to unify China later.

c. **The combination of warships, weapons, rivers, and fire attacks in the war battle**: The Battle of Huangtiandang is not only an important battle between the Song army and the Jin army in the early Southern Song Dynasty, but also one of the famous water battles in the history of China. In 1129, after plundering a large number of properties in Lin'an by a long march from the distant northern China, the Jin army prepared to return to the north along the Yangtze River. On the way back, they were confronted with Song army led by Han Shizhong(Fig. 5-2), a famous anti-Jin general in the Southern Song Dynasty, who has made careful deployment in Zhenjiang to intercept the Jin army, and the two sides engaged in a fierce battle on the Yangtze River. Liang Hongyu, Han Shizhong's wife, beat drums to encourage the Song army. The huge size of the Song army's warships, usually several times larger than those of the Jin army, have enabled the Song army to prevail over Jin, who at last fled hurriedly into Huangtiandang(Fig. 5-3), a dead water port in the northeast of Jiankang under the pursuit of the Song army since they are not familiar with the waterway in the Yangtze River. Han Shizhong ordered the fleet to block the only water passage into the Yangtze River within Huangtiandang. In addition, he also ordered craftsmen to forge a large number of iron ropes and hooks considering that Jin army was mainly equipped with small and light ships. With everything prepared, the Song army launched attacks in two ways when the Jin army rushed out from the Huangtiandang: one way is to collide with Jin's light ships, and the other is to ask strong soldiers to throw hooks to flip the light ships. Due to the Song's tight defence, Jin army's several attempts to break out of the encirclement failed, and their request for reconciliation was also denied by Han Shizhong.

One month after being besieged, the Jin army paid heavily to residents to get a piece of important information that there was an old irrigation river nearby that could lead to the Yangtze River. Digging all night, they successfully went back to the Yangtze River. However, they were still defeated by the Song army at the same time suffering great losses. They failed in attempts to cross river and were trapped for 48 days.

Hopeless in breaking out of the siege, Jin army paid heavily to seek solutions to defeat warships of the Song army. A guy with the surname of Wang, from Fujian, taught the Jin army to fill the boat with earth and lay flat wooden boards on it to add weight to the light ships to prevent them from bumping in the wind and waves and flipping caused by Song's iron hooks. Furthermore, he also taught Jin to install oars on both sides of the boat to speed up the ship's speed and facilitate mobile attacks. Jin also rushed to make rockets overnight, and dug a new river in Bailuzhou, southwest of Jiankang. By using the new passage, unnoticeably, Jin outflanked the enemy and proceeded to the upper reach of the Song army. One day, the Jin army secretly approached the fleet of the Song army with light boats carrying good archers, lighting the canopy of the Song army. Attacked by rain-like arrows and covered by dense smoke, the Song army was badly defeated. By taking advantage of this opportunity, the Jin army successfully escaped.

Figure 5-2　The Statue of Han Shizhong①

Figure 5-3　the Ancient Battlefield of the Battle of Huangtiandang

---

① Han Shizhong: (1089-1151) was a Chinese military general, poet and politician of the late Northern Song Dynasty and the early Southern Song Dynasty.

In the battle of Huangtiandang, the Song army led by Han Shizhong has created a miracle in the fight against Jin by using only 8,000 water soldiers to confront 100,000 Jin army and besieging the enemy for as long as 48 days. This successful attack has forced the enemy to give up their plan to cross the Yangtze River for 30 years. Factors like natural conditions of the Yangtze River, large-sized strong warships and the appropriate use of weapons and tactics contributed to the victory. In comparison, as a losing side at the beginning of the battle, Jin army also made a successful and wonderful escape by timely transforming ships, dredging new water passages, and using fire attack at the right time. Huangtiandang battle was an excellent example in bringing the advantages into full play and at the same time avoiding the disadvantages in the battle. The commanders of both sides competed fiercely in their bravery, wisdom and war tactics, leaving a wonderful battle in the military history.

Unlike what happened in the history, currently, it is not very possible to have large-scale invasion of foreign enemies, but the possibility of local wars and armed conflicts caused by external factors cannot be neglected. In this case, the war in rivers and lakes within the territory will no longer be the main form of water war, while wars in the sea to safeguard the sovereignty and maritime rights and interests of China will become the dominating form of water war. The experience and lessons of ancient water war and sea war in the history of China will provide good references for Chinese people to deal with those emergencies.

Section II   Water-aided War

Water is different from other substances, that is to say, water is the only substance in nature that exists in forms of liquid, solid and gas at the same time, and it is also transformable among the three forms if meteorological and hydrological conditions permit. This characteristic of water is often used to assist military operations, and sometimes even determines the outcome of the war. Ancient Chinese strategists attached great importance to this characteristic of water, not only in theory, but also in practice. Mozi once advocated that in the defensive battle the well outside the city should be "completely drained to leave no drinking water for enemies". By the time of the Northern Song Dynasty, Zeng Gongliang also emphasized the importance of drinking water in the book of *General Military Principles*: for example, he thought when defending a city, "trees shall be cut, bridges and houses burnt, wells buried, and springs poisoned within 500 steps outside the city (about 300 m)", the strategy aims to weaken the enemy by destroying the drinking water outside the city. Water has created many wonders in assisting wars and left many successful war cases in the history.

1. Water-aided War

Liquid state is the most common form of water, which widely exists in rivers, lakes, oceans, swamps, wells and pools. At the same time, it appears in rainfall, condensation, tide and other weather hydrological phenomena. In ancient wars, rainfall had a significant impact on military operations. Positively, it could cover the march of troops, while it also had more negative effects. For example, at the age of cold weapons, when bows and arrows were drenched with rain, the strings loosen, resulting in a shortened range and reduced lethality. Li Tao recorded a battle that Khitan cavalry was defeated by the Song army due to the failure to use bows and arrows because of the bad weather in his book *A Sequel to History as a Mirror*: In the 4th year of Xianping, Emperor Zhenzong of the Song Dynasty (the 19th year of Tonghe, Emperor Shengzong of the Liao Dynasty, in 1001), the Song army led by General Zhang Bin was confronted with Qidan calvary, their enemy, at the mouth of the Great Wall. A steady rain left the leather strings on bows of the Khitan cavalry wet, resulting in reduced elasticity and therefore greatly weakening Khitan's fighting capacity. The Song army defeated them and killed many Khitan soldiers. At the age of hot weapons, however, the rain also influences military operations. Firearms and gunpowder cannot be set off after being showered with rain. The rainfall brings great inconvenience to the march of the army, grain transportation, and camping of the army. Serious flood caused by rainstorms even destroys the road, breaks the river bank, submerges the camp and engulfs the army. The surging water surface once caused a fatal blow to Jin army in the history, who was not good at water war. In 1222 (the second year of Yuanguang, Jin Dynasty), Jin took advantage of the opportunity of shallow water in Huaihe River to cross the river and invaded its south bank; while on their way to the north in May, a heavy rain overnight raised the water level of the Huaihe River, and finally drowned all the Jin army, which was recorded in the *Story of Shiqing*, the 117th Volumn of the *Jin History*. In the ancient war history of China, the Zhuolu Battle between the Yellow Emperor and Chiyou, and battle of Guanyu's successful flooding his enemy during the period of the Three Kingdoms were all successful cases of using rainfall to get the victory. In ancient times, the sea battles or landing operations across the sea were also greatly influenced by tides and rainfall. Zheng Chenggong's battle to recover Taiwan, Shi Lang's battle to conquer Penghu were all successful examples of making full use of the wind and tide.

Shi Lang's military success in conquering Penghu and Taiwan afterwards was a successful landing operation by using tide(Fig. 5-4).

On June 22, 1683, General Shi Lang of the Qing Dynasty(Fig. 5-5), commander in chief of Fujian Navy while enjoying the honorary title of Prince tutor, led more than 20,000 sailors on more than 300 ships and 230 small and medium-sized warships to start from Tongshan of Fujian Province. They sailed all the way to target Penghu Islands, a strategic outpost of Taiwan, and the only barrier for Zheng army in Taiwan to defend against enemies. General Liu Guoxuan, the commander-in-chief of the Zheng army, deployed the main forces in Penghu and built solid fortifications including 14 artillery stations, about ten-kilometer-long of high walls and deep trenches along the sea equipped with guns aiming at a decisive battle with the Qing army. Faced with the strict guarding of the Zheng army, Shi Lang divided the Qing army into three parts with the

Figure 5-4　A Drawing Depicting the Scene of Shi Lang's Conquering Penghu

Figure 5-5　Shi Liang (1621-1696)

left and right wing checking the enemy, and he himself led the main force composed of 56 large warships to attack Niangmagong Palace, an important military stronghold in Penghu. Taking advantage of the favorable southwest wind, the Qing army used the five-point plum blossom array to encircle one Zheng army ship with several warships until finally destroying it. The way of concentrating forces in defeating enemy proved to be highly successful. In Penghu battle, Qing army led by General Shi Lang succeeded in burning, sinking, and capturing 37 large warships and 107 other ships. On the contrary, Liu Guoxuan, commander-in-chief of the Zheng army, had lost several opportunities in attacking by waiting for the hurricane, which led to a disastrous defeat. More than 300 military officers were killed and injured, and about 12,000 soldiers were killed and wounded. Dead bodies were floating all over the sea. Only 31 boats fled back to Taiwan.

Shi Lang's success in taking Penghu and defeating the elite troops of Taiwan army opened the door of Taiwan Island. On July 27th, Zheng Keshuang, owner of Taiwan, submitted instrument of surrender to Qing government. In 1864, Taiwan Province was officially set to be subordinate to Fujian Province. Qing government also garrisoned troops to be stationed there, hence, Taiwan and the mainland was completely reunified.

The reason why Qing army can win the battle lies not only in their well-equipped warships and brave soldiers, but also in the wise command of General Shi Lang. As recorded in the biography of Shi Lang in the *History of Qing Dynasty*, Shi Lang, a good master of tactical deployment of troops, ran his army strictly. He knew well the rules of tide and wind in the sea, hence excel in water battle, as shown in Shi Lang's choice in the time of sailing across the sea and his departing port. Instead of choosing the northeast wind season, a traditional choice, Shi Lang chose to sail across the sea in the middle of June, when the southwest wind started. This move helped to ensure the safe anchorage of the Qing navy before launching the general attack. When choosing the route, Shi Lang departed from Tongshan, instead of the traditional choice of Jinmen or Xiamin, thus the Qing navy could take advantage of the southwest wind to take the unprotected islands in the south of Penghu as a base, and then turn northward into the Penghu Sea area. When sailing along this route, the Qing navy were always in a favourable position along the wind and the current. Shi Lang's victory over Penghu was a typical case of tidal hydrology, which provided a useful reference for the later sea crossing and landing operations.

In modern war, water can still help people win the initiative in the war. Shajiabang Lake is a place where reeds are densely distributed, so it became an important base to resist Japanese invasion(Fig. 5-6).

Figure 5-6   The Reed Marsh in Shajiabang

In May 1939, the sixth regiment of the New Fourth Army marched eastward in the name of "Jiangnan Anti-Japanese volunteer army" and assembled in Yangcheng Lake water network area of southern Jiangsu Province to carry out Anti-Japanese guerrilla warfare under the cover of reed marshes. Ye Fei, commander of the sixth regiment of the New Fourth Army, recalled, "there are numerous harbours and numerous water networks, which are quite similar to the Liangshanpo described in the *Water Margin*. According to local people, the terrain of the reed marsh is very complicated, and it is impossible to get in or out of the reed marsh without the help of a guide." The modern Beijing Opera *Shajiabang* was created on this background. Today's "Shajiabang" has long been synonymous with Changshu, and it is even more popular than the name of Changshu.

2. War with the Help of Snow and Ice

Rivers and lakes will freeze, and snow or frost will appear at very low temperature, which will negatively influence war operations. In ancient China, famous generals have left many classical cases by taking advantage of this weather condition in combination with their tactical deployment. In 775 A. D. An Lushan[①], leading a troop of 180,000 soldiers, started a rebellion. In December, he planned to cross the Yellow River to move southward. However, the mighty river has presented them with huge difficulties. It would take nearly 10,000 boats to transport his soldiers, which would be time-consuming and laborious. Moreover, the prolonged journey will make it easy to be noticed by the Tang army, and corresponding defending would be therefore organized to fight against them. In order to avoid such results, An Lushan decided to cross the Yellow River during its freezing period. In this case, he ordered the troops to use shabby boats tied with thick ropes and woods to slow down the flow rate of the river, thus speeding up the formation of the ice. Then he led the troops to quickly cross the river and went into the hinterland of the central plains, which caught the Tang emperor by surprise. The war started and the prosperity of the Tang Dynasty was ended.

Another typical example in this regard is made by Li Su, a high-ranking official in Tang Dynasty. In the fight against the rebels in Caizhou, due to his insufficiency in soldier number and supply, Li Su decided to launch a quick attack based on the high fighting spirit of his soldiers and the long-term reconnaissance of the rebels. He finally took the advice of Li You, a surrendered general, to lead the troop to run to Caizhou in the snowy night to attack the unprepared enemy. Finally, the initiative of the battle was firmly held by him.

Another famous case is about the battle in Suicheng between the Song and the Liao armies. In the winter of the 17th year of Tonghe during the reign of Emperor Shengzong of the Liao Dynasty (the second year of Xianping, during the reign of Emperor Zhenzong of Song Dynasty in 999), Khitan, an ancient ethnic group in China went down to the south to attack Song army. Both parties

---

① A general in the Tang Dynasty who is primarily known for instigating the An Lushan Rebellion.

battled in Suicheng, where it was freezing cold. The Song army took full advantage of the cold weather by pouring the city wall with water so that the wall was all covered by ice, which has scuppered Liao's siege plan and in turn forced the Liao army to withdraw its troop. The case is recorded in the *History of the Song Dynasty*. It said "In the winter of the second year of Xianping, Khitan disturbed the border, Suicheng, where Yanzhao was stationed. The city is too small to be well equipped, so it was encompassed by Khitan for several days. Each time when Khitan tried to start the war, the Song army was scary. Yanzhao then organized the young male adult to guard the wall by equipping them with armours and weapons. The weather at that time is freezing. Yanzhao ordered his men to pour the city wall with water. Next morning, cold weather has turned the water into ice and therefore made the city wall too slippery to be climbed, which has left Khitan nothing to do but to withdraw from Suicheng. Song army got victory at last. " Cold weather should have been more favourable for Khitan cavalry, but the wise use of ice by Song army has changed the results.

At the end of the Northern Song Dynasty, the Jin army also successfully made use of the snowfall weather in attacking Kaifeng City. In winter of 1126 (the second November of the first year of Jingkang of the Northern Song Dynasty according to the lunar calender), Kaifeng was extremely cold. Wang Zao, a literati in the Song Dynasty, recorded in *JingkangYaolu* (a record of big events happened in the year of Jingkang) that on the 24th day of the month, "the snow was several feet deep. "The next day, as recorded in the *Collection of War Related Records with Jin Army of the Three Emperors in Song Dynasty*, compiled by Xu Mengxin, the heavy snow still continued. Wanyan Zonghan, commander of the Jin army told his subordinates that "such a heavy snow is equal to 200,000 new soldiers. " The Jin army took advantage of the heavy snow to launch a fierce attack on Kaifeng City. Finally, Kaifeng City fell into the hands of the Jin army.

3. Fog-aided War

Vapor could condense into fog, the gaseous state of the water. In the eyes of an artist, fog is beautiful. However, in the eye of military experts, fog, dense fog, has a fatal impact on military operations. It can reduce visibility, making it difficult to locate the enemy's target and hinder the effective attack. Fog, on the other hand, has advantages, which can be used to cover the trail or confuse the enemy. The legend had it that during the war between the Yellow Emperor and Chiyou, Chiyou made a fog lasting for three days and nights, negatively influencing the Yellow Emperor. Inspired by the Big Dipper, Fenghou, a minister of the Yellow Emperor, invented the southward pouting cart, leading the troops out of the fog. As is known to all, the story of Zhuge Liang's borrowing arrows from Cao Cao with straw boats is about the skilful use of fog to achieve the purpose of military action(Fig. 5-7). The novel of *The Romance of the Three Kingdoms* has shaped Zhuge Liang as a legendary figure. In a war against Cao Cao, armies led by Sun Quan and Liu Bei have formed an alliance. Zhou Yu, the chief general in Sun Quan's army, planned to kill

Zhuge Liang, the military adviser of Liu Bei's army, since he was jealous of Zhuge's ability. Zhou's plot is to appoint Zhuge Liang to make 100,000 arrows in ten days. If Zhuge failed to fulfil the task, Zhou Yu would have the excuse to kill Zhuge. In this case, he has set many obstacles to stop Zhuge from performing the task smoothly. Clearly knowing Zhou Yu's plot, Zhuge Liang made a plan to "borrow" arrows from Cao Cao with the help of fog, which he predicted to appear in three days by observing the astronomical phenomena. Zhuge Liang took the order, which has made Zhou Yu very happy. In a foggy night, Zhuge Liang led several boats filled with straw to fake an attack against Cao army. Without clear visibility, Cao Cao ordered the soldiers to shoot more arrows instead of fighting at shorter distance. All the arrows had been shot into the straw on the boats, so Zhuge Liang easily "borrow" more than 100,000 arrows from Cao Cao and completed the talk. Unable to break his promise, Zhou Yu had to give up his killing plan, and signed "Zhuge Liang is so wise and witty that I am unable to compare with him."

Figure 5-7　A Drawing Depicting Zhuge Liang's Borrowing Arrows from Cao Cao with Straw Boats

4. Stimulate the Army Morale with Water

Chinese has many idioms related with water. Xiang Yu, a general in late Qin Dynasty, once broke the cauldrons and sank the boats after crossing the river to show his determination by cutting off all means of retreat; Zu Ti, a general in the East Jin Dynasty, stroke the ship's rail with his paddles to promise to defeat the enemy, otherwise, he would never return; Han Xin, a general in the Han Dynasty, led his troops to fight by river to stimulate the army morale since there was no retreat. In those stories, water is used as a hopeless situation. Faced with it, soldiers must be determined to fight for the victory, since there was no alternative. Han Xin's popular story of fighting to win or die is such a typical example.

In 204 A. D. , after climbing over Taihang Mountain, Hanxin, planned to go eastward to attack the state of Zhao, Xiang Yu's subordinate state. On the way, there was a very narrow pass called Jingxingkou, which is ranked as one of the eight important passes in Taihang Mountain. Within it, there was a narrow post road with the length of 50 km, making it very difficult for troop movement since it is easy to be defended but difficult to be attacked. Li Zuojun, a counsellor of the king of Zhao State, proposed to defeat Han Xin by blocking the entrance of Jingxingkou on the one hand, and sending troops to take a side road to cut off supplies of the Han army on the other. However, after denying the advice, the commander-in-chief of Zhao insisted in fighting head-on with the Han army, since he was quite confidence about his military advantage.

Knowing about the strategy of the Zhao, Han Xin was greatly relieved. He came up with an idea. Firstly, he ordered the troops to camp 15 km away from Jingxing pass, and let the officers and soldiers have some snacks. He promised them that they could have a good meal after the victory. Then, he sent 2,000 light cavalry to advance quickly but secretly toward the Zhao army's camping site to replace the Zhao's flag with that of the Han army once the Zhao army left. In addition, he dispatched 10,000 soldiers to lure the the Zhao army by arranging military array against the river.

At dawn, Han Xin launched the attack and two sides were soon engaged in a fierce battle. After a while, the Han army lured the the Zhao's to wholly leave their camp by a fake retreat to the riverbank, where the main force of the Han was waiting for them. Han Xin's troop fought bravely since they have to had the determination to win or to die. The Zhao army could do nothing but to go back to its camping site. To their surprise, the banner of the Han army had been planted in the camp, which has shattered their morale. Continuing the pursuit of the defeated enemy, the Han army, led by Han Xin, has made a great victory.

The Battle of Jingxing served as a crucial one in Liu Bang and Xiang Yu's fight for hegemony. After that, the Han army, led by Liu Bang, gradually gained strategic advantage over the Chu army, led by Xiang Yu. Han Xin's skilful master of tactics recorded in the *Sun Tzu Art of War* written by Sun Wu contributed to the victory. Sun Wu knew well of the psychology of soldiers, in the book, he wrote "soldiers will be fearless if put in an extremely dangerous situation; they will be firm if no alternative could be provided, and they will be brave in fight if they had to choose between victory and death. " In the battle, Han Xin's army only numbered 10,000, while his enemy had soldiers of more than 200,000. He deployed his military formation against the water, leaving no retreat for soldiers, which has solidified his army's determination to win. The battle itself also became a model in ancient Chinese military history for its feature of conquering the most with the least.

With the development of social productivity and the progress of military science and technology, war has evolved from cold weapon, hot weapon to mechanized and information war. However, weather conditions, such as rain, fog, snow, ice and tide, are still important factors for the victory of modern warfare. Whether it is the army's tanks and other weapons, or the air force's aircraft, whether it is the navy's warships, missiles, and other guided weapons, they are still greatly affected by different states of water. Therefore, it is still an indispensable tool to prevent modern war. Efforts still need to be devoted to take full advantage of water and avoid its harm in the time of war. At the same time, people can also develop hydro meteorological weapons with the help of the characteristics of water, such as artificial fog making, fog eliminating, artificial rainfall, acid rain making, which will cause difficulties to the other side, bring serious losses to the enemy, therefor help to achieve victory.

Section III   Water as Soldiers

Water, without a fixed state, is both beneficial and harmful. It is either soft or rigid when applied differently, which can be used as both solid defending tool and powerful attacking weapon in the war. In ancient China, strategists sometimes conquered the city or defeated the enemy by either creating artificial floods or bringing natural disasters after digging up canals, embankments or dams to bring the kinetic energy and the potential energy of water into full play. This way is known as "substituting water for soldiers" or "water attack" in the history.

In the history of the Chinese nation, it is common to substitute soldiers with water especially at times of social turbulence and country division such as the Spring and Autumn Period, the Three Kingdoms Period, the Southern and Northern Dynasties, the Five Dynasties and Ten Kingdoms Period. This way of attacking usually brought serious consequences. The rivers frequently used were mainly the Yellow River, Huaihe River and Haihe River. The Yangtze River and the Zhujiang River were less applied. Sometimes, even the man-made Grand Canal was used. During the northern expedition of the Taiping army in Qing Dynasty, the Qing army led by Senggelinqin dug up the canal twice to flood the Taiping army, causing failure to its northern expedition.

Water soldiers' strategies can be divided into the following types.

1. Using Continuous Rainfall, Rainstorm, and Other Natural Floods to Substitute for Soldiers

This needs the right time and the right place. For example, during the period of the Three Kingdoms, Guan Yu flooded the Wei army, which was the use of continuous rainfall and rainstorm to substitute water soldiers.

During the reign of Emperor Wu of Liang Dynasty, the Northern Wei army was defeated badly, and the river surge was an important factor. In 506 (the fifth year of Tianjian period of Emperor Wu of the Liang Dynasty), general Yuan Ying of Wei Dynasty led the army to attack Zhong Li, while Cao Jingzong and Wei Rui of Liang Dynasty led soldiers to defend Zhong Li. A stand-off was reached between two armies. Next March, spring brought water surge to the Huaihe River by more than 2 meters. The Liang army took the opportunity to go aboard the warships to fight the Wei army. The Wei army, on the other hand, had to abandon their weapons and armors and committed suicide by jumping into water, because their battle bases have been watered to collapse. The dead Wei soldiers were so much that the Huaihe River was blocked. There were thousands of Wei soldiers found dead and more than 50,000 soldiers captured alive. In addition, The Liang army has got countless weapons, grains, cattle and horses. Taking advantage of the flood, the Liang army defeated the Wei army and won the most brilliant victory in the war between the north and the south.

Rainfall also showed its power in the war attacking Zhongxingfu City, the capital of the Xixia State, by the Mongolian army. Zhongxinfu City, the economic centre of the Xixia, prospered because of its advanced irrigation system, which was similar to many cities in Ningxia today, an autonomous region in China. At first, it's very difficult for the Mongolian army to take the city. However, a disaster soon changed the picture. Finding that the autumn rainfall has caused a rise of water level in the Yellow River, Genghis Khan, commander of the Mongolian army, ordered to build a dam to introduce the Yellow River water into the city, which in turn has caused serious casualties and property losses. Facing this dilemma, the Xixia had to send for help from Jin Dynasty. Many ministers and generals of the Jin Dynasty advocated sending troops to relieve the siege. They thought that once the Xixia was completely conquered, the Jin Dynasty would become the next target. But Wanyan Yongji, the new Emperor of the Jin Dynasty, believed that the Mongolia and the Xixia were both enemies of the Jin Dynasty, so he ignored Xixia's plea. It was not until January 1210 when the wall of Zhongxingfu City was on the verge of collapsing that the Mongolian army's encirclement was relaxed. Then the accumulated river water suddenly burst out of the dike outside of the city and flooded the surrounding flat land, forcing the Mongolian army to retreat to a higher place. Despite the defeat in the siege of the Zhongxingfu City, Genghis Khan firmly believed that the harsh reality caused by the siege would force Li Anquan, the head of the Xixia State, to compromise, so he sent a delegation for negotiation in the city. The extremely severe situation in the capital city was thus exposed to the Mongols. Li Anquan, the leader of the Xixia State, had to marry one of his daughters to Genghis Khan in exchange for Mongolian's withdrawal from the Xixia.

2. Building Artificial Weirs or Dams in the Upstream or Downstream of the River, and Using the Water Level Difference to Substitute for Soldiers

A low-lying terrain or that close to the river could bring a lot of convenience to urban traffic and people's daily life, which, however, could also offer the enemy with opportunity to perform water attack.

In the Yellow Emperor era, which was 5,000 years ago, there was the earliest record about replacing soldiers with water. Legend has it that Yinglong, the eldest son of the Yellow Emperor, could open his huge mouth to spray water to rout his enemy by drowning them in great amount of water(Fig. 5-8). When a faceoff was reached between the Yellow Emperor and Chiyou, Yinglong secretly went to the upper reaches of Lingshan River Valley in the south of Chiyou City to store water. When the river water accumulated to a certain level, Yinglong burst the dike and flooded Chiyou City, causing considerable losses to Chiyou.

Figure 5-8 Yinglong Dragon, the Eldest Son of the Yellow Emperor in Tales of Legends

During the Spring and Autumn Period and the Warring States Period, there was a fierce annexation war among different states. Those states not only "block and defend all rivers for their own benefit", but also use water as a powerful weapon in war. Therefore, water attack was very common, especially in the Warring States Period. In 279 B. C. , Bai Qi, a general of the Qin Dynasty, attacked Yancheng City of the State of Chu (Now, Yancheng City is in the southeast of Yicheng City, Hubei Province), and was resisted by the Chu army. After several failed attempts, Bai Qi began to used Yishui River (Yishui is now known as Qingjiang River, a tributary of the Yangtze River) to perform water attack. Yishui ran south-eastward from the long valley in the Xishan Mountain in Yicheng City, the State of Chu. Fully taking this advantage, Bai Qi built a dam within the valley of Xishan Mountain of Yicheng, a hundred miles west of Yancheng City, and a long canal connecting Xishan Mountain and Yancheng City. Then he burst the dike to flood the city. As a result, thousands of people were drowned in the city, and the Chu army suffered heavy losses.

Such case was even more popular after the late Tang Dynasty. As recorded in *Zizhi Tongjian*

(*A General Reflection for Political Administration*), Qian Liu of the Wuyue State attacked Kunshan City from March to September in the first year of Guanghua (in 898). Qin Pei, commander of the Kunshan garrison, defended the city with 3000 troops. After both armed attack and enduction of capitulation failed, Gu Quanwu, a general of the Wuyue State, diverted water to drown the city, incurring catastrophic damages. Finally, Qin Pei was forced to surrender due to the lack of food in the city. The separatist forces in the late Tang Dynasty were quite familiar with the tactics of replacing soldiers with water. Such record can still be found in the historical records during the Five Dynasties Period. For example, in September of the first year of Longde in the Post Liang Dynasty (in 921), Jin soldiers "crossed Hutuo River, surrounded Zhenzhou City, and dug up canals to flod the city."

The "Great Wall of Water" built in Hebei Province in the Northern Song Dynasty played an important role in defending the attack of the Liao Dynasty. It was He Chengju, a high-ranking official of the Northern Song Dynasty, who first put forward the proposal. According to *Brush Talks from Dream Brook* by Shen Kuo, "the Waqiaoguan pass is adjacent to the Liao State in the north, without any rivers as barrier. In the past when He Chengju served as commander of the Waqiaoguan garrison, he proposed to stock water to build military fort." The time when He Chengju was appointed was just the time when a northern expedition was defeated. The failure shocked people in the Song so much that He Chengju began to think seriously about the proposal. In order not to leak this idea, He Chengju pretended to invite his colleagues for boating and flowers appreciation, among which they have also made poems. He ordered to paint his activities into a painting and sent it to the capital. No one knows what it really meant. In fact, his actions were disguised investigation, and the painting he drew was the map for the water. In the fourth year of Yongxi (in 987), Emperor Taizong of the Northern Song Dynasty inquired the officials about the frontier defence plan. Song Qi, an official, proposed that the north bank of the Yellow River can be dug up to use the flood as defence tools, or to build a great wall between Cangzhou and Dingzhou like Emperor Qinshihuang. He Chengju didn't think the two ideas wise, since firstly, flood cause by digging up the Yellow River would destroy the fertile land and displace thousands of local people; secondly, it was the plain lying between Cangzhou and Dingzhou, hence, there was no favorable topographic condition like mountainous area to build the great wall. What's more, building such a great wall on the plain would also cost a lot of money and labour, since the plain was punctuated with lakes, rivers and ditches. In this case, he suggested "we should open a mouth on Yihe River in the west of Shun'anzhai (now known as Anxin County), and introduce the water flow eastward to the sea, thus a water channel with the width of 25-35 km and length of around 150 km will be formed. If we build dikes to store water, there would be more farmland opened on the one, and there would be an effective defence against the cavalry of the Liao State on the other". Following his father on the journey to fight enemies at a very young age, He Chengju not only knew well of the topological conditions of Hebei Province, but also understood natures of the Khitan nationality quite well, who were nomads, good at riding horses and shooting arrows, thus riding horses in the battle on the plain was their strengths, while fighting on ships was their weakness. That's why He Chengju made such proposal which was fully accepted by Emperor Zhao Guangyi. With the emperor's support, the Great Wall of Water was soon completed, forming a deep-water barrier for the Khitan cavalry. Then, on the Great Wall of Water, "26 frontier passes, 125 forts, 11 officials, and more than 3,000 soldiers were placed on the water, and there were also 100 boats patrolling in the water", posing a great threat to the Khitan cavalry, who was not good at water attack.

3. Breaking the Embankment of the Upper Reaches of the Yellow River to Flood the Enemy Troops or Cities

"The Battle of Jinyang" in the Warring States Period is an important example of water attack. In 455 B. C., Zhibo of Jin State led Han Kangzi and Wei Huanzi to attack Zhao Xiangzi. Zhao army was completely outnumbered and retreated to Jinyang City, which was besieged by Jin army for one year and three months without any successes. In 453 B. C., Zhibo ordered his soldiers to build a dam on the upper reach of the Jinshui River to form a reservoir. Then the water in the reservoir was poured into Jinyang City. Zhibo thought he has got the victory and boasted that "Today, I know that water can destroy one country." After hearing this, Han and Wei worried that Zhibo would use the same method to flood their cities in the future, so they rebelled against the enemy and joined Zhao. The allied army flooded Zhibo's troops by digging up Jinshui River. As a result, Jin army was completely defeated, and Zhibo was killed, so was all his family members. Jin State was divided by Han, Wei and Zhao, which was known in the history as "Dividing Jin into Three States".

In 225 B. C., the State of Qin attacked the State of Wei. Daliang (now known as Kaifeng), the capital city of Wei, has been besieged by the Qin army for a long time without any successes. Wang Ben, general of Qin, ordered his troops to dig up the Yellow River to flood Daliang City, which was fallen three months later and afterwards Wei State came to an end.

During the Wei, the Jin, the Southern and Northern Dynasties, the frequency of water attack was even higher. Especially in the Sorthern and Nouthern Dynasties, the most frequently used way of fighting between the two sides was to flood the city with water, which occurred nine times in the Liang Dynasty alone, and seven times in the period of Emperor Wu of the Liang Dynasty.

To make up for the shortage of soldiers, the Chen Dynasty used water attack instead of soldiers five times. Post Jing's rebellion at the end of Liang Dynasty got victory on the use of lake water. In the third year of Taiqing of the Liang Dynasty (in 549), Hou Jing broke Xuanwu Lake and poured water into Taicheng City, hence Emperor Wu of the Liang Dynasty was captured alive and then starved to death. In the Five Dynasties Period, to fight for hegemony, the ruling class never hesitated to dig up rivers to use water attack instead of soldiers without thinking of great damages caused to the people. According to the records in the *New Book on History of the Tang Dynasty*, "in February of the fourth year of Zhenming, the Post Liang Dynasty (in 918), Xie Yanzhang, the general of the Post Liang Dynasty, came to attack Yangliu. They built strong ramparts for defence and broke the river to resist the troops of Jin State". *A General Reflection for Political Administration* also recorded that "in the third year of Longde, the Post Liang Dynasty (in 923), at that time, the Post Tang army has conquered Yunzhou, Duan Ning, the general of the Post Liang Dynasty, broke river in Suanzao and introduced water to flow into Yunzhou to resist the Post Tang army. The water was therefore called Emperor Protecting Water." Man-made river breaking has led to many floods in these areas, leaving farmland barren and agriculture production damaged, thus seriously threatening local people's survival.

From the Five Dynasties Period to the end of the Northern Song Dynasty, the Yellow River had three major breaches due to military and natural disasters. The rolling water has formed a big lake after connecting with the ancient marshes at the foot of Liangshan Mountain (Fig. 5-9), which is known as "eight hundred Li Liangshanpo Lake". The lake was described in *Heroes of the Marshes* as "with thousands of river branches and covers an area of 800 Li". This was just the place where heroes of Liangshan staged their chivalrous stories including "gathering in the mountains, building camps, fighting against violence, killing the rich to help the poor, and acting on behalf of heaven".

Figure 5-9 Liangshan Marsh

After establishing their own country, the Jin State, originating from Northeast, conquered the Central Plains and captured two emperors, Huizong and Qinzong, bringing the Northern Song

Dynasty to an end. In the winter of 1128 (the second year of Emperor Gaozong's reign in the Southern Song Dynasty), Du Chong, a general of the Southern Song Dynasty, who remained in Kaifeng, dug up the Yellow River in ligudu, Huaxian County, Henan Province in an effort to stop the Jin army. As a result, the Yellow River flowed eastward into Huaihe River from Sishui River. However, this strategy did not stop the Jin army's attack at all but brought serious damages to the people living on the reaches of the Yellow and Huaihe Rivers. Furthermore, it also caused the great diversion of the Yellow River, which has occupied the waterway of Huaihe River to flow into the sea, bringing far-reaching impact in the history.

The most typical example of digging up the Yellow River and substituting soldiers with water was the mutual water attack between the Ming army and Li Zicheng[①]'s army in the east years of the Ming Dynasty. In 1642, the uprising army of Li Zicheng attacked Kaifeng City for the third time. This time, Li Zicheng adopted the strategy of long-term siege, while the Ming army chose to defend the city till the last minute. Four and a half months later after such a stand-off, Kaifeng City was in a terrible situation: the officers and soldiers have to live on some herbal medicines such as yam, Poria cocos, Polygonum multiflorum, angelica, cinnamon and plantain seed; while the citizen could only feed on aquatic plants, water insects, faecal maggots, clay or horse manure, and later the situation was so severe that people even began to eat the dead body of human being. The worse situation drove the Kaifeng garrison to break Zhujiazhai, a part of the embankment of the Yellow River, attempting to drown the Li Zicheng's army at one stroke. As a result, ten thousand Li Zicheng's soldiers camping in the southeast of Kaifeng City were killed in the flood. Li Zicheng, deciding to adopt the same method, sent people to dig up the Majia levee on the Yellow River to flood the city. It was September at that time, when it rained heavily. Water of the Yellow River burst out from the two openings, broke the north gate of the city and left through the southeast gate, leaving the whole city drowned in deep water killing more than 340,000 soldiers and citizens among the total number of 370,000. Many historic sites, such as Baogong Temple, Kaifeng Mansion and Prince Zhou's Palace of Ming Dynasty, were buried together with Kaifeng City by the sand brought by the Yellow River. This water attack drowned the most amount of people in Chinese history.

In Chinese modern history, there is another typical example of substituting water for soldiers by Chiang Kai Shek when he cut the Yellow River Dike at the entrance of Huayuankou to block the Japanese invaders, but Chiang still suffered great failure. In early June of 1938, after occupying Kaifeng City, the Japanese invaders approached Zhengzhou, to attack Wuhan. In order to prevent the Japanese army from attacking, Chiang Kai Shek ordered to breach the Huayuankou riverbank in the north of Zhengzhou City and the Zhaokou riverbank in the northwest of Zhongmou to use the flood to stop the enemy from advancing westward. Although the artificial flood temporarily blocked

---

① Li Zicheng: (1606-1645) was a peasant rebel leader who overthrew the Ming Dynasty in 1644 and ruled over northern China briefly as the emperor of the short-lived Shun Dynasty before his death a year later.

the Japanese army's westward move, China still paid an extremely heavy price. When the Yellow River broke, about 54,000 km² of land in 44 counties and cities in Henan, Anhui and Jiangsu Provinces became a desolate land (Fig. 5 – 10). 890,000 people were killed in the flood, and 12.5 million people were displaced (Fig. 5 – 11). The tragic scene was just like the picture depicted in Du Fu's poem "Long time has passed, white bones were still left unattended. Ghosts lingering for ages cried loudly, upsetting those of the newly dead. Cloudy sky, wet rain, and grieving ghosts, what a miserable picture!"

In addition, draining the moat is also a way for the besiegers to attack enemy who dig trenches for self-defence. *A General Reflection for Political Administration* records that in the fourth year of Qianning of the Tang Dynasty (in 897), Zhu Wen conquered Zhuxuan in Yunzhou. "Being lack of food and soldiers, Zhu Xuan refused to have face-to-face battle but introduced water into deep trench for defence." In order to defeat his enemy, Pang Shigu a general of the Bian, built a floating bridge and made efforts to drain the moat. After all the preparations, he attacked Zhu Xuan's army by night. As a result, Zhu Xuan abandoned the city and fled to Zhongdu.

In ancient China, the power of substituting soldiers with water was no less powerful than the atomic bomb in modern wars, which always brought catastrophic consequences. Like the contemporary prohibition of the use of nuclear weapons, ancient politicians tried to ban water attacks by treaty. However, these prohibitions were not really observed in the wars of all dynasties. On the contrary, the substitution of water for soldiers became more and more frequent, and therefore becoming a commonly used method in ancient Chinese wars.

Figure 5-10 The Breaking Place of Huayuankou of the Yellow River

Chapter Five Water and Wars

Figure 5-11 Homeless People after the Breaking of Huayuankou①
Levee of the Yellow River

---

① Huayuankou: During the Anti-Japanese War, Guomindang troops under the leadership of Chiang Kai-shek broke the levees holding back the river near the village of Huayuankou in Henan Province in an effort to stop the Japanese army, causing great damages to local people.

Chapter Six Water and Water Conservancy Projects

Sima Qian① (Fig. 6-1) wrote in *the Records of the Grand Historian* that "Water control is significant in influencing people's lives." and "since then, people in charge are keen in developing water conservancy projects". This is the first time in Chinese history that someone has put forward the concept of water conservancy, and the idea that it could bring benefits and eliminate harm for people. Since then, the phrase "water conservancy" has the meaning of irrigation, shipping and flood control. From ancient times to the present, numerous water conservancy projects have been built by the Chinese nation. This chapter mainly explores water culture content contained in the water conservancy projects from the three aspects of irrigation, canal, and embankment projects.

Figure 6-1 Sima Qian

Section I Irrigation Projects

Irrigation project is a general term of projects and facilities built for irrigation of farmland. In ancient China, great emphasis was laid on agricultural production. To ensure that, ancient Chinese has constructed many irrigation projects and therefore accumulating abundant experience and technologies. In ancient China, people used water from river, lake, pond or well

---

① Sima Qian: was a Chinese historian of the early Han Dynasty (206B. C. -220A. D.). He is considered the father of Chinese historiography for his *Records of the Grand Historian*, a general history of China in the Jizhuanti style covering more than two thousand years beginning from the rise of the Legendary Yellow Emperor and the formation of the first Chinese polity to the reigning sovereignty of Sima Qian's time, Emperor Wu of Han Dynasty.

spring for irrigation. The north mainly used river water, while the south pond water. No matter which way is used, it is necessary to build water diversion channels and distribution facilities.

1. The Dujiangyan Dam

Among the numerous irrigation projects in China, Dujiangyan Dam is the most famous and representative one (Fig. 6-2), which has different names in different historical periods. However, its original name had no record, and it was used to be called Fupeng, Fuyan and Du'an Dayan after the Han and Wei Dynasties. It was also known as Fuweiyan Dam in the Tang Dynasty and eventually Dujiangyan Dam since the Song Dynasty.

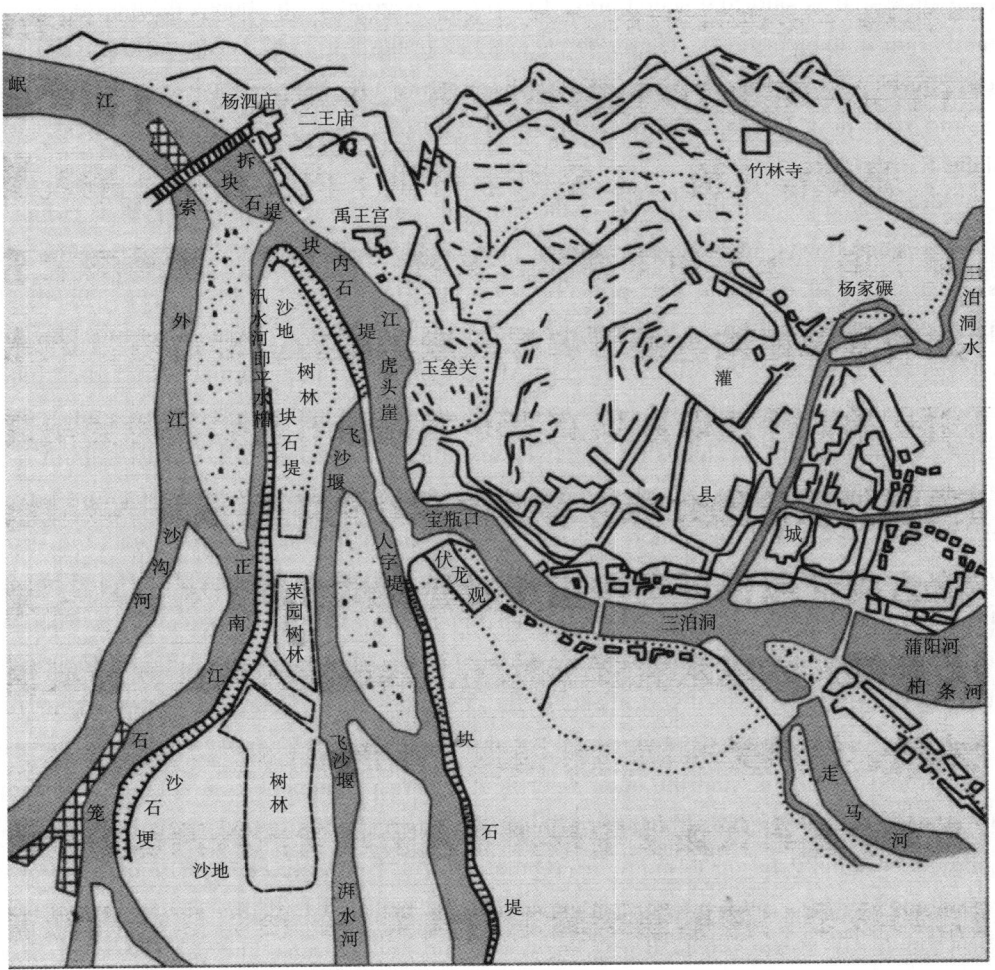

Figure 6-2 The Drawing of the Channel Head of the Dujiangyan Dam

Located in Guanxian County (now Dujiangyan City), Sichuan Province, where Minjiang River enters Chengdu Plain, Dujiangyan Dam, a water diversion project without a dam, built in 256 B. C., enjoyed the longest history of more than 2,200 years in the world. Till now, it is still full of vitality and plays a role of moistening the earth and benefiting local people.

However, before the construction of Dujiangyan Dam, flood and drought were very serious on Chengdu Plain. The Minjiang River, also known as the Wenjiang River, Chengdu River or Dujiang River in ancient times, is the most abundant in water among tributary of the Yangtze River in Sichuan Province. There is a great drop height on its upper reaches from its origin to the Guanxian County, with a drop of more than 3,000 m among the length of 340 km, so the current is turbulent. However, the drop decreases sharply, and the velocity slows down when the river enters from the Guanxian County to Chengdu Plain. Such a structure easily leads to frequent floods. It is said that sometimes, it could be as great as the floods during the Periods of Yao and Shun in ancient times. Therefore, as early as in the Spring and Autumn Period, people of ancient Shu State have dug a river channel connecting the Minjiang River and the Tuojiang River, and named it Jiangtuo Channel, to divert part of water in the Minjiang River into the Tuojiang River.

Li Bing was appointed the prefect of the Shu prefecture in about 256-251 B. C. when there were still serious floods due to heavy rain in mid-summer on Chengdu Plain. Therefore, during his six years as prefect of the Shu prefecture, Li Bing organized the local people of all ethnic groups to vigorously build Dujiang water conservancy projects, so as to give full play to the advantages and overcome the disadvantages. At that time, the main projects included: blocking the river to build a watershed dike, crossing the Pijiang River and Jianjiang River and chiseling Lidui (an isolated hill). By blocking the river to build a watershed dike, Li Bing built a large weir on the Minjiang River, so as to divert a part of water in Minjiang River to the east of the Yulei Mountain to facilitate irrigation and shipping on Chengdu Plain. At that time, the structure of the weir was relatively simple, but it was well-designed. It made full use of the sand bar in the middle of Minjiang River. Firstly, it transformed the top tip of the sandbank into a Fish Mouth shape to easily separate the water. Secondly, a weir body is built between the tail of big sandbank and the isolated hill, so as to divert a part of the Minjiang River water into Baopingkou. In this way, Minjiang River is divided into inner river and outer river. The inner river is at the east of Fish Mouth and Sandbank, and the outer river is at the west. After the completion of the project, there was not major flood and drought any longer on Chengdu Plain, and agricultural production was guaranteed, thus it began to enjoy the reputation of a "Heavenly Land of Plenty". In order to commemorate Li Bing's achievements, later generations not only built the Erwang (Two Greats) Temple (Fig. 6-3) to worship Li Bing (Fig. 6-4) and his two sons, but also revered Li Bing as the Master of Sichuan.

Dujiangyan Dam has benefited local area for over two thousand and two hundred years. The hidden cultural wisdom in it lies in the fact that it embodies the traditional Chinese philosophy of

Chapter Six   Water and Water Conservancy Projects

Figure 6-3   the Erwang Temple

"maintaining harmony between man and nature, and Tao following the nature", which has enabled the project to integrate with the ambient environment and also corresponded with the modern notion of "sustainable development" as well as "promoting harmonious coexistence between human and nature".

Firstly, the head of Dujiangyan Dam canal is located at the mouth of the Minjiang River. Surrounded by mountains, this area forms a circular terrain and circulating water potential. In addition, the drop of nearly 300 m between here and the downstream Chengdu Plain has created unique natural conditions for the construction of water conservancy projects featured by diversion channel without dam and gravity irrigation.

Secondly, the setting of the three main works of Dujiangyan Dam covering Fish Mouth, Feishayan weir and Baopingkou makes good use of the terrain. In the upper reaches, the Minjiang River is divided into inner river and outer river by Fish Mouth. After flood and sediment discharge by "Feishayan Weir", the Minjiang River enters into "Baopingkou", and then water is diverted through "Baopingkou". In

Figure 6-4   The Statue of Li Bing

this way, the three major projects complement each other and achieve the magical effects of water diversion and irrigation, flood diversion and disaster reduction, sediment control and siltation prevention.

The six key Chinese characters to describe flood control in Dujiangyan Dam are translated as "deep clean riverbed, maintain low weir" (Fig. 6-5). The so-called "deep clean riverbed" is an annual repair system. Every winter, local staff will be organized to remove the silted sand and gravel in the inner river of the Minjiang River to ensure that the project will not be silted up. In the annual repair work, the most special tools used to block the river are Macha (used as abatis) and the bamboo cage (Fig. 6-6).

Figure 6-5 Six Key Characters on Flood Control in Dujiangyan

Figure 6-6 Bamboo Cage and Macha

Macha is a river blocking tool made of three thick wooden piles as a tripod, and three thin wooden piles as its beam. Bamboo cage is a cage made of bamboo, which is filled with many pebbles to prevent the bamboo cage from being washed away easily by the current. The closure started at the Fish Mouth of Dujiangyan. Before the start of construction, three iron guns and firecrackers were fired. Then, boats full of Macha, bamboo cages and pebbles came to the river. As the boat approached the dike, dozens of strong men would jump on board, and another board of strong men would jump into the river and line-up in a row. On the boat, three people in a group, hold up Macha and passed it over; in the river, people, also three in a group, after taking over the Macha, put it into the river. At the same time, boats full of bamboo cages and pebbles approached

Macha. People put bamboo cages at the foot of Macha, and then put the pebbles into bamboo cages, and finally added the water baffle plate. After finishing those actions, a row of Macha turned into a solid stone dam, and the inner river from the Fish Mouth to the opposite bank would soon be blocked. The section from Fish Mouth to Baopingkou would in turn become a dry riverbed. At this time, the farmer labourers would seize the time to remove the silted sand and gravel in the river. The silt removed from the river will be used to repair the broken dam on the site. The ancients have also made a standard on the degree that the silt in the river channel is removed, that is, "dig up the river sand until you see the iron pile." The ancients buried three iron piles in the Fengqiwo section of the river bed as a bench mark, commonly known as "lying iron". If the "lying iron" is seen in the dredging work every year, it will be regarded as the work meets the standard. The so-called "maintain low weir" in the six key Chinese characters is to control the height of the Feishayan weir (Fig. 6-7). After the Minjiang River was diverted, the water flowing into the inner river was thrown against the bank due to the blockage of rocks by riverbank. Thanks to the function of circulating current for sand elimination at the bend, a large amount of gravel and stone mixed in the water were thrown to the side of the Feishayan weir, achieving the purpose of automatic sand elimination. Therefore, the height of Feishayan weir cannot be too high, and it is good if it is 2 m higher than the riverbed.

Figure 6-7 Feichayan Weir

　　The annual repair work generally started from the last month of the year on lunar calendar and ended before the ploughing work began next spring. A grand ceremony, commonly known as "Water Disemboguing" (Fig. 6-8), would be held from the completion of the annual repair of Dujiangyan Dam to the start of spring irrigation in Tomb-sweeping Day. The water disembodying ceremony was presided over by local senior officials. The day before the ceremony, people would first go to Wang Cong Temple in Pixian County to offer sacrifices to Emperor Wang and Emperor Cong. On the morning of the day when the ceremony was held, the honour guard, led by the presiding official and other participants and accompanied by drum beating and music, would carry the sacrifice to Erwang Temple from the Yuleiguan Pass to offer sacrifices to Li Bing and his sons. With the voice of the master of ceremony, the chief official would loudly read *the Song of Welcoming Gods*. Afterwards, all would stand in silence and sing *the Memorial Song*. After the song, people should present flowers, silks, wine, and food. The chief official would read the congratulatory song and people would bow to the statue of Li Bing. Then, wine would be presented, and silks would be burnt as sacrifice. A shrine would be set up, and *the Farmer Labourers Song* would be sang to bid Gods farewell. The chief official would later bow to the statue of Li Bing three times again, and finally fired three guns of salute. After that, they would go to Yangsi Temple to offer sacrifices to those who had made contributions to the maintenance of Dujiangyan Dam in the past dynasties, and to offer sacrifices to river gods in the red tent beside the river. The climax of the ceremony would come when the Macha was cut open to discharge the water. At the command of the chief official, three guns of salute were fired, and gongs and drums were blaring. River workers would forcefully cut off ropes tying up the Macha before the Fish Mouth, and people on the beach would pull the rope hard, as a result, Macha would be dismantled, and water would roar out. Young people would run along with the water and throw stones to the front of the current, which is called "hitting the first wave of water", because it was believed that disaster could be eliminated and happiness could be achieved by doing so. At this time, some people would also put down ducks at the weir head, attracting young people on both sides of the riverbank wading into the water to fight for "ducks at the first wave of water". There

Figure 6-8　Water Disemboguing Festival in Tomb-sweeping Day

would be many women along the riverbank to scoop "the first stream of water" to offer sacrifice to the gods and wish for a smooth year.

After the ceremony, the chief official should get to Chengdu before the water arrived. If he fell behind, his folk men would think the water that year may not be enough. This ceremony lasted until the 1950s and was then canceled after the introduction of electric gates. It was not until the 1990s that the ceremony was resumed, and its name was changed to "Water Disemboguing Festival". Nowadays, the "Water Disemboguing Festival" in Dujiangyan Dam has become China's intangible cultural heritage and a must see show for tourists visiting Dujiangyan Dam(Fig. 6-9).

Figure 6-9 The Show of Water Disemboguing Festival in Tomb-sweeping Day

2. The Zhengguoqu Canal

After the completion of Dujiangyan Dam, the State of Qin built another large-scale farmland irrigation project in Guanzhong area, Zhengguoqu Canal (Fig. 6-10). At that time, the scale of Zhengguoqu Canal was larger than that of Dujiangyan Dam and its strategic position was more important. Zhengguoqu Canal was built during Qin's war to unify the six states. Its construction has a complex historical background.

In the middle of the third century B. C. , the State of Qin became increasingly powerful, thus posing a great threat to many eastern states. Frightened by the strong Qin State, the Han State, relatively weaker, planned to adopt a strategy to exhaust the Qin state by sending Zhengguo, a hydraulic engineer, to go to Qin as a "spy" whose aim was to lobby the Qin to develop some large-scale water conservancy projects. In this case, manpower and material resources of the Qin State would be squandered as the Han State had planned, which in turn could stop Qin's step of invading

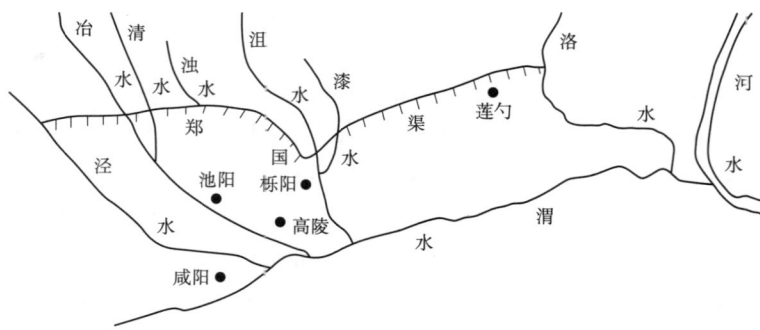

Figure 6-10　The Drawing of Zhengguoqu Canal

eastward. After shouldering such a crucial task, instead of paying a rash visit to the king of Qin, Zhengguo sneaked into the Qin State and dressed up as ordinary people. Secretly, he has investigated all the mountains and rivers in Guanzhong area, observed the topography, and finally planned for the construction of a large-scale water conservancy projects for irrigation by diverting water, and then he presented this plan to the king of Qin.

Qin fell into the trap, but in the process of construction, the conspiracy was discovered, so the king of Qin tried to kill Zhengguo. Zhengguo argued that "at the very beginning, this plan was a plot. However, this plan can also bring great benefits to the Qin State. What I have done can only win several years of peace for Han but would bring long-lasting contributions to Qin". The king of Qin acknowledged his words and continued to send him to oversee the construction. After ten years of hard work, a large-scale irrigation project of diverting water from the Jingshui River was finished, and it was named "Zhengguoqu Canal" after the name of its designer, Zhengguo.

Figure 6-11　Relic of Canal Head of Zhengguoqu Canal

The information about Zhengguoqu Canal was first recorded in the section of "Records on Rivers and Canals" in *Historical Records*, but it was very brief. It said that "Zhengguoqu Canal cut open the Jingshui River from Hukou located at the western foot of Zhongshan Mountain, run along the Beishan Mountain and finally arrived at the Luoshui River with a total length of about 150 km." This record only indicated the head (Fig. 6-11), direction, length and the end point of Zhengguoqu Canal.

Judging from the perspective of landform, the main canal of Zhengguoqu Canal ran from west to east at the elevation of 450-370 m, and was built on the highest line of the second terrace of the Weibei Plain. The vast plain in the south of the canal is within its coverage, therefore the gravity irrigation across the whole area could be realized and favourable irrigation benefits could be obtained.

Zhengguoqu Canal has adopted different solutions when meeting natural rivers on its way to the Luoshui River. Some used the original "Overpass" technology to separate them from each other to avoid interference; some diverted all the river water into the canal to become the irrigation source; some used the constant flow of the river to force the flood flow into the downstream channel through the confluence of the canal and river. This series of measures increased the water source of Zhengguoqu Canal and made the canal run smoothly.

Zhengguoqu Canal is one of the largest irrigation projects in ancient China. The whole irrigation area started from the Jingshui River in the west, reached the Luoshui River in the East, the Yuanjiao in the north and the Weishui River in the south, covering an area of 1100 km^2. According to records in *the Records of the Grand Historian*, more than 40,000 hectares of farmland was irrigated at that time, which showed that this was a large irrigation area. At that time, the land was not leveled, and flood irrigation was used. The actual irrigation area accounted for about 70% of the total land area. The Guanzhong area belongs to the loess area. The loess itself is rich in potassium, phosphorus, and lime, which has good natural fertilizer effect. Once irrigated, its potential fertility can be brought into full play and become fertile soil.

Zhengguoqu Canal not only brought water from the Jingshui River to moisten a large area of land, but also warped the saline alkali land with irrigation water. The Jingshui River is a river with high sediment content, and its average sediment concentration is as high as 180 kg/m^3 for many years. The sediment from the Longdong Plateau is rich in organic matter as well as nitrogen, phosphorus and potassium. Therefore, after diverting water from the Jingshui River, the soil fertility was increased, the halogenated soil was improved, and a large area of "saline land" which could not be planted crops was also turned into high-yielding farmland.

Since the Zhengguoqu Canal irrigation has many benefits such as fertilization, infiltration and improvement of saline alkali land, after the completion of Zhengguoqu Canal, the Weibei Plain has become a "fertile field", and the dry land agriculture has been transformed into irrigation agriculture, and the crop yield has been greatly increased. According to the records of *Historical Records*, the irrigation area was "more than 120,000 hectares" at that time, and the yield was high.

Sima Qian once evaluated the significance of the completion of Zhengguoqu Canal that "after the completion of the canal, Guanzhong area has become a place with fertile land and without any bad harvest years. The Qin Dynasty became rich and powerful since then and finally annexed other states"Later, Ban Gu, a famous historian in the Han Dynasty also commented that "Qin opened the Zhengguoqu Canal to enrich the country and strengthen the army. ""The land to the west of Shangluo area and to the east of Long is fertile, that's the reason why Qin captured Xirong, a western ethic group and conquered other states to the east of the mountain. " These statements profoundly revealed the far-reaching influence of Zhengguoqu Canal on politics and economy of the Qin State. Among the many reasons, the opening of Zhengguoqu Canal was significant in promoting agricultural development in Guanzhong area. Taking Chengdu and Guanzhong economic zones as important pillars, the Qin State accelerated its steps in defeating Xirong ethnic group and annexing other states, and finally completed the great cause of unifying China in 221 B. C. .

3. The Karez Well

The Karez Well is a well-known irrigation project located in Xinjiang where there are many ethnic groups (Fig. 6-12). Karez Wells are mainly distributed in Hami and Turpan basins of Xinjiang. During its heyday, the total length hit 10,000 Li (5,000 km), therefore being called "the Underground Great Wall". It is listed as the three major projects in ancient China together with the Great Wall and the Beijing-Hangzhou Grand Canal.

Figure 6-12 The Bird-view of Karez Wells

Xinjiang has a vast area, but with very scarce water resources. The Hami and Turpan basins where Karez is located are situated at the southern foot of the Tianshan Mountain, where it is rich in snow water under the ground. If the underground snow water in the northern edge of the basin could be introduced to the south by digging canals, the gravity irrigation would be realized thanks to the slope in the basin. However, the precipitation in this place is very rare, only 20 mm in the whole year. In comparison, the annual evaporation is as high as 3,000 mm, 150 times of the precipitation. If the open channel irrigation was adopted, the channel water would be mostly evaporated. To avoid this result, local people invented a way of digging underground ditches to let the water flow under the ground.

The length of each Karez Well is about 3 km, and the longest one often includes several connected Karez Wells, the length of which could reach tens of or even hundreds of kilometeres. It is generally composed of four parts: a culvert, a vertical shaft, an open channel and a water storing dam (Fig. 6-13). Among them, the culvert (Fig. 6-14) is the main body of the Karez Well. Its function is to block the groundwater and lead it out, so the water flows under the ground in this section. The shaft is used by the construction workers to excavate, ventilate, access lights, and determine the flow direction and slope of the culvert, which was set up every 20 m. The depth of the shaft varies from several meters to hundreds of meters, depending on the depth of the aquifer, the amount of shaft ranges from several to about 300 on each culvert. The open channel (Fig. 6-15) is a channel connecting the outlet of the culvert and the farmland, introducing the underground water from the culvert to the farmland. There is also a water storing dam at the junction of open channel and the culvert. It is, in fact, a reservoir, built at the outlet of the culvert, where local people store water flowing out of the culvert. There are three functions of this dam: firstly, it is to store water. Agricultural production stops in Xinjiang in winter due to the very cold weather, while Karez Well continues to deliver water. The dam can then store the water in winter for further use in the coming spring. Secondly, to warm water by sun. The main source of the groundwater flowing through Karez Well is snowmelt, thus with very low temperature. If it is directly used to irrigate the farmland, the low-temperature water would seriously affect the growth of crops. Only after sun warming in the dam, can the irrigation benefit the crops. Thirdly, it is convenient for unified allocation of water for farmland.

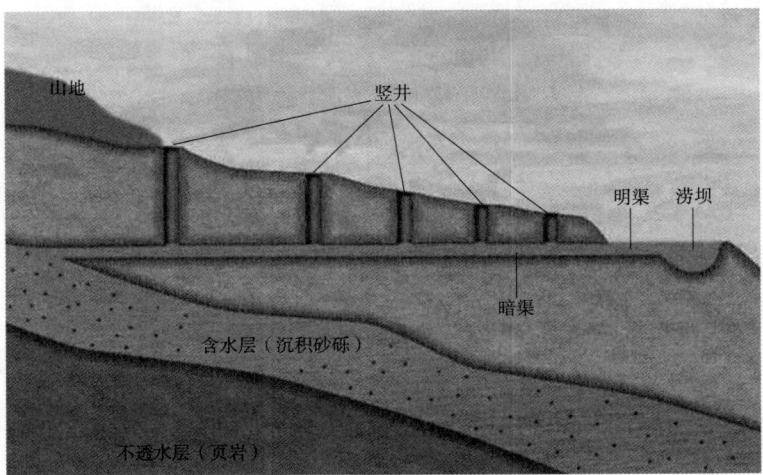

Figure 6-13 Structure Drawing of the Karez Well

There are three theories about the invention of the Karez Well. Most scholars believe that it can be traced back to the Western Han Dynasty. The reason is that since the reign of Emperor Wu of the Han Dynasty, the Western Han Dynasty began to perform political ruling in Xiyu (the

Figure 6-14　The Culvert

Figure 6-15　The Open Channel

western regions), stationed troops and developed farmlands in Luntai, Quli (within the Korla area today) and Cheshi (within the Turpan area today). There is little rainfall in this area, so water conservancy projects must be built to facilitate the government strategy. Those scholars believe that the technology of digging Karez Well had already been mastered when the Longshouqu Canal (Fig. 6 – 16) was built before the Han developed Xiyu. According to *the Records of the Grand Historian*, during the reign of Emperor Wu of the Han Dynasty, people excavated water diversion channels near Shangyan Mountain by Luoshui River in Dali County, Shaanxi Province. Because the banks of Luoshui River were often flooded by the river, the construction of diversion channel was often affected. To solve the problem, wise craftsmen at that time invented a way to open a kind of "well canal", that is, to dig a shaft at the fixed distance, with the depth of about 130 m, and then connect the bottom of the shafts to form a culvert allowing water to flow through it. In this way, people can not only control the water resources, but avoid the collapsing of canals. This kind of underground channel excavation technology was known as "well channel method" in the history. After the Han Dynasty built connections with Xiyu, this technology was passed

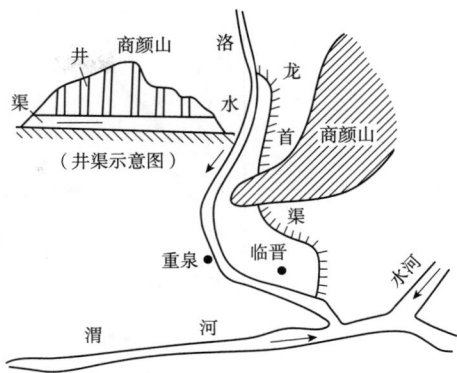

Figure 6-16 Drawing of Longshouqu Canal

to the local people. Later, after the transformation of the people of all ethnic groups, they finally developed that into the Karez Well suitable for the geographical conditions of Xinjiang.

Some scholars believe that the construction technology of Karez came from Central Asia. In ancient Persia, Karez had been used before 500 B.C., which was also used in some neighbouring countries near Xinjiang, including Afghanistan, Pakistan and other Central Asian countries. Therefore, it was believed that Karez technology in ancient Xiyu was introduced from ancient Persia along the Silk Road. Some scholars point out that Karez is the translation of Persian Karez. They believe that Karez originated from ancient Persia, and the area with Karez Well now belongs to the place within the influence reach of Persian and Iranian culture.

However, in recent years, more and more domestic scholars began to support the third view, that is, the Karez in Turpan Basin was the creation of the local an cient people. The view was universally agreed by Uygur scholars and famous Karez craftsmen in Turpan. They pointed out that Karez Well is essentially different from well canals in Guanzhong area in the Han Dynasty. The "well canal" is an underground structure, while the Karez Well is a water intake project to bring underground water to the surface with the help of gravity by using the relationship between the terrain gradient and groundwater hydraulic gradient.

Figure 6-17 Lin Zexu

Historically, the Karez Well got great development in Xinjiang in the late Qing Dynasty. Thanks to the efforts of some key officials then including Lin Zexu (Fig. 6-17) and Zuo Zongtang, the scale of Karez has been rapidly expanded (Fig. 6-18).

When Lin Zexu was transferred to Xinjiang, he was

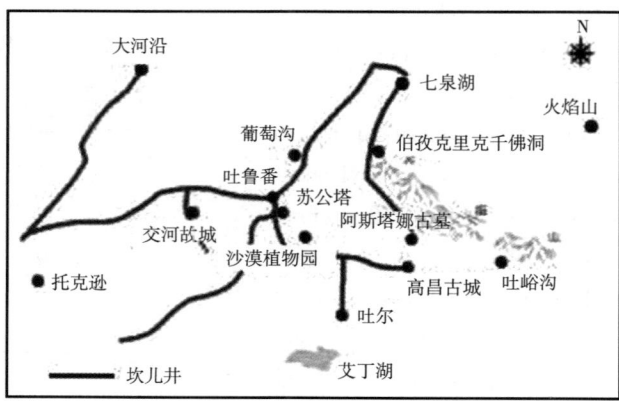

Figure 6-18 Distribution of the Karez Wells in Xinjiang

reguested by general Buyantai of Ili area to build water conservancy projects in southern Xinjiang together with the Minister Quanqing of Kalashar affairs. They vigorously expanded the Karez project there, from Turpan to Tuxeon, Iraliq and other places. Later, although Lin Zexu was transferred back to the inland by the Qing government, his practice of developing Karez Wells still received the attention and support of his successors. As a result, the number of officially built Karez Wells in Turpan Basin increased from 30 to more than 100, and local people were also encouraged by local government to build this kind of project. This has helped to turn Turpan's vast wilderness into fertile land. The local people were so grateful for Lin Zexu that they called the Karez Well as "Lingongjing"(The well of Lin).

Figure 6-19 The Portrait of Zuo Zongtang

The second great development of the Karez Well was after Zuo Zongtang[1] (Fig. 6-19) defeated the invasion of Agubai in 1878. Zuo Zongtang regarded the restoration and development of local water conservancy projects as one of the important contents of the rehabilitation work, so in just three years, great achievements have been made. In addition to repairing the official Karez Wells in Turpan, 185 new official wells have been built, and local people were also very active in this construction. Ten years later, thousands of Karez Wells were built on places within the Turpan Basin to the west of Muqin.

---

[1] Zuo Zongtang: (November 10, 1812–September 5, 1885) was a Chinese statesman and military leader of the late Qing Dynasty.

In Turpan, at its peak, there were 1,237 Karez Wells with a total length of more than 5,000 km, covering more than 30,000 hectares of farmland and orchards, accounting for 67% of the total cultivated land. This is equivalent to 1.5 times the length of the Grand Canal, 28 times the length of Suez Canal, and 60 times the length of the Panama Canal. With such a large scale, it is no wonder that Lin Zexu wrote the exclamation of "It is truly beyond my imagination" after he first saw the Karez Well. After investigating the Karez Well, Maodun, a famous modern Chinese writer, signed that "the great scale of the project is beyond my imagination."

The Karez Well in Xinjiang is not only a unique and magnificent underground irrigation project, but also one of the symbols of ancient Chinese water culture. The Uygur people here call Karez as "jiangbulak", which means "the source of life". Since ancient times, people in Turpan Basin have formed a unique ecological culture centering around Karez. Twelve Muqam (Fig. 6-20), a large traditional music unique to Uygur people, describes the digging and use of Karez, as well as the close relationship between local people and Karez. In recent years, studies have also found that the social structure, livelihood style, folk customs related to marriage and funeral, and the use of land resources of Uygur villages in this area before 1949 are closely related to the construction of Karez and the use of Karez water. Only with Karez can people have Turpan oasis and oasis civilization. Therefore, Turpan culture is Karez culture. In Turpan, many towns, administrative villages and residential areas are named after Karez. When measuring the farmland, instead of using the traditional measurement unit "Mu", local people adopted the unit of "well". For example, "ten-Mu field" is called "ten-well field" by local people. This phenomenon also proves the importance of Karez in local people's minds.

Figure 6-20 Twelve Muqam

Section II Canal Projects

Water conservancy projects, especially the canal project, can also provide convenience for people's transportation. The canal refers to the artificial waterway constructed by manual excavation based on some natural rivers or other ditches.

China's terrain is featured by being high in the west and low in the east, therefore major rivers in China, including the Yellow River, Huaihe River, Yangtze River and Pearl River flow from west to East, which leads to a convenient water transportation in this direction. However, it is difficult to use water transportation from north to south, hence demands to dig canals connecting the north and the south arise. Fortunately, there are many north-south tributaries of the major rivers including those of the Yellow River, Huaihe River, Yangtze River and Pearl River, and distance between them are usually not far apart. In addition, in the middle and lower reaches of these rivers, the land is flat and abundant in lakes. With a little modification and connection, the artificial river channels can be formed. As a result, most of the canals in China are in the north-south direction.

China is one of the earliest countries to build canals in the world, therefore with a long history. In ancient times, canals were mainly built for military purposes. For example, at the end of the Spring and Autumn Period, the State of Wu in the south grew stronger. In order to fight for hegemony in the Central Plains, the king of Wu ordered people to build Hangou, the earliest canal in Chinese history, connecting the Yangtze River and Huaihe River basins.

In the Warring States Period, King Weihui built the Honggou[①] twice for the sake of the war (Fig. 6-21), and connected the Yellow River and Huaihe River systems. After the Qin State annexed the six other states, another famous canal was built to meet the needs of the war. That is the Lingqu Canal.

1. The Lingqu Canal

The Lingqu Canal (Fig. 6-22), located in Xing'an County, Guilin, Guangxi, is known as "the three major water conservancy projects in the Qin Dynasty" together with Zhengguoqu Canal and Dujiangyan Dam. Mr. Guo Moruo, a famous Chinese modern writer, once praised the Lingqu Canal as: "Together as world wonders, it echoes in the South with the Great Wall in the North." This conservancy project built in the Qin Dynasty also has its unique historical background.

In the 26th year of the Shihuang of the Qin Dynasty (221 B.C.), Qin Shihuang sent 500,000 Qin

---

[①] Honggou (8th-5th centuries B.C.), the longest one of that period according to *the Records of the Grand Historian*.

Chapter Six Water and Water Conservancy Projects

Figure 6-21   The Relics of Honggou

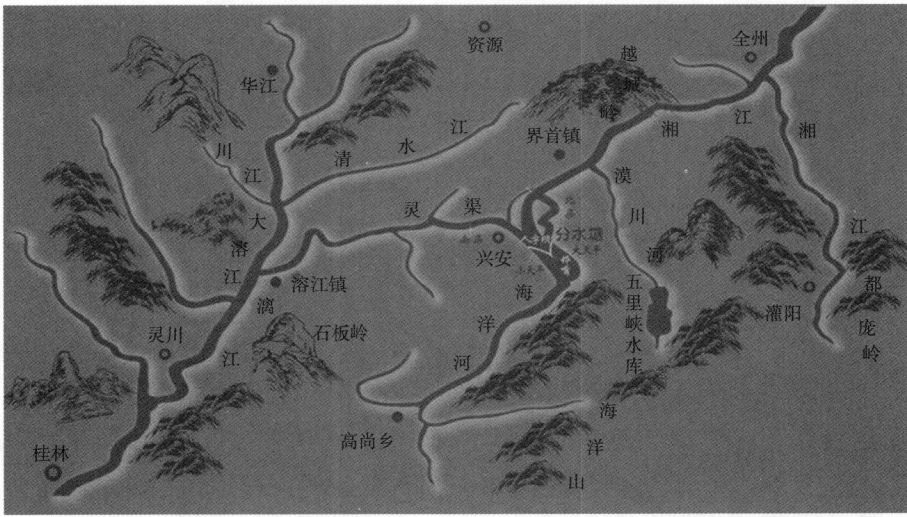

Figure 6-22   Geological Position of Lingqu Canal

troops to advance southward on five routes. One troop went to the mountains of Tancheng, one guarded the fortress of Jiuyi, one was in Panyu, one guarded the frontier of Nanye, and one was stationed by Yugan River. The Qin army, which advanced toward Lingnan (South of the Five Ridges), met the tenacious resistance of the local Yue leaders. The Qin army spent three years in hard fighting. At the junction of Guangxi and Hunan, the mountain road was extremely rugged, bringing great difficulties to transportation. At that time, Lu, a person-in-charge for transporting the army's provisions, was left helpless when faced with the problem.

Two years later, Qin Shihuang, after crossing the Huaihe River and the Yangtze River, came to Hunan, which related to the front lines. He deployed the war to unify Lingnan. In order to solve the problem of grain transportation, starting from the needs of unifying and developing the South of the Five Ridges, the first emperor Shihuang made a major decision to "let the supervisor to dig canals to transport grain". In ancient times, it was customary to take the official position as the surname. Therefore, the censor named Lu was called Shilu. After five years of hard construction, they finally built the Lingqu. Lingqu not only opened the Xiangjiang River and the Lijiang River, but also connected the Yangtze River and the Pearl River, which relieved the difficulty of the Qin army's grain supply. Then emperor Shihuang quickly unified Lingnan and completed the great cause of unification. In the "*Huainanzi · Ren jan xun*", it is mentioned that "to let the supervisor unable to transfer the funds, but also to dig the canal to transport the grain." This is the earliest record of digging Lingqu Canal in *Historical Records*.

It was recorded in the history that there were totally 26 times of renovation on Lingqu Canal ranging from the Qin to Qing Dynasty, including once in the Eastern Han Dynasty, twice in the Tang Dynasty, three times in the Northern Song Dynasty, three times in the Southern Song Dynasty, twice in the Yuan Dynasty, three times in the Ming Dynasty and twelve times in the Qing Dynasty. Lingqu Canal project includes the South Canal, the North Canal, Huazui, Datianping and Xiaotianping Dikes (used as barrage), Qindi Dike, Doumer Gate and large and small spillway dams, which is shown in the following chart. (Fig. 6-23).

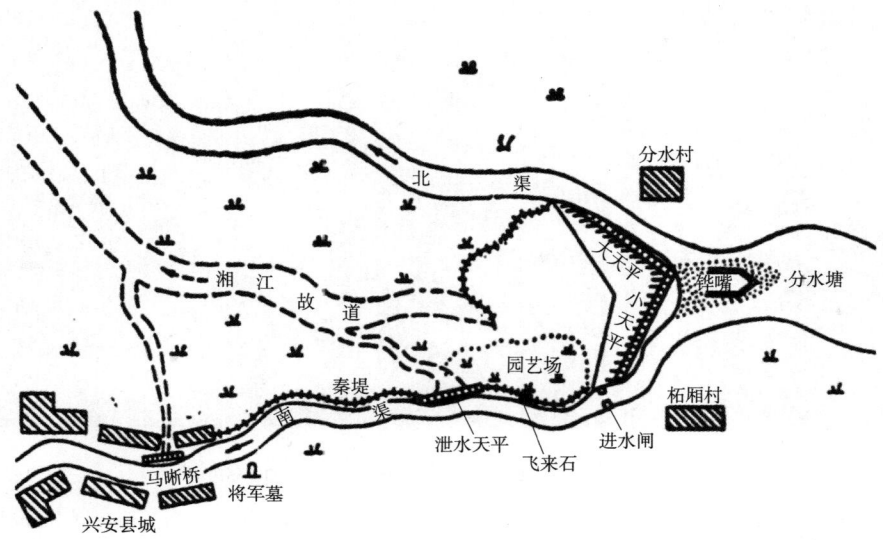

Figure 6-23 Head of the Lingqu Canal

The South and the North Canals constituted main body of the project, with a total length of about 34 km. Huazui as well as Datianping and Xiaotianping stone dikes adopted the Y-shaped structure, serving as key projects of diverting water and introducing water from Xiangjiang River to Lijiang River. Huazui was located at the front of the Y-shaped stone dike, which was named as

Huazui (the mouth of the plough) because it was sharp in front and blunt in the back, looking very similar to the front end of a plough. Huazui was used for water diversion, like the function of Yuzui in Dujiangyan Dam. Datianping and Xiaotianping stone dikes were located behind the Huazui and played the role of blocking, separating and discharging water together with it. Because the stone dam "can effectively separate water just like the weighting scale", they were both named Tianping (scale) in Chinese. Its working mechanism was as follows: firstly, the Datianping and Xiaotianping stone dikes blocked and raised the water level, and then they separated water in the upper reaches of Xiangjiang River with a share of 30% and 70% by using the 108° angle formed between them. Under the normal water level, 70% of the Xiangjiang River water was diverted into the North Canal to flow northward up into the Xiangjiang River, while the left 30% into the South Canal to go southward down into the Lijiang River. When the flood season came, Huazui can also reduce the impact of the flood on the two stone dikes and distributed the pressure to both sides. The flood above the dam surface was discharged into the old channel of Xiangjiang River. Such a mechanism was efficient in adjusting water level and balancing water quantity.

There were two spillway dams on the South Canal. One was large and the other small. The large one was set on the dike on the east bank of the South Canal, which was slightly lower than the surplus water in the canal. Water flew out from the large spillway dam and converged into the old channel of Xiangjiang River through a small ditch. In fact, it was a flood discharging gate, only without water volume regulating gate. When the flood rose sharply, both Datianping and Xiaotianping failed to discharge all the flood, and too much water crowded into the South Canal, it would be used to discharge flood, to avoid the flood over-topping the dike and causing damages. The small one was located in Xing'an City (Fig. 6-24) with the length

Figure 6-24 Xiaotianping Remains

of about 12m. It also served as a flood discharging gate, where was also the place the South Canal met the Shuangnujing stream from the southwest. Shuangnujing stream flew pass the Mashiqiao and went eastward into the old channel of Xiangjiang River. The flow was very small in dry season. However, during rainstorm period, flood in the stream was mainly discharged by the small spillway dam to avoid possible damages when flood crowded into the South Canal.

As a cultural relic with a history of more than 2,000 years, the Lingqu Canal contains rich water culture. Among them, the first is the scientific and technological water culture as embodied in Lingqu canal. In the process of repairing the Lingqu Canal, Doumen Gates were designed and constructed (Fig. 6-25). Doumen Gate was an important tool for raising water level, storing water, and therefore facilitating boat transport in the Lingqu Canal. The reason why it was used lied in the geological position of the Canal. The Lingqu Canal was in the middle of high mountains with large height difference. The gradient of the North Canal was about 1/300, and that of the South Canal from Nandoukou to Lingshanmiao village was about 1/900. In some places, the water level would rise or fall by 1m every 160 m, making it impossible to sail boats at all. If the river channel could be extended, the sharp height difference could be reduced. However, the river length needs to be prolonged by 20 times to achieve this purpose, total engineering amount thus added would be beyond people's imagination.

Figure 6-25 Doumen Gate of the Lingqu Canal

As a solution, the wise ancients invented the device of Doumen Gates located in places where the water level difference is large. When a ship entered the Doumen Gate from the upstream, people would set up steep bars on the stone caves of the Doumen, and put a few blocks at its feet to stop the water, which in turn would raise water lever. The ship could then move forward steadily. In this way, it can climb up the mountain step by step and vice versa (Fig. 6-26). In terms of its working mechanism, Doumen Gate is like a multi-level ship lock in modern times. In comparison, the earliest ship locks did not appear in Europe until 1375 in Netherlands. Therefore, experts from the International Dam Commission think that the Doumen Gate of Lingqu Canal is the earliest ship lock in history, the earliest ancestor of modern electric gate, which can be given the title of "the father of ship locks in the world".

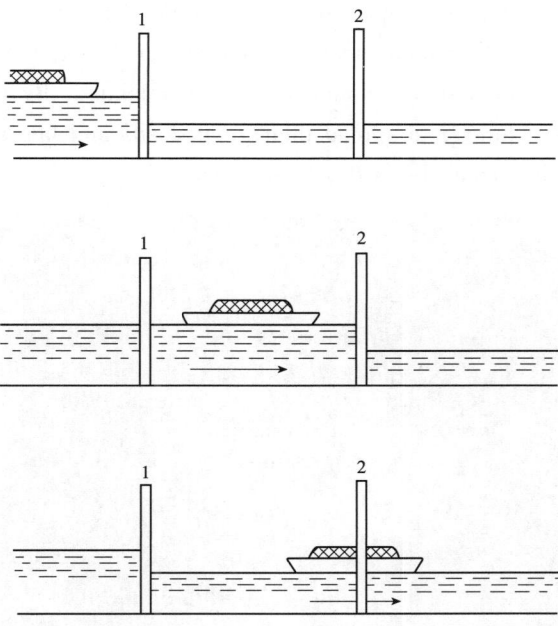

Figure 6-26　Sketch Map of the Ship Passing through Doumen Gate

In addition to abundance in water culture in science and technology, there was also a special water worship culture about Lingqu Canal. There is a tomb of three generals near Xing'an County where Lingqu Canal is located (Fig. 6-27). Legendary has it that Shihuang Emperor successively sent two generals, Zhang and Liu, to build the canal. General Zhang was killed by the emperor because of his failure in solving problem of water level difference in the Lingqu Canal. General Liu, on the other hand, was very intelligent and invented the Doumen Gate as a solution. However, he was also killed because he did not finish it on schedule. Later, General Li was sent to continue the task. After successfully building the canal, instead of being happy, he felt quite ashamed because he thought the success was made based on previous experiences. Unwilling to steal others' fruits, he committed suicide. Local people buried three generals together and called the tomb as "Three Generals' Tomb" to commemorate their contributions. Now, the tomb is located on the south bank of Lingqu Canal near Sujiaqiao in Xing'an County, Guangxi Zhuang Autonomous Region, which has been granted as a sacred tomb by imperial court of the Ming Dynasty. The inscription on the tombstone was carved during the reign of Emperor Qianlong of the Qing Dynasty. It said "There was a long history behind the Three Generals' tomb. However, it is a pity that we cannot find a detailed record about their deeds. Legendary has it that they were granted the title of Zhenguo General (a high-ranking title for officials in Ming and Qing Dynasties) because of their great contributions to building dams. After died, they were buried together at the south of the mountain in the northeast of this place. Three generals were helpful to their country and people before the death, and they were believed to become gods to bless their country and people. To worship them, people in this place built two temples. Although there were inscriptions on the tombstone, its content was quite brief. The long past years have brought serious damages to the tomb, which nearly collapsed to the ground. Bearing their great contributions to this land in mind, we cannot leave it unattended. By rebuilding the tomb, we sincerely wish it could last forever to spread their great deeds and famous names to the coming generations. We also wish it could bless this land forever."

Figure 6-27　Three Generals' Tomb

In the history, there were many poems left by famous poets when they went to visit Lingqu Canal, the great water conservancy project. The earliest one was *Lingqu*, written by Hu Zeng, Tang Dynasty, it said "Mountain splitting to invite waves of Xiangjiang tumbling in, flow from the sky above, attracting magpies to cross, build a bridge for aspiring lovers to meet upon". The most famous one was *Xing'anqu Canal* written by Xie Jin, a famous scholar and poet in Ming Dynasty, who topped the three most brilliant intellectuals at his times. The poem was written when he passed Lingqu Canal after being demoted to Guangxi. It said "Stone channel connects Xiangjiang in the north and Lijiang in the south, so deep the water splitting dam is, an embankment laid below, had Qin ruled the country scores of years more, ships in the canal would have sailed to the end of the earth." In addition, A poem by Su Zongjing, a scholar in Qing Dynansty, said "at the end of Lingqu, a water street emerges in Xing'an, ship sails in the city, across bridges one by one, an easy touch of water rows me on, a smile to the window by water bank, a bottle of wine can be bought, how smooth the trip is, I am looking forward to my journey ahead.", showing that Lingqu has become a famous place of interest at that time attracting many famous literati when they visited Guangxi.

2. The Grand Canal of China

With the development of economy and society, the function of the canal has changed from the initial military supplies transportation to the service of commercial trade. In this context, the ancients built a more magnificent grand canal.

The Grand Canal of China is a miracle created by people in ancient China. On June 22, 2014, at the 38th World Heritage Conference, it was announced that the Grand Canal in China was successfully selected into the world cultural

Figure 6-28 Xie Jin

heritage list, becoming the 46th world heritage project in China. Beijing-Hangzhou Grand Canal, a major part of the Grand Canal starts from Beijing in the north and ends in Hangzhou in the south, passing through Tianjin, Hebei, Shandong, Jiangsu and Zhejiang, and connecting Haihe River, Yellow River, Huaihe River, Yangtze River and Qiantang River, with a total length of 1,794 km, 10 times longer than that of Suez Canal and more than 20 times the length of Panama Canal. Till now, it has had a history of over 2,500 years starting from the digging of Hangou (Fig. 6-29) by Fu Chai, the king of Wu State, the expansion in Sui Dynasty to the perfection during Yuan and Ming Dynasties. Therefore, among the canals in the world, the Grand Canal is second to none in terms of its length and long history.

The earliest section of the Grand Canal was excavated by the State of Wu in the 34th year of King Jing of Zhou Dynasty (486 B. C.). After defeating the State of Yue in 494 B. C., Fu Chai, king of Wu State, wanted to lead his army northward to the Central Plains to fight with Qi and Jin States for hegemony. But at that time, there was no connection between the Yangtze River and the Huaihe River. In order to go northward, Wu's navy had to detour to the sea from the Yangtze River and then went to the Huaihe River from the sea. This way not only prolonged the voyage but also bring more difficulties to the journey. Therefore, in 486 B. C., before the official attack, Fu Chai recruited soldiers and civilians, and built Hancheng near Yangzhou, Jiangsu Province, and then dug Hangou (Fig. 6-30). It was designed to introduce water from the Yangtze River near Guazhou, Yizheng, Jiangsu Province, and then diverted water northward. After passing through Sheyang Lake, the canal reached Huai'an in the north and flowed into the Huaihe River from Mukou, thus building a connection between two major rivers, and laying a foundation for the shipping on the Grand Canal.

Figure 6-29　Scenery of Water Splitting Dam

Figure 6-30　The Relic of Hangou

After the establishment of the Sui Dynasty, Emperor Wen ordered the opening of Guangqu from Chang'an to Tongguan and Shanyangdu from Yangzhou to Huai'an in 587, which was actually a comprehensive renovation and dredging to the old Hangou canal. This laid the foundation for the establishment of the canal network. During the reign of Emperor Yang, in 605, the government recruited more than one million labors and opened Tongji Canal in order to connect Luoyang with Jiangdu (now Yangzhou). Tongji Canal started from Bianhe River and connected with Hangou through Huaihe River. In this way, ships can reach Jiangdu directly from Luoyang. Besides, to strengthen the defense of the northern border, Emperor Yang ordered to guard Zhuojun as an important military fort. In the fourth year of Daye (in 608), he recruited more than one million people from Hebei to open Yongji Canal, which diverted water from Qinshui river in the south to the Yellow River, arrived at Tianjin in the north, and then turned northwest to Zhuojun (now south of Beijing). In the sixth year of Daye (in 610), Emperor Yang again put a great amount of labor forces in building the canal in South China on the basis of the existing canals in Dongwu of the Three Kingdoms. The canal starts from Jingkou (now Zhenjiang City) to Yuhang (now Hangzhou City), connecting the Yangtze River and Qiantang River.

After choosing Dadu (now Beijing) as the capital of the Yuan Dynasty, the political centre of China was transferred here, and the canals dug in the Sui Dynasty were not applicable anymore. Guo Shoujing, a famous water conservancy expert in the Yuan Dynasty, proposed a plan accordingly to reform the Grand Canal to shorten the traffic distance between Dadu and Southeast China, which in turn could facilitate the transport of the grain and materials from South China to Dada. According to this plan, the canal of Jizhou River, Huitong River and Tonghui River were built. The Beijing-Hangzhou Grand Canal was officially completed, and the once fan shaped canal was charged into a straight-line transport route without the need to detour to Luoyang and take a big turn to the West (Fig. 6-31). The reconstructed Grand Canal went southward directly from Beijing to Hangzhou, shortening more than 700 km.

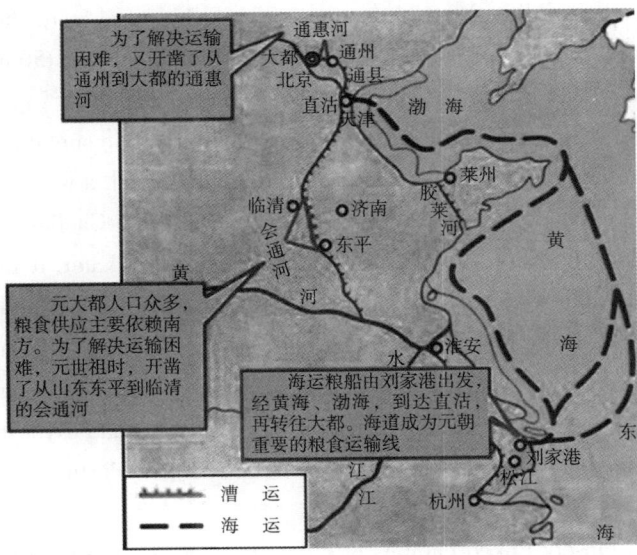

Figure 6-31 The Rebuilding of the Grand Canal in the Yuan Dynasty

The Beijing Hangzhou Grand Canal was excavated and connected by different sections in different dynasties. Each section has its own name: the one from Tianjin to Linqing was called the South Canal; the one from Linqing to Taierzhuang was the Lu Canal; the one from Taierzhuang to Huaiyin was the Central Canal; the one from Huaiyin to Yangzhou was the Li Canal; and the one from Zhenjiang to Hangzhou was the Jiangnan Canal.

Grand Canal was abundant in ancient wisdom in terms of engineering technologies, and Baifu Water Diversion project designed by Guo Shoujing was an excellent example. In 1275, the central government of the Yuan Dynasty began to rebuild the Grand Canal, only to find that there were no ready-made waterways from Dadu to Tongzhou and from Yuhe River to Wenhe River in Shandong Province. To fill in the vacancy in Shandong section, Guo Shoujing was ordered to investigate the main rivers in the southwest of Shandong, such as Sishui River, Wenshui River and Yuhe River, and finished the design accordingly.

However, the problem in Dadu was somewhat tricky. The opening of Huitong River near Dadu could only helped to bring transported goods to Tongzhou, and then road transport had to be used to take goods from Tongzhou to Dadu, which was time consuming and cost ineffective. There were many attempts from the past dynasties to solve the problem, only resulting in a failure due to the topography of being high in the west and low in the west, which led to severe water shortage and high sediment content in the river. After learning from the experience, Guo Shoujing proposed to build a canal from Dadu to Tongzhou. Instead of diverting muddy water from Yongding River, he designed to divert clear water from Baifu Spring in Shenshan Mountain (Fenghuang Mountain today) at the northwest of Dadu. However, the spring water could not be directly introduced south-eastward to Dadu since there were two valley lowlands of Shahe River and Qinghe River between Dadu and Changping hindering on the way. When faced with such a special terrain, in his miraculous design, instead of directly going south-eastward, the canal went the opposite way to go westward to the foot of the Xishan Mountain, and then ran along the 50m contour line to go southward to avoid the valley lowland. Along the way, it intercepted water in the upper reach of the Shahe River and Qinghe River as well as the springs in the two mountains, and then flew into Wengshanpo (now Kunming Lake) in the southeast. Along the canal, a weir was also built with the name of Baifu weir. The canal continued its way south-eastward into Gaoliang River, and arrived at Jishuitan Pool in Dadu City, where it was used as a parking port. Later, it flew eastward through Tongzhou City by the old waterway of Zhahe of Jin Dynasty to meet the Grand Canal in Gaolizhuang at the south of the city. This project not only facilitated goods transportation, but also was helpful in flood prevention in Dadu and irrigation in suburbs. The day when the project was completed was also the day when Kublai Khan, emperor of the Yuan Dynasty, returned to Dadu from Shangdu. He immediately named the canal as "Tonghui River" (the river that is beneficial) (Fig. 6-32).

The Grand Canal closely linked capitals of different dynasties and the richest areas in China, playing an important role in economic development, cultural exchange, and national unity. In addition to promoting economic prosperity, it also fundamentally changed the customs on both sides of the river. According to records in the *Travels of Marco Polo* (Fig. 6-33), in the Yuan Dynasty, it was busy and busting at places near Yindingqiao Bridge and Yandaixiejie Street. There were so many ships parked in Jishuitan that the water surface has been covered. Prosperity on both sides of

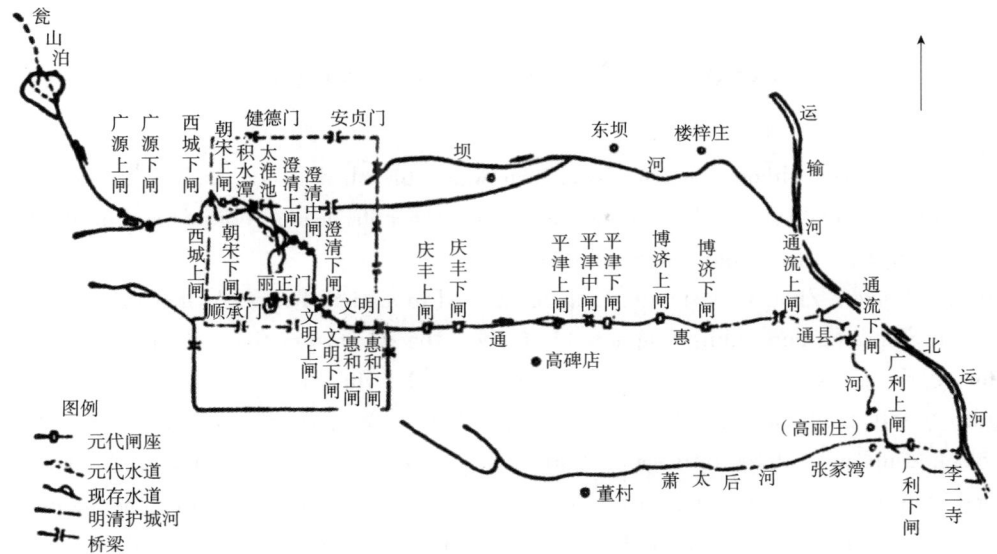

Figure 6-32　Drawing on Position of the Gate of Tonghui River

the Grand Canal together with its beautiful scenery have attracted many visitors, including many famous poets (Fig. 6-34), who have left behind a large number of poems paying great tribute to the Grand Canal. For example, after making a tour to the Canal, the Emperor Qianlong of the Qing Dynasty showed his admiration by saying "Goods transported to the capital from afar via the Grand Canal, bathed in warm spring, I ride a horse wandering on the dike with unparalleled joy."

Figure 6-33　Marco Polo

Figure 6-34　The Picture of the Prosperous Suzhou

177

Section III Embankment Projects

In ancient times, although people lived near water, they had to live high to avoid the flood. Later, with the population growth and land development, people began to build small-scale dikes to resist floods, which is the original form of dikes.

In the Western Zhou Dynasty, dike was mentioned in ancient books. At that time, there was a story about Shaogong persuading Emperor Li of Zhou Dynasty to practice enlightened government by allowing the grass roots to express their opinions freely. He said that "If the grass roots were forbidden to talk freely, it would be like to build a dike in the river to prevent flood. If the river were blocked up and collapsed, it would hurt more people." This famous saying, which was later included in *National Languages*, sent a warning signal to feudal rulers of many generations.

During the Spring and Autumn Period as well as the Warring States Period, all the vassal states built dikes in the Yellow River and Huaihe River Basins. It is said that during the reign of Qi Huangong (Duke Huan of Qi), the most powerful one of the five tyrants in the Spring and Autumn Period, the State of Chu invaded the States of Song and Zheng, and built dams on the Sui River, causing flood to the upper reaches. As the overlord, Qi Huangong sent troops to intervene, demolished the barrage, and coerced the State of Chu to sign a peace treaty, in which there was a clause meaning that it was not allowed to build dikes that would harm other countries.

Since the emergence, dikes have been built continuously in the past dynasties with growing scales, which almost covered all the main river systems in the nation. The embankment systems in the nation gradually came into being including the Yellow River Embankment (Fig. 6-35), the Yangtze River Embankment, the Huaihe River Embankment and the Yongdinghe River Embankment, etc.

Figure 6-35 Bird View of the Yellow River Embankment

1. The Yellow River Embankment

Among the major river embankments projects, those along the Yellow River were the earliest and the most complete ones with the largest scale.

The lower Yellow River Plain covers an area of about 250,000 km^2. This vast plain was formed by the sedimentation of the Yellow River, so it is categorized as alluvial plain. The Yellow River is rich in sediment, so its riverbed is silted up. Once there is flood, it could be tens of meters higher than the fields on both sides. In this case, the channel of the Yellow River has become a watershed between the north and the south. To the east of Zhengzhou, there are no other tributaries flowing into the Yellow River except rivers in Dongping and Pingyin mountains. The water to the north of the Yellow River flows into the sea through rivers such as Weihe River and Tuhai River. The water to the south of the Yellow River flows into the sea through rivers such as Yinghe River, Woshui River and Sishui River. The special terrain indicates that once the Yellow River bursts, there will be a risk of diversion. The breach in the north may cause the water to invade the Weihe River to arrive at the sea in Tianjin, and the breach in the south may cause the water to seize the channel of the Huaihe River to flow into the Yangtze River. In the past 3,000 years, the Yellow River has burst more than 1,500 times, and changed its route on a large scale 26 times, five of which were the greatest, posing serious threats to the people in the lower plain.

In this case, starting from the day Gun, the father of Dayu, began to use the way of blockage to control floods, the embankment system of the Yellow River has been continuously improved in the process of harnessing the Yellow River. The embankment system was quite unreasonable during the Spring and Autumn Period as well as the Warring States Period because different vassal states acted in their own ways. However, it still laid the foundation for the dike system of the lower reach of the Yellow River. After the unification of China, Qin Shihuang (the founding emperor of the Qin Dynasty) began to adjust the unreasonable dikes. In the Han Dynasty, dike projects were further strengthened, and stones were used in building dikes at many river sections, which was so solid that they were called as "golden dike". Especially during the reign of Emperor Wu of Han Dynasty, the Yellow River burst in Huzi (now southwest of Puyang, Henan). To block the breach, Emperor Wu of the Han Dynasty came to the site to lead the project in person. He sank white horse and jade to show his determination. Finally, under the joint efforts of the government and the people, the flood was brought under control. In order to commemorate the success, Emperor Wu (Fig. 6-36) wrote two poems of *Huzi* to express his excitement. Deeply touched by the magnificent scene and Emperor's poems, Sima Qian sighed in *Shiji* (Historical Records) that "Water control is significant in influencing people's lives."

In the Song Dynasty, efforts have been transferred from large-scale construction to dike reinforcement, thus technologies on breach blockage have become mature. Almost all kinds of technologies in this regard have come into being. Technologies like Saogong (a way of water conservancy technology by using wooden material and earth in different layers) have become very developed. In the early Ming Dynasty, after moving the capital to Beijing, Ming government reopened the Grand Canal to facilitate grain transportation from south to north. Xuzhou-Huai'an section of the canal borrowed the channel of Sishui River that was occupied by the Yellow River. To safeguard the smooth transport of the Grand Canal, the policy of "Harness the Yellow River to safeguard transport of the Grand Canal" was formed at this time. In the fourth year of Emperor Hongzhi (in 1491), Liu Daxia, a high-ranking official, formulated and implemented the Yellow River control strategy of "Building Dikes on the Northern Bank Only". He built a 360 km-long dike from Zuocheng to Xuzhou at the north of the Yellow River. After the formation of the northern embankment, it prevented the river from flooding the north and ensured the smooth flow of the canal. However, floods to the south bank of the river were left unchecked, which had brought many water disasters to this area and the increase of southward branches to the lower reach of the Yellow River.

Figure 6-36　Emperor Wu of the Han Dynasty

Later, Pan Jixun (Fig. 6-37), a famous river governing expert, led the river controlling projects four times. During this period, based on predecessors' thoughts and river management experience, he summarized a general strategy of "harnessing water to flush sand" when managing the Yellow River. That is to say, water in the river was first kept by using the dike, and then released to scour the riverbed in order to increase the storage capacity, therefore achieving the purpose of flood control and transportation safeguarding. The key to this strategy lied in the building of dikes. Pan Jixun proposed and practiced the idea of "double dikes" (Fig. 6-38). He designed and built a set of prevention system on both sides of the Yellow River, which is composed of remote dikes, low dikes, lattice dikes, moon-typed dikes, and reducing dams on the remote dikes.

During the reign of Emperor Kangxi in Qing Dynasty, Jin Fu became the governor of the Yellow River. Facing the unfavorable situation of "the Huaihe River collapsed in the east, the Yellow River burst in the north, and the transportation dried up in the middle", Jin Fu followed Pan Jixun's strategy of comprehensively managing the Yellow River, Huaihe River, and transportation. In order to practice the strategy of "harnessing water to flush sand", he built an intake channel on both sides of the River from Huai'an to Haikou. The dike building area was wider than that of Pan Jixun. In addition to repairing the old dikes, he also added dikes to river sections where no embankments were built before.

Figure 6-37 Pan Jixun

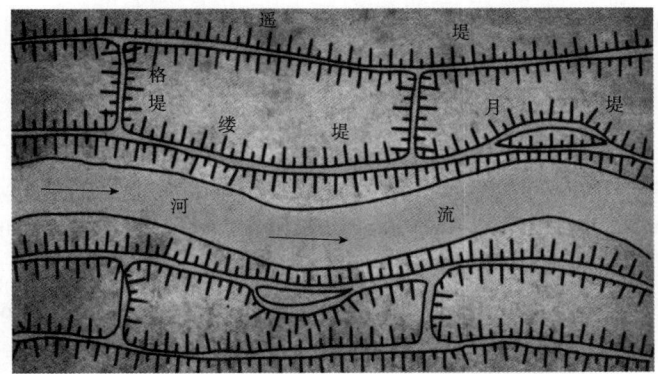

Figure 6-38 Schematic Diagram of Double Dikes

During the reign of Emperor Daoguang in Qing Dynasty, a section of the embankments was named after a person, Lin Zexu, a national hero in Qing Dynasty. That is the Lingong Dike located in Kaifeng, a commemoration to his contribution in harnessing the Yellow River. After being removed from his position due to his destroying of opium in Humen, Lin Zexu was demoted to Yili in Xinjiang. On the way, a piece of news came declaring that the Yellow River burst in Zhangjiawan, Kaifeng. Due to the recommendation of ministers of the central court, Emperor Daoguang ordered Lin Zexu to go to Kaifeng to help control the flood, since Lin was also a great water control expert.

When Lin Zexu arrived at Kaifeng after traveling day and night, Kaifeng City had been besieged by floods for more than two months. The flood broke through the city protection dike and rolled into the city. Serious flood together with several days of heavy rain have left people in the city in a terrible situation. Without dry clothes and enough food, people could do nothing but cry. Touched by this sad scene, Lin Zexu determined to save Kaifeng City at all costs. After great efforts of tens of thousands of laborers for more than five months, the Yellow River was finally forced to its old channel. Kaifeng City, which has been besieged by floods for eight months, has been preserved. Finally, Emperor Daoguang still insisted that Lin Zexu go to Yili without delay. After he left, people in Kaifeng did not forget his achievements, so the dike built by Lin Zexu was affectionately called "Lingong Dike".

For thousands of years, a lot of folk culture has been formed related with the Yellow River Embankments, among which one of the most representative music forms is the famous Yellow River Haozi chant. It belongs to the labor chant, a kind of sound with certain rhythm and fluctuation gradually formed by the Han nationality ancestors in their fighting together against the flood. Different labor divisions in harnessing the Yellow River brought about different kinds of Haozi such as rescue Haozi, ramming Haozi and boatman Haozi. Those Haozi chants have great charm, which also played an important role in the history of Chinese modern music. For example, in the famous Yellow River Cantata, composed during the Anti-Japanese War period and inspiring millions of Chinese people during that difficult time, the first chapter, the Yellow River Boatman's song, was in the form of boatman Haozi. Now Yellow River Haozi Chant has been listed as a national intangible cultural heritage, which will be well protected and inherited.

2. Jingjiang Embankment

In China, Yellow River Embankments in the north and Yangtze River Embankments in the south are equally important. An old saying goes like this "Among the 10 thousand-km long Yangtze River, the most dangerous section lies in Jingjiang River" (Fig. 6-39). In this case, Jingjiang Embankment (Fig. 6-40) tops the most dangerous and representative section on the north bank of the middle reach of the Yangtze River, known as the "Great Wall on Water".

Jingjiang, another name for the section on the middle reach of the Yangtze River starting from Zhicheng, Hubei Province to Chenglingji, Yueyang City, Hunan Province. A place called Ouchikou divides this Section into two parts: upper Jingjiang River and lower Jingjiang River. Rich sediment deposition and the great number of branches have caused the Jingjiang River to wind its way into a complicated curve, both sides of which are low-lying, leading to frequent floods in the past dynasties. In the past, Jingjiang River was relatively spacious, with sandbanks scattered in the river, branches mature in development, and relatively stable riverbed. There were many outfalls distributing water on both sides of the river. In *Shuijingzhu*, a famous book on ancient Chinese geography written by Li Daoyuan, it was recorded that there were more than 20 water diversion outfalls. According to the record in the Inscription of Reopening Ancient outfalls "there were nine

Chapter Six Water and Water Conservancy Projects

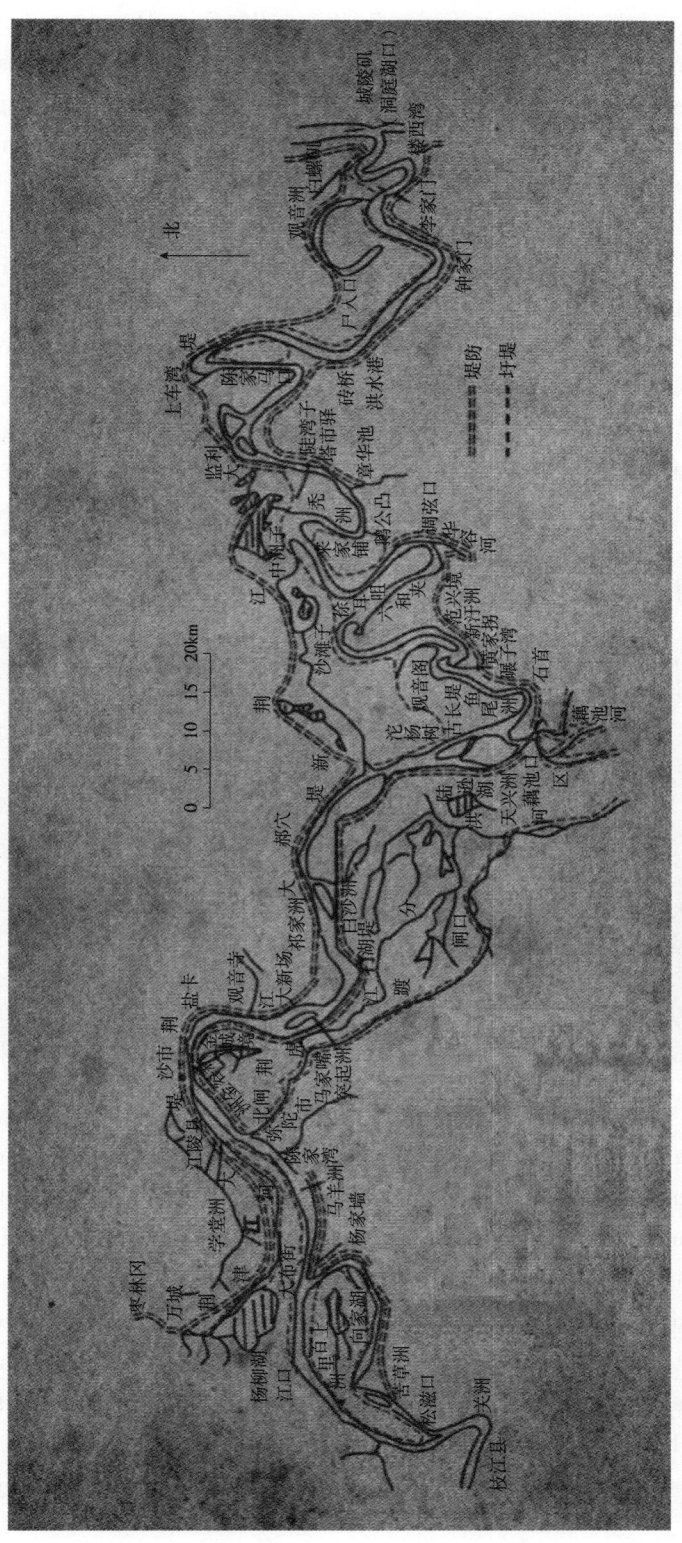

Figure 6-39 Water Conservancy Projects on Jingjiang River

outfalls and thirteen mouths in ancient times. " "Before the Song Dynasty, all the outfalls were unblocked, so there was little water trouble in the river. " In the early Yuan Dynasty, the mouth of the outfall had been basically silted up, therefore the flood in Jingjiang area became increasingly frequent. In the Yuan Dynasty, six of them were excavated again, but they were gradually blocked by the end of the Yuan Dynasty. In the early Ming Dynasty, Haoxue outfalls in Jiangling County and Diaoyuan outfall in Shishou County were reopened; during the reign of the Emperor Jiajing in Ming Dynasty, Haoxue outfall was blocked again. During the reign of Emperor Longqing (1567 – 1572), there were only two outfalls distributing water southward in Jingjiang left behind: Hudu and Diaoxian. In Qing Dynasty, frequent floods occurred to Jingjiang River, and several diversion holes were formed on the south bank. In the twelfth year of Emperor Tongzhi(in 1873), four diversion holes of Ouchi, Songzi, Taiping (Hudu) and Diaoxian were formed. However, instead of being helpful in flood control, this situation further deteriorated the crisis, especially on the north bank of Jingjiang River, since what lied on its north bank were rich Jianghan Plain and some large and medium-sized cities such as Wuhan and Jingzhou. Once flood occurred, there would be heavy losses to those places.

Figure 6-40　A Bird-view of Jingjiang Embankment

　　In fact, Jingjiang Embankment refers to the one on the north bank of Jingjiang River ranging from Zaolin'gang, Jiangling County (Fig. 6 – 41) to the south of Jianli City, Jianli County, Hubei Province. Its total length is 182. 35 km, with the vertical height of 14–16 m, and the water level of Jingjiang River is more than 10 m above the ground outside the embankment during flood period, posing great threat to its surrounding areas. Jingjiang Embankment is a great barrier protecting more than 500, 000 hectares of cultivated land and tens of millions of people in Jianghan Plain and some big cities such as Wuhan and Jingzhou. As the most important and the most dangerous section of the Yangtze River Embankments, Jingjing Embankment, historically known as "embankment with missions", has always been the focus of flood control of the Yangtze River by government at different levels.

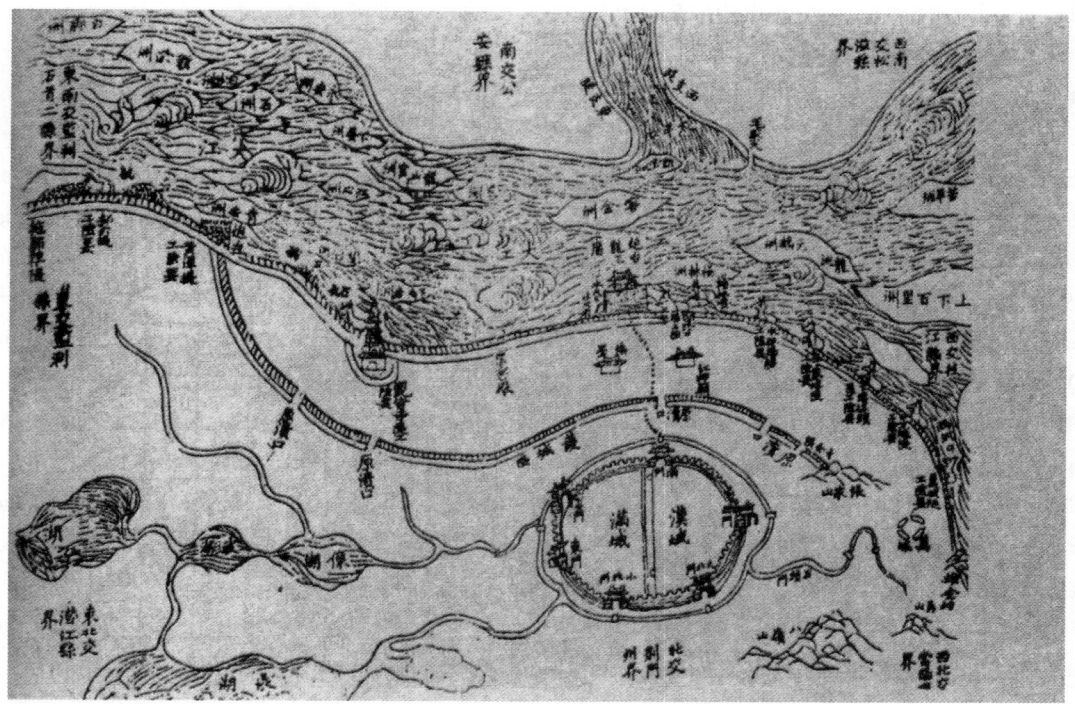

Figure 6-41 Jiangling Section of the Jingjiang Embankment (in Annals of Jiangling County during the Reign of Emperor Guangxu in Qing Dynasty)

Jingjiang Embankment, originally known as Jindi Embankment, was built in 345, the first year of Yonghe in the Eastern Jin Dynasty, by Chen Zun under the command of Huan Wen, the governor of Jingzhou. During the Kaiping period of the late Liang Dynasty (907-911), the Cunjin dike of Jiangling was built at the downstream of the Jindi Embankment built in the Eastern Jin Dynasty; in the Northern Song Dynasty, Zheng Xie, the governor of Jingzhou, presided over the construction of Shashi dike; in the Southern Song Dynasty, Huangtan dike was built and Cunjin dike was added. After the expansion and reinforcement of the Song Dynasty, the Jingjiang Embankment has basically taken shape. In the 21st year of Emperor Jiajing of Ming Dynasty (in 1542), the north bank of Jingjiang River and Haoxue water diversion cave were blocked, so the 124 km-long dike from Duijintai to Maobu was connected, which was called "Wancheng Dike" in history and later "the Great Wancheng Dike". During the reign of Emperor Qianlong and Daoguang of the Qing Dynasty, Cunjin dike was prolonged to connect with the Shashi dike. In 1918, the Great Wancheng Dike was renamed "the Jingjiang Embankment".

Although had basically taken shape in the middle of the Northern Song Dynasty, the Jingjiang Embankment suffered great damage at the turn of the Northern and Southern Song Dynasty. Starting from the Southern Song Dynasty, great efforts have been made on its maintenance and reinforcement. Lu You, a great patriotic poet in the Southern Song Dynasty, once passed by Jingjiang area at the turn of summer and autumn in the sixth year of Emperor Qiandao (in 1170).

He recorded what he saw in the book of *the Travel to Shu* (Sichuan Province now) by saying that "many sections of the Jingjiang Embankment have been damaged, and repaired work has never stopped for years."

After Yuan Dynasty, Jingjiang Embankment became vulnerable. Due to its thin structure and the frequent breaches in the history, the flood occurred frequently in Jianghan Plain, posing a threat to the safety of Wuhan and Jingzhou as well as the transportation on the Yangtze River. According to statistics, during the 390 years from 1559 (the 38th year of Emperor Jiajing of Ming Dynasty) to 1949, Jingjiang Embankment had burst 36 times, especially in 1788, 1931 and 1935. The tough problems forced the rulers to frequently organize the overhaul to the Embankment. In Ming Dynasty, continuous construction and repair projects had been done to Jindi, Lijiabu, Cunjin, Shashi, Huangtan, Wencun, Xinkai and Zhougong dikes. In 1542 (the 21st year of Emperor Jiajing), after the Embankment was connected into a whole, the flood washed it away many times. The government had to organize forces to overhaul it and formulated the "Embankment Law" in the first year of Emperor Longqing, employing dedicated laborers to engage in dike maintenance, namely, 7,300 people on the north bank and 3,850 ones on the south bank.

In 1788 (the 53rd year of Emperor Qianlong in Qing Dynasty), the flood broke the embankment, drowning 36 counties in Hubei Province. About 6-meter-deep water in Jiangling City have killed more than 1,700 people and left 40,000 houses collapsed. In addition, the flood rushed downstream to Wuchang and changed the city into a hell with countless dead bodies floating. The water was over 6 meters deep and didn't ebb until February the next year. People in Hanyang must go to the city by boats. The severe flood shocked the imperial court so much that Emperor Qianlong appropriated 2 million kg silver from the state treasury and transferred many officials to perform the comprehensive maintenance and reinforcement in accordance with the trace of the former Wancheng Embankment. He also set up stone ruler as the mark of the water level and left records stipulating the guarantee period of the embankment. He also changed the management system of the embankment, upgrading it from civil one to the state one under the control of the state government. Two years later, he ordered to repair the 1,000 km long embankment and build the east and west dikes in Fengcheng. In the 4th year of Emperor Daoguang (in 1824), all the projects below Hengtang of Wancheng Embankment in Jingzhou were also repaired. Therefore, after the middle of Qing Dynasty, Jingjiang Embankment became more and more solid. In July 1935, the flood raised the highest water level in Shashi to 43.97 m, and broke Jingjiang embankment at Mabuchang at the east of Desheng. Although it was not a dangerous section, there were still tens of thousands of casualties. Therefore, the governments of all dynasties laid great emphasis on maintenance and protection of the Jingjiang Embankment, and took it as a key project for flood control of the Yangtze River (Fig. 6-42).

Since the construction of Jingjiang Embankment went into operation, it has started the history of fighting against the flood of the Yangtze River. One of the most brilliant pages occurred in 1998 (Fig. 6-43). At that year, a once-in-a-hundred-year flood occurred in the Yangtze River. The

Chapter Six   Water and Water Conservancy Projects

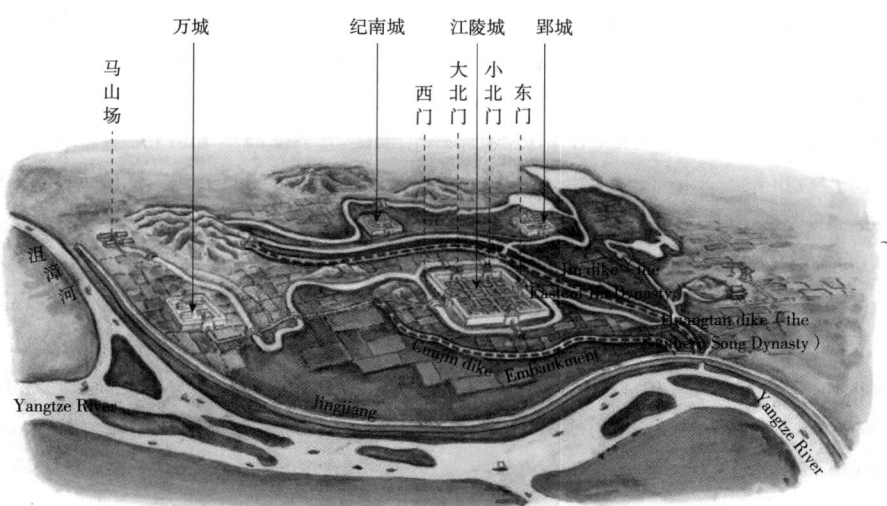

Figure 6-42   Construction of Jingjiang Embankment in Past Dynasties

highest flood level of Jingjiang hit 45 m, more than ten meters higher than the ground elevation of Jingzhou. To fight against floods and rescue the affected people, Chinese Central Military Commission had deployed 320,000 officers and soldiers into the campaign, which is the largest scale of military build-up after the year of 1949. Hundreds of thousands of officers and soldiers fought on the front line of flood fighting, and many touching stories were remembered by Chinese people.

Figure 6-43   Fights against the Flood in 1998

Due to the frequent floods near the Jingjiang Embankment for thousands of years, a series of worship culture has been gradually formed for people to prey for safety. The third of March of the lunar calendar is the legend birthday of the Dragon King, which is a great event for people living by the Jingjiang River. Because at this time of the year, people will give sacrifices to the Dragon King and pray for good weather. In the sacrificial activities, people will invite a Taoist to read the sacrificial texts, bow three times to the Yangtze River, then light and throw the texts into the river. The people around him will quickly put the prepared eels and loaches into the river to release them free, and some people would throw their Children's clothes into the river. Why is that? In fact, these clothes are ones no longer worn by children. The reason for this behavior is to tell Dragon King that those clothes are substitutes of their children. In this case, it is believed that children would be protected by the Dragon King and would not encounter any accidents when they play by the river.

In the years of frequent disasters, people could do nothing but to pray for the gods to lock the river and subdue the flood. Till now, there are still several iron cattle with special poses on the Jingjiang Embankment, which are the famous River Subduing Iron Cattle. In the 53rd year of Emperor Qianlong (in 1788), Jingzhou was flooded. After the ebb of the flood, Emperor Qianlong ordered to cast nine cattle. The reason why iron cattle was selected could be found in the *Records of Jingzhou Wan Cheng Dike*, "in November of the 53rd year of Emperor Qianlong, the emperor said "it has been a tradition for many years to put iron cattle on the dangerous and important areas along the river. According to Chinese philosophy, dragon is afraid of iron, and cattle have the feature of earth, which can stop water. In this case, iron cattle are needed to put on the embankment to subdue floods. " Therefore, Bi Yuan, the governor of Hubei and Hunan Provinces, cast 9 iron cattle according to the command of the emperor, which were located on 9 important sections of embankment including Wancheng, Zhongfangcheng, Shangyubudou, Lijiabu, Zhongduyang, Yanglinji, Yulukou, Heiyaochang and Guanyinji. However, those 9 iron cattle do not exist anymore. In the 25th year of Daoguang (in 1845), another cast iron cow was placed on the Lijiabu Dike. In the 9th year of Xianfeng (in 1859), Tang Jisheng, the governor of Jingzhou, made another iron cow and placed it on Haoxue cave in Jiangling. Till now, those two iron cattle still exist and become famous (Fig. 6-44).

Haoxue Iron Cow was also known as Zhen'an Temple Iron Cow, because the place it was located was originally named as Zhen'an Temple Bay. It was cast by Tang Jisheng, the governor of Jingzhou. Being shaped as an unicorn, the cow stands on the front legs and crouches on its hind legs. It perched on the embankment, overlooking the Yangtze River. It is 3 m long and 1.8 m tall, being solid outside and empty inside, with the weight of about 2 t. There are 126 characters on the back of cow (Fig. 6-45), which means "it is of high virtue, so it can protect the river from damages of violent waves and floods. It can protect and benefit people for thousands of generations. "

At the foot of the west wall outside the South Gate of Jingzhou, there is a 35 m long and 22 m wide mound, which is called "Xirang Soil" by local people. There are four stone pillars on it as protection marks. Legend had it that the mound was the place where Dayu buried his flood control tools. At that time, Dayu brought water from the upper reaches of the Yangtze River to Jianghan,

Chapter Six Water and Water Conservancy Projects

Figure 6-44　Haoxue Iron Cow

Figure 6-45　Inscriptions on the Cow Back

diverting water into the river and finally into the sea, and therefore turning the vast ocean of Jianghan into a fertile oasis. When he came to Jingzhou, he found that there was a water hole pouring water out without stop. This water hole was connected with the Yangtze River. If the holes were not blocked in time, the fertile farmland oasis in Jianghan would become a vast ocean again, and his success in flood control would be changed into a failure, so Dayu resolutely put his water control tools into the cave, sealing the hole tightly, and then the water stopped.

In *Shanhaijing*, an ancient Chinese book recording many fairy tales in ancient times, there was a record that "Yu stopped the flood with Xirang Soil". The records of Xirang in *Yutang Xianhua*, a book in Song Dynasty, were more detailed. It said that "outside the South Gate of Jiangling, under the inner wall of Yongmen, there is a small room, which is about a foot high. When being asked, local people said it was Xirang Soil. After successfully bringing floods under control, Yu found that there was a sea hole pouring water out without stop. Yu then engraved a Stone Dragon Palace and put it in the hole to seal it. Xirang soil means the soil can grow forever." In *Jianghan Congtan* written by Chen Shiyuan of the Ming Dynasty, it is said that "Xi means living, and Xirang Soil means that the soil can grow unceasingly." There was a legend during the reign of Emperor Kangxi of the Qing Dynasty: "In Jingzhou, when the weather was dry, the local people tried to dig up the Xirang soil. As a result, it rained heavily at that night and has continued for more than 40 days. Heavy rain caused serious flood, and it nearly broke Wancheng embankment and drowned Jingzhou."

3. Qiantang River Seawall

Seawalls are also known as sea embankments or sea weirs, distributed in coastal areas of Jiangsu, Shanghai, Zhejiang and Fujian Provinces. They served as important coastal projects to resist tide invasion and therefore preventing coast collapse. Among them, most typical of them is the one in western Zhejiang Province.

Qiantang River, with the length of 668 km, arrived at the East Sea from Hangzhou Bay (Fig. 6-46). The trumpet shaped bay together with tidal phenomena created the famous surging tide to Qiantang River. The past thousands of years have witnessed local people's great efforts on the construction of seawalls on both sides of the estuary, which has become a famous man-made wonder in China. Qianjiang tide and the ancient Qiantangjiang Seawall, one world heritage in nature and one in human culture, have long enjoyed a great reputation, among which the ancient Qiantangjiang Seawall is an important architectural heritage of water conservancy projects in China. Situated on both sides of the estuary, it has a history of repeated destruction and repeated construction for more than 2,000 years, winding its way along the coast for more than 300 km. Long building history, complicated construction technologies and rich architectural remains have made it equally famous as the Great Wall and the ancient Grand Canal, the greatest ancient projects in China.

The total length of Qiantangjiang Seawalls on both sides of Qiantang River is 306 km, of which more than half are made of stone, and the others are made of earth. Among stone seawalls, there are different types including large fish scale typed stone dam, big stone dam, fish scale typed dam with 5 vertical and 5 horizontal stone slabs and concrete dam in modern times. The length of the stone seawall is the longest in China, and its types are also the most varied in China.

Qiantangjiang Seawall has a long history. It had been built in different dynasties, and the

Figure 6-46 Qiantang River and Hangzhou Bay

large-scale construction and mainlenance happened in the Ming and Qing Dynasties. However, there were few records on its construction before Tang Dynasty, and its specifications were even less recorded. Therefore, the construction of the seawalls before the Tang Dynasty can only be regarded as the initial stage, and a systematic history only started after the Five Dynasties.

There is no historical record on when the construction of Qiantangjiang Seawalls began. There were only legends in the Han and Wei Dynasties. Records about seawall like buildings can be found in the West and East Jin Dynasty. In the Southern and Northern Dynasties, a few scattered trustworthy records appeared, but the earliest one of Qiantang can be found in the records at the foot of Lingyin Mountain in the late Han Dynasty. There was a story in *Shuijingzhu* saying that: "The tide prevention seawall is 500 m away from the east of the county, which was proposed to be built by Huaxin, an official in the county. At the start of the project, the one will be paid one thousand copper coins if he can carry 60 kg of soil to the construction site. Within one month, people swarmed to the site. However, the seawall was not completed, and soil carrying people were not paid accordingly, so they abandoned their soil into water. Unexpectedly, a seawall was formed. People then gave it a name "Qiantang", "Tang" means seawall, and "Qian" in Chinese refers to money, which probably means the wages not paid to people in the above-mentioned story.

Although this historical record has been widely cited, the saying that Huaxin proposed to build seawalls has long been refuted as unbelievable. According to *Zhai Junlian's Haitanglu* (Records of Seawalls) in the Qing Dynasty, "in *Shiji* (Historical Records), in the 25th year of the first emperor of Qin Dynasty, Kuaiji county was established as the 26th county. Qiantang already existed at that time. How can it be possible to be built by Huaxin? He also told his friend that: "the Chinese character of the Tang was different from that after Tang Dynasty, and the meaning of it is 'road', which can be proved by the poem in ancient times. In this case, the saying that Qiantang was named by Huaxin was again proved to be wrong."

However, although the story recorded in *Shuijingzhu* cannot show that the seawall originated in the later Han Dynasty, it was very reliable to prove that there was a seawall in Qiantang County before the Six Dynasties. Unfortunately, this story only introduced the beginning of its construction, but failed to provide records on its position and engineering technologies.

In the Sui and Tang Dynasties, there were still very few historical materials about the seawall project. However, some brief records could still show that the coast at that time had basically taken shape, and the seawall project in the coastal area of Jiangsu and Zhejiang Provinces had been gradually completed. Moreover, in the southeast of Haiqiao, embankments were also built to contain water, which guaranteed the agricultural production.

In Sui and Tang Dynasties, records about Hanhaitang Seawall in Yan'guan and Fanghaitang Seawall in Shaoxing appeared. In the book of *Introduction of Seawalls*, it cited one part from *Records on Geography in The Book of the History of Tang Dynasty* saying that "In the 7th year of Wude during the reign of Emperor Gaozong in Tang Dynansty, Yan'guan County was removed and brought under the management of Qiantang County, which was recovered in the 4th year of Zhenguan during the reign of Emperor Taizong in Tang Dynasty. There was a Hanhaitang Seawall in Yan'guan with a length of 72 km, which was rebuilt in the first year of Kaiyuan." *Records of the History of Shaoxing* also cited from *Records on Geography in The Book of the History of Tang Dynasty* saying that "Fanghaitang Seawall started from Shangyu and ended in Shanyin, with a length of nearly 50 km. In the 10th year of Kaiyuan, Li Junzhi was ordered to expand it. In the 6th year of Taihe, Li Zuoci, the head of the county, was order to expand the seawall again." The two historical records proved that seawalls in Zhejiang Province have existed on both sides of the estuary of Qiantang River before the year of Kaiyuan (during the reign of Emperor Xuanzong in Tang Dynasty), and it was rebuilt in the year of Kaiyuan.

Detailed records on engineering technologies and specifications were absent in Tang Dynasty. However, it can be inferred from the technical level at that time that Qiantangjiang Seawall could only passively prevent the invasion of tides. It was only a line of seawall made of earth which cannot be counted on to actively protect the coast from tide erosion. In this case, faced with problems when sea water eroded the coast, local people could do nothing but to refer to the help of gods, which is why Bai Juyi, a famous poet in Tang Dynasty, wrote a piece of writing praying to God for blessings in Qiantang River when he was the governor of Hangzhou.

However, both sides of the Qiantang River were vulnerable to sea erosion. Once extremely disastrous weather occurred to the sea, tens-of-kilometres wide lands would collapse into the river in a few months. The passive way of tide prevention cannot protect the lands on both sides of the estuary from the sea threat. Therefore, starting from Qian Liu (Fig. 6-47), King of Wuyue State during the Five Dynasties (a period with 5 dynasties and 10 states in China after Tang Dynansty), an idea of actively preventing land collapse began to dominate the maintenance and the construction of Qiantang Seawalls.

According to the *Records of the History of Lin'an in the Year of Xianchun of Emperor Duzong in Song Dynasty*, Hangzhou was appointed as the capital of Wuyue State in the Five Dynasties, but there were many tide troubles in the city. In this case, in August of the 4th year of Kaiping in Liang Dynasty, Qian Liu, the king of the state, ordered to build Hanhaitang Seawall outside of Houchao Gate and Tongjiang Gate. However, the surging tides easily wash away the rammed earth, seriously hindering the progress of the project. The king then ordered to prepare many strong bows to shoot the head of tides. He also ordered to plant big wood and to wave bamboo network and put big stones in to replace the rammed earth. In this case, the

Figure 6-47　Qian Liu

seawall was finished and later became the place where the busy city streets were situated. The flat land today was the river in the past.

It can be seen from the records that Hanhaitang Seawall built by Qian Liu was the start to build seawalls in the suburb of Hangzhou, marking the transfer from passive defence against tides to active collapse prevention. At the beginning, rammed earth was used, but it turned out be a failure due to the loss sand contained in soil excavated in places near the river. After that, people must turn to some superstitious methods such as offering sacrifices to the God of the river and shooting the head of tides.

The legend about King Qian's shooting tide has been widely spread. According to Yang Rong's *Brief Introductions to Seawalls*, "King Qian Liu shot tide to force it to retreat, then the seawall was completed. The iron arrow was as big as a pestle, which was first unearthed in Xinqiao. It was so big that people can only shake it but cannot manage to pull it out." It is of course impossible to pull out an arrow as big as a pestle. The significance of burying it outside of the bank of the construction site is to subdue tides to protect the base of seawall from being washed away by surging tides.

Qian Liu also invented the way of waving bamboo network to hold stones to replace rammed earth. This way added the weight of seawalls, therefore providing better protection against tides. In addition, the way of planting big wood pillars was also applied to alleviate the scour at the foot of the seawall to avoid its collapse.

There were records on the big wood pillars planted in front of the seawalls in *Mengxi Bitan*, written by Shen Kuo in Northern Song Dynasty. It said that "There were stone embankment along Qiantang River, and tens of rows of wood pillars planted outside of the embankment with the name of Huangzhu. During the year of Baoyuan and Kangding of Emperor Renzong in Song Dynasty, some people proposed to take the pillar to get the wood. The general in Hangzhou agreed and ordered to pull the pillars out of water, only to find that all the wood have been rotten and useless. However, the absence of wood pillars led to frequent floods later, since the striking and erosion of tides on seawalls have been increased."

Qian Liu's method of building seawalls with bamboo cage and wood pillars were inventions to the construction technology(Fig. 6-48). The bamboo cage was tens of meters long, and the wood pillar was several meters high. Many bamboo cages with big stones in it were piled together to build into seawalls, and long and thick pillars were planted deeply into the beach, indicating that the construction technology had reached a high level at that time. The former method was still used in later generations, and the latter one was abandoned due to the easy decay of wood pillars.

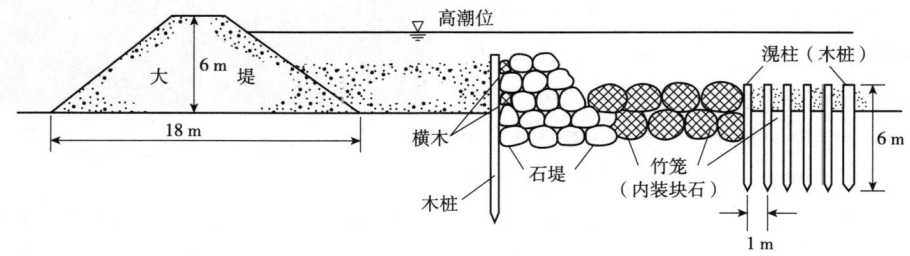

Figure 6-48　Drawing of Seawall Built with Bamboo Cages

During the Northern Song Dynasty, the focus in seawall building was still laid in Hangzhou, and its important project was the stone dike along the main river in Hangzhou. The most creative technology was the application of Saogong (a kind of water conservancy technology by using firewood and earth in different layers) and the replacement of bamboo cages with firewood and earth. In the early years of Song Dynasty, bamboo cages filled with stones were still popular in seawall maintenance. During the years of Dazhongxiangfu (during the reign of Zhenzong Emperor of Song Dynasty), Chen Yaozuo (Fig. 6-49), the governing official in Zhejiang, began to adopt firewood and earth as building material in seawall protecting projects. This was recorded in *Dongdushilve* (A Record of History in Eastern Capital), which said that bamboo cages filled with stones were easily damaged by tides in Qiantang River, hence overhaul would be needed every several years. Chen Yaozuo proposed to replace the old method with firewood and earth, which was firstly questioned, and then proved to be efficient in the projects.

Figure 6-49　Chen Yaozuo

Chen Yaozuo's method was not accepted at that

time, but it was later proved to be more effective than sand for the purpose of emergency rescue, and more convenient than piling of stones in bamboo cages. Compared with King Qian's construction method, it saved a great amount of huge wood and stones, so later generations applied this method to build Chaitang Seawall in appropriate places.

In the Ming Dynasty, focus in building seawall was laid in Haiyan. Starting from the years of Hongwu (during the reign of Taizu Emperor in Ming Dynasty), seawalls were gradually built in other places, so that in the Ming Dynasty, coast in Haiyan and Pinghu were basically built with stone seawalls. According to records in *A Brief Introduction to Seawalls*, during 276 years of Ming Dynasty, there were 21 times of seawall building in Hanyan and Pinghu County, among which large-scale projects happened at the 3rd year of Hongwu, the 13th year of Chenghua, the 14th year of Jiajing, the 3rd year and the 16th year of Wanli period.

In Ming Dynasty, seawall projects in Haiyan were not only large in scale, heavy in investment, but innovative in construction technologies, among which important creations included Yangtang seawall invented by Wang Xi, Potuotang seawall (Fig. 6 – 50) by Yangxuan and five-vertical-and-

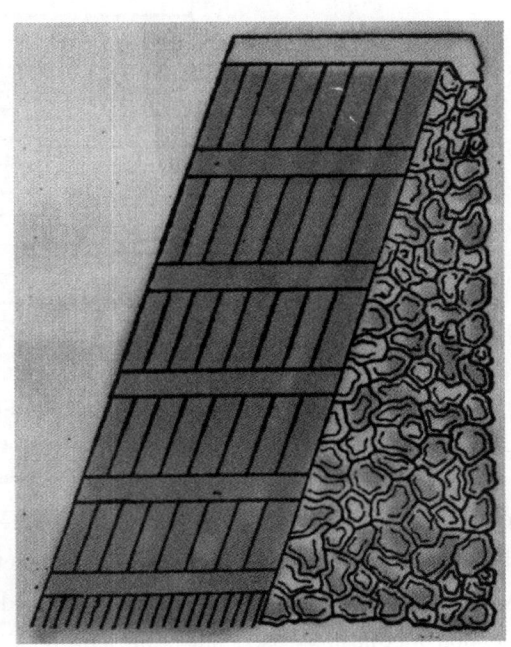

Figure 6-50　Potuotang Seawall

five-horizontal scale-typed seawall (Fig. 6-51) by Huang Guangsheng.

In the Ming Dynasty, there were many improvements in seawall construction methods, from Hongwu's outer-vertical-and-inner-horizontal seawall to Huang Guangsheng's five-vertical-and-five-horizontal scale-typed seawall. Starting from then, considerations were given to factors including not only the local soil quality but also the local tidal potential when building seawall projects. In this way, different construction methods can be flexibly selected according to different locations and conditions.

In the Qing Dynasty, great number of construction experiences have been accumulated since the vertical-and-horizontal-stacking stone seawall were built in Haiyan in Ming Dynasty, which has laid good foundations to build large-scale stone seawall along the coast of Haining. However, the projects of scaled-typed seawalls in Haining and Renhe were not started until the 59th year of Emperor Kangxin (in 1720).

Seawall construction personnel in Qing Dynasty were left with the most difficult section to build. Accordingly, measures they adopted should be the most solid one. Based on the experience from Ming Dynasty, they were also very innovative in creating many new engineering methods. They not only emphasized waterproof construction but also attached importance to reform flow potential of

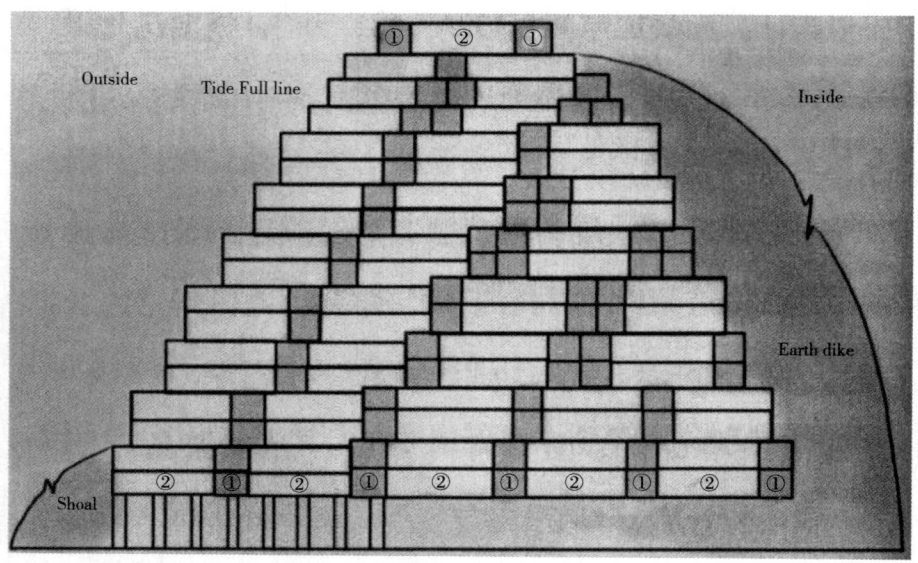

Figure 6-51 Five-vertical-and-five-horizontal Scale-typed Seawall
①Horizontal: The stones were placed horizontally.
②Vertical: The stones were placed vertically.

the water flow or even the river lines. New technologies appeared in this period including the solidest scale-typed seawalls, protective projects at the food of seawalls, stone dams of water diversion, and the sand cutting project of river diversion. Although the sand cutting project of river diversion was no long used later, the data obtained through the small and medium sized gateways were still very valuable.

In the Qing Dynasty, scale-typed stone seawall dominated in section from Haining to Renhe. Furthermore, there were also temporary buildings including slope protection seawall made of gravel and earth and seawall made of firewood and earth for the purpose of emergency repair before the completion of main works. There were also temporary repair seawalls in places that were not directly flushed by sea tides. In addition to the main structure of seawalls, there were also some important basic projects such as protective projects at the foot of seawalls to prevent the silt from being directly scoured by the sea tide, and a soil berm built inside seawalls to prevent seawater infiltration. Scale-typed stone seawall was a large-scale and heavy project in China. On each 3-meter-long seawall, 17.5 m^3 of strip stones were used, weighing more than 47 t. On the basis of the method of vertical and horizontal stacking in Ming Dynasty, it absorbed the method of inlaying putty into stone joints and connecting strip stones by using iron curium from water conservancy projects built in the 40th years of Emperor Kangxi, which made small stones connect into big stones and the whole seawall stonework connect into a whole, thus becoming the strongest seawall in China.

The construction of the scale-typed seawalls started during the reign of Emperor Kangxi, but were tested during the reign of Emperor Yongzheng, while the large-scale construction started in years during the reign of Emperor Qianlong (Fig. 6-52). In the 59th year of Kangxi, more than

1,600 m-long seawalls were first built. During the reign of Emperor Qianlong, the first round of construction on a large scale started finishing over 20 km-long seawalls, the second round finished over 13 km long, and the third round finished over 7 km long. Seawalls reformed during the years of Emperor Qianlong totalled 2.1 km. Seawalls finished from Emperor Kangxi to Qianlong has hit more than 44 km.

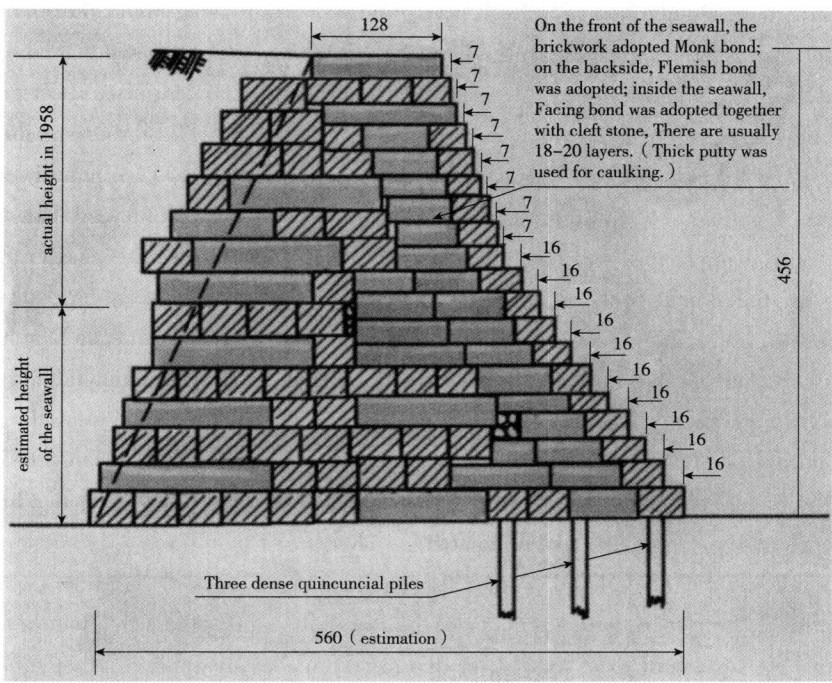

Figure 6-52 Scale-typed Seawall in Qing Dynasty (chi: about 0.3 m)

In the Qing Dynasty, the focus of seawall construction in Zhejiang was in Renhe and Haining, thus seawalls in the two places were basically completed during the reigns of Emperor Kangxi, Yongzheng and Qianlong. Since its completion, there have been few marine disasters in the two places. Sometimes, it was also influenced by the wind and tide, resulting in some minor damages. Except for a few times, it was generally not too serious. In the late Qing Dynasty, due to the frequent foreign invasion and the poor state treasury, the government was unable to provide financial support for the construction of seawalls, resulting in several dangerous areas. Fortunately, the scale-typed seawall were so strong that no serious problems were caused.

The ancient seawall of Qiantang River has been formed for a long time. In the process, people on both sides of Qiantang River Estuary have created and accumulated rich cultural heritages in terms of literature, folk culture, technology, and ecology, with far-reaching influence.

When it comes to the value of literary heritage, the magnificent scenery of Qiantang River has attracted and inspired countless writers to create many masterpieces, either to sing high of the natural scenery, or to describe flood and drought disasters, or to praise the great achievements of people's efforts in building the great seawalls.

Great amount of folk culture was also developed during the development of the seawall including legends, worship culture, production customs, taboo customs, and special products. These cultural connotations are an important part of the seawall heritage.

The place where Qiantangjiang Seawall was situated was an estuary, and there is Taihu Plain to its north and Ningshao Plain to its south. The whole area is abundant with lakes, therefore topics such as flood control, land improvement, water conservancy projects building, and transportation development have always been the main contents of local people's lives. Accordingly, there were many water related legends such as stories about water gods popular in Xiaoshan on the Ningshao Plain, or stories about seawall building and tide subduing. Those stories showed people's eager to control flood on the one hand, and commemorations to the great historical figures who had made contributions on the other. In addition, they also recorded the progress of the development of seawalls, thus with great value.

In order to commemorate the legendary or historical figures who controlled flood and subdue surging tides, people worship them and offer sacrifices to them every year, including Dayu, Wu Zixu, Qian Liu and Zhang Xia, and Mazu, who stabilize the tide and protect the people's livelihood. In addition, the historical figures who contributed to the construction and management of seawalls and even sacrificed their lives are also remembered. The worship, on the one hand, supplement the history of seawall, on the other hand, enrich the connotation of seawall cultural heritage. What's more, it inspires later generations to manage the seawalls more scientifically and wisely, and continue work hard to benefit local people. In this case, the seawall worship is not superstition, but historical heritage.

The construction of seawall needs scientific labour organization. In the process, the production custom has also become an important historical relic bearing great heritage connotation. The chant of seawall laborers in Haiyan is a typical representative in this respect. On the one hand, it records the organizational procedures of labour and the seawall construction history. On the other hand, its libretto, tone, and melody have become the composition of literature, music and dance, and the films with complete records become excellent comprehensive cultural products. In addition to the construction of the seawall, the production customs concerned with the salt drying and fishing around the seawall have also become an important cultural heritage, which is worth deeper research.

Section IV Water Diversion Projects

Water resources are distributed unevenly spatially, which could be efficiently reallocated by water diversion projects. Water can be transferred across river basins and regions to meet the needs of water supply, irrigation and ecological water demand. China is one of the earliest countries in the world to construct water diversion projects. As mentioned above, Dujiangyan and Karez have the function of water diversion. After the founding of the people's Republic of China, several water diversion projects with large water transfer volume and long distance have been completed, such as the Hongqiqu Canal and the South-to-North Water Diversion Project.

1. The Hongqiqu Canal

The Hongqiqu Canal was built in Linxian County (now called Linzhou City) of Henan Province. Linxian County is in Taihang Mountain area, at the junction of three provinces including Henan, Shanxi and Hebei. Although Zhanghe River flows through the county, severe drought and water shortage caused by blockage of high mountains have lingered on for hundreds of years. Historical records proved that more than 100 natural disasters and over 30 times of zero harvests because of droughts occurred for 514 years ranging from the first year of the Ming Dynasty to the founding of the People's Republic of China. Sometimes, rivers and wells dried up in successive years of drought (Fig. 6-53), therefore no crops were harvested, leading to serious hungry problem, and some local people were even forced to survive by eating others' dead bodies. At that time, a local idiom was popular by saying that "water is as expensive as oil, and harvest is impossible in nine out of ten years", a vivid portrayal of Linxian County then.

Figure 6-53 Dry Well in Linxian County

From October in 1944 when Linxian County established CPC government to the end of 1950s, the CPC Linxian County Committee organized local people to carry out many large-scale water conservancy projects. However, a bottleneck problem still existed. That is the lack of sufficient water resources, hence water shortage has not been solved despite the above-mentioned efforts. To find an ultimate solution, a plan to divert water in nearby Zhuozhang River into Linxian Country

Water and the Chinese Culture

Figure 6-54 People in the March to Build the Hongqiqu Canal

has taken shape.

In the 1960s, people in Linxian County began to build Hongqiqu Canal, planing to transfer water in the Zhuozhanghe River from Shanxi Province to Linxian County along the Taihang Mountain. On February 11, 1960, also the Lantern Festival in China, 37,000 peasant workers, carrying their tools, luggage, pushing carts and carriages, started from 15 communes in the whole county at the same time (Fig. 6-54) to march toward Zhuozhanghe River, where Shanxi, Hebei and Henan Provinces converge.

It was destined to be an arduous struggle from the first day to build Hongqiqu Canal, since the year of 1960 also saw the start of three years of extreme economic difficulties in China. People in Linxian County had to start from scratch to continue the construction without support of any machinery equipment or adequate food. Self-reliance was the only way that they can refer to. When faced with fund shortage, people there converted their payment into workload, which would be calculated according to their own benefited area. Peasant workers brought their own tools and food, and only got compensation from the grain reserves of the production team if the food was insufficient, to save every cent. When faced with material shortage, people there began to pool their own intelligence into developing self-made explosives (Fig. 6-55), lime (Fig. 6-56) and cement (Fig.

Figure 6-55 People Making Explosives

6-57). Without adequate accommodations, workers then lived on cliffs(Fig. 5-58), in stone or earth caves(Fig. 5-59), mats or even slept in the open air. Without any data to refer to, technicians had to make designs by in-the-field investigation despite all kinds of difficult geological conditions and extreme weather conditions.

Figure 6-56　People Producing Lime

Figure 6-57　People Making Cement

　　In the process of the canal construction, the people of Linxian County cut mountains and dug canals, opened holes, and set up troughs, which embodied the spirit of unity, cooperation and selfless dedication. During the closure of the canal head dam, peasant workers jumped into the cold

Figure 6-58 People Living on Cliffs

Figure 6-59 People Living in Stone Caves

river and built a "human wall" to stop the torrent, which made the closure successful (Fig. 6-60). During the project on Yingwuya Cliff, the general headquarters decided to organize 15 communes to take part in the construction according to the survey situation. More than 5,000 young men formed a difficult tackling team in the fight, who had manually drilled hundreds of holes to put explosives with steel chisels and hammers. Qingniandong Cave is the throat project of Hongqiqu Canal. To cross the steep cliff of Langya Mountain, a tunnel with a length of more than 600 m must be drilled. However, the quartz sand on the mountain was as hard as steel, and a hammer down can only leave a spot. After 17 months of hard work, the young fighters finally dug the cave through the hard rock.

The main canal of Hongqiqu was built among mountainous area, making it extreme difficult and dangerous. People have overcome great difficulties in finishing this project. However, no matter how difficult it was, no one illegally spent any cents for personal purposes. Every year, after the autumn harvest, the young man took his iron shovel and pushing carts up the mountain to build the canal, and went back home in spring, and went up the hill again the following year. In this way, with the spirit of hard work, people in Linxian County have worked hard for 10 years, flattened 1,250 mountains, and drilled more than 200 tunnels. It is said that if the excavated earth and rock could be built into a wall 2 m wide and 3 m high, it would be long enough to connect Guangzhou and Harbin.

Figure 6-60　River Closure by Barricade Formed by People

It took almost ten years ranging from February 1960 to July 1969 that the construction of Hongqiqu Canal was completed. On the 1,525.6 km long canal, the brave people of Linxian County built 48 reservoirs, 364 ponds and 12,408 buildings for different purposes, including 211 tunnels, 151 aqueducts, and various small hydropower stations and water pumping stations on each branch canal. The irrigation system with Hongqiqu canal as the main body has basically taken shape here. People's dream for water spanning over 1,000 years has finally been realized (Fig. 6-61).

During the 10 years of the construction of Hongqiqu Canal, many heroes have emerged, and 81 people have sacrificed their lives, among whom the oldest is 63, and the youngest is only 17.

Wu Zutai, the chief designer of Hongqiqu Canal (Fig. 6-62), conducted detailed field survey without stop after taking the designing task regardless of any dangers and difficulties, even the great blow of losing his wife (sacrificing her life to save others). On the afternoon of March 28, 1960, on hearing that the cracks on the top of the Wangjiazhuang tunnel dropped soil, he went straight into the tunnel to check the dangerous situation. Unfortunately, he was hit by a huge rock falling from the top of the tunnel and lost his young life.

At the beginning of 1960, he participated in the design of Hongqiqu Canal. To draw a blueprint for the project as soon as possible, he worked with other engineering and technical personnel to carry out field survey over many difficulties. As a result, he drafted the first blueprint of Hongqiqu Canal titled *Preliminary Design Book on Zhuozhang River—Linxian Country Water Diversion and Irrigation*

Figure 6-61 Bird-view of Hongqiqu Canal

Figure 6-62 The Portrait of Wu Zutai

Project within a short period of time. Since the project had to pass through the cliffs and rivers, the topography is very complex. He and his colleagues have solved many engineering difficulties in their work and designed many efficient solutions. For example, on the section of Qingnianjian, it was originally planned to dig an open channel around the mountain, which would incur great amount of workload and bring great difficulties. After repeated consideration and comparison, Wu Zutai improved the design scheme and adopted the method of digging a tunnel to let the channel pass through the cliff. In order to figure out ways to let the main canal cross Zhuozhang River, he visited the old people in the nearby mountain village for more information, carefully studied geological and hydrology data of the river, and finally worked out an optimal design of the "hollow dam" with his colleagues, allowing the canal water to pass through the dam core and the river water to overflow from the dam top, thus solving the problem between the canal water and the river water.

In February 1960, after the project started, Wu Zutai served as the deputy chief of the engineering department and was responsible for the engineering design. He had to not only draw the design drawings of each project according to the actual survey, but also take care of safety measures of each section. His work was very busy, but without any complaint. One day, he went to the construction site of Fenghuang Mountain in the south of Panyang Village and found that the channel the workers had dug for five and six days was not in line with the design. He felt very guilty and corrected the deviation in time. The lesson of this incident was deeply engraved in his heart.

Once, he found several cracks in the Wangjiazhuang tunnel, and immediately studied the risk prevention methods with peasant workers. In order to ensure the construction safety, he changed the original design of "single tunnel" into "double tunnels". This improvement can not only reduce the span of the tunnel top, but also make the tunnel more solid.

Ren Yangcheng, praised as "Flying Tigers and Eagles" (Fig. 6 - 63), took part in the building of Nangudong Reservoir with his 90-odd villagers by responding to the call of the government on "Reshape Rivers and Mountains of Linxian County" in 1958. On the construction site, he willingly shouldered the most difficult or the most dangerous job, and therefore joined the CPC on the site because of his excellent performance.

Figure 6-63 The Portrait of Ren Yangcheng

In the process of construction, the use of explosives would bring many loose stones to fall, which would in turn hurt the peasant workers building canals under the cliff. To ensure the safety, the project headquarter decided to set up a team to get rid of dangers beforehand. Ren Yangcheng was the first to sign up and was elected as the leader of the team. From then on, after tying a rope around the waist, he led the team members to fly down the cliff to remove dangerous factors all the day (Fig. 6-64). That's why he was called "Flying Tiger and Eagle" by the people. Once, he climbed up to Tongtiangou ditch to get rid of dangers, but sadly fell into a cluster of thorns. When he struggled to get up,

Figure 6-64 Removing Dangers down the Cliff

his back was covered with sharp thorns. Painfully enduring the pain, he climbed up the cliff again, and continued to remove dangers. In the evening, when the landlady and her daughter-in-law picked thorns for him, they took one hour and picked a handful of thorns from his back, but he was so brave that he didn't say a word. Once again, in Hukou cliff, when he was about to plunge into the concave eaves, a stone fell from the top of the eaves and hit him on the mouth, making his three teeth loose. There was a deep pain and blood flowing down the corner of his mouth. He pulled out his teeth and endured the pain until he finished the task. The next day, by wearing a mask, he put on a rope on his back and went up the mountain to continue his job again. In this way, he has been flying from cliff to cliff for many years. A circle of blood marks has been made on his waist by the rope, and his flesh and blood often sticked to his body, and he can't even take off his clothes. His dedication to his job has always been praised by everyone. In 1965 and 1966, when the main canal and the three main canals were completed, he was rated as the model and super model of Hongqiqu Canal.

Although the construction was difficult, the completion of Hongqiqu Canal has brought great economic benefits to the people of Linxian County. At the same time, the spirit of Hongqiqu Canal has become a precious cultural wealth in China.

Since the founding of the People's Republic of China, many large-scale water conservancy projects have been invested by the state, but Hongqiqu Canal was mainly financed by collective funds. People in Linxian County has created such a great miracle through practising self-reliance. Without waiting for help or depending on others, they have only one firm ambition, that is to "work hard all my life to create happiness for future generations. "This great cause has reflected the courage and wisdom of the Chinese nation, as well as the spirit of being the master of history of the working people in the new era. Premier Zhou Enlai praised Hongqiqu Canal as a "River from the Sky" and regarded it as an outstanding representative of the achievements of new China's engineering projects together the Nanjing Yangtze River Bridge. In 2006, as a contemporary water project, Hongqiqu Canal was listed as a national key cultural relic protection unit, showing its importance with great cultural value.

Hongqiqu Canal spirit is a monument of Chinese national spirit. Builders of Hongqiqu Canal summarize the spirit into several sentences as "it is for the people and by the people; when doing jobs, we need to dare to think and do, we need to seek truth from actual facts; the spirit of self-reliance, hard work; unity and cooperation as well as selfless dedication shall be valued". Chinese leaders also praised the spirit as "the soul of the Chinese nation". In terms of spiritual value, Hongqiqu Canal belongs not only to Linzhou, but also to every Chinese people. So far, the spirit has cultivated and inspired generations of entrepreneurs. Now, hundreds of thousands of people are attracted to visit Hongqiqu Canal every year. They are also inspired and encouraged by the great spirit of the project. The construction of Hongqiqu Canal embodies the CPC's ruling idea of bringing benefits to the people and leading the people to create a new life, and shows the builders' ambition and respect for science. The Chinese spirit and national spirit contained in the project is an eternal spiritual monument in the great cause of China's national rejuvenation.

Although formed in the 1960s, Hongqiqu Spirit has now accumulated into a cultural tradition and cultivated generations of children in China. Back then, thousands of people in Linxian Country fought bravely in Taihang Mountain. After the reform and opening up, thousands of people in Linxian County marched out of Taihang Mountain to a broader market. With their exquisite construction technology and conscientious and responsible spirit, they contracted construction projects all over the country and even overseas, making Linzhou a famous hometown of craftsmen, creating good economic benefits and promoting the second time of take-off in economy. At the beginning of the 21st century, the people of Linzhou (formerly known as Linxian County) began to make great efforts to develop ecological agriculture and tourism. Hongqiqu Spirit has become a cultural tradition, which will be carried forward by generations of people in Linxian county.

2. The South-to-North Water Diversion Project

The South-to-North Water Diversion Project is a major strategic infrastructure to alleviate the serious water resources shortage in North China. It is the largest water diversion project in the world and an equally important one with the Three Gorges Project. This project is of great significance to China's social progress and sustainable economic development. As a critical large-scale project, its construction requires higher on the rational allocation of water resources, the improvement of the comprehensive utilization rate of water resources, the enhancement of environmental protection awareness and the improvement of social public welfare responsibility.

As early as the founding of the People's Republic of China, Chairman Mao Zedong has put forward the great blueprint of borrowing water from the south to the north. Since then, the planning and research of the project has kicked off. 50 years of investigation, planning and research have seen the finalization of the planned three water diversion areas in the lower, middle and upper reaches of the Yangtze River respectively, and the deciding of the East, Middle and West water diversion routes included in the project based on comparisons of over 50 kinds of schemes. Through communications of the three routes with the four major rivers, namely the Yangtze River, Yellow River, Huaihe River and Haihe River, four horizontal and three vertical routes have been planned to allow north to south water allocation, thus realizing mutual compensation between the east and west part of China.

The project, with the length of 4,350 km, aims to alleviate water shortage in North China, particularly the area within the reach of the Yellow River and Huaihe River, which is estimated to benefit 438 million people. By the year of 2050, the average annual water diversion scale of the East, Middle and West routes will be planned to hit 14.8 billion m^3, 13 billion m^3 and 17 billion m^3 respectively, with a total volume of 44.8 billion m^3.

Among them, the East Route draws water from the Yangtze River near Yangzhou, and then lifts and transfers water to the North step by step by using the Beijing-Hangzhou Grand Canal or expanding it at some sections. On its way, the route passes through Hongze Lake, Luoma Lake, Nansi Lake and Dongping Lake, crosses the Yellow River near Weishan, then flows by itself, and ultimately reaches Tianjin through Weilin Canal and South Canal. The East Route aims to compensate water for North China. The area it benefits includes the following: the lower reach of the Huaihe River Plain in Northern Jiangsu Province except the belly part of the Lixia River and its East and North highlands; both banks of the Huaihe River to the west of Bengbu in Anhui Province, area located at the both banks of the Xinbian River to the east of Huaibei City and some areas of Tianchang County; the surrounding areas of Nansihu Lake, Hanzhuang Canal and Liangji Canal in Shandong Province, some cities in Jiaodong region and the non-Yellow River irrigation area of North Shandong Province; the Yundong region of Heilonggang in Hebei Province; Tianjin City and the nearby suburbs. The water supply scope of this route benefits five provinces (cities) including Jiangsu, Anhui, Shandong, Hebei and the City of Tianjin. In addition to such function, the project is also designed for purposes of shipping and flood control.

The Middle Route diverts water from Danjiangkou Reservoir of Hanjiang River. The main water transport canal starts from the head gate of Taocha Canal, runs along the plain in front of Funiu Mountain and Taihang Mountain, the west side of Beijing-Guangzhou railway, crosses the four major river basins of Yangtze River, Huaihe River, Yellow River and Haihe River and finally arrives at Beijing and Tianjin. The length of the main canal is 1,246 km, and the length of Tianjin trunk canal is 144 km. Its water supply scope covers Beijing, Tianjin, North China Plain and part of Hubei and Henan Provinces along the line. The main function of this route is to supply water for urban life and industry, as well as for agriculture and other purposes, but not for shipping.

The West Route includes three diversion lines, namely, Yalong River, Tongtian River and Dadu River. This route is designed to divert water from the main stream and tributaries on the upper reach of the Yangtze River to that of the Yellow River. The diversion project is planned to build dams and reservoirs on the upper reaches of the three main rivers, and then introduce water to the Yellow River by using a diversion tunnel that will cross the Bayan Har Mountain, the watershed between the two major rivers. The water supply scope of this route is designed to benefit Qinghai, Gansu, Ningxia, Inner Mongolia, Shaanxi and Shanxi. Its main function is to compensate water for the Yellow River and satisfy water demands of daily life, agricultural and industrial development in northwest China and west part of North China. If necessary, it can also supply water to the lower reach of the Yellow River. Up to now, the Middle Route Project and the first phase of the East Route Project have been completed and have begun to transfer water to the north.

The South-to-North Water Diversion Project is the achievement of the collective wisdom of the Chinese nation and a comprehensive ecological project to benefit Chinese people. It greatly improves the quality of water resources and carrying capacity of the water environment of areas along the project, supplies water to more than 100 cities along the line, and returns part of water resources, formerly used by cities, to its original agricultural and ecological purposes. In a sense, this is re-feeding of the industry to the agriculture and that of cities to countryside, which is the vivid embodiment of the scientific outlook on development in the aspect of water resources security.

The project transfers the abundant water resources of the Yangtze River Basin to the north to alleviates the water shortage and ecological environment deterioration in the north. It is not only a major strategic decision made by the state to coordinate the regional and economic and social development, but also an embodiment of harmonious development between man and water, man and nature.

Historically speaking, the decision-making process of the project was a major innovation. On October 30, 1952, Chairman Mao Zedong went to inspect the Yellow River. After hearing the report of Wang Huayun, director of the Yellow River Water Conservancy Commission, on the idea of diverting water from Yangtze River to Yellow River, he said: "there is more water in the south than in the north. If possible, it is OK to borrow some water. " Thus, the grand idea of South-to-North Water Diversion was put forward for the first time. In February, 1953, Chairman Mao went to inspect places from Wuhan to Nanjing. On the 19th, after hearing the work report of Lin Yishan, director of the Yangtze River Water Conservancy Commission, he proposed again that "there is more water in the south than in the north. Can we borrow some water from the south to the north? " He also pointed to the map with his pencil on places like Hanjiang River and Danjiangkou, and inquired about the possibility of diverting water. After the meeting, Mao Zedong instructed people to make further study on the water diversion scheme on Hanjiang River, organize personnel to carry out investigation and write to him after any headway was made. On the 22nd, Chairman Mao Zedong told Lin Yishan: "We still need to make more considerations on the Three Gorges project, but the one to transfer water from the south to the north need to be sped up. "

In March 1958, at the enlarged meeting of the Political Bureau of the CPC Central Committee held in Chengdu, Chairman Mao Zedong once again put forward the idea by saying that "we can open the Tongtianhe River, the Bailongjiang River and the Taohe River to borrow water from Yangtze River to Yellow River, from Hanjiang River to Yellow River at the Danjiangkou, from Yellow River to Weihe River, and eventually build connections with Beijing. " Premier Zhou Enlai then organized a meeting to have detailed discussions on the project by adhering to principles of combining plan and available resources, goal and steps, vision and the near future, overall strategy and actual methods. In August of the same year, at the enlarged meeting of the Political Bureau held by the Central Committee of the Communist Party of China in Beidaihe, Zhou Enlai said "there are four water diversion routes. Plans to divert water at the upper, middle, and lower reaches of the Yangtze River are all feasible, thus a comprehensive plan should be made. " The meeting passed and issued a document named Instructions on Water Conservancy Work, which clearly stipulated that "the long-term water conservancy planning of the whole country, will give priority to divert water in the south (mainly refers to the Yangtze River) to the north, that is, to link major rivers in China covering Yangtze River, Huaihe River, Yellow River, Hanjiang Haihe River and so on into a unified water conservancy system. " This is the first time that the term "South-to-North Water Diversion" has appeared in the official documents of the central government. During the three years from 1958 to 1960, the central government has held four national meetings on the project, formulated the work plan from 1960 to 1963, and proposed the goal of completing the preliminary planning report of the project within three years.

After the reform and opening, facing the increasingly severe situation of water shortage in North China, the CPC Central Committee and the State Council continued the overall and strategic considerations on the possibility of the project. In December 1979, the Planning Office of the South-to-North Water Diversion Project was set up by the Ministry of Water Conservancy to lead the implementation of the project. In March 1991, at the fourth session of the Seventh National People's Congress, the Outline of the Ten-year Plan for National Economic and Social Development and the Eighth Five-year Plan was promulgated, which stated that the project would start during the period of the Eighth Five-year Plan. In June of 1999, when addressing at the Symposium on the Yellow River Management and Development, Mr. Jiang Zemin, the General Secretary of CPC, pointed out that "in order to fundamentally alleviate the serious water shortage in North China, it is necessary to build the South-to-North Water Diversion Project. A feasible blueprint print needs to be made based on scientific comparison and detailed planning. "

The history on the formulation of the project suggested that a step-by-step approval was made ranging from the agreeing of the master plan and the overall feasibility study report, the establishment of the leading organization of the project construction to the raising of funds. Every work needs to go through many links, through the coordination of many departments and provinces. Without the support of the leadership of the Central Committee, it is impossible to carry out the project.

Residents' resettlement caused by large-scale water conservancy project is a worldwide difficulty involving tight schedule and great amount of compensation. In addition, unwillingness of local people caused by passive choice and the need to resettle people at nearby areas also compound the situation. In the past several large-scale projects, it took 17 years to relocate 370,000 for the Three Gorges Project, and 11 years to relocate 146,000 for Xiaolangdi Project on the Yellow River. There are totally 330,000 local residents in Danjiangkou Reservoir area needed to be resettled for the South-to-North Water Diversion Project (including 162,000 in Henan Province and 181,000 in Hubei Province). However, the project construction committee of the State Council determined that "Four years of work needs to be accomplished in two years. "That is to say, the resettlement needs to be finished in 2011, two years ahead of schedule, making the job even more difficult.

During the process of residents resettlement, a kind of "Immigrant Spirit" was formed, which firstly comes from the patriotism of local residents and people working in the project who were willing to sacrifice their own interests for the greater benefits of the country. It also shows people's hard-working and self-reliance spirit. Hu Minrui, a worker of the publicity centre of the South-to-North Water Diversion Project, believes that "patriotism" is the core of the "Immigrant Spirit", and "dedication" is its root. Li Chunlin, deputy editor-in-chief of *Guangming Daily*, believes that the national spirit with patriotism as its core is the psychological basis for the formation of "Xichuan Immigrant Spirit".

Figure 6-65 Relocated Residents of the South-to-North Water Diversion Project

It's always hard to leave one's hometown, and hard to abandon one's homeland(Fig. 6-65). "A hometown can be called so only when there are lands to cultivate on, relatives to help with each other, ancestors to worship, and local accent to hear. What buries under the water is the deep love of thousands of immigrants to their hometown and the land, which would become a permanent attachment in their nostalgic hearts. In addition, home is even more important to an ordinary person. Relocation can restore the immigrants' tangible properties in a short period of time or make them even better than before. However, the intangible ones such as their social network and geographical kinship, are difficult to recover, which are also hard to measure by numbers and compensate by money. More than 50 years ago, most of the immigrants in Danjiangkou Reservoir area have made sacrifice by leaving their own homes for the greater interests of the country. However, today, 50 years later, they must make the sacrifice again. An old man said, "Northerners are thirsty. We must move!" Those words expressed a bit of helplessness, but most of the feelings showed are pride and deep love to the country and to people living in the north. One 91-year-old immigrant moved together with his coffin in order to "quench the thirst of Beijing". He said "I am proud that Beijing people can drink water from our Danjiang River." Those words, no matter how simple they are, have shown the immigrants' great selfless love.

Over the past 50 years, several generations of Xichuan immigrants have been repaying their motherland wholeheartedly when they are "needed by the country". The power of this kind of spirit is, in essence, the power of morality. Many touching stories have emerged. He Zhaosheng, a villager of Yanjiang Village, Cangfang Town, Xichuan County, have been relocated three times spanning a half century. At the age of 23 (in 1958), construction of Danjiangkou Reservoir resettled him in

Qinghai Province. A few years later, unable to endure the local poor living environment, his family return to Xichuan after going through all kinds of hardship. In November 1964, the restart of the first phase of Danjiangkou Project resumed work relocated his whole family including his parents, wife and three children again in the 14th Production Team, Liming Brigade, Shilipu People's Commune, Jingmen, Hubei Province. At that time, he was 30 years old (in 1966). They lived in thatched cottage built by the government for relocated residents. Several years later, poor economic situation forced him to move back to Xichuang again with his family. On Jun. 26th, 2010, due to the start of the South-to-North Water Diversion Project, at the age of 75, he left his hometown for the third time together with thousands of home fellow to Yanjiang Village, Changcun Town, Huixian County, Henan Province, which is located on the north of Yellow River, at the foot of Taihang Mountain, and 500 km away from his hometown. The old man has traveled three provinces and four places in his life, who can be called the "most typical immigrant" in China and the "walking dictionary" of immigrants in Danjiangkou Reservoir area. Before moving for the third time, the old man only enjoyed his life in the new western-style house in his hometown for more than one year. However, without any complaints, he moved to Huixian County with the leek root dug from his hometown. When he left, he said, "No matter my hometown has golden or silver mountain, I will move as long as the country needs me to move."

Xianghua Town is known as the "Hong Kong" of Xichuan County. Wu jiao'e, a 70 year old villager living in Yuguan village, Xianghua Town, settled down here from Dachai Lake in Hubei Province. In the resettlement plan, six of her nine children would move to three different resettlement sites. Holding back the pain of separation, she said to the child, "it's our honour that Beijing can drink our water. Don't bring any trouble to the country. Let's go." To guarantee national interests, safeguard the construction of key projects, and make sure that people in the north can drink the sweet water from the Yangtze River, the immigrants have sacrificed their own benefits to ensure the greater interests of the country. When preparing for departing, they quietly pack up their belongings, demolished their own houses, relocated their ancestral graves, bid farewell to their relatives and friends, and left their hometown with endless nostalgia. It is just because of the patriotic dedication of tens of thousands of immigrants like He Zhaosheng and Wu jiao'e that this worldwide difficulty has been successfully solved.

Chapter Seven Water and Confucianism

Water serves as not only the source of life, but that of civilization, and philosophy. Ancient Chinese philosophers kept deep interest in water, believing that truth could be perceived by observing water related phenomena, and it was applicable to the whole world. Therefore, the imprint of water can be seen in many schools of thought. It's reasonable to say that water played a crucial role in the development of ancient Chinese philosophy. Confucianism, the mainstream thought in China, has many famous expositions related with water.

Section I The Wise Delight in Water

There are two famous maxims recorded in Chapter 6 of *The Analects of Confucius*, saying that "The wise delight in water while the good delight in mountains. The wise love mobility while the good love tranquillity. The wise live happy while the good live long." Confucius①(Fig. 7-1) , the founder of Confucianism, showed a special love for water. He thought that man and nature are inseparable, so qualities of mountains and water were also reflected in characteristics of human being. Among the ever-changing nature, the mountain remains stable, unchangeable and tolerable, thus trustworthy and can always providing the most reliable support; unlike mountain, water is changeable without stable appearance. It is both soft and sharp, being good on the one hand, and maybe evil on the other. Like the water, the wise could always perceive the development

Figure 7-1 Confucius

---

① Confucius (551-479 B.C.) was a Chinese philosopher and politician of the Spring and Autumn Period who was traditionally considered "the paragon of Chinese sages."Widely considered one of the most important and influential individuals in human history, Confucius' teachings and philosophy formed the basis of East Asian culture and society and continue to remain influential across China and East Asia today.

of things, and change accordingly instead of sticking to some unchanged rules, thus they could always get success by avoiding ignorance and difficulties, as depicted in the famous Chinese saying "knowing well the changing rule of things, change with the changes." Even if they cannot succeed, the wise, like the water, could still keep active and optimistic. They would adapt themselves well to different circumstances and seek other chances. Like the mountain, the benevolent is calm and stable, unlikely changed by external things. They treat people and things with love. Like the mountain, they stand very high, thus far-sighted; they open their arms to all things like the mountain welcoming everything, thus tolerant and kind. They are not slavery to physical demands, thus not influenced by them. They can all live a longer life since they have neither worry nor terror in their minds.

Inspired by Confucius, Xunzi, a successor of the Confucianism, said that "When finding the mighty water, the intelligent man must go and appreciate it." Mencius, based on the sentence "the wise love mobility while the good love tranquillity" by Confucius, proposed the way to appreciate water by saying that "there is a way to appreciate water: observing its waves."

These three masters of Confucianism all compared water to the wise and gentlemen, and endowed water with human nature and morality, which had a far-reaching impact on later generations. Why do Confucians like water so much?

Professor Sarah Allan thinks that the reason why early Chinese philosophers liked to meditate on water is that they thought rules suggested by water related phenomena applied to the whole universe. That's to say, the reason that the masters of Confucianism loved, and worshiped water so much lies in the realization of Tao from water. Then what kind of law of nature can be contained in the water?

1. The Law of Nature

In Chapter 9 of *The Analects of Confucius*, the Master, standing by a stream (Fig. 7-2), said "Time passes away night and day like running water." Judging from the literary meaning, Confucius, inspired by the flowing water in the mighty river, said so to sigh for the quick elapsing of time and short span of life, which imposed great impact on the coming generations. From then on, Many Chinese poets have expressed their sorrow on the flying of time. There is a poem in Yuefu of Han Dynasty, saying that "The river flows all the way eastward, when will it come back? Without working hard, a young adult will soon turn old, nothing accomplished but sighing hard." In Jin Dynasty, Tao Yuanming, a famous poet, wrote "the most energetic age will be gone without return, A morning passes, a day can never bring it back turn, work hard, because time waits for no man. In Tang Dynasty, the poet Wang Zhenbai had a famous metaphor "One inch of time is as valuable as one inch of gold."

However, by saying "Time passes away night and day like running water", Confucius was actually perceiving the Tao of Heaven, that is life, like the running water, will never end, neither does the running of the world. Xunzi said in his book that "water, like Tao, is exhaustible." The

Figure 7-2 Standing by a Stream, the Master Said "Time Passes away Night and Day Like Running Water"

Tao of Heaven, in other words, the natural law, runs without stop. Day is succeeded by night, and four seasons circulate without stop. Water, like the natural law, is exhaustible in watering things in the world, thus all things grow, and life is endless. That's the root of the Tao of Heaven. An intelligent man shall learn from this Tao and make great efforts to devote himself in pursing the truth. Zhu Xi, a famous Confucianist in the Southern Song Dynasty, also said that "In the nature, the past is succeeded by the coming. The process is endless, which is the core of Tao." Only by following this natural law, can people make some accomplishments. The similar thinking was also reflected in the sentence of "If you can make things better for one day, you should make them better every day and never stop doing this!" by Tang, the first emperor of Shang Dynasty, which is recorded in *Daxue*, a famous Confucianism work.

2. The Tao of the Intelligent Man

Mencius[①], based on the sentence "the wise love mobility while the good love tranquillity" by Confucius, proposed the way to appreciate water by saying that "there is a way to appreciate water: observing its waves." This idea is identical to the maxim of "the wise delight in water" by Confucius. The wise delight in water, particularly the flowing water, which is because they can perceive similar qualities of the intelligent man from the flowing water and the up-and-down waves. In addition, they can also figure out knowledge on the society and life from the natural appearance

---

① Mencius: (372-289B.C.) was a Chinese confusion philosopher who has often been described as the "second Sage". He is part of Confucius' fourth generation of disciples. Mencius inherited Confucius' ideology and developed it further.

and function of water. For example, before filling up pits and holes, water won't flow forward. If an intelligent man determined to pursue the truth, they won't make any progress unless they study hard day and night. Advance in knowledge and one's career is just like the flowing water, which not only need efforts day and night but also the realization that it won't grow unless it is full in the first place.

Mencius thought that the reason why water is inexhaustible lied in its source, from which he perceived that the intelligent man must stick to basic principles of Confucianism so that obtain further development. When pursuing truth and perfecting one's virtue, an intelligent man should learn from water, that flow eastwards without any stop and fill up pit and holes on its way in the first place and then seek further growth. Only by this, can he develop into an ideal intelligent man as required by Confucianism.

After observing water, Xunzi understood qualities of an intelligent man. In his book, he wrote, "Water is as fair as a sage, since it is level and not inclined under all circumstances." He also compared the learning spirit of an intelligent man to the characteristics of water, which became Xunzi's unique contribution in water metaphor. It said that "ice, frozen from water, is cold than water." He also said: "if you don't accumulate small streams, you can't make rivers and seas." Those two characteristics summarized by Xunzi are often used to teach people that knowledge cannot be increased and abilities cannot be improved if without hard work with perseverance. The two maxims also become important mottoes to inspire Chinese to study hard.

3. The Tao of Life

The Confucianists delight in water, because they were pleased by the natural beauty of mountains and rivers. They liked to pursue the Tao of life while bathed in the beauty of nature.

In Chapter 11 of *The Analects of Confucius*, Confucius asked his disciples about their ambitions. In a nice spring morning, Zi Lu, Zeng Xi, Ran You and Gongxi Hua sitting in attendance, the Master asked them to talk out their future goals. Zi Lu, Ran You and Gongxi Hua made impassioned speeches, expressing their idea of managing the state in order. Without evident judgement, the Master turned to Zeng Xi, who, pausing as he was playing on his twanging lute, put it aside and said "In late spring I would put on my newly made spring dress and go with five or six grown-ups and six or seven young men to purify ourselves in River Yi, enjoy the breeze at the Rain Altar and come back singing." The Master said with a sign, "I would like to go with you."

What Zeng Xi has depicted is a moving picture, in which people sing happily while bathed in river and enjoying the breeze. In the eyes of Confucius, having a bath in the Yishui River and clearing one's mind are indispensable pleasures in life. Confucius lived in an era when rites and music, that he attached great importance to, were gradually abandoned. Ground by daily trifles, he must feel exhausted both physically and psychologically. In this case, it is pleasant to have bath in river and enjoy the breeze at the Rain Altar. At the same time, this open and clear picture must be the vision of the great harmony world that Confucius has been longing for in his life.

Throughout his life, Confucius took it as his own mission to rejuvenate rites of the Zhou Dynasty. To promote the Confucianism, he travelled around the states with his disciples. However, what welcomed him was only indifference and criticizing from the local authority."In Song State, the big tree under which Confucius preached his ideas to his disciples was cut; In Wei State, he was ignored; On the way to Chen, he was put into custody; He was also stuck between Chen and Cai States, starving; He was also humiliated by Ji family and Yang Hu in Lu State. He was sad until death."Facing all the difficulties, the Master couldn't help expressing his complaints of "If the truth I preach were not followed, I would float on the sea by a raft. Who would then follow me but Zi Lu?"

However, those words are not his true intention, but only the complaint to Confucius, showing his helplessness and disappointment after scores of years of fruitless efforts at the age of 70. However, inspired by the words, many Chinese intellectuals, feeling disappointed with their own careers and lives, began to retreat to forests, mountains, and water to find comfort for their souls.

The wise delight in water, while the good delight in mountain. If as persistent as a mountain and as brave as water, this person must be the one with high virtue, great values, and happiness, thus living a longer life. Until now, Chinese people still treat qualities perceived from mountains and water as their life model. The love for mountains and water remains popular among Chinese people.

Section II Comparing Water to People's Virtue

The typical aesthetic view of people before the Qin Dynasty was to compare characteristics of natural scenery to people's virtue. It is believed that the beauty of natural scenery lies in the fact that it embodies the beauty of human spirit, that is, the beauty of human personality. When observing mighty rivers, Masters of Confucianism tried to find connections between water and virtue of human being. They attached great importance to find people's virtue in water. From this, the Confucian principles, and principles of living in the world were derived, and the concept of "Comparing Water to People's Virtue" was formed.

1. The Virtue of an Intelligent Man

When teaching students, Confucius usually brought his disciples to the nature to inspire them instead of confining them in one room reading bundles of books made of bamboo slips.

Once, Confucius brought his disciples to the bank of Sishui River outside Qufu for an outing, when was just the spring with red pear blossom and green willow trees. The air was full of fragrance of flowers. Water level also rose. All the disciples were intoxicated in the beauty of nature.

Only Confucius stood by the galloping Sishui River meditating. Zi Gong asked: "Master, why do you like observing mighty rivers whenever you met them?" Confucius asked Zi Gong to gather all the disciples together and told them "Water, like the virtue of people, is so unselfish that it waters and nurtures everything in the world. When it flows, no matter which direction it goes, it always sticks to its own way, which is like Yi, the natural rule. When it runs, it seems to be inexhaustible, which is like the Tao. It runs down to deep valley without terror, it is like the bravery of people."

"When poured into the measuring instrument, its surface must be flat, which is like the law; It can keep its surface flat without resorting to external forces, which is like the fairness of the intelligent man." It is gentle and can reach all the subtle places, which is the clear observation of a gentleman; it is the ambition of a gentleman to roll indomitably from its origin.

"Water can seep into all the subtle places, which is like the clear observation of an intelligent man. Water flows all the way eastward from its origin with no return, which is like the ambition of an intelligent man."

"After being washed in the water, everything becomes clean, which is like the enlightenment of an intelligent man."

"With all those virtues combined in it, I like to observe it whenever I meet it."

Confucius's descriptions about water depicted an ideal image of an intelligent man in his mind, involving nine virtues of morality, goodness, Tao, courage, law, righteousness, discriminating, ambition, and enlightenment. It's because water has so many virtues like an intelligent man that Confucius likes to observe mighty rivers and ponder on it.

2. The Doctrine of the Mean

When Confucius was inspecting the ancestral temple of Duke Huan of Lu, there was a vessel that inclined to one side. Confucius questioned the temple caretaker about it: "What kind of vessel is this?" The caretaker replied: "I believe it is the warning vessel that sat on the right of the emperor." Confucius said: "I have heard of such a warning vessel (Fig. 7 - 3): if empty, it inclines; if half full, it is upright, and if completely full, it overturns." The warning vessel Confucius talked about is a vessel with a special design: it can be hung up by rope tying on ears at its both sides. Its bottom is thick and sharp, thus staying inclined if empty. Its mouth is thin and open, which is conducive to fill in a large amount of water and overturn. Above it there is a device dripping water to it at a constant speed, so it forms an automatic process: after being filled up,

Figure 7-3　The Warning Vessel

the vessel will overturn, and water will be poured. After being half full, it goes back to be upright receiving water drops.

Turning to his disciples, Confucius asked his disciples to give it a try. His disciples drew off some water and poured it into the vessel. When it was half filled, it became upright; when it was filled, it overturned; and when empty, it again inclined. Lu said: "May I ask whether there is a way to maintain complete fullness?"

Confucius replied: "Brilliant intelligence and sage-like knowledge should be guarded by the appearance of stupidity; meritorious achievements covering the whole empire should be guarded by an attitude of deference; courageous power comforting the age should be guarded by fear and riches encompassing all within the four seas should be guarded by frugality. This is what is called the way of 'drawing off and reducing'." From this warning vessel, Confucius tried to reveal a truth to his disciples and people that one should be always humble, otherwise, damages could be incurred.

In addition, Confucius also explained the Doctrine of Mean, which is very profound in its meaning. The warning vessel expressed at least two meanings: to overdo is no better than to underdo.

Chapter 11 of *The Analects of Confucius* recorded such a story: Zi Gong asked about Zi Zhang and Zi Xia, "Which of them is better?" The Master said, "Zi Zhang has overdone and Zi Xia underdone." Zi Gong asked, "Is Zi Zhang better?" The Master said, "To overdo is no better than to underdo."

There is another story about Confucius. When travelling around the states, Confucius and his disciples were busy in driving the carriage to Lvliang for half of the month. One day, they passed a small village and asked direction to an old man, "How many days do we still need to arrive in Lvliang?" Seeing the carriage, the old man gave an interesting answer "If driving fast, three days will be enough; if driving slowly, one day will be enough." Although puzzled, the anxious Master ordered his disciples to go fast. Suddenly, the axle of the carriage was broken, and they cannot move any longer, but stay in the mountain to repair the carriage. After pondering on what has happened, Confucius finally realized the meaning of the strange answer of the old man, that is "More haste, less speed."

"Grasping the two extremes and taking the mean" came from *The Doctrine of Mean* in *the Book of Rites*. This doctrine was applied in the governance of the country. The warning vessel was always put on the right of the emperor's seat to warn him to be humble and impartial. In fact, this truth also applies to daily life. For instance, when making friends, neither being too close or too cold is good. Following a natural process could make the friendship last longer.

3. The Good and Evil Nature

Exploration on human nature served as basis of Confucian moral theory before Qin Dynasty. Both Mencius, advocating that human nature was good, and Xunzi, advocating that it was evil, liked to compare qualities of water to human nature.

Gaozi, living in the same era as Mencius, thought that there was no good or evil in human nature. He argued with Mencius by citing water as evidence, saying that human nature was like a turbulent water. If an opening was opened in the east, water would flow eastward; if the opening was in the west, water would flow westward. Human nature is neither good nor evil, just like the flow of water without fixed direction. It sounded quite reasonable.

Mencius, on the other hand, advocated that human nature was good also by taking water as supporting evidence. He said, "It is true that water can flow either eastward or westward. How about the direction of upward and downward? It's well known that water must flow downward, so is the human nature. It is always good." However, if the water is beaten, it could be higher than people's forehead. The water can also be introduced up to the mountain if it is blocked by the outer force. It is the special situation that forces water to change. Likely, the reason why people do bad things lies in the fact that their human nature is forced by the outside force. Logically speaking, Mencius' statement was not persuasive enough, but he is quite intelligible to support his arguments by using the water qualities. From then on, this argument together with human nature of compassion, shame, modest and telling right from wrong have become the foundation of human virtue including benevolence, righteousness, propriety, and wisdom.

Xunzi also thought that human is born evil, and he supported has ideas by citing water qualities, too. Xunzi thought that people's mind is like a basin of water. If the basin is put upright, dirty things will naturally settle down, thus the water above it will be clean and clear enough to be used as a mirror. On the contrary, if water in the basin is stirred, the dirty things will make the clean water turbid, thus it cannot be used as mirror anymore. It's the same with people. If guided by right methods, a man can be well cultivated and become discriminating between the right and wrong. In this case, Xunzi attached great importance to the restraint and enlightenment of the rites.

To sum up, comparing water to virtue is not only the aesthetic value before Qin Dynasty, but also an important form for Confucianists to express their own thoughts. Thus, a special water image is formed in China, and it also became a moral standard for later Confucianists, bringing profound impact on Chinese politics, society and culture.

Section III Comparing Water to Country Governance

Water worshiping philosophy started by Confucius not only expounded the way to become an intelligent man but was used by ancient Chinese thinkers and politicians to express their political opinions.

The earliest record on comparing water to country governance is about Shaogong's admonishing Emperor Liwang in Zhou Dynasty. Shaogong said, "The way you forbid people to express their opinions is just like that you block rivers. When blocked, accumulated water in rivers will burst out from the broken embankment, hurting millions of people, so are the people. In this case, when managing rivers, a better way is to dredge them to let the water flow freely; likewise, a better way to govern people is to encourage them to freely express their opinions." From then on, comparing water to country governance has become increasingly frequent, and Confucianists emphasized such way, which covers the following forms.

1. Water and Relations between the Monarch and Common People

Confucius, Mencius and Xunzi have always stressed the "people-oriented" thought, that the people are the foundation in the relationship between the monarch and the people and the foundation for the development of the country. The emperors should obey the public opinion, regard the interests of the people as the fundamental interests of the country, and take the people as their own service objects. Therefore, the most representative view to describe the relationship between the monarch and the people is to compare it with boat and water, which has become a fixed and symbolic metaphor. The relationship between boat and water properly reflects the interdependence and mutual restriction between rulers and people. The boat cannot move forward without water, which means that the ruler can only rely on the people to stably hold the managing position; and the water can overturn the boat, so is the relationship between the ruler and the people. The power of the people can overthrow tyranny and drive the ruler out of power.

In fact, the earliest record on this metaphor is done by Xunzi, saying that, "The relationship between a monarch and the common people is like that between a boat and water. It is on water that a boat floats, and it is in water that a boat may capsize." The most popular story about this theory is the story between Li Shimin, Emperor Taizong of Tang Dynasty, and the wise minister Wei Zheng. In the sixth year of Zhenguan, Emperor Taizong discussed with his ministers the way of the rise and fall of the dynasty. Emperor Taizong sighed that "if the emperor runs the country with Tao, people will actively follow him; otherwise, people will abandon him. This is really frightening." Taizong's words showed his ability in reflection, which were just like a maxim by Mencius "A Just Cause Enjoys Abundant Support While an Unjust Cause Finds Little Support." Wei Zheng replied: in the past, those emperors at the end of each dynasty, living long time in peace, have forgotten dangers, ignored contradictions and turmoil, so they could not last for a long time. If you can pay attention to the way of governing the country and keep a cautious attitude like walking on thin ice, your governance will be long-term. I have also heard an ancient saying: "The relationship between a monarch and the common people is like that between a boat and water. It is on water that a boat floats, and it is in water that a boat may capsize." This dialogue touched Taizong very much. He quoted and warned himself in many places. He attached importance to people's power, and finally turned Tang Dynasty into a strong and prosperous one.

2. Administration Thought and Water

Inspired by the nature of water, the Confucianism advocates that the ruler should perform benevolent administration. Benevolence is an important part of Confucius' political thoughts. "The people need benevolence", said the Confucius, "more than water and fire. I have seen people drowned in water or burned to death in fire, but none die in benevolence." Water and fire meet the most basic needs of human material life, while benevolence meets the needs of human spiritual life. Material needs sometimes hurt people, while the constant pursuit of spirit will only make a person better, instead of incurring any harm. A Chinese idiom "Die to Achieve Benevolence" does not mean one man is killed by benevolence, but to dedicate oneself in the attainment of benevolence. Benevolence itself, therefore, shall not be blamed, which, however, is the spiritual support of the common people.

Mencius supplemented and developed Confucius's thought and put forward "benevolent administration". "Water" in Mencius's statement had become a tool to explain the "benevolent administration". Mencius advocated human-oriented idea, and thought the ruler can only run the country successfully after winning the hearts of the people. "The people's aspiration of benevolence," Mencius said, "is like the water's running downward, and the beast's going wild. On the contrary, otters try to catch fish only to drive them to deeper water, and sparrow hawk try to catch sparrows only to drive them into bushes. Likely, Jie, the last emperor of Xia Dynasty, tried to run the country, only to find that his people was forced to Shang Tang, the first emperor of Shang Dynasty, and the same happened to Zhou, the last emperor of Shang Dynasty." By this contrast, Mencius tried to warn rulers that only benevolent administration can help them to win the support of their people, like the water's running downward.

Similarly, the rulers should have firm confidence in performing "benevolent administration". Mencius believed that it is an inevitable trend for the world to return to "benevolence". Just as water will eventually put out the fire, "benevolence" can eventually trump "inhumanity".

Mencius also illustrated the essence of benevolent administration by speaking highly of Dayu's achievements in flood control for the benefit of the people and his merits and virtues of carrying out kingcraft. A water conservancy expert Bai Gui of Mencius's contemporaries once told Mencius that his contribution to flood control was better than that of Dayu: "the flood control by Dan is better than that by Yu."Dan is Bai Gui's name. Mencius criticized him and said, "you are wrong. Dayu managed the flood by following the law of water flow, and channelled the flood into the sea. He used the four seas as the gullies for water storage. On the contrary, you take neighbouring countries as gullies for water storage. Once the water is blocked, the flood will run rampant. Thus, your activity is opposed by the virtuous." Mencius pointed out that Dayu's flood control embodied the spirit of benevolent administration since he followed the natural law of water flow, while giving priority to the benefits of the common people. Unlike the selfish and indifferent Bai Gui, "Yu the

Great" Mencius said, "felt like he himself was drowned when he found that there were still people who would be drowned to death." In order to control the flood, Dayu took the lead despite his pains. He is too dedicated to his work to go back home even if he passed by the door several times. His achievement, therefore, only lied in flood control but also a showing of spirit of benevolent administration of attaching great importance to the country and the people, which is also the core of Mencius' benevolent administration.

Section IV Unity of Man and Nature

1. Monarch's Conduct and Water

In ancient feudal autocratic society, the strengthening of the centralized system led to the supremacy of the monarchs. The moral character of a person in charge is also crucial to the political environment of the whole country. Therefore, political thinkers and social critics who are good at using metaphors naturally have a lot of statements to compare water with the virtue of the monarch.

Xunzi[1] said that: "The ruler is the sundial, and the people are the shadow. If the form is upright, then the shadow will be upright. The ruler is the bowl, and the people the water. If the bowl is round, then the water will be round; if it is square, then the water will be square." According to Xunzi's statements, conduct of the ruler can directly influence behaviours of his people. In ancient China, King Zhuang of Chu was fond of small-waisted men, consequently his court was composed of men who starved themselves since they were afraid to lose the favor of the lord. Every morning, after getting up, his ministers must hold the breath to tighten their waist bank. They can only stand up with the support of the wall. Next year, the court is full of officials with unhealthy complexion. As suggested by Xunzi, the ruler is the wellspring of the people. If the wellspring is pure, then the outflow will be pure; if the wellspring is muddy, then the outflow will be muddy. As a ruler managing a vast country with billions of people, serving as a moral model is crucial to his administration.

What's more, a successful monarch shall be the one with virtue, who shall be broadminded, inclusive and respectful to talents. According to Xunzi, the more tributaries a river has, the more abundant its water will be. Similarly, a ruler can run the country well only after taking advice from all sides. In addition, he shall also remain impartial like the water since "water is perfectly level. Its correctness cannot be made to tilt to one side. When the operations of the mind are like this, they resemble the sage." Being impartial also helps to create a harmonious political atmosphere for

---

[1] Xunzi (310–235B.C.) was a Chinese Confucian philosopher and writer who lived during the Warring States Period and contributed to the hundred Schools of Thought. A book known as *the Xunzi* was traditionally attributed to him. His works survived in an excellent condition, and wore a major influence in forming the official state doctrines of the Han Dynasty.

a country. Last, a ruler needs to be modest. There were many examples on how an arrogant ruler ended up in failure, so the ruler needs to learn lessons from the history. A modest attitude is helpful in maintaining a good governance.

2. Theological Politics and Water

In addition to analogize water to the relationship between the monarch and the people, political strategy and moral conduct, the mystery and sanctity of water are also used by rulers and those who oppose them.

In ancient China, the new ruler would be described as the choice of the heaven when dynasty changed. In fact, there was a theory of "Five virtues" in ancient politics, integrating the traditional theory of five elements covering gold, wood, water, fire, and earth into the historical law of dynasty replacement. It is believed that each dynasty has its own "moral sign", just as everyone has his own zodiac sign. The five elements of gold, wood, water, fire and earth support each other on the one, and hinder each other on the other. The replacement of dynasties follows the same rule. The theory of five virtues came into being in the Warring States Period, and became popular staring from Qin Dynasty, since Qin Shihuang, the first emperor of Qin, needed a theory to legitimate his reign. Qin Shihuang thought that Qin Dynasty was in the position of "water virtue", and Zhou Dynasty "fire virtue". Qin ended Zhou's reign, which was as natural as water extinguished fire. Therefore, all subjects should obey his rule. Since it is in the position of "water virtue", it is necessary to implement "water morality". As a saying goes that "water dominates Yin, and Yin is characterized by severe punishment and kills". Therefore, the Qin Dynasty implemented the rule by law featured by strict punishment and severe law. It is believed that "water virtue" emphasize the colour of black and the number of six. Officials in Qin Dynasty preferred black clothes. When they wore hats, it needed to be as high as six inches. When taking carriages, six horses would be necessary to pull it. A stride needed to be measured as six feet when walking. Qin Shihuang's adoption of this theory is to make his subjects believe in and obey his administration. One ironical fact was that he didn't admit the five elements were restricted and checked in sequence, and claimed that Qin's water virtue was the last one among the five ones, hence it could last forever.

Such theory was gradually perfected in the Han Dynasty. From then on, each dynasty would legitimate their reign by finding a corresponding "moral sign".

In early days, people thought that the nature and human world were dominated by the supernatural sacred "heaven". Natural disasters such as floods, droughts, hails, locusts, earthquakes, landslides, pestilence were regarded as punishment for the monarch for wrongdoings, which leads to the theory of natural punishment. In his book of *Chunqiu Fanlu*, Dong Zhongshu fully discussed this theory together with the thought of the unity of heaven and man. He thought that "If one country fails in performing Tao, the Heaven will punish it by making natural disasters as warning signals." Some special natural phenomena are regarded as warnings to emperors, and water is an important aspect of natural disasters.

In the event of a major flood or disaster, the emperor should issue an imperial edict to make apologies and reflect on his own mistakes. Such an activity was typical idealism, since natural phenomena exist objectively and have no inevitable connection with the emperor's immorality. However, in the feudal society, because the emperor's rights were supreme, the theory of heaven's punishment, to a certain extent, was meaningful in restricting the emperor's rights.

In a word, water, an element of nature, has a very important position in the minds of ancient Chinese politicians and thinkers. They endowed water with political life, ranging from the origin of the world to the personal conduct. Appearing a little bit old-fashioned nowadays, those thoughts, however, are still significant in such social issues as properly handling the relationship between the CPC and the masses, protecting the people's interests, and carrying out the anti-corruption campaign within the CPC.

Chapter Eight Water and Taoism

Section I The Highest Good is Like that of Water

Confucius and Laozi[①] (Fig. 8-1) represented two different philosophy systems, namely, Confucianism and Taoism. However, both liked to compare water to people's virtue. When seeing water, Laozi signed: "The highest good is like that of water. Its goodness lies in facts that it benefits everything; yet itself does not scramble." In comparison, Confucius's comments were "Time passes away night and day like running water." Water has greatly enlightened ancient Chinese philosophers.

Figure 8-1 Laozi

[①] Laozi was an ancient Chinese philosopher and writer. He is the reputed author of the *Daodejing*, the founder of philosophical Taoism, and a deity in religious Taoism and traditional Chinese religions.

1. Water is Near to the Tao

Through thousands of years of world civilization, there are several major breakthroughs in philosophy. Some of them took place in China. Many schools were created by ancient Chinese philosophers in the pre-Qin Dynasty Period, among whom Laozi was an extraordinary one. Mr. Zhang Dainian, a famous Chinese modern philosopher, thought that Laozi was the founder of ontology of ancient Chinese philosophy. The core of Laozi's philosophical thoughts is Tao. What is the Tao? Laozi thought that "Tao that can be told of is not an unvarying Tao. The name that can be named are not unvarying names…The origin of Tao we can but call the Mystery, or rather the 'Darker than any Mystery', the Tao whence issued all Secret Essences." All in all, the Tao is "incommensurable and impalpable." Laozi's explanation of Tao has confused many people, so he compared the Tao to water that was familiar to everyone.

Shuowen Jiezi (*Origin of Chinese Characters*) explained that "Tao is the road people walked on." The original meaning of "Tao" is road, and then understood as rule of things. One feather of water is that it flows along its way. When springing out of its source, water doesn't scatter around but follow one way. "Tao" shall also be understood like this, and that's also the reason why Laozi compared Tao to water. This vivid explanation of Tao has made the once complicated concept much easier to understand. By following Tao, it means that everything in the world develops by following natural rules.

2. Water Benefits Everything without Scrambling

In *Daodejing* (also known as *Laozi*), Laozi said that "The highest good is like that of water. The goodness of water is that it benefits everything; yet it does not scramble but is content with the places that all men disdain. It is this that makes water so near to the Tao." Benefiting everything without scrambling and staying at the humblest place are two distinctive features of water admired by Laozi.

In details, "the highest good" means the best virtue, i. e., people can bring great benefits to others; "without scrambling" means without fighting for interests such as fame or fortune. People who act by following the Tao will be called sage by Laozi.

Water is everywhere moistening everything. It is the same case with the Tao, which is why Laozi compared Tao to water.

3. Remaining in the Humblest Place

"Water is content with the places that all men disdain. It is this that makes water so near to the Tao." People with virtue are willing to contribute silently as paving stone for others. Their behaviors are those by following the Tao.

Laozi thought that the sea was inclusive because it was in a lower place, thus becoming big, and therefore can water all things in the world, which was the essence of Tao. The essence has consisted of two qualities of water: one is being in humble place, and the other is inclusive, two of which have relations of cause and effect. Because water has the quality of running downward, and therefore inclusive. The sea is located at a lower place, so it can receive hundreds of rivers and becomes immense.

4. Other Virtues of Water

In *Daodejing*, Laozi summarized the virtue of water as the following: "It is located in a good place, always remains still, values gentleness in friendship, and truth in words; it is fair and upright, it is effective within its reach and act with good timing."

By "locating in a good place", it means that water likes to remain at places disdained by others, showing its humble attitude.

By "remaining still", it means that the water is as calm down as deep water, and outside forces won't influence it. As compared to people, men need to stay free from the influence of personal gains or losses.

By "valuing gentleness", it means when making friends, men shall be sincere.

By "valuing truth in words", it means that men need to be integrated.

By "being fair and upright", it means that men need to be upright and fair when doing deeds.

By "being effective within its reach", it means that men need to do things that are within their reaches. Mencius said, "Jumping across the North Sea with Taishan Mountain under one's arm is beyond human being's ability. People don't do it because they cannot accomplish the task. However, if one refuses to give a help hand to the elderly. It's not because he cannot do it but he is not willing to do it."

By "acting with good timing", it means that people should be good at grasping opportunities, doing the right at the right time and stopping when it is needed. Otherwise, people always face failure.

The above seven qualities of water embody the highest requirements on the perfect human personality by Laozi. Almost nobody can have all of them, but people can cultivate themselves toward such goals.

The analogy of water is a common thinking characteristic of ancient Chinese thinkers. Some use water to describe people, or to compare morality with water, Tao with water, or war strategies with water. Compared with other thinkers in the pre-Qin Period, Laozi's understanding of water is obviously more profound. He did not simply use the metaphor of water to compare his ideal personality but found out its internal law and logical relationship from the characteristics of water, and constructed a relatively complete ideal personality with water as the main clue. Laozi's statements related to water have become an important origin of Chinese culture in comparing water to people's virtue.

Section II Models with Virtue of Water

Based on Laozi's description on human virtue after comparing to water qualities 2,500 years ago, Chinese people have concluded a Chinese virtue as "The highest good is like that of water, being inclusive and bearing great virtue", which has also become the highest virtue standard pursued by Chinese people.

Laozi has said that "Water has great virtue since it benefits everything; water is humble since it never scrambles while benefiting everything; water is also inclusive since it is content with the places that all men disdain." From his statement, it can be concluded that Laozi thought staying humble was an ideal human nature. A humble person is likely to be inclusive, which in turn can win a lot of support for him. In other words, one's achievements are proportional to his degree of tolerance. If one want to learn from water qualities, he should be broad-minded just like water that is very soft but can tolerate the whole world.

1. People Accomplishing Great Achievements Advocate Modesty and Tolerance

From ancient times to the present, all those who have made great achievements have the moral quality of modesty and tolerance. Let's take Liu Bei in the Three Kingdoms Period as an example. When starting his fight, Liu Bei had no army, no city as his base, and no high talents. But he was broad-minded with firm faith and the character of humility and tolerance. Finally, it was his good qualities that attracted many excellent talents to support him, and Liu Bei has ultimately became the emperor of the Shu Kingdom. The story of his visit to Zhuge Liang for three times is well-known to Chinese people.

Another good example is Cao Cao. Even though he was suspicious, he also has extraordinary tolerant character, which was shown in the Battle of Guandu. After defeating Yuan Shao, many letters were found, which were written to Yuan Shao before the war by people from Xudu, Cao Cao's base. Cao Pi, a son of Cao Cao advised him to arrest those people, but Cao Cao said that "Even I could not protect myself then, let alone others." Finally, he threw the letter into the fire without even reading it.

Cao Cao appreciated Guan Yu's bravery, and after he was captured, he was rewarded with many valuable presents and treated with great courtesy. However, Guan Yu still had no intention to surrender to him, since he cannot forget his pledge to share weal and woe with Liu Bei. When Cao's generals heard that Guan Yu had left, they asked Cao Cao to send troops to pursue and kill him.

When Cao Cao learned of the news, he did not kill Guan Yu. Instead, he allowed him to go alone for thousands of miles, kill six of his generals through five passes, and even let all levels of passes let him go. It was Cao Cao's magnanimity that made Guan Yu let him off on the Huarong Road after losing the Battle of Chibi. Finally, Wei Kingdom, led by Cao Cao, became the most powerful one in the Three Kingdoms.

2. Ultimate Goal of an Excellent Member of the Communist Party of China: Serve the People

The motto of "The highest good is like that of water, being inclusive and bearing great virtue" is not only pursued by intellectuals, but also the moral standards of an excellent Communist. The aspiration of the CPC since its foundation has always been bringing benefits to the working masses. As early as 1944, Chairman Mao Zedong put forward the idea of "serving the people", taking it as the fundamental purpose of the CPC, which showed that the great undertakings led by CPC aimed at bringing benefits to the majority of people.

Over the past 90 years, CPC has always shared the same breath and the same destiny with Chinese people. By adhering to the people-oriented principle, CPC has performed its administration by relying on the people and ultimately for the people.

In the 19th CPC National Congress report, general secretary Xi Jinping stressed the need to "Strictly adhere to the fundamental purpose of serving the people wholeheartedly, and carry out the party's mass line into the country governing activities"; "all the work of the party must take the fundamental interests of the overwhelming majority of the people as the highest standard. We should persist in taking the trivial matters of the people as our major affairs, start with the jobs that the people care about and those that satisfy the people, and lead the people to create a better life."

Jiao Yulu is a good example of "a good member of the party", "a good servant of the people", and a model of the Secretary of the CPC Committee at the county level. In the 1960s, although suffered from liver cancer, he still persevered with his work in leading the people of Lankao to fight against the sandstorm and to alleviate harms caused by sand, flood and saline-alkali soil. He always put the interests of the common people in the first place and made great efforts to build Lankao. With his own practical actions, the "spirit of Jiao Yulu" was forged and an eternal monument to serve the people was built.

An excellent manager should also be like water, tolerant and modest to his subordinates. Only in this way can he unite talents to form an efficient team. A man with this character can always succeed, because he can do what others don't want to do, and he is willing to go places disdained by others.

Section III Actionless Administration

"Staying actionless" is one of the core thoughts of "Tao". Laozi not only explained Tao with water, but also described the norms and requirements for rulers by observing and analysing the nature of water. In *Daodejing*, he said "Tao never does, neither does the water." Water, although unconsciously and unintentionally, flows from its source and nourishes all things. We are so used to its existence that we fail to realize its importance all the time. It seems that water never does. In fact, People's life is inseparable from water. Similarly, rulers should stay actionless like water, so that the people can become self-disciplined.

In Chinese history, actionless administration was performed by Shun when he was in power. Shun followed Yao's ideas in administration without any changes. In fact, it means to conform to the natural changes, and do not act rashly, so that the world is duly regulated. This idea was thereafter referred to enlighten people with virtue.

1. Inactivity

There are two layers of meanings of "Inactivity": Firstly, people need to behave by following natural trends. Laozi said "the Sage rules by emptying his people's hearts, and filling their bellies, weakening their intelligence, and toughening their sinews". It means that the ruler shall feed his people well and toughen their bodies, so that they will not need to struggle for life.

"Inactivity" does not mean doing nothing, but behaving without too much artificial interference, so that people's creativity could be brought into full play. In addition, "Inactivity" also means behaving without subjective actions. When ruling, needs and demands of the common people shall be respected and followed, and the wills of the minority shall not be imposed on the majority.

2. Taking Actions

The second layer meaning of "Inactivity", on the contrary, is taking actions. "Inactivity" does not mean do nothing, but to take actions in a restrained and selective manner like the way water does. Only by this way can people stay focused on what needs to be done, which is also the thought advocated by Taoism.

In Chapter 37 of *Daodejing*, Laozi said "Tao never does; yet through it all things are done. If the barons and kings would but possess themselves of it, everything would at once be transformed." It means that Tao seems to stay actionless, but it turns out to get everything duly regulated. Barons and kings, when ruling their own countries, shall not be too arbitrary in pursuing personal fame. Then natural rule will serve as an invisible hand to guide people and everything to be duly disciplined, therefore peace and prosperity can be attained.

Judging from the history, such a rule always works. King Zhuang of Chu State during the Autumn and Spring Period was a good example on his way to become one of the five hegemonies.

One night, Duke Zhuang of Chu treated his officials with a banquet, and his concubines also attended the feast. During the banquet, Duke Zhuang asked Xu Ji and Mai Ji, two of his most beloved beauties, to toast the generals in turn. Suddenly, a gust of wind blew, and all the candles on the banquet went out, leaving the hall to be dark. At this time, a general ventured to stretch out his hand and attempted to touch Xu Ji in the dark. Xu Ji was very angry, but also very tactfully pulled off the tassel belt on the man's hat as evidence. Then Xu Ji complained in front of Duke Zhuang of Chu and asked him to light the candle and look at the hats of the people to find out the person who offended her. After hearing this, Duke Zhuang of Chu announced in a loud voice, "Please take off your tassel on hat to enjoy your food and drink." Everyone obeyed his order, then the Duke ordered to light candles and drink with his officials until the banquet was over.

Three years later, in the war between Chu State and Jin State, a general fought very bravely in every battle. Finally, he dedicated the head of the enemy general to the Duke of Chu. The Duke was so surprised that he couldn't help asking "I don't usually give you any special favour. Why do you fight so hard?" The general replied, "I was the man whose tassel was pulled off in the feast. I should have been punished and died at that time, but you were so generous in forgiving me, which makes me guilty for a long time. Today, what I have done is to show my appreciation for your generosity." It was this seemingly inaction, but in fact, very tolerant practice of King Zhuang of Chu that finally made the State of Chu strong.

Laozi said: "So long as I do nothing, the people will of themselves be transformed, so long as I love quietude, the people will of themselves go straight; so long as I act only by inactivity, the people will of themselves become prosperous; so long as I have no wants, the people will of themselves return to the ' state of the Uncarved Block'." In the administration, the ruler shall benefit people rather than bossing them. With Tao in action, everything will be duly regulated, as seas and mighty rivers can attract bricks flowing toward them. In this case, Laozi suggested to rulers that virtue of water including generosity, unselfishness and modesty was needed to run the country.

Section IV The Enlightenment of Actionless Administration

The followings are enlightenment got from actionless administration.

1. On Environmental Protection

After the reform and opening, more efforts are devoted to economic development over ecological protection in many parts of China, leaving no harmony between man and nature. Such irrational tap of natural resources led to serious smog and pollution of rivers and lakes. The reason underlying is the failure of human being in following natural rules. Actionless administration like water should have been applied in tapping natural resources, rather than the adoption of arbitrary, excessive, and unreasonable way of exploration. There are spirits in every mountain and water, and feelings in every plant and tree. The rational development and utilization of natural resources is allowed, but we can't plunder and destroy it relentlessly. On the contrary, natural rules shall be followed by bringing peace back to nature, so that every living being can coexist. Only when human beings cherish the natural environment on which we live, nature will always nourish us like a loving mother and continue to contribute selflessly for us.

In September 2013, when delivering a speech at a university in Kazakhstan, President Xi Jinping said, "We not only need golden and silver mountains but also lucid water and lush mountains. If an alternative must be chosen, we would pick the latter one rather than the former one. In fact, lucid water and lush mountain are themselves valuable silver and golden mountains." Such statement has conveyed to the world the concept of China's green development and vividly expressed the distinct attitude and firm determination of our party and government to vigorously promote ecological protection.

Accelerating the reform of ecological civilization system and building a beautiful China is an important conclusion put forward in the report of the 19th National Congress of the Communist Party of China. General Secretary Xi Jinping pointed out in the report that "lucid water and lush mountain are valuable silver and golden mountains".

We would rather abandon the economic development that destroys the ecological environment, to ensure the ecological civilization. We should protect the environment on the one, and develop the economy on the other, to achieve both goals.

Principles of respecting, following, and protecting of nature shall be strictly adhered to. To build a beautiful China and realize socialist ecological civilization at the new era, efforts need to be made to carry out basic policy of resource saving and environmental protection and to include ecological protection into the process of economy, politics, culture and social development.

2. On the Building of a Clean Government

An old saying goes like this "Please don't expect to make a fortune if you work as an official, and if you want to become rich, don't work as an official", which fully embodies the norms and constraints required by actionless administration on the leadership. It is an indispensable ideological resource and has profound implications for the building of a clean government.

Let's look at a man, Li Dakang, who is one of the main characters in the popular TV series "the Name of the People" in the first half of 2017. It can be said that he is a double-sided man. In his life, he is boring and appears to be indifferent in many regards. He denied the requests of his wife, Ouyang Jing, for many times, refused to take care of his old friends' business, and rarely paid for the living expenses of his daughter studying abroad. Finally, he divorced his wife, and his family broke up. In his work, he is very vigorous in solving difficulties. For the interests of the common people, he rejected the unreasonable request of Zhao Ruilong, the son of the former Secretary of the Provincial Party Committee. He resolutely refused to approve a pollution project and transformed a marshland into a scenic spot. He was praised highly as a model in reform by Sha Ruijin, a Provincial Party Secretary.

Li Dakang is a contradictory role, but he is also dialectically unified. His behavior is just in line with Laozi's "Inactivity" theory. On the one hand, when faced with his relatives, he seems to have done nothing, but it is his "Inactivity" that has helped him to achieved his great achievements——serving the people all the time, and achieving a Communist's thought of building the party for the public and assuming power for the people. Therefore, the CPC leadership should behave like Li Dakang in doing nothing in seeking personal interests.

Corruption is the tumour of the society. Punishing corruption and restricting power coincides with the concept of "actionless administration". Its essence is to encourage social autonomy. In areas where social autonomy can be achieved, the government should try not to intervene. Do nothing, if necessary, corruption can be reduced since there is no excessive power. Since the eighteenth Congress, the Party Central Committee, with Xi Jinping as its core, has promulgated the "eight provisions" to further promote anti-corruption campaign, which is quite decisive in performing. This campaign is like the thought of Taoism in advocating frugality and opposing extravagance.

3. On Our Lives

The thought of "Inactivity" can also be used to guide our study and life. Almost every step we take in life will encounter resistance. However, to achieve the main goal of life, we must sacrifice or abandon a lot of things. For example, if you want to achieve good academic results, you may have to sacrifice the time of dating or online chatting. An unyielding spirit like the flowing of water needs to be taken in the study. In addition, when making efforts, things we want to accomplish need to be selected and restricted. Only when you have something to give up, can we achieve our goal in life.

Section V   The Soft Triumphs over the Hard

1. The Implication of "the Soft Triumphs over the Hard"

In 2012, a statue of Laozi was set up in Suzhou Industrial Park, incurring heated discussion. In the statue, Laozi sticks out his tongue and shows his teeth (Fig. 8-2). Many netizens said that the sculpture is ugly, which has vilified the sage. There are also some people believing that this is not a vilification. There is a story behind it. One year, Confucius, with his disciples, went to Luoyang, capital city of the Zhou Dynasty, to visit Laozi for Tao. Laozi opened his mouth and asked, "Do I still have the teeth", "no" answered Confucius, "How about my tongue?" Laozi continued, "yes!" answered Confucius. Then Laozi stated that "What is stiff and hard is a 'companion of death', what is soft and weak is a 'companion of life'; the teeth is hard, so they are gone earlier; the tongue is soft, so it is still here."

Figure 8-2   The Statue of Laozi

In this story, Laozi used the tongue to show that the soft can conquer the hard. In the book, Laozi used water to explain this truth. One important feature of water is that it is soft. Laozi thought that "nothing under heaven is softer or more yielding than water; but when it attacks things hard and resistant there is not one of them that can prevail. For they can find no way of altering it." In this case, Laozi advocated to behave like water, so that the soft could triumphs over the hard and the weak over the strong.

What Laozi has advocated has the following two layers of meanings.

(1) Staying Soft can Protect Oneself

Firstly, staying soft can protect oneself. Laozi proved his theory by observing the life of human being and plants, he said "When he is born, man is soft and weak; in death he becomes stiff and hard. The plants and trees are supple and soft while they are alive, but they become brittle and dry when they are dead. Truly, what is stiff and hard is a 'companion of death', what is soft and weak is a 'companion of life.'" "The reason why the hard is easily damaged is that it is too prominent to avoid shock from the outside force, which is also the reason why an old Chinese saying says that if one tree is taller than others in the forest, the wind will destroy it. On the contrary, the grass, tender as it is, is easy to protect itself when attacked by the wild wind.

Laozi thought that protecting one's life is paramount. Since the soft conquers the hard, it is a good choice to stay soft to protect oneself in the battle. Let's take the story of an American soldier as an example. In war, American soldiers are allowed to surrender. In the Korean and Vietnamese wars, American soldiers had a surrender letter in their pockets, printed in 13 languages. Chinese was the most prominent. It said "I am an American. Please don't kill me and try to send me back. I will pay you, through the U. S. government." Chinese people call it the letter of surrender, while the U. S. military call it the letter of life saving. In the eyes of American soldiers, it is not shameful to be a prisoner, and to live is the most important thing. This is also in line with Laozi's philosophy of valuing life.

(2) The Soft can Conquer the Hard

Laozi thought that protecting oneself was still not the ultimate purpose of staying soft but conquering the hard. He said that "What is of all things most yielding can overwhelm that which is of all things most hard." The same rule applies in the water. In daily life, we can observe a fact that the drips, with its long-time persistence, can penetrate a hard stone. It shows that the weak, despite its weakness, can finally achieve the goal by relying on the long-term persistence.

When enough water is accumulated, it has amazing power. When the flood is overflowing, the fields and buildings will be inundated, and the buildings will be destroyed. Nothing solid can resist it. It can be seen that the weakness mentioned by Laozi is not really weak. It contains indomitable confidence and tenacious will and can finally achieve the goal of conquering the strong.

Water, being soft and never compete for anything, seems to be subordinate to the hard. In fact, it can finally conquer the hard. Staying soft can protect oneself on the one and overwhelm the hard on the other.

2. The Enlightenment of "the Soft Triumphs over the Hard"

The following is the enlightenment drawn from the truth that the soft triumphs over the hard.

(1) Seizing the Chance to Attain the Goal

In our life, when we are weak, the first thing to do is to protect ourselves, and then realize our dreams with long-time persistence; when we build enough power, we need to seize the chance in time and get to where we admire at once.

The story of Duke Zhuang in Chu state during the Spring and Autumn Period was a good example. Three years after he was in power, he did nothing. One of his officials criticized him that "I have met a kind of bird who does not practice its wings, nor fly or chirp for three years. Your majesty, do you know what its name is?" The king knew well that it referred to him, so he argued that "without practice its wings for three years, they are growing; without flying or chirping for three years, it is observing people's attitudes. Although it does not fly now, it will fly high into the sky someday; although it does not chirp now, it will shock everyone when it begins to do in the future." Half year after the dialogue, the king performed large-scale reforms including abolishing ten old criminal regulations, killing five corrupt officials, starting nine new regulations beneficial to the future development of the Chu state, and appointing six talented people as his aids. Thanks to the reforms, Chu State had become stronger and began to enjoy the hegemony among other states.

There were many cases in which the weak conquered the strong in Chinese history, which have become important parts of Chinese wisdom. It includes the story of Gou Jian, the king of the Yue state, who endued all the humiliation and hardships after being defeated by Wu State and finally realized his retaliation. Another example is Liu Bang, the founding emperor of Han Dynasty, who was weak at the beginning when battling against army led by General Xiang Yu, and finally got victory.

(2) Staying Flexible

Laozi thought that water had great flexibility since it was tender. When it is still, it is as horizontal as an instrument, precipitating impurities, clarifying itself, and perfectly reflecting the foreign objects; when it flows under normal conditions, it is square when it meets a square, a circle when meeting a circle. No matter what kind of environment it is in, it can always protect itself and easily adapt itself to the surroundings; when the torrent is surging, it can burst into a kind of amazing power, which can carry mighty mountains, penetrate stones, and destroy gold. Huge waves can even capsize big boats. Under abnormal conditions, it can be either as hard as steel or be dispersed into steam, presenting in an almost invisible state, but can arrive at every place.

In daily life, many praises are given to appreciate the strength of the strong since the strong can always win over the weak. However, an appreciation of the long-standing persistence of the weak is often absent, hence, a peaceful mindset and a restrained manner are also absent when dealing with matters. For instance, road rage has happened from time to time in recent years, leading to tragedies like what has happened in Chengdu. Lu, a female driver, was beaten violently by a male driver Zhang because she changed lanes several times while driving, resulting in Lu's bone fractures at several places. Zhang was also sentenced to have eight months' imprisonment and one-year long probation for intentional injury. The incident was started by a small matter. However, it is the short temper and unnecessary anger that upgrade it into a tragedy.

  The intense anger is not a solution to a problem. A calm but firm attitude may be a better choice to simply tell the other people that he or she is wrong. In the incident above, Zhang's performance was too strong. Provided he could step back a little bit, he could not only save himself from the pain of staying in prison but save others from physical hurt.

Chapter Nine Water and Guanzi's Ideology

Abundant water culture could be seen in all pre-Qin philosophies[①], among which the thoughts involving water culture of Guanzi School embodied with unique features, systematically reflected in the book *Guanzi*. The philosophies and statements concerning water and conservancy in *Guanzi* were concentrated in several articles, such as *Shuidi*, *Dudi* and *Chengma*, especially the most representative one named *Shuidi*, the 39th article. Water culture in Guanzi's (Fig. 9-1) ideology mainly manifests in the following aspects.

Figure 9-1　Guanzi

Section I　Water is the Origin of the World

Water is the origin of the world, without which neither can life exist or everything show vibrant. The philosophy that water breeds the universe is acknowledged by almost the entire

---

① Pre-Qin philosophies: The philosophies before Qin unified China in 221 B.C. are called pre-Qin philosophies. It includes multiple philosophy systems and schools reflecting benefits of different classes of people.

Chinese nation. The author of *Guanzi* was a typical representative who owned such perception. In *Guanzi*, water is regarded as the origin of the world and the root of everything. It was stated in *Guanzi* that "What is water? Just the origin of the universe, and forebear of all living creatures", "Nothing survives without water", "Water is such thing that can fill anything and stay anywhere. Water can gather on the ground or in the sky, contained in everything"(*Shuidi · Guanzi*).

In *Guanzi*, it is believed that human is made of water. "Human is water. Man and woman blend together then embryo is formed through water flow." It shows that the body or embryo of human is formed through water flow. It further explains that the formation of fetus undergoes three phases: the phase of "three months", "five months" and "ten months". The fetus in the phase of "three months" can absorb five tastes, i. e. , five internal organs. The sour taste corresponds to the spleen, the salty taste the lung, the pungent taste the kidney, the bitter taste the liver, and the sweet taste the heart. Five internal organs being formed, then five internal structures come into being. Membrane is shaped following the formation of the spleen, bone follows the lung, brain follows the kidney, skin follows the liver and flesh follows the heart. The formation of five internal organs is followed by the creation of nine orifices. The nose gets into shape from the spleen, the eyes from the liver, the ears from the kidney, other orifices from the lung. The body is formed in the phase of "five months", and then baby is born in the phase of "ten months". In *Guanzi*, it also says that "After birth, baby can see by eyes, hear by ears and think by heart. What the eyes can see are not only mountains, but also tiny things. What the ears can hear is not only the thunder, but also little voice. What the heart can think are only something big, but also the subtle issues."

It is believed in *Guanzi* that man and woman blend then embryo is formed through water flow. After three months, the fetus will be able to absorb five tastes, after which five internal organs are formed, followed by the formation of nine orifices. After five months, the body will get into shape. After ten months, the baby will be born. Both the feeling and thought are all produced from water including the sight, hearing, thought, nine orifices and feeling of five sense organs.

In *Shuidi · Guanzi*, apart from the statement that "water" is the origin of everything, it proposes that "land" is also the essence of the universe. "Land is the medium of all living things." "Medium" means the place where everything takes root. Then it says "Water, being the blood of the land, flows like the vein in human's body." It means water circulates in the ground like blood vessels in human's body. That's why it says water possesses everything.

Section II Water and Self-cultivation as well as Statecraft

1. Water and Self-cultivation

It is nearly the most common metaphor for pre-Qin philosophers to use water as a metaphor for human's virtue. *Shuidi · Guanzi* states that "water being plain, human is righteous; water being clear, human is affable; human being righteous, desires are uncontaminated; human being affable, behaviours are innocent." "Water being righteous" indicates that composition of water is single and pure, while "water being clear" means the nature of water is clean and transparent. Therefore, that is to say, if the water quality is pure, human will be of integrity; if the water quality is clear, human will be approachable. With impartial human heart, there will be no filthy lust; with affable human heart, there will be no evil behaviours. Here Guanzi realized the relations between water and moral character of human. On the basis of stating the thought that water is the origin of the universe, *Guanzi* evolved the characteristics of water into that of morality, putting forward the concept of "using water as a metaphor for morality".

In *Guanzi*, water is extremely admired and characterized by personification and ethicization. Water is highly praised as "God" possessing everything with "both utility and beauty", for which Guanzi asked people to learn from water. In *Shuidi · Guanzi*, it says "Water possesses everything. How to know that? Being soft and clear, water can wash off dirty, which shows its benevolence. Though it looks dark, water is actually white, which shows its honesty. If measuring water, it stops the inflow when container is full, which shows its justice. Man struggles upwards while water flows downwards, which shows its humility. Humility is where Tao embodies and manifests the tolerance of emperors." These statements indicate five moral characters of water including benevolence, honesty, righteousness, justice, and humility. The aim is to admonish people to learn from water by emulate its selfless benevolence and achieve the realm possessing both kindness and beauty. Moral characters are used as metaphor in *Guanzi* to describe water from different angles according to its distinct functions and properties. Similarities can be seen between such metaphor and the Taoist concept "greatest virtue is like water" and the Confucian theory "water is likely to be used by a man or woman of virtue to compare to his or her own moral characters".

2. Different Water Characteristics Determine Various Folk Customs and Morals of the Local People

As the old saying goes "The unique features of a local environment always give special characteristics to its inhabitants", water in different places cultivates people of different types. *Shuidi · Guanzi* gives detailed statements on the relationship between characteristics of the local water at that time and people's nature and "What is water? ... Beauty, ugliness, virtuousness, disgrace, stupidity, talent are all born from it." It is stated in the book that water gives birth to different moral characters, in which examples are listed to show different water cultivates people with various characteristics and folk customs. "As water in ancient State of Qi flowed urgently, people in Qi showed greedy and rude. As water in ancient state of Chu flowed mildly, people in Chu seemed nimble and bold. As water in ancient State of Yue was muddy and erosive, people in Yue were stupid, jealous and dirty. As water in ancient State of Qin was stagnant and turbid, people in Qin showed greedy, brutal and cunning with favour in slaughter. As water in ancient State of Jin was bitter and mixed, people in Jin showed flattering and hypocritical with greed in money. As water in ancient State of Yan were weak, stagnant, and mixed, people in Yan seemed innocent, steadfast with no fear of death. As water in ancient State of Song were light and clear, people in Song seemed simple and friendly with fond in justice.

Through the understanding of nature of rivers in different places, *Guanzi* connects characteristics of water with temperament and moral characters of local people, holding that the sages enlighten the public in different ways according to different characteristics of local water, by which they could finally achieve the goal of governing the country. Although there may be biases, it is no matter an opinion of simple Materialism explaining humanity with the material nature of water, which is much more scientific compared with the transcendental theory of humanity.

Section III　Water and Governance

Guanzi finds the key to governing the country from the relationship between nature of water, humanity and folklore, and further believes water plays an essential role in the governance of a country lying in that the ruler's understanding of water is the foundation of governing the country. In *Shuidi · Guanzi*, it is said that "When the sages govern society, they do not conduct enlightenment from door to door". It means that the sages govern society by mastering nature of water instead of admonishing everyone or persuading each family. That is the point. *Guanzi* discusses the relationship between water and country governance in great detail. It says: "Those who are good in governing country must first eliminate the five hazards, … one is flood; one is drought; one is severe weather; one is pestilence; and the other is insect. These are the so called five hazards, among which flood is the worst one. After the five hazards have been eliminated, people can be governed well." (*Dudi · Guanzi*) [1] This sentence clearly points out that floods are the country's biggest disasters. Those who are adept at governance must first deal with the floods. The success of water conservancy is the prerequisite for the prosperity of a country. Only by vigorously building water conservancy facilities can allow the agriculture to develop, the economy prosper, and the country be strong. In *Guanzi*, it says "If the ditches cannot be dig through and water in the dams overflows to disaster, the country will be in poverty; conversely if the ditches are dig through and dams store water well, the country will be in prosperity."(*Lizheng · Guanzi*) [2] It is believed in *Guanzi* that the enactment of national laws and regulations must follow the laws of water, combining legislation with the philosophy of water. "The decree shall be issued like the source of the flowing water. The people shall be put on the position with no disputes. The decrees

---

[1]　*Dudi · Guanzi*: the 57th article of *Guanzi*.
[2]　*Lizheng · Guanzi*: the 4th article of *Guanzi*.

issued conform with common aspiration of the people. *Following people's will, the decrees could be implemented.*" (*Mumin · Guanzi*) ① It means that the country must enact and issue decrees like flowing water, naturally following the will of the people, so that the decrees could be implemented nationwide. When it comes to how to deal with the relation between governors and the people, the tactic called "releasing and blocking" are recommended in *Guanzi*. "If the people are too closed, they must be channelled, and if the people are too open, they must be blocked. Just like the flowing water, we shall build a dam to make it flow and block it to stop the flow." (*Junchen II · Guanzi*) ② "Governing the people without understanding the tactic of releasing and blocking is like making the water flow back." "Governing people is like controlling the water. If the monarch himself can act according to the rules, the officials will obey the orders." (*Qifa · Guanzi*) ③ "If the monarch's behaviours follow the rules, the people will submit to the authority. If not, the people will not either. This is like a surging wave that will fall when reaching the top, which is an inevitable trend." (*Junchen II · Guanzi*) From Guan Zi's point of view, if the water nature is understood, the monarch will know about the public sentiments and then find the key to governing the country.

Water resources are the basic material conditions for the existence and development of a country. According to the source and flow conditions, *Guanzi* divides rivers into five categories namely Jingshui (main river), Zhishui (branch river), Gushui (seasonal river), Chuanshui (artificial river) and Yuanshui (lake and marsh), which provides a scientific division for the development and utilization of water resources. It is said, "Rivers have differences in size and distance. Those originate flow the mountains and flow into the sea are called Jingshui; Those separate from others and flow into rivers and sea are called Zhishui; Those lie in valleys and sometimes disappear are called Gushui; Those originate from the underground and flow into rivers and sea are called Chuanshui; Those originate from the underground without flowing out are called Yuanshui." (*Shuidi · Guanzi*) Regarding the different ways in which water resources exist, *Guanzi* believes that we must proceed from the characteristics of water, make best use of the situation, and adapt measures according to local conditions in order to achieve the desired effect. As it says "Along with their flows, these five kinds of rivers can be guided and can also be blocked" and "The nature of water lie in that when flowing down from a high place, it will be so fast that it can move the stones; while going up from below, it will not move on. Therefore, we could raise the upstream water level and guide it down with potteries. The pottery tilts down three-tenths per foot, and the water can travel 49 li in a hurry. Then the water can flow to farther places." (*Dudi · Guanzi*)

Guanzi puts forward some specific measures on how to make use of water resources effectively and prevent natural disasters like floods. One is to set up an administrative organization. Water conservancy is a major issue of manpower and material resources, which must have highly developed organization and management technology. *Lizheng · Guanzi* proposed to set up a water

---

① *Mumin · Guanzi*: the 1st article of *Guanzi*.
② *Junchen II · Guanzi*: the 31st article of *Guanzi*.
③ *Qifa · Guanzi*: the 6th article of *Guanzi*.

management organization and clarified its main responsibilities. It said: "In order to keep the safety of the reservoir, we should discharge the ponding, dredge the ditches, and repair the dikes and dams. So that when there is too much rain, it is harmless to the grain. And when the year is dry, there still has a good harvest. This is the duty of Sikong①." It further stipulates the specific responsibilities and division of labour of water officials: "To eliminate the five disasters water disaster is the primary one above all. To set up a water officer and appoint a person who is familiar with water to administrate it. To appoint a minister and a minister assistant to take charge of the principals and all the official assistants. Each of the water officer's left and right subordinates select one person as the leader of hydraulicians. They were sent to inspect waterways, walls, dikes, rivers, ditches, government offices, and state capital. And they appropriate funds to officers for all the places to be repaired". (*Dudi · Guanzi*) To organize and manage an efficient institute is the principal guarantee for water conservancy activities.

The second is to take preventive measures. For flood control, prevention is more important than settlement after it happens. *Dudi · Guanzi* puts forward specific preventive measures on how to prevent floods. It says "In late autumn, a civil census should be conducted to check household registration and land, verify the population, and count the numbers of men, women, old and children separately. Those who cannot be engaged in water control work shall be exempted; those who are unable to work because of sickness shall be treated as patients; those who can only do a little work shall be treated as half-workers. After a general investigation, the soldiers from various places were selected, and the total number of soldiers serving in the military should be reported to the officer. As for the tools for controlling floods, preparations should be made during the winter slack. For every ten soldiers, there should be six baskets, spades, clamp spates and wooden rams, one earth cart, and two rain-proof canopies. And there should be two sets of food utensils for each soldier to keep in case of damage or loss. Then the water control officials and the foremen should be often required to check such preparations together with the local officials called Sanlao, Liyousi and Wuzhang (county-level officials). During the winter slack, soldiers are sent to gather firewood and store next to the water. Therefore, preparations are made when there is no flood and used when the flood occurs. So that the flood can be controlled with less harm. This is called being always prepared and taking preventive measures." It is pointed out that at the end of autumn, the water conservancy construction team should be organized according to the number of people, the amount of land, and the actual situation. And the team roster should be reported to the government. Various construction tools and materials should be prepared to prevent problems before they occur.

Guanzi regards the construction and maintenance of dikes as an important preventive measure to prevent floods, and believes that the construction of dikes should be conducted in the proper season. It was said in *Dudi · Guanzi*, "In the three months of spring, dry weather is accompanied by less water. At this time, being dry with less water, the weather is getting warmer, and the coldness is

---

① Sikong: an official title in ancient China who oversaw water conservancy and civil construction.

fading away. Everything comes back to life. The previous year's farming has finished, and the new year's farming has not yet begun. Young shoots of the grass have already grown to be edible. The lengths of day and night tend to be the same along with changes in warmness and coldness. After the length of night equal to that of day, the night will get shorter, and the day will become longer. Just then it is beneficial to construct dikes because the embankment is getting stronger and stronger." And "In the three months of summer, the natural world changes greatly. As the Great Heat[①]comes, everything flourishes. Weeding of farmland should be done well. Thus, the decree should not interfere with farming, and the corvee should not be too long. Currently, it is not conducive to construct dikes because of the obstruction to farming. The geotechnical work makes no progress because of the labour cost." It also states that "In the three months of autumn, mountain springs gush out of the underground with heavy rains and frequent mountain torrents. And it is difficult to drain the water into sea due to distance. The autumn rain goes on and on, the heaven and the earth blending. At this time, we should pay close attention to the autumn harvest so that the grains can be gathered to the warehouse." It says at last, "In the three months of winter, the heaven and the earth are separated as the rain stops. It's too cold, and everything is ripe. It is unfavourable to do geotechnical work currently with the price of seven-tenths of the labour cost. And the soil is frozen, being difficult to do any work." *Guanzi* believes that in spring the weather is dry, the soil moisture content is appropriate, and it is in the agricultural slack period, which make spring the best season for dike construction. However, in summer, autumn and winter, construction may be unfavourable due to busy farming or uneven soil moisture content.

Guanzi's understanding of the characteristics of water flow has reached a very high level, which seems to be in line with scientific truth even today. It describes the phenomenon of water flow caused by canal water passing through an inverted siphon. "When the water flows to a tortuous place, it stops and retreats. When the place is full of water, the water flow is pushed forward. It flows smoothly in the terrain with small drop, while it flows intensely in the terrain with great drop." Then it describes two kinds of damage phenomena brought by canal flow. "The water will destroy the land when it flows to tortuous terrain. If the terrain is too tortuous, the water flow will leap. Leaping causes bias flow; bias flow causes whirlpool; whirlpool causes concentration; concentration causes sentiment; sentiment causes blockage; blockage causes river diversion; river diversion causes intense flow; and intense flow finally causes disorder." (*Dudi · Guanzi*) The two extremely destructive water flow phenomena are water whirling and water leaps, both of which will cause serious damage to the channel, resulting in flood. That is why we must strengthen the maintenance of the embankment.

Guanzi believes that it is necessary to dispatch water conservancy officials to patrol the river banks regularly. We should often send water officers to inspect the dikes and dams in winter, and immediately report to leaders the problems that need to be repaired. The dikes are usually fix in

---

① Great Heat: one of the 24 solar terms.

spring when there are few things to do. After the dikes are built, they should be inspected frequently. If the dikes are damaged in case of the heavy rain, we will send people to protect them by sections. If they need to be repaired, we will assign them to complete. In the heavy rain, the dikes need to be covered in time; In the flood, the dikes need to be blocked as soon as possible. Throughout the year, the effect of water control work is to keep the dikes in good condition. This is also the so-called "being prepared at ordinary times, where does the trouble come from?"(*Dudi · Guanzi*) It can be seen from this paragraph that to ensure the safety of dikes and achieve the goal of being solid and undamaged throughout the year, it is necessary for water officers to inspect dikes in winter, report problems in time when finding problems, and repair dikes in defect of farming in spring. If dikes are damaged or caught in a heavy rain, they must rush to repair and protect the dams. In addition, it is also advocated to build flood storage areas to cope with the surplus water resources when flooding occurs. It said that: In the barren land nearby, we must dig out the reservoirs. Dikes are repaired for large reservoirs and dams for small reservoirs, so that dikes surround the reservoirs to prevent the damage to crops. The dikes and dams should be repaired year by year, and thorns and shrubs should be planted on them to reinforce the soil. We also need to plant some tall trees such as cypress and poplar to prevent the floods. (*Dudi · Guanzi*) Guanzi's water conservancy thoughts also have reference significance for the development of modern countries. Under the condition of serious shortage of water resources in China and uneven distribution in space and time, it is necessary to scientifically understand water resources and take appropriate and effective measures to ensure the sustainable utilization of water resources and maintain the sustainable development of social economy.

Section IV   Water and Choice of Residential Environment

The ancestors of ancient China have already realized that the ideal living environment is inseparable from water, and they regarded water as the most important part of the living environment. The book *Guanzi* shows deep understanding of this. It is pointed put in *Dudi* that "To build a capital city, the sage must choose a stable and reliable place. The place must be fertile. It backs on to mountains surrounded by rivers and lakes. In the city, there are well-built ditches for drainage, which flow into great rivers. In this way, natural resources and agricultural products are abundant to feed the people and breed livestock." It means that the sage must choose a stable and fertile place to build capital where there are mountains and lakes. Inside the city, net of canals and ditches is built so as to drain wastewater to great rivers. That will be favourable to the existence of human beings and other living things. In *Chengma · Guanzi*[①], it is said that "All the capitals, no matter big or small, were built either at the foot of mountains or nearby the rivers. Those in the

---

① *Chengma · Guanzi*: the 5th article of *Guanzi*.

highlands should possess sufficient water resources, while those in the lowlands should not be close to depressions for saving the cost of building dikes." The layout of urban construction should suit local conditions, depending on the terrain and water environment conditions. It is not necessary to stick to a certain architectural model.

Guanzi also believes that water is like human's blood as it says "Land is the medium of all living things. Water, being the blood of the land, flows like the vein in human's body." The importance of blood to the human body is conceivable, so the importance of water to the earth is self-evident. This is also the keystone of so called "To settle down in places with water is the best" in Feng Shui (also known as Chinese geomancy, refers to a Chinese philosophical system intended to harmonize people with their environment).

The above-mentioned statement on urban site selection in *Guanzi* is a summary of the ancients' experience of survival "environmental selection", which also clearly reflects the Chinese nation's advocacy of "harmony between man and nature" and the pursuit of a beautiful living environment in which man and the natural environment are in harmony. It can also be seen that human civilization and wisdom shine and glimmer. The ecological value of such site selection consists in the backing of mountains or slopes, which can block the wind in winter and enjoy the coolness in summer, giving people a sense of stability as well as accounting the needs of flood control. Being close to water is an essential condition for human settlements, because, on the one hand, it is convenient for human life and communication, on the other hand, water can also create a pleasant and vibrant ecological environment. Today, with the rapid development of urbanization, the "reinforced concrete forest" has become the main character of the city. Urban rivers and lakes are destroyed, buried, and polluted frequently, and the problem of ecological environment deterioration has become increasingly serious. In order to solve this chronic problem, experts and scholars have put forward the concept of building a "landscape city" based on the traditional Chinese view of landscape and nature and the philosophy of harmony between man and nature. Guanzi's city location concept provides meaningful reference for modern society.

Chapter Ten Water and Mohist Ideology

The Mohism founded by Mozi (Fig. 10-1) was one of the most important schools during the Warring States Period. It had a wide range of influence at that time, once called the "manifest school" together with the Confucianism. The Mohist thoughts are concentrated in the book *Mozi*, which almost includes all kinds of knowledge at that time, involving philosophy, ethics, politics, economics, management, military, education, and natural sciences. It can be called "encyclopaedia", which also contains quite a wealth of water culture.

Figure 10-1 Mozi

Section I Manners of Yu and Universal Love

"Universal love" is the most important political proposition in Mozi's thoughts, which is the core and fundamental feature of Mozi's ideological system. Mozi believed that the root of unrest in the family, the country and the world was that everyone did not love each other but hated and did harm to each other. In order to change this situation, the only way to achieve the great rule of the world is to "practise universal loving and multilateral benefiting". In particular, rulers should have the idea of universal love. In order to publicize his thought of universal love, Mozi especially admired Yu's spirit of harnessing water, and believed that Yu's deeds embodied the great spirit of saving the world, which was an example for future rulers to follow.

Mozi's admiration and praise of Yu was narrated in *Tianxia · Zhuangzi*. "Mozi praised: ' In the past, Yu fought the floods by guiding water into the sea to connect the lands including Siyi① and Jiuzhou②. He controlled 300 large rivers, 3,000 tributaries, and countless small rivers. Yu personally held basket and shovel to converge rivers of the world. He worked so hard that even the hairs on his legs were worn off. No matter it blew or rained, Yu fought the floods and finally settled the world. Being a great saint, Yu still worked so hard for the world. ' Therefore, Mozi demanded that Mohist followers of later generations use animal skins and coarse cloths as clothing, wear wooden clogs and straw sandals, work without rest regardless of day and night, and take self-suffering as the criterion. He said: ' If you can't do this, it's not the way of Yu, and you are not qualified to be a Mohist. '"

Mozi thought that Yu's experience in harnessing water was the concrete practice of universal love, and Mohists must imitate Yu's hard-working spirit and strive for the interests of the people all over the world. The words and deeds of Mozi and Mohist really embodied the "manners of Yu" in their mind. Mozi was eager to save the world. The basic contents of his theory, such as Esteeming sages and Esteeming accordance, Universal love, Non attack, Economize on use and burial, Tianzhi, Minggui, Feiyue, Feiming and so on, are all salvation techniques, which are in line with Yu's spirit of harnessing water and benefiting the people. From the action point of view, Mozi and his disciples followed the example of Yu, who operated on his own and braved the water and rain, practiced to death. Most of them are laborers who directly participate in the production work. They cultivate the land and do the work personally, especially manual manufacturing, which is often engaged in by Mohists and a basic skill that must be mastered. Mozi himself is a craftsman proficient in mechanical manufacturing. Mohism not only took part in production and labour personally, but also lived frugally, assiduously, and selflessly. "Serving the interests of others at great self-sacrifice"(*Jinxin* I· *Mengzi*). It was full of selfless dedication and fearless sacrifice spirit. The spirit and quality of the above behaviours, such as consistent words and deeds, personal practice, strict discipline, and courage to sacrifice, were also the concentrated embodiment of Yu spirit. Mohism not only took Yu as a model in his heart, but also tried to follow his example and showed his admiration.

In *Mozi*, there can be seen many praises for Yu's achievements and spirit in controlling flood and benefiting people. Mozi indicated that: "To love and benefit each other is the law of the saint and the rule of the world." (*Jianai* II · *Mozi*③) He also quoted a large number of Yu's stories in

---

① It means four tribes, the general name of ethnic groups around the Central Plains in ancient China.
② The ancestors of the Han nationality divided the original settlement into nine regions, which later became the alternative name of the ancient China.
③ *Jianai* II · *Mozi*: the 15th article of *Mozi*.

water management, explaining that the idea of "universal love" was based on the political practice of Yu and other holy kings. "To love and benefit each other is completely different, which was ever adopted by the ancient holy king. How do you know that? In ancient times, Yu ruled the world, dredging the West River in the west to discharge Qu River, Sun River and Huang River. While in the north he dredged Fangshui, Yuanshui and Gushui to flow into Zhaozhi Mansion and Hutuo River, diverted the rivers in the Huzhu Mountain in the Yellow River, and dig open the dragon gate to benefit the people of Yan, Dai, Hu, Mo and Xihe area. In the east, Dayu blocked the circuitous water passing through the mainland into Mengzhuze (a lake in ancient times) and divided it into nine rivers to limit the flood for the benefit of the people of Jizhou (one of the nine regions). In the south, he dredged the Yangtze River, Han River, Huaihe River and Ru River to the east into the sea, thus irrigating the lands for the benefit of the people of Jingchu, Wu Yue and Nanyi. This is the deed of Yu, and we must now practice universal love in this spirit."

Mozi also cited the example that "Gun (father of Yu) and Yu both fought floods, while one failed and the other succeeded" to illustrate the truth that only by selecting the virtuous and appointing the capable can the country be in peace and prosperity. "For example, in the past, Gun, the eldest son of the emperor, corrupting the emperor's merit and virtue, was soon killed in the placed named Yujiao, which was beyond the light of the sun and the moon. The emperor did not love him."(*Shangxian* II · *Mozi*[1]) Although Gun was of noble birth and had a high official position, he not only lost his position, but also was killed by Shun because of his lack of talent and failure in flood control. Mozi went on to state that "Well, who is the virtuous person appointed by the emperor? The answer was: Yu, Ying and Gao Tao. Yu regulated floods and named mountains and rivers." After Gun was killed, Yu, who had both ability and integrity, was appointed in the midst of crisis. He led the people to control floods, overcoming thousands of difficulties and dangers, and finally defeated the flood. Yu became the holy king of great virtue.

Mozi's thoughts and actions fully reflect the "manners of Yu", carrying forward the spirit of Yu's flood control, which together constitute the important characteristics of Chinese culture, especially water culture.

Section II   Self-cultivation through Clarifying Morality by Water

In Mozi's political thoughts, it is particularly important for those in power to strengthen their own moral cultivation, which is the foundation of governing the country. Rulers must strive to carry out his own moral cultivation. "If the roots are not strong, the branches will be in danger. He who is brave but pays no attention to moral cultivation will be lazy later. If the

---

[1] *Shangxian* II · Mozi: the 9th article of *Mozi*.

water is dirty at the source, it will no longer be clear. And the reputation of those who act unfaithfully will fade away."(*Xiushen · Mozi*①) Here, Mozi used an example that the source of the water is dirty and the whole river will be muddy, which vividly illustrated that if the officials ignored moral cultivation, they would tend to be greedy and evil. Many acts of unrighteousness will lead to self-destruction, and after a long period of time, they will be trapped in the abyss of filth, leading to the evil consequences.

"Qinshi" is one of the ten political propositions of Mozi. He believed that to govern the country well, the monarch must keep close to and appoint the virtuous persons. He pointed out that "A good bow is not easy to open, but it can shoot high; a good horse is not easy to ride, but it can travel far with heavy goods. Talented people are not easy to master, but they can help kings gain respect. That is why the great rivers increase the amount of water as they accept streams. That is why the water in great rivers do not come from the same source. Is there a reason to adopt the same opinions as yours and not to accept opinions that are different from your own? This is not the way to unify the world. So the narrow streams become dry quickly, and the shallow lakes dry up easily." (*Qinshi · Mozi*②) It is believed that only when those in power are broad-minded like great rivers accept small streams, can they recruit talents in all fields; only when those in power are good at adopting different opinions like the rivers with countless sources, can they listen to opinions of all sides. The monarch and his ministers are of one heart and one mind to protect the country. Conversely, if the monarch is narrow-minded and unable to embrace everything, he will eventually end up lonely betraying the relatives and breaking up the country, just like the narrow streams drying up.

The above thoughts of Mozi also reflect his understanding of modesty and tolerance in moral cultivation. "The great rivers increase the amount of water as they accept streams. The water in great rivers do not come from the same source." This shows that during the development, things essentially realize the qualitative changes through the accumulation of quantitative changes, especially the moral cultivation.

Mozi also realized the transformation of the opposites, putting forward the proposition that "the peak is difficult to last long". He said, "The sweet wells are the easiest to dry up, the tall trees are the easiest to be cut down, the effective turtles are the first to be captured for divination, and the miraculous snakes are the first to be exposed to the sun for rain. So if it is on the peak, it will not last long."(*Qinshi · Mozi*) These phenomena that "the peak is difficult to last long" are quite similar to "the golden mean" of the Confucianism and the saying of Laozi as "Good fortune follows upon disaster; disaster lurks within good fortune." In Mozi's view, people and things must have a grasp of the "degree", being not "too prosperous". Otherwise, things will often turn to the opposite, resulting in very serious consequences. It can be seen that Mozi has realized the law of mutual transformation between the opposites from some specific phenomena in nature and society, and

---

① *Xiushen · Mozi*: the 2nd aricle of *Mozi*.
② *Qinshi · Mozi*: the 1st article of *Mozi*.

regarded such law as an important aspect of moral cultivation. Mozi takes the characteristics of water as an example to clarify the point of view, which illustrates Mozi's profound philosophical thinking brought by water.

Section III　Water and Non-attack

Mozi was a pacifist in the Warring States Period strongly opposing wars. He travelled among the vassal states all his life, advocating "non-attack" and objecting the war. In order to prevent the outbreak of war, he strongly advocated active defence, that is, used defensive war to oppose the aggressive war achieving "armed peace". According to the book *Mozi*, Mozi successfully prevented three upcoming wars of "Qi attacked Lu", "Lu attacked Zheng" and "Chu attacked Song", which showed his wisdom and courage. Mozi did not blindly rely on preaching to stop the attack. He knew well that some wars were hard to avoid when princes competed for hegemony. Therefore, he led his disciples to create a military doctrine of active defence. These theories were mainly recorded in 11 articles in *Mozi* such as *Beichengmen* and *Beishui*, which discussed in detail the relationship between water and war.

During the Warring States Period, the scales of wars grew increasingly, so did the measures used. Water was particularly favored by the initiators of war due to its destructive power, for which the surging rivers and billowing torrents became tools for the vassals to replace soldiers with water and carry out annexation wars. In response to the frequent water attacks at that time, Mozi led his disciples to develop a relative systematic defence mechanism against water attacks: "Path with width of 8 bu should be built around the moat to prevent the enemy from flooding the city with water. We must carefully examine the surrounding terrain. In the low-lying areas, we should give orders to dig channels. While in the lower-lying areas, we should give orders to dig deep well so that the channels could connect with each other, and water could be diverted. The instrument "Zewa" should be placed in the wells to measure the water level. If the water depth outside the city is more than one foot deep, water canals inside the city should be excavated. Every two boats are connected to form as "one lin". Then the boats are formed as "ten lin". Each lin is equipped with 30 people, all of whom are good at archery. Four out of ten people must wear shoes. We must be good at using this kind of ship as a "Fenwen" (car crash) to destroy the enemy's embankment. Twenty boats are formed as a team. Thirty soldiers are selected for a combined boat, twenty of whom each prepare a hoe and wear armour and leather boots. The remaining ten have spears in their hands. Of course, we should support the brave people's lives in advance, and provide another house for their parents, wives, and children. When it is found that the dikes could be broken, the two boats were used in parallel to form the "Fenwen" to break the outer dike. At the same time, the shooting machines should be quickly used to shoot arrows at the enemy to cover the fleet that break the dike."(*Beishui* · *Mozi*[①])

Here, Mozi clearly expounded the tactical strategy responding to the water attack from the enemy: on the one hand, channels should be dug in the lower parts of the city, and wells should be dug in the lower parts of the city, so that they can be collected, and the water can be leaked. Meanwhile, the instrument "Zewa" should be placed in the wells to measure the water level at any time. If the water depth is more than one foot, the canals should be dug to discharge the water. On the other hand, 300 well-trained soldiers and 20 fast ships are selected to form a dike-breaking commando, unexpectedly rushing out of the city and breaking the dikes to release water. To strengthen the attack force, every two ships are juxtaposed together called "one lin". Each lin is equipped with 30 powerful and skilled soldiers, and armed with crossbows, spears, hoes, helmets and armours. With the help of darkness at night, the soldiers rush out of the city under the cover of a transducer, dig the embankment with a hoe, and drive boats to break the dike. In this way, the enemy's strategy of attacking the city with water can be overcome. To oppose the war, Mozi made a profound analysis and practice on the role of water in the war and how to defend against water attack, thus forming a unique water and war culture.

[①] *Beishui* · *Mozi*: the 58th article of *Mozi*.

Chapter Eleven Water and Literature

Section I Water and Poetry

Water-chanting poems are splendid in the kingdom of poems. Poets chant water, praise water, and express their emotions through water, leaving a galaxy of splendid and immortal poems. This section will discuss poetry: water that expresses emotions. First of all, we need to know what "poetry expresses emotions" is.

1. Poetry Expresses Emotions

That "poetry expresses emotions", which was called "the first guiding principle" by Mr. Zhu Ziqing (1898 – 1948, Chinese modern writer) (*Analysis of Poetry Expressing Emotions*), is the foundation of classical poetics theories in China. It is recorded in the *Book of History* that Shun once said: "Poetry expresses emotions, songs are languages that are chanted, the five tones are set down according to the songs, and the six pitches harmonize the five tones." It is said in *Zhuangzi* that poetry is what is used to express emotions."

According to the textual research of Mr. Wen Yiduo (1899–1946, Chinese modern writer): originally, "shi (poetry)" and "zhi (emotions)" were written as the same character, whose upper part of the Chinese character "zhi (emotions) is shi (poetry)", and the lower part of it "xin (heart)", meaning staying over one's heart, in fact, that is memory. After the creation of characters, and with the help of literature, nobody resorted to rote memory, and all written records were called "zhi (annals)", namely poetry. What stays in mind is "zhi", and when it is expressed in words, it is called poetry. Investigated from the perspective of exegetics, the basic meaning of "zhi" is interlinked with "poetry". As early as in the Han Dynasty, most people explained "poetry" as "zhi". For example: in *Origin of Chinese Characters—Chinese Radical Yan(讠)* by Xu Shen's: Poetry is emotions. Emotions are expressed in words (Yan), so its meaning follows words (Yan), and its pronunciation is like that of Chinese character "si (temple)".

After knowing that "poetry expresses emotions" means "what stays in mind is 'zhi (emotions)', and when it is expressed in words, it is called poetry." we can conclude that "poetry expresses emotions" is actually expressing emotions with poems. In this section, we'll talk about two specific forms of water that expresses emotions from the human perspective, which actually refers to ambitions here. We'll discuss the poets' ambitions about the people, nation and the world from their outward ambitions, followed by gentleman's ambitions from their inward ambitions.

2. Water Expresses Ambitions

(1) Ambitions of Family, Nation and the World

When speaking of Cao Cao (Fig. 11-1), what would you think of? You may think of Defining a Hero While Drinking, the Battle of Chibi, or the Battle of Guandu? But there was an important battle that was critical to Cao Cao, which you may not know. It was Northern Expedition to Wuhuan, which was immediately after the Battle of Guandu. The main mission of the Northern Expedition to Wuhuan was to mop up the remaining force of the Yuan Shao in the North.

Wuhuan, some people call it "Wuwan", is a name of a tribe in ancient China. It is one of Eastern Hu ethnic groups. It is also called "three counties in Wuhuan", Liaoxi, Shanggu and Youbeiping, and it is a branch of Xianbei ethnic group.

Figure 11-1　Cao Cao

Why did Cao Cao make this expedition to Wuhuan (Fig. 11-2)? At the Battle of Guandu, Cao Cao utterly defeated Yuan Shao. Frightened, Yuan Shang and Yuan Xi, two sons of Yuan Shao, fled to Liucheng day and night. They went and sought refuge with Wuhuan. Yuan Shao had a close relationship with Wuhuan, and now his two sons went to collude with them. It eventually would be a disaster. How could Cao Cao let it be like that? Besides, the home front of Cao Cao would be consolidated by conquering Wuhuan, and so would the whole northern territory. Then Cao Cao and his troops could keep marching southward and rule the world. So, the "Northern Expedition to Wuhuan" is clearly important to Cao Cao. Cao Cao therefore determined to make this northern expedition to Wuhuan. At that time, quite a few people were opposed to this risky expedition because the trip to Wuhuan was full of steep mountains and precipitous paths, and the troops would be exhausted when arriving there. Any slight mistake would lead to complete annihilation. Only Guo Jia, a famous counselor, supported Cao Cao. With the opposition of the majority of people, Cao Cao commanded all his troops of 200,000, thousands of chariots and almost all the elites of his civilian officials and military officers, such as the counsellor of Guo Jia, Generals of Zhang Liao, Zhang He, and Xu Huang, and Cao Zhi, his son of great talent …He was determined to take a gamble on it.

Figure 11-2 Northern Expedition to Wuhuan

Finally, Cao Cao waged a bloody war with the cavalrymen of Wuhuan at the foot of Bai Lang Mountain. Wuhuan suffered a crushing defeat, and the Northern Expedition was a complete victory. This warfare lasted for over a month, and stretched for 400 kilometres, completely removing the threat of the powerful and prosperous Wuhuan to China, wiping out the remaining forces of Yuan family, and unified the north. After this victory and in September of the same year, Cao Cao and his troops got back from Liucheng. When passing by Jieshi (now in Hebei Province), Cao Cao climbed up the mountain on the back of the horse, looking into the Bohai Sea. Looking back on his unprecedented achievements and with high spirits, Cao Cao composed the famous poem named *The Sea*.

> *I come to view the boundless ocean*
> *From Stony Hill on eastern shore.*
> *Its water rolls in rhythmic motion,*
> *And islands stand amid its roar.*
> *Tree on tree grows from peak to peak;*
> *Grass on grass looks lush far and nigh.*
> *The autumn wind blows drear and bleak;*
> *The monstrous billows surge up high.*
> *The sun by day, the moon by night*
> *Appear to rise up from the deep.*
> *The Milky Way with stars so bright*
> *Sinks down into the sea in sleep.*
> *How happy I feel at this sight!*
> *I croon this poem in delight.*

I travel eastward on the back of the horse, climbing up the summit of Jieshi Mountain, and looking down at the sea. The waves of the boundless sea roll in rhythmic motion, and surging with great momentum, the islands tower over the vast sea...The cold autumn wind helps intensify the strength of billows and waves like rolling mountains. The movement of the sun and the moon seem to set out from the vast ocean. The star-spangled galaxy seems to be produced from the vast ocean as well.

Look, Cao Cao chose the most magnificent sights in Mother Nature—the sun, the moon and the galaxy in his poem, but he made people strongly feel that the sun and the moon seem to rise from and fall into the sea; The stars and galaxy were so splendid that they both seemed to have sprung out from the bosom of the sea. In other words, even the most magnificent sight in Mother Nature starts from the sea. How profound and tolerant the sea is! In this way, he described the extraordinary scene of the vast and deep sea from a broader vision. In the Qing Dynasty, Shen Deqian (a famous poet and scholar) commented that this poem "has a cosmic atmosphere" (*The Wellsprings of Old Poems*). The ability to describe the sea in such an extraordinary way lies not only in his writing skills, but also in his generosity in mind. Hu Yinglin said that: "Cao Cao had great talent in both deployment of troops and composing poems, which were bold and unconstrained, influencing the world" (*Shisou*). Poets writing on the sea shall have a mind as broad as the sea and a spirit like the sea. The vastness of the sea rightly portrayed the bosom of the poet, and the broad mind of the poet in turn endowed the sea with broad atmosphere. Cao Cao linked the vast sea with the boundless cosmos, and framed against the sun, the moon and the galaxy, he described the majestic momentum of the sea, showing the broad mind of the poet and the enterprising spirit of caring about the world as embodied in "The water can never be too deep, and the mountain too high". In short, he had dominant temperament. Shen Deqian thought Cao Cao "would show his dominant temperament from time to time", alluding to such ambition and mind. Liu Xie (Literary critic of the Southern Dynasties) said in the 26th Chapter of *The Literary Mind and the Carving of Dragons*: "Standing on the mountain makes one's emotion spread all over it, and watching the sea by it makes one's imagination overflowing." "Climbing up high to enjoy the magnificence between heaven and earth", the complex about one's family and country is the emotion of "spiritual self". Poets place their ambitions in water and show their ambition and mind.

Meng Haoran (a poet of the Tang Dynasty) also expressed his "ambition about families, nation and the world" through "the water of Dongting Lake" in *To Prime Minister Zhang from the Bank of Dongting Lake*: "In August, the lake is full to the brim; The limpid vastness melts into Heaven's rim. While vapours envelope the ancient Yun-meng Lakes, Waves roar ahead to rock the ancient Yueyang City. I yearn to cross, yet no boat's waiting for me; It's a golden age and I sense shame to this retreat I flee. Sitting to watch those anglers with satisfied looks, I can only feel envious of their heavy hooks." This is a poem aiming at self-recommendation, "The poem was inspired by Dongting Lake, and the poet hoped to be recommended by Zhang Jiuling"(a poet of the Tang Dynasty) Wan Dajin sold that the poem indirectly showed the poet's intention of being recommended by Zhang Jiuling through his exclamation while facing the vast Dongting Lake but there was no boat to wade him through the lake as well as his complex of irresoluteness. The first four lines depicted the magnificent scene of Dongting Lake and its majestic momentum, and the last four lines expressed the poet's political passion and wishes. The whole poem was inspired by watching Dongting Lake, through the transition of "I yearn to cross, yet no boat's waiting for me", the poet made an elaboration on Dongting Lake like painting splashed-ink landscape, although intended to make signification through the lake, showing the vast and majestic sight of Dongting Lake that stretched for 400 km and achieving heart-shaking artistic effect, so as to make the poem a masterpiece depicting the landscape.

When the country was faced with crises and during difficult times and when people suffered, poets expressed their "ambition about their families, nation and the world" through water in a profound and forceful way. For example, the frustration in Du Fu's (the famous poet of the Tang Dynasty) poem "On war-torn land streams flow and mountains stand; In vernal town grass and weeds are overgrown". Wen Tianxiang the famous politician and litterateur of the Southern Song Dynasty, wrote in *Sailing on Lonely Ocean*:

Delving in the Book of Change, I rose through hardship great,
And desperately fought the foe for four long years.
Like willow down the war-torn land looks desolate,
I sink and swim as duckweed in the rain appears.

For the perils on the Perilous Beach I have sighs,
On Lonely Ocean now I feel dreary and lonely.
Since olden days there's never been a man but dies,
I'll leave a loyalist's name in history only.

In the late Southern Song Dynasty, Wen Tianxiang became a captive in a battle against the Yuan army in Chaozhou. While he passed by the estuary of Lingding Bay, the Yuan army forced him to summon the Song army firmly defending Yashan Mountain to surrender, and he wrote down this poem. The meaning of the poem is that he had commanded his troops and resisted the Yuan army for four years, but rebels answering his calls were few and far between all around. The territory of Great Song was like willow catkin in the wind, on the brink of ruin. His fate was like the duckweed on the water buffeted by the rain, so lonely and forlorn. He had retreated his troops on Huangkong Beach and was now deeply concerned with the destiny of his country; now he was at the estuary of Lingdingyang River and exclaiming about his bitter circumstances. Since the ancient times, nobody could run away from death, as long as his loyalty could go down in history, he was satisfied. The poet expressed his ambition with his poem and showed his exemplary conduct and noble character affronting death and his heroic spirit with a strong sense of righteousness.

Du Fu would unconsciously integrate his thoughts about his families and country and his nostalgia of the nation while showing the images in Mother Nature. Therefore, the "water" depicted by Du Fu was not only about the graceful scenery in nature, but also placed with his worries about the social realities and care for people, to give "water" broader connotation and a more profound deposit. For example, he gave vent to his dissatisfaction with the luxury and vanity of the royal nobility in a peaceful era with "By the riverside so many beauties in array" in *Satire on Fair Ladies*, expressed his longing for security in the society and people's living and working in peace and contentment with "The scene of prosperity is like the placid pool water can " (*Written on the North Bridge in Xinjin*) and "Politics and civilization are as still as peaceful water" (*Capable of Drawing*). Throughout his lifetime, Du Fu had been concerned with politics and worried about society. He frequently linked the depiction of natural scenery with the prospects of society and the fate of his country, writing down a lot of poems that exclaim about the current affairs through "water". For example, in *Two Poems on the Yangtze River*, although the lines were all about the Yangtze River, the poet placed his endless longing for the unification of his country: "All waters converge in Fuwan(Fuling and Wanxian Counties, now in Chongqing City) and strive for one gate in Qutang. Ministers pull together and bandits shall respect the royal court. The solitary stones are like batted steeds, so dangerous and horrifying; the apes drooped to drink water, so disgusting. A heart longing for return won't be stopped by the flipping waves so easily." (The first stanza of *Two Poems on the Yangtze River*) "The formidable river won't stop and is about to reach the East China Sea. All streams want to return to the sea, just like all countries want to serve the emperor." (The second stanza of *Two Poems on the Yangtze River*) Du Fu showed water's intention of worshiping the royal court through the convergence of all rivers in Fuling and Wanxian County while striving for Kuimen (now in Chongqing City) before flowing into the sea eastward, further signifying that people should be just like the water in terms of the intention of respecting the royal court and serving the emperor. In fact, the two poems of Du Fu are targeted at the struggle between Guo Yingyi and Cui Gan in the second October of the lunatic calendar of the first year during the reign of Emperor Yongtai (765 A. D.). At that time, the royal court of the Tang Dynasty experienced chaotic warfare for a long time, and the laws of the imperial court were neglected. The forces separating the government and military power were gradually taking form, so Du Fu was very worried about this. He showed his own stance through praising Yangtze River: people who acted against common senses were doomed to die. Just like the flipping water in the river wouldn't stop people from coming over and pledging allegiance, the bandits separating regime couldn't stop the unification of the country. Here, "water" is no longer a purely objective image, it is entrusted with Du Fu's concern with his family and country, to be specific and of great realistic value.

Water of the Yellow River written by Gao Qi in the Ming Dynasty also expressed the poet's deep perception of the bitterness suffered by people and his loud cries:

The Yellow River comes from the West and wound for five hundred kilometres. After winding and being cut for four times, it returned to the Bohai Sea, and the turbid waves are deep and bottomless. According to legend, the Yellow River used to be clear for three thousand years, and the sage came out to make the world peaceful. How rare it is for the water to be clear! When will the optimal governance return? How I wish the river to stay clear all year around, the sage can be alive, and sacredness can be revived, so that the world will be peaceful for tens of thousands of generations.

Harnessing the Yellow River and making the river water limpid are the strong wishes of people, therefore, the poet hopes for a peaceful scenery where the Yellow River is clear, sage appears, and the world becomes peaceful. Although this hope is placed upon spiritual force, it reflects the requirements of the masses after all, bearing positive significance.

If the ambition about families and country is the outward pursuits of poets through chanting about water, then expressing "gentleman's ambition" through water is their inner pursuits.

(2) Ambitions of Gentlemen

According to *Record of Yidu* by Yuan Shansong, the litterateur of the East in Dynasty: "if the mountains and rivers were alive, they would be amazed with meeting confidants for such a long time". For mountains and rivers, people are like "beauties", for people, mountains and rivers are like "amazed confidants". The poet and the landscape are confidants to each other. They reflect and understand each other as embodied in "I feel that the blue mountains are amiable and beautiful, and I guess the blue mountains think about me in the same way". Water being amazed with confidants is the ambition of a gentleman and the way of cultivation.

Figure 11-3 *The Book*

Zhu Xi, a famous scholar of the Song Dynasty had a poem that read like: "There lies a glassy oblong pool, where light and shade pursue their course. How could it be so clear and cool? For fresh water comes from the source." (Zhu Xi, *The Book*) (Fig. 11 - 3). The pond that covered half of one mu is like a bright mirror, reflecting the shining light of the sky and shade of the clouds. If you want to know why the pond is so clear, you should look at the fresh water flowing all the time from its source. The poem had a deep implied meaning. It compared learning to the fresh water coming from the source and urged people to keep absorbing new knowledge to make progress and bring about new changes. By the two lines of "How could it be so clear and cool? For fresh water comes from the source" the poet implied that people shall study hard and supplement new knowledge from time to time to have a clear mind by showing that the water was limpid because of the continuous infusion of fresh water from its source, accounting for people's frequent use of these lines to imply that only through continuously learning new knowledge can they attain a new atmosphere and praise the learning and artistic achievements of a person.

Readers can also be inspired by this poem. Only when their mind is always active, accepting different thoughts and fresh knowledge with their open and broad mind can their talent be reserved like fresh water flowing for a long time. These two lines have been condensed into an idiom meaning "flowing water", used to compare to the source and driving force of the development of things. This seemingly scenery-depicting poem in fact contains the personality ideal about water. Water was endowed with the meaning orientation of moral ethics and became the carrier of the personality of Confucius culture.

Throughout history, the Chinese culture has always been rich in legends about gentlemen, and water happens to be an excellent symbol of gentlemen. Poets admire the generosity of interacting with the heaven and earth without being prideful towards everything, free and affectionate. Noble character is just like beautiful jade and is an important content of "morality". And poets always show their ambition as gentlemen through "water".

For example, *The Ode of Qi'ao* in the *Book of Songs*: "Where the river flows past, the bamboos their shade cast. The lord stands there refined, like ivory polished, like precious stone finished…", meaning that planting bamboos at the winding place of the river, the green bamboos are so slender and beautiful. The river and green bamboos signify seclusion in mountainous forests and hidden stream, highlighting the noble character of a gentleman, and maintaining the true personality, thereby becoming associated with the nobility of gentleman's morality as beautiful as jade.

During the Spring and Autumn and the Warring States Periods, there used to be a *The Ode of Canglang River* in the Chu State: "Canglang River is so limpid, Wherewith I wash my tassel; Canglang River is so turbid, Wherewith I wash my feet." In Chu Ci, the old fisherman used to chant these four lines to persuade Qu Yuan to become a hermit for self-preservation indirectly so that he could reconcile himself to his situation. Afterwards, "Canglang River" became frequently a way of praising the image of seclusion, the maintenance of personal independence and nobility. According to Bai Juyi's *Poem Composed on the Way of Being Dispatched to Hangzhou as a Cabinet Minister in the Second Year during the Reign of Emperor Changqing while Passing by Blue Creek*, "Suddenly I take interest in the lake and sea and admire the water of Canglang River so often." The so-called "interest in the lake and sea" referred to the poet's thought of seclusion, and "Canglang water" referred to the place of seclusion. According to Du Mu's *Fisherman*: "Being gray-haired on Canglang River, forgetting about all rights and wrongs", the "fisherman" here takes on the image of a hermit standing aloof from worldly success. Chao Duanli of the Song Dynasty wrote down *Courtyard Full of Fragrance* that went like: "The endlessly beautiful scenery in River Blue makes me want to spend the rest of my life here under my straw hat." expressing his life temperament and interest of finding seclusion in all corners of the country in his declining years.

According to Cen Shen's *Song of Hun Monks in Taibai*: "His mind is as clean as the flowing water, and his body doesn't even contend with the floating clouds." He compared the limpid stream to the integrity and aloofness from the world on the part of the Hun monks. Du Fu also composed *Beautiful Lady*: "The spring water in mountains is clear but turbid out of the mountains."

So, it is Wang Wei's *Autumn Evening in The Mountains Abode* that contained the lines of "Among pine trees bright moon beams peer; Over crystal stones flows water clear", making up a quiet and pure natural scenery. At this moment, the poet seemed to feel that he had been washed clean as well. The beauty of nature and the beauty of his mind were completely integrated, creating a purely beautiful poetic conception as bright and pure as water, the moon, and the mirror, full of Zen mood. The quietness in the mountains contrasted sharply with the external filth. The longing for life in mountains and the praise of the limpid brook showed the poet's disgust with the officialdom outside the mountain. Wang Wei wrote down in his *Chanting Four Men of Virtue in My Abode in Jizhou*: "I won't rest in the shade of bad wood and all the water I drink definitely has a clear source", he also said: "I would rather rest in the wild forest and drink from the streams in mountains than bowing to the nobility to get delicious food." (*To Shixing gong*[①]) The poem rightly showed the noble ambition of the poet. The pines in the moon and the brook on the stones were the ideal personality he pursued and the ideal conception of his life.

"The Yellow River flows down directly into the central plains vigorously, and a gentleman's broad mind shall also be contained here." Historically, poets expressed their ambition in their poems, and gave vent to their complex about their families and country, chanting the personality of gentlemen while containing the connotation of water.

Section II Water and Lyrics

Find emotions in poems and feelings in lyric poems. "Lyric poems were originally played with wind and stringed instruments, dissipated music" (*General Catalogue Summary of Imperial book Collections of Four Series · Summary of Music Collections*), "Lyric poems are amorous materials", and lyric poets could finally write on "love" at their hearts' content and "complexes in life".

First, let's look at the water of tender and reserved feelings. Although lyric poets could boldly write on "love", most of the lyric poetry was about long steady love.

1. Water and Tender Feelings

"Water" can be used to express the endless softness and sweet love between two loved ones when they come together. Qin Guan's *Immortals at the Magpie Bridge* was a lyric poem of this type, containing the lines of "Their tender love flows like a stream; Their happy date seems but a dream. How can they bear a separate homeward way?" "Water" was often used to symbolize feminine things similar to water. Here, "water" represented a gentle aesthetic image "signifying love and temperament".

[①] Shixing gong refers to Zhang Jiuling, a famous prime minister of the Tang Dynasty.

See the Northern river flow, And the Western river flow! By Gua Islet, mingling waves, they go. My love, please go slowly, I'm waiting for you at Louwailou(a famous restaurant in Hangzhou City).

The above are the lyrics of *Norther River Flows*, the ending song of a costume TV series named "Love against Kinship". People who know about this lyric poem must find it familiar. This song was adapted from Bai Juyi's lyric poem, *Everlasting Longing*.

Let's have a look at this lyric poem:

See the Northern River flow, And the Western River flow! By Gua Islet, mingling waves, they go. The Southern hills dotted with woe. O how can I forget? How can I not regret? My deep sorrow will last till with you I have met, waiting from moonrise to moonset.

The Northern River referred to in the lyric poem originated from Henan Province, and the ancient branch of the Northern River flowed eastward from Kaifeng to the present Xuzhou, converging in the Western River, connected with the canal, passing through Guazhou Ferry (Fig. 11-4) south to Yangzhou and Jiangsu before flowing into Yangtze River and farther places.

Figure 11-4 Guazhou Ferry

This lyric poem is literally all about the scenery of flowing water. Let's look at the first stanza. In the first three lines, a young woman's husband went away, travelled southward along the Northern River and Western River to a remote place. The fourth line of "the Southern hills dotted with woe" indirectly showed the young woman's sorrow upon missing her husband with the rhetoric device of personification. The author lightly touched on "woe" to cause tremendous changes on the conception: to start with, the Southern Hill was no longer beautiful, only the sorrow of the people there was as heavy as mountains; Secondly, the mountains would also be sorrowful due to people's sorrow; Thirdly, the mountain is sorrowful, so the "Northern River" and "Western River" mentioned before were also full of regret, "there is so much to regret in life like the water flowing eastward, not to return again". People tent to take the first three lines as just the depiction of scenery. But as we know, all words of scenes are those of sensations. "Northern river flow, and Western river flow" is to depict the flowing water literally, but it is actually about the drifting husband of the young woman like flowing water, typically comparing flowing water to people while indicating that the heart of the young woman drifting away with the flowing water after her husband's traces.

In the second stanza, the author came straight to the point, and expressed the young woman's regret for her husband's long-term absence. The first three lines were about her thoughts that were like flowing water. In the boudoir, her thoughts were endless since she couldn't see the person she was missing. Her thoughts and regret were both endless. The word "long" signifies flowing water and indicates human feelings. The last line, "waiting from moonrise to moonset", was painting landscape and also about feelings. The whole lyric poem wraps up with these words, to indicate that the thoughts about rivers and mountains above, the missing and regret were what was on the woman's mind when she was looking at the moon; The painting that was like sketches showed her missing while looking afar confusedly. Her longing for her husband was like the long flowing water in front of her. Her husband wouldn't return. She regretted it, she was sorrowful, helpless with loneliness and solitude.

The entire lyric poem was framed against the tender flowing water below the moon, symbolizing the leisurely and continuous parting sorrow, profound reverie and the bitterness thereby produced, the clear moonlight, rolling water, dotting remote mountains were weaved with the leisurely thoughts and long regret, forming an extremity like floating clouds and flowing water while adding to her lasting sorrow and highlighting an atmosphere of melancholy and sadness.

On the other hand, Li Qingzhao, a famous woman poet of the Song Dynasty, expressed her deep love for her husband who travelled far away in a brief lyric poem containing the bitterness of a couple missing each other while being far apart from each other: "The faded pedals are scattered away, the water is flowing smoothly. Must we share the same longing in two places? This love, I am unable to evade: For when my eyebrows banish it, it overruns my heart."

In addition, Qin Guan also compared his slight sorrow to water in his lines, "Falling pedals, leisurely, carefree, as in a dream; The endless rain, sad as my grief at parting; While pearl curtains hang idle on silver hooks." Li Zhiyi's *To the Song of Divination* went like: "I'm living upstream and you, downstream. Day by day, you are the one I am missing. Even if we can't meet, we are of the same river. The time when the water stops flowing is the time of the end for my grief. I'm wishing your heart were also missing me, then my pining for you has a meaning." With no need of detailed explanation, this was about two lovers living downstream and upstream of Yangtze River respectively. Although they couldn't meet each other day and night, both "share" the "Yangtze River water" that only belongs to them and they were immersed in the happiness that only existed between them.

There is not only tender emotion, but also exclamation with lofty sentiments in this lyric poem.

The content of lyric poems grew richer and richer through the development of Su Shi and Xin Qiji and other famous lyric poets. The feelings contained became loftier and loftier gradually as well. Let's move onto the second point: Lofty and Sentimental Water.

2. Water and Heroism

Xin Qiji (the general and poet of the Southern Song Dynasty) depicted the vastness of water with "The southern sky for miles and miles in autumn dye, and boundless autumn water spread to meet the sky" (*Water Dragon's Chant*). Zhu Dunru depicted the remoteness of water with the lines of "The setting sun sinks to the earth's level: The Yangtze River in its onward flow." (*Joyful Reunion*) and Fan Zhongyan wrote about the continuity of water through "Hills steeped in slanting sunlight, sky and waves merged" (*Waterbag Dance*). Between such wide and magnificent heaven and earth, with the mood of "Boundless waters and skies merging into a single entity, a lonely wild goose is now in sight, now out of sight." (*A Blessing at Hand* by Zhu Dunru), lyric poets created their water of lofty sentiments.

Let's appreciate Zhang Xiaoxiang's *From the Huai I Gaze Afar*:

From the Huai I gaze afar, how rank the weeds, how rank they are. Dust veils the pass now, all is silent but, a strong frosty sough. With my gloomy stare, I think hard of that year's affair that had been destined, no man could change, never. At Sishui River and the Zhushui River, through Land of Music flow, stained with bloody woe. Mongol camps over there stand; Cattle and sheep come through afterglow, where guard posts dot the land. The chieftain leads hunting at night, the horsemen swaying torches bright. The lutes and drums sound loud, which gives one a fright.

The Huaihe River was the boundary between the Song Dynasty and the Jin Dynasty. The lyric poet looked afar at the Huaihe River that stretched out. The vast plains had become the frontier defense, and he couldn't help feeling downcast on seeing such a bleak sight. The coast of the Sishui River and the Zhushui River used to be places of rite and benevolence, but they were now invaded by the soldiers of the Jin Dynasty as well, permeated with the atmosphere of bloody woe. On the northern bank of the Huaihe River, there were guard posts dotting the land. The hunting fire shone on the wilderness, and the horsemen swayed torches bright. People in the Jin Dynasty wouldn't give up destroying us, and it was such a terrifying sight, but the author failed to fulfil his great aspirations, like a hero with no place to display his prowess.

The first part depicted the confrontation between the Song and Jin troops in Jianghuai basin. The characters "Chang Huai" referred to the borderline between the two states at the time, containing exclamation. Since November in the 11th year during the reign of Emperor Shaoxing, the Song Dynasty "made peace with the Jin state, entered into a treaty of alliance, agreeing to setting the middle streamline of the Huaihe River as the border" (*History of the Song Dynasty · Biography of Gaozong*). The Huaihe River that used to be an artery now became a border area. Just like Yang Wanli exclaimed in *Upon First Entering the Huaihe River*: "One becomes depressed after reaching the Huaihe River", "North to the middle streamline of the Huaihe River there will be the end of the world!" The border of the state was shrunk like this, leaving half of its original size alone. Looking as far as one could, there was no screen defending the southern coast, leaving only the vast plains. Within the region of Jianghuai, the prospect of expedition looked dim, the frost and the wind were bleak and harsh, adding to the forlorn sight after war.

Standing at the long coast of the Huaihe River and looked as far as one could, one would see that the bushes and wild grass on the border pass were vast wild plains. The expedition northward had become dim, the cold autumn wind was blowing hard, and the frontier was solitary. I gazed and felt depressed. Thinking of the sinking of the Central Plains in the past, it might have been written, not to be altered by manpower; on the banks of the Zhushui River and the Sishui River where the apprentices of Confucius used to study, the land of music was now stained with bloody woe. Across the river, there were the camps of the enemy, at dusk and sunset, cattle and sheep returned to their hutches, and the guard posts dotted the land. The soldiers and generals of the Jin troops ordered hunting during night-time, and horsemen held torches, shining over the whole plain, the lutes and drums gave out sad sound, making people scared and frightened.

This lyric poem is about the feelings upon watching the Huaihe River, through an overview of the territorial situation, the author criticized and condemned the royal court's policy that seeks momentary ease, and expressed his strong wish to serve the country, showing his loyalty and giving vent to his indignation.

In *Buddhist Dancers: Written on the Wall of Zaokou, Jiangxi*, Xin Qiji exclaimed: "Blue mountains can't stop water from flowing; Eastward the river keeps on going." There were countless blue mountains, and the poet exclaimed that they obscured the capital, while further indicated that they couldn't stop water from flowing, referring to the enemy with blue mountains. In the subconscious of the lyric poet, the blue mountains should refer to the capitulators. "Eastward the river keeps on going" particularly deserve appreciation. "All streams want to return to the sea, just like all countries want to serve the emperor", therefore, he must be indicating something, signifying where justice inclines with the east-flowing river. Justice will conquer evil in the end, which is certain in history and unstoppable by all.

In Wang Anshi's *Fragrance of Laurel Branch*: "The running water saw the Six Dynasties pass, but I see only chilly mist and withered grass." He indicated changes in the times through the natural passing of water, leaving readers feeling sad. The second types of lyric poems indicate the irreversibility of history. For example, *Tune: The Charms of Niannu* by Su Shi: "The endless river eastward flows; With its huge waves are gone all those Gollant heroes of bygone years" and *Partridge Sky* by Xin Qiji: "Blue mountains can't stop water from flowing; Eastward the river keeps on going", all showing the poets' celebration of the heroic feats in the ancient times on the one hand, and exclaiming over the shortness of life, enlightening posterity. Liu Yong's *Eight Beats of Ganzhou Song*: "Everywhere, a bright red becomes dull red. Leaves turn yellow, and some are even browned. The beauty of nature—fading away. Only the Yangtze River flows on quiet, eastward bound." These examples taking water as the conception of time showed the importance people in the Song Dynasty attached to the special object of water and tried to indicate the rational meaning accumulated in the object of water, so as to add to the volume of signification of the lyric poem, making it profound in meaning and remote in feelings. Meanwhile, the implication that the image of water has not only made the poem more reserved and refined in signification, but also makes it broader, more profound, and magnificent in conception, showing the special perceptions lyric poets in the Song Dynasty for nature and the society.

Jiang Jie's *Listen to the Rain · to the Tune of Yu Mei Ren* (Fig. 11-5) was, on the other hand, an exclamation over his life:

When I was young, I listened to the rain in singsong girl's boudoirs, the red candles casting a dim light on the brocade canopy. When I was middle-aged, I listened to the rain in travelers' boats: The cloud low, the river wide, in the west the stray geese cried. Now I listened to the rain in monasteries, my temples specked with grey, joy and sorrow, parting, and re-union—They do not affect me so much anymore. Let the raindrops drip, on the doorsteps till morn.

Figure 11-5 *Listening to the Rain*

His abundant and intricate life was fully shown in the flow of time day and night. Raindrops became the life of Jiang Jie. The flowing water is chronological, and everything lives in the stream of life; The flowing water is also full of life. Therefore, water is interconnected with the time consciousness through life consciousness. Wang Anshi perceived the rise, fall, success, and failure of history from the water flow while exclaiming the history in the line "The running water saw the Six Dynasties pass" from "the limpid river, belt-like, flowing a thousand miles" (*Fragrance of Laurel Branch*). "The waves of the mighty river flowing eastward have swept away the brilliant figures of a thousand generations" (*Tune: The Charms of Niannu*), Su Shi not only saw the historical time, but also saw the tens of thousands of lives active in history. People who can see time and history in water flow are either heroes or philosophers: "In the vast land of ages, no one can find a hero like Sun Zhongmou", "All gallant deeds now sent away by driving wind and blinding rain" (Xin Qiji's *Joy of Eternal Union*). This is not only the perspective of a philosopher, but also a projection of the self-consciousness of heroes. Moreover, this is the profound exclamation of heroes in the face of driving wind and blinding rain.

If heaven had feelings, it would too age; If water had feelings, it would last forever. There is tenderness, implications in lyric poems, lofty sentiments, and exclamations in lyric poems.

Section III Water and Fu[①]

We often feel excited after appreciating a famous painting, enjoying a piece of classical music, watching a classical opera, or reading a collection of masterpieces. We cannot express accurately or vividly. What we can do is only sigh: "It can be sensed but not be expressed in words!" Huang Kan, a scholar in Qing Dynasty, said about the literary form of Fu: " It can pass on the difficult meaning, explain the unreadable article, write the untraceable form, and express the sub audition." Liu Xie also said in Chapter 37 of *Wen Xin Diao Long*: "Where words are spoken, boasting endures." Yongshuifu includes a spectacular sight of exaggeration, and this section will discuss about Fu: the water of exaggeration.

Why is there so much exaggeration in Fu? It is not only to praise, but also write the untraceable form by exaggeration which cannot be described by nature.

1. Water and Exaggeration: Delineating the Connotation

Most of us have seen great rivers and oceans. Our heart will be rising and falling like waves when we are facing the spectacular view of nature. Have you thought about how to describe nature?

Let's take a look at *The Composition about Shanglin* by Sima Xiangru, which depicted how the rivers and lakes merge eastward into Taihu Lake:

Those expansive rivers' water, flowing to different directions, is very changeable. Some flows to the East or West, some flows to the North or South, running and crisscrossing with one another… strikes huge stones, pounds against the sand bank, the sounds and flows are fierce, the waves are sweeping and surging. The whole picture was powerful, showing a forward, unstoppable momentum. The writer combines his cultural feelings for the mighty Han Empire into the magnificent natural aesthetic feeling and artistic expression of the mountains and rivers, thus forming such a thrilling artistic conception.

---

① Fu: a style of writing in ancient China, which embraces the characteristics of both poetry and prose.

In *Qi Fa*, Mei Cheng (Fig. 11-6) advised the Prince to watch rivers and depicted waves vividly and heart-stirringly.

When rivers began to surge, the torrent flew down, like a flying egret gliding down. When it grew a little bigger, the water was vast and white, like a white horse driving a vegetable cart, with a hood curtain on it. And when the waves tumbled like clouds, it rose like armies and marched forward in garrisons.

In depicting the three stages of variation of waves, the author vividly reproduces the great wonders of rivers and seas by using this ink-focused approach, which can extend infinitely to space, and is suitable for the difficult-to-write theme of mountains and rivers.

Figure 11-6　Mei Cheng

In *Ode to the Sea* the author said:

The sails suspended, the wind blowing, the boat moving farther and farther in the sea, gradually became a black spot like a bird, and finally disappeared at the end of water. This section of the scene is quite picturesque. The realm is expansive and intelligent, which can be regarded as one of the competitive works.

Ode to Jishui River by Cao Pi was the first writing that praised Jishui River. It wrote on the visit of Jishui River, describing the three aspects of it: the unique scenery of water, which was marvellous and spectacular; wonderful stuff, like a frolicking tortoise, groups of warblers, beautiful jade, and glowing pearl; and the third is delightful people, who so greatly enjoyed this place that people lingered on and wouldn't go back until sunset.

Another example is *Ode to the Wo River* by Cao Pi. The preface of it says after ascending the stone, Cao Pi went to Bozhou City to worship his ancestors. On the way back, he took a horse tour of the Wo River. Along the road, he saw the green trees shady, swirling water and rippling blue waves, so he stopped and wrote:

The green river flowed eastward like a girl who had just woken up. As soon as the spring wind blew, green weeping willow fluttering along the two sides. Hundreds of birds singing on the branches, waves sparkling, and fish are intimate... The beautiful scenery of the meandering Wo River presented itself alive on the paper. Historically, the beauty of Wo River is famous, although she is not as magnificent as the Yangtze River or the Yellow River, she has the girl-like beauty and elegance. This writing shows the quietness, the decency, and the gentleness vividly, which has become an eternal masterpiece praising Wo River, Bozhou City.

The grandeur of rivers can expand literatus' minds, satisfy their emotional needs to certain extent, and bring them great aesthetic pleasure. Therefore, it is inevitable that the Fu writers often have a certain feeling in the Fu of river. Moreover, compared with the sea, rivers have a closer relationship with people's life. During the Period of Wei, Jin and Southern and Northern Dynasties, wars broke out everywhere. The patriotic literatus, unwilling to see the nation disintegrated, would seek the natural landscape symbolizing the orthodox Huaxia culture. And the river with a long history and majestic momentum is bound to be the object of praise. The Fu writers have made a great effort to brag about them, at the same time, it also showed the high-spirited mind, great ambition, and subtle thoughts in their hearts. Of course, these thoughts are in praise of the shock of the river landscape.

My heart shows my feeling. What literature should show is the author's thoughts and feelings. And Fu can pass on the difficult meaning by exaggeration.

2. Water and Exaggeration: Passing on the Unutterable Feelings

"Face the sea, with spring flowers blossoming." "Mayflies are so tiny, like an individual in front of heaven and earth, and the sea." When facing waters, poets usually employ exaggeration to present the unutterable affections.

In *Ode to the Yellow River*, Cheng Gongsui first gave positive praise to the Yellow River in the history of Chinese literature, with only about 100 words.

Looking at all the majestic splendour of the hundred rivers, the grandeur of the Yellow River is matchless. Its undercurrents at the the steepest part of Kunlun Mountain, running between the towering hills of Jishi Mountain and Longmen, run out of the gorge eventually, and yellow wave tumbles and runs south for thousands of miles. As Li Bai wrote, "Running from the west and bursting out of the gate". The quietly flowing Huayin River and Qu'e River (which are respectively in Shanxi Province and Jiangsu Province today, and Junshui River is in Kaifeng City, Henan Province today), stands like a pillar mountain in the Yellow River rapids, the water waves fly when passing by Luoyang City. The author describes the Yellow River by using verbs like "潜" (Qian, means run quietly), "登" (Deng, means climbing up with difficulty), "游" (You, means swim), "拂" (Fu, means brush gently) and human-like manner to write the momentum of the Yellow River. The magnificent scene of the Yellow River has been vividly presented on the paper. The author writes all the way from Kunlun Mountain, the source of the mother river that once nurtured the Chinese nation, to the end of the Yellow River—Ocean, shows the long history and grandeur of the Yellow River. In addition, it also shows the historical and cultural allusions of the Yellow River, including empires of Yin, Wei, Zhao, Qin, etc. and extolled the innumerable merits and virtues of the Yellow River. Finally, it ended with "exclaiming over the sage ancestors and their virtue of noble character and like broad mind like the Yellow River", which also showed nostalgia and expressed the deep history and culture of the Yellow River, the birthplace of Chinese civilization.

Ying Yang's *Ode to the Linghe River* not only praised the long flow of the Yellow River, but also showed his deep sympathy to the suffering people. In the wartime of Han and Wei Dynasties, his works naturally showed his sympathy to the people of the difficult time.

Ode to the Huaihe River by Wang Ji and Cao Pi, the background of which was recorded by VolumeI of *The Three Kingdom* that in July of the 14th year of Emperor Xian, Cao Cao took an eastern expedition to Empire Wu starting from the Wo River, passing by the Huaihe River and Feishui River. At that time, Wang Ji and Cao Pi followed the army along the Wo River into Huaihe River, seeing the sails as dense as woods on the Yangtze River and Huaihe River, they made their works with the same title for expressing their sentiments. Wang Ji's writing of scenery was bright and lively, which showed his excited mood for taking part in the battle. Ending with the military achievements, his works shared the same expression results with different approaches from Cao Pi. Their works portrayed the landscape as well as expressed the warship, which can really be regarded as characteristic compositions of the kind.

Guo Pu's works of *Ode to the Yangtze River* in the East Jin Dynasty which could be taken as the grandest works in the Fu of rivers. Li Shan, by quoting *The Book of Mid-term of Jin Dynasty* wrote *Ode to the Yangtze River*. It could be seen that although these works were devoted to the description of scenery, it also contains abundant political significance. Guo Pu said that the beauty of the Yangtze River has a positive intention to stabilize people's heart. In Guo's heart, the Yangtze River was not only significant scenery, but also the symbolization of Hua Xia culture. Although he had cynical and high-hearted thoughts, Fu was filled with the idea of worrying about the country. It was quite glorious in the literary world at that time. As the central power and cultural centre of ancient China were in the Central Plains of the Yellow River Basin, people knew little about the Yangtze River. Even in *Yu Gong*, there was only a simple description. Guo Pu's *Ode to the Yangtze River* is the first eulogy of the Yangtze River in an all-round way, with a total length of 1682 words, and is a typical work . It described the origin and process of the Yangtze River, accounted of the Yangtze River and its' two sides topography, animals, plants, fruits, immortals, and histories in detail. Thus, praising the long history, vast territory and momentum, rich property, and magnificent scenery of the Yangtze River Basin.

It emphasized the importance of the Yangtze River at the beginning from five aspects, "The combination of the five talents was the primate of water virtue". And then it wrote about the rush of water and the danger of topography of the Yangtze River, grand and magnificent, soul-stirring. Then Guo Pu described the fantastic things and variety of treasures in the sea. Since Guo Pu himself is a naturalist and has made a note on *Shan Hai Jing*, the introduction of the strange scene in the sea was easy for him. The water was interlaced and dazzling, expanding the capacity of past river Fu. Finally, the author describes the life scene between wind driving boat and fishermen on the river, many of these paragraphs are vivid.

The literary form of Fu, has widely reproduced the beauty of the landscape and inspired people to love mountains and rivers for the enjoyment of beauty, it also deeply revealed the utilitarian value of mountains and rivers, enlightened people to understand the natural attributes of mountains and rivers, so as to transform and utilize it; Meanwhile, Fu writers were good at merge themselves in nature when they describe the mountains and rivers, in order to attract people to embrace nature.

The heart of Fu writers, including the universe and characters. They talk about the concept of governance and cite the masterpieces of predecessors.

Section IV Water and Essay

It was said in *Shu Yi Ji* that: "Since the death of Pan Gu, creator of the universe in Chinese mythology, his head became mountains, his eyes became sun and moon, his skin became rivers, and his hair became woods." It showed that the magnificent rivers and mountains on the earth are the blood of the ancestors and the land on which the Chinese nation depends for its survival and reproduction. Both man and mountain depend on each other.

"The natural beauty of lakes and mountains is countless". Because of the Chinese ancient essay pays attention to the inornate trick, the mountains and rivers in essay are often inornate in the same way.

1. Water and Peacefulness

The essay pays more attention to description of water in inornate form and of quiet places. Let's look at *The Small Tarn West of the Knoll* (Fig. 11-7) written by Liu Zongyuan (a famous

Figure 11-7 *The Small Tarn West of the Knoll*

litterateur of the Tang Dynasty):

When Liu Zongyuan described the small tarn, he started with the sound of water. Over a hundred steps westward from the knolls, he heard the sound of water across the bamboo forest. What did the water sound like? Listening with carefulness, the crisp sound was like a jade pendant colliding with a jade bracelet. Appealed to the sound, he was immediately in delightful mood. Then, he followed the sound of water, cut down the bamboo, trying to open a road and find the cold water. He indeed, saw a small pool in which water was truly clear and cold. This paragraph describes the quiet scenery and atmosphere of the small tarn.

The full text was written in a lonely, quiet, and depressed tone. It seemed to be a scenic description, in fact, it showed the author's inward world. With few lines of description of swimming fish in the pool, the author while presented an accurate and vivid depiction of the clear pool water and the shape and spirit of the fish.

Besides, the writing of swimming fish in the pool was tactful. No description of water was mentioned, but only describing fish as " they seemed to be gliding through empty space without support", the clarity of the water and the vividness of the fish were all wonderful. The artistic conception was so deep that people were amazed.

The author tried hard to depict the silence of the small tarn, even immerse into people's heart. "All the scenery words are sentimental". This essay vividly described the beauty and tranquility of the place, expressing the author's feelings of loneliness after being demoted.

A Letter to Zhu Yuansi(Fig. 11-8) by Wu Jun was one of the quiet environment models. This essay depicted the blue-water and green mountains from Fuyang to Tonglu in the west of Zhejiang Province. The blue-water and green mountains mingled with the cries of the animals vividly.

The author described the blue-water and green mountains along the field of the Fuchun River, implying his deep attachment to the nature of the mountains and rivers, and his heartfelt boredom of the official career. "Drifting along the river aimlessly." A leaf of canoe freely floating along the river. The author was also clarity in his heart. The author and the surrounding around him were so

Figure 11-8 *A letter to Zhu Yuansi*

empty, so pure, symbolizing the harmony between the heaven and the man. "The water was blue" drew a picture of fish swimming in the clear and deep water, colourful pebbles, all experience visible, showing the silence of the abyss. He wrote about drifting along the river: the Fuchun River had the torrent dangerous beach when the boat moving. "急湍" (Ji Tuan, means torrential) described the rapidity of the turbulent current which was faster than the arrow of the high string and the white wave surged like the galloping of the horse, having its own magnificent beauty, highlights the posture of the water and the strange clouds.

This essay depicts the scenery from the vivid visual and auditory portrayal of mountains and rivers. Hu Huaichen said: "The depiction of the mountain, water, bamboo, trees, birds and fish were all well-organized. With only a few lines, it presented endless artistic conception with people. It was so beautiful and vivid. Was it a painting or a writing?" Just like the essay said that there are pictures in the text, words in pictures. Zhang Chao said in *The Shade of a Dream* that the writing and painting are intermingled.

2. Water and Seclusion

Actively participating the social activities can help realize the scholars' ideal of family regulating, state ordering and the world peacefully governing, and improve their sense of achievement. But in the concrete process of implementation, there may be variety of hardships and difficulties which may distort their personality and disposition. Therefore, the landscape and idyll are the best places for them to send peace of mind, preserve temperament, and verify the value of personality.

Wang Siren, who lived in late Ming Dynasty, depicted a beautiful picture of the mountains and waters in *Shan Xi*. The first scene was about the first night of the San Jiezhi village:

The night view of a riverside village was represented: mutual reflection of the lights on the fishing boats, lights of the village and the moonlight, mingled with the beautiful serenade, which constituted a world of clarity and serenity. In the end, the author would move to the "end of the boat for a deep sleep", which showed the author's elegant feelings and interest of seclusion. Liu Changqing said: "There are many secluded officials in Shan Xi".

Let's take a look at Tao Hongjing, who was called the "Prime Minister in the Mountain". He retired from Maoshan Mountain at 37 and lived in Lin Quan for over 40 years. With the beautiful landscape of the south of the Yangtze River, Lin Quan was his ideal spiritual home. *A Letter to Xie Zhongshu*(Fig. 11-9) was also an essay directly description of landscape of the beautiful scenery of mountains and rivers, and the thoughts of seclusion.

The beauty of mountains and rivers has been frequently talked about. The high peaks are as high as clouds. The streams are clear. The stone walls on both sides of the strait are gorgeous. The green mountains and bamboo are reflected on each other. Such is the beautiful scenery throughout a year of four seasons…With sun setting, the fish prance in river, which is really a rare wonderland in this world of desire.

Figure 11-9　*A Letter to Xie Zhongshu*

We will find that Tao Hongjing describes beautiful landscapes as "The Wonderland of The World of Desire". In Buddhism, "The World of Desire" is the lowest one of the three divisions of the universe, the place where all living beings are addicted to food and lust. Look at the Fuchun River, which was regarded as the "仙" (immortal) by the author. What is "仙"? Let's look at the word "仙" (Xian), which consists of radical of left part, with meaning of people, and right part, with meaning of mountain. That is to say, a person, living in mountains, divorced from the secular desire and indulging in the beauty of mountains and rivers, can be called "仙人" (immortal).

The author witnessed the social upheaval and participated in some events of regime change. He was deeply touched by the secular struggle for power and interests, and he lived in seclusion in the mountains in search of liberation.

It was said in *A New Account of the Tales of the World* that "Emperor Jianwen visited Hualin garden and said to his attendants that: It is not necessary to go far away to the fairyland. With woods that are lush and beautiful mountains and rivers, you will naturally have the idea of being as leisurely as at Haoshui River or Pushui river, thinking that birds and fish would come to get close to people by themselves."

Being able to appreciate the mountains and rivers, Xu Xun enjoyed touring mountains and rivers, and was regarded as the elegance of gentleman. So, people praised him. Wei Yong knew few about mountains and rivers, then Sun Chuo laughed at him: "He knows nothing about mountains and rivers, how can he write an essay?" The Wei and Jin Dynasties are an era of "literary consciousness", people of that time discovered the beauty of natural, and found the deep feelings of human beings inward. Since Wei Yong didn't know about mountains and rivers, people just wondered if he could write an essay. People questioned his aesthetic taste.

A New Account of the Tales of the World · *Literature* said that after reading Guo Pu's lines "There is no still tree in the forest or no stop in the river", Ruan Fu sighed with emotion, "The raging stream and the howling wind are indeed indescribable. Every time I read this poem; I feel like my mind is out of this world."

Seemingly depicting the scenery, but in fact it contains the philosophy that everything is changing, and things are impermanent, and the poet's deep emotion about life. With just eight characters, great potential is presented.

A New Account of the Tales of the World · Language said that Gu Changkang came back from Kuaiji mountain, and people asked his impression of the mountain. He replied that: "Hundreds of rocks are of different shapes, thousands of rivers surge forward. Towering woods are spectacular like clouds."

The ancient scholars' love of leisurely landscapes. If people do not understand "the unity of nature and man, the culture of seclusion," the dilemma of Chinese traditional intellectuals in far away from common customs and accession to the society, or the eastern philosophical method of calming down their grievances, healing their wounds and winning freedom in the beauty of the lake and mountains, it is then difficult to understand Chinese landscape literature, especially the essay of the water of recluse.

The ancient Chinese essay expresses the beauty of the scenery and the seclusion from the world in water of recluse. My heart is not tired and in case of peace. Walking outside the world of mortals, my heart is between the water and clouds. *Laozi* also said: "The universe is created by nature without doing anything."

The world is so vast that I want to look at the quiet mountains and rivers and enjoy the leisure of life.

Section V Water and Novel

Water images frequently appear in ancient poems and poems, and novels are also inextricably linked with water. Although Chinese myths and legends are not novels in the true sense, they already have rich contents of water myths and legends, such as Jingwei Filling the Sea, Kuafu Chasing the Sun, The Legend of the Yu the Great, etc. Water-related novels are of great variety, such as The Eight Immortals Crossing the Sea, Legend of the White Snake, Story of Liu Yi, the four classic novels of Chinese literature, etc., and even the modern and contemporary literature writer will praise water, such as Shen Congwen's *The Border Town*, Wang Anyi's *Light Rain*, *People of the Yellow River*, and Mo Yan's *Wine* and so on, all related to water.

The novel has three elements of character, plot and set, among which the character is the core. This section will discuss about the core characters of the novel, and mainly focus on the four classic novels of Chinese literature, *Romance of the Three Kingdoms*, *the Outlaws of the Mush*, *The Journey to the West* and *Dream of the Red Chamber*, to analyze the imitation of human water in the novel.

1. Water as Medium

Water is the source of life, who gives birth to life, and man is the spirit of all things.

Therefore, characters in novels often have the characteristics of water, and water, as a medium, is closely related to the background and living environment of characters.

Water has many properties, and flow is a natural property of water. Thus, in people's aesthetic taste and feeling, this attribute can be transformed into the characteristics of life, which is, "humanized nature", and the material water then has symbolic meaning. In the face of water, we will reflect on the past in the light of the present and sigh with history. This is to see history as living, flowing "water", such as the beginning of *Romance of the Three Kingdoms*:

The Yangtze River symbolizes the history of the Three Kingdoms, which is surging and changing like the Yangtze River, and finally passes away like the flowing water, expressing the author's sigh about the vicissitudes of history. At the same time, the flowing water causes the illusion of life history. History is eternal and changing, which reflects the cyclical view of history that "the world will separate after long time united and also will do the opposite after long time splitting".

Another example of *The Journey to the West*, for scripture team: Tang monk, Monkey King, Zhu Bajie, Sha monk, the White Dragon Horse, every one of which has something to do with water.

The birth of Tang monk (Fig. 11-10) is a famous "baby flowing on the river" story. In the novel, his father was murdered on board when he was on the way to take up an official post, and his mother kidnapped. After his birth, he was placed on a plank in the river by his mother and floated along the river. He was rescued by the elders of Jinshan Temple and named Jiang Liu. Tang monk was a real person in history and a great religionist. Both the old and new *Book on the Tang Dynasty and Continuation of Eminent Monk Biography* have written biographies of him. From the late Tang

Figure 11-10 Tang Monk

Dynasty to the Song Dynasty, with the spread and deification of scripture stories among the people, Tang monk was also deified. The life story of the Tang monk "baby flowing on the river" is a literary story that combines the relevant contents of ancient Chinese mythology, Tang and Song novels, Song and Yuan operas and folklore. Water appears in many abandoned child myths: some babies are abandoned by water or ice, while others are simply thrown into the river, which forms a very typical "baby flowing on the river rive" paradigm. *Si Xing and the Miserable Baby*, *Three Blondes*, the legend of Sargon, and the story of Moses in *The Bible* all have plots of abandoning babies in water (or near water). In addition, many similar legends can be found in Chinese literature and classics. For example, the story of King Xu Yan, written by Zhang Hua of the Jin Dynasty, "Maid of honour Xu's gave birth to a baby, who was abandoned by the water because it was considered unlucky" and was carried back again by dogs. In *Records of Huayang Kingdom · Nanzhong*, a woman washed clothes on the riverbank. A big bamboo flowed into between the woman's feet. She wanted push it off but failed, then she broke the bamboo and got a baby boy, and when he grew up, he became an emperor. There is also an extension of the child-abandoning myth, in which sages or heroes are not only born in bad circumstances, but also have been plagued by bad luck and suffering since they grew up and before (or even after) their achievements. At the same time, this kind of deity is also influenced by the method of historical transmission. In the development chain of the tradition of historical transmission, those who have made great achievements, such as emperors, sages, and heroes, etc. , who are admired by people, are endowed with divine power when they are born to highlight their transcendence. Therefore, because of the identity of "baby flowing on the river", Tang monk obtained the same transcendence of life as his disciples Monkey King, Zhu Bajie and Sha monk, and made the origin of this scripture collection team all have the same divinity and solemnity, which contains the profound ancient mythology, and all these are with the help of "water".

The birth of Monkey King is more related to "water". He was born on a fairy mountain, Mount Huaguoshan, surrounded by water on all sides.

There is a famous mountain in the sea called Mount Huaguoshan. This mountain is the ancestral vein of ten continents. Three islands originated from the very beginning. What a nice mountain! As proofed in the following Fu:

With greater potential than the oceans, and Yaohai seat, all the fish went to home. There seemed to be the fairyland. There was an island in the southeast of the East China Sea, and the Mount Huaguoshan was the highest mountain on the island. On the Danya Mount, golden pheasants sang pleasantly; In front of the wall, the unicorn lied alone. People could frequently hear the golden pheasants singing and watch the dragon swimming through the Longmen. There were deer and foxes of longevity in the forests, and immortal birds and cranes in trees. The immortal flowers and grass never withered, and the pine and cypress remained green all the year round. Peach tree always bore lots of fruits, and tall bamboo towered up to the sky. A ravine was covered with vines, with newly grown grass all around. What a sky reaching pillar to which all the rivers' head and the origin of all things in the world.

Mount Huaguoshan, created in *The Journey to the West*, has rich cultural connotations. It is a paradise for apes and a home of freedom for humans. It is a paradise for recluses and for rebels. While Mount Huaguoshan is more than that. It is a unique existence formed by the synthesis of many factors (including the living habits of apes), and is the essence of heaven, earth, and ocean. The habitat is "Water Curtain Cave", with a waterfall outside the cave as a curtain.

Monkey King (Fig. 11-11) was not only born in the world of water, but also borrowed the weapon he uses, the Golden Cudgel, from the Dragon Palace. At the same time, the origin of this Golden Cudgel is more closely related to water. It is the magic pin left by Yu the Great to control the flood, which has its origin with the myth of controlling the flood. In addition, the 72 changes of Monkey King are also related to water. He can change into fish, snakes, and other aquatic animals.

Zhu Bajie (Fig. 11-12) has a similar origin with water. Pigs are aquatic animals and they like water. Ancient people regarded them as aquatic animals. In addition, the bathing habit of pigs had some connection with rainfall. In ancient times, they mistakenly believed that rainfall was related to pigs, so they were regarded as aquatic animals and deity of water. *In Mao Biography* by Zheng Jian: "Vermin, aquatic animal"; Zheng Xuan said, "Pig, aquatic animal". It is said in the *Book of Changes* that "Kan means water." He Bo, the god of water, has an image of Pig. Before being banished, Zhu Bajie was Marshal Tianpeng in the heaven who oversaw the sailors and the Tianhe. In the war of Liusha River, Zhu Bajie introduced himself by saying that: "I used to govern of the Tianhe and oversee eighty thousand sailors."

Figure 11-11 Monkey King

Figure 11-12 Zhu Bajie

Water and the Chinese Culture

Figure 11-13 Sha Monk

Sha monk (Fig. 11-13) is a water monster in the Liusha River. The environment of the Liusha River in which he lives is described in the novel as: "It's vast and deep river on which even goose feathers cannot float, and the fall of the reed must sink to the bottom." " waves surging las high as mountains". Even the dharma name that Avalokitesvara Bodhisattva gave to him was related to water. In the book, it says, he named River as his family name. He and I gave him a dharma name, Sha Wujing.

The White Dragon Horse (Fig. 11-14), the mount of Tang Priest, is transformed by a white dragon. The story introduced the white dragon through Monkey King, who said, he is a horse, but not common one. He was originally the son of Ao Run, the Dragon King of the West Sea. He was the Third Prince named White Dragon Horse. Just because he set fire and destroy the pearl and was regarded as disobedience. Avalokitesvara Bodhisattva saved him, and he waited for his master for a long time in the steep stream. Avalokitesvara Bodhisattva visited him again and took off his scales and horns and picked the beads under his neck. Then he transforms into a horse. The ancient people took the horse as one of the models of the dragon because of the horse, which originally constituted the local features of the dragon. Not a horse on land, but a hippo in the water. In ancient times, the Yellow River Basin had a mild climate, there were elephants, rhinoceros,

Figure 11-14 White Dragon Horse

hippopotamus, and other animals. The hippopotamus is regarded as the god of water because it lives in water. The dragon horse in the legend is the embodiment of this kind of hippo: "Fuxi has the kingdom, and the dragon and horse are drawn from the river"(*Notes to the Book of Documents*); "There is a deep pond in the Shenma Mountain of the western Gansu Province, born of the dragon and the horse"(*Geography Book of the Han and Tang Dynasties*); "The dragon horse is the essence of the river"(*Ruiying Tu*). The legend of the dragon and horse living in the water, said that the dragon first integrated the object for the hippo. However, due to the many similarities between the hippo and the horse on land, the ancient people did not strictly distinguish the animal itself, so they tend to regard the hippo and the land horse as the same kind. The most distinctive feature of the dragon's appearance is the horse's head.

All the characters in the scripture collection team, including White Dragon Horse, are related to "water".

2. Water and Character's Personality

The core of a novel is to create characters; therefore, character is the key. And many of the characters have the features of water. "Softness and sentiment" are descriptions of women, while for bad women, we will also use the character related to water: "skittish". Not only female, but also male characters are closely related to water.

Water Margin, for example, uses a variant of water, "wine", to create characters. The author tends to connect characters with wine, to shape and present people's character with wine, to develop the plot, to reflect the social reality. In Chapter 3, Lu Zhishen, a monk, drank ten bowls of wine in the first place, then had dog meat together with garlic sauce, which really stunned the shopkeepers. Then there was the farce of on Mount Wutai. All those showed his unrestrained character that was not bound by religion and pursuing freedom. In Chapter 10 of "Lin Chong went to Liangshan on a snowy night". Lin Chong drank three or four bowls of wine in the Zhu Gui Hotel. Because he had to go to Liangshan by water but had no way to find a boat, he was upset. He drank another few bowls, and then he wrote down the eight lines of heroic words, showing his determination to go to Liangshan with revenge. When water is not strong enough to show the vitality, the "wine" may be employed. Water is necessary for human survival, but wine is the substance that sublimates the passion of life. Compared with wine, water is more of a life of scattered inaction, wine is a wild struggle, it is the savage life of the spontaneous play. When drunk, human nature is easier to show, so are the spirits of passion and struggle. Compared with the Greeks, the spirit of wine is not as strong as them.

In *Romance of the Three Kingdoms*, Liu Bei (Fig. 11-15) is directly written with the word "water". For example, in the 31st Chapter, when Liu Bei was about to confer with Liu Biao, Sun Qian went to Liu Biao's to persuade him, and mentioned Liu Bei: "General Liu of Jingzhou treat worthy men with courtesy, and the men of talents pay allegiance to him, like the rivers flowing to

Figure 11-15　Liu Bei

the east." The metaphor of "water" shows Liu Bei's appreciation and respect for talents. Cao Cao also used "water" as a metaphor for human beings when he commented on Liu Bei. Cao Cao said, "Liu Bei is an outstanding person who didn't get his opportunity. Now he's got Jingzhou today, like the dragon getting into the sea. How couldn't I be worried!" Cao Cao took Liu Bei as a dragon, who was simply unable to flourish because he was not given favourable conditions. All his life, Cao Cao regarded Liu Bei as his strongest rival. However, Liu Bei had no base of his own in his early years. After capturing Jingzhou, Liu Bei was like a dragon entering the sea. Therefore, Cao Cao was determined to despoil Jingzhou. But Liu Bei also made a comparison of the relationship with Cao Cao. Xuande (Liu Bei) said, "Cao Cao is my strong opponent, and we two are like water and fire. If Cao Cao is impatient, then I will be relaxed; if he is grumpy, then I benevolent; if he is deceitful, then I faithful. Only if I behave inversely, then I will succeed. I cannot bear to betray the people just for petty profits." Liu Bei compared his relationship with Cao Cao as "water and fire". Liu Bei was "water", and Cao Cao was "fire". Like the mighty water, Liu Bei, giving the enemy an impression of weakness, while overcoming the strong with soft method, and finally ascended the throne.

Liu Bei is portrayed in the novel in the form of water variant, and the most typical is "tears" and "crying". In fact, "tears" is used to show his benevolence, righteousness, morality, and other respected conduct, at the same time, through "tears" to show his fate, and rough and difficult life. For example, in Chapter 19, Liu An, the hunter, "wanted to find game for food, but failed, so he killed his wife to eat." When learning of this, Liu Bei "was overwhelmed with sadness, and got on his horse with tears". The "tears" were out of human nature. There are many other examples of "tears" in the book for the purpose of depicting his character, praise his personality. For example, when getting to know that Xu Shu was going to Cao Cao to look for his mother, Liu Bei "burst into tears" and "looked at him with tears pouring down his face". This is to show Liu Bei's talents, which eventually touched Xu Shu. Although he was "in Cao Cao's camp, his cared about Han, and he never set a single plan for Cao Cao in his whole life."

In the section of Liu Bei abandoning Fancheng, it says:

People on both sides burst into tears. Xuande (Liu Bei), mourned bitterly by seeing this: "Because of me, the people of the city suffered so much. Why was I born!" He tried to commit suicide but was stopped by his attendants. People learning of this were all touched. When the ship reached the south bank, he looked back at the people and cried again when seeing the people who didn't come with him.

Hundreds of thousands of people followed Liu Bei, and Liu Bei could not bear to abandon the people, so thus appeared the aforementioned tragic and stirring scene, "benevolence, virtue" the image of the king was vividly presented.

In addition, Liu Bei even threw his baby at Changbanop (now in Yichang City) because his general Zhao Yun risked his own life to save his baby. Liu Bei "sobbed" while doing so. Here this "sob" just showed his "selflessness" and "love" for his general. When Liu Qi (Liu Bei's nephew) died, Liu Bei cried. When Liu Bei married the daughter of the King of Wu State, he cried. During the dispute about Jingzhou (now in Hubei Province) he covered his face and cried. When Liu Zhang (Liu Bei's cousin) surrendered to Liu Bei, Liu Bei held his hands crying: "I did not mean to do so." When Guan Yu, his brother and general died, Lie Bei was heart-stricken for days, with no appetite at all. Before Liu Bei died, he saw Guan Yu in his dream, sat up, trying to grasp him, and cried. Liu Bei finally completed his "righteousness" of dying on the same day of the same year.

Other characters, such as Zhuge Liang, are also related to water. The novel first wrote Zhuge Liang's seclusion environment—"a high mountain with the running water", "running water with flying stone", "water is not deep but clear", by using the description of the environment to show how Zhuge Liang's different from others. Ancient masters often live in saclusion at the beautiful mountains and rivers, such as Xu You at Yingshui River, Gui Guzi of enjoying seclusion in Qingxi Stream, and Jiang Ziya at Panxi Creek. By living among the mountains and rivers, those hermits easily showed their noble character. After that, Liu Bei paid several visits to invite Zhuge Liang and treated him as a teacher, which caused the displeasure of Guan Yu and Zhang Fei. Xuande said, "I get Kongming (Zhuge Liang), just like a fish in water." It also showed Liu Bei's affirmation and trust in Zhuge Liang's talent and gratitude. Zhang Fei therefore was dissatisfied. Later, he said to Liu Bei, "Why don't you send the 'water' to fight for you?"

A Dream of Red Mansions is also closely related to water. The world of Grand View Garden is the world of women. "Women are made of water and men are made of mud. When I see a daughter, it is refreshing, and when I see a man, I feel muddy and smelly." Cao Xueqin connects the world of women and the world of water virtually.

One of the main characters in the book is Lin Daiyu (Fig. 11-16). The writing about her appearance says, "a pair of eyes with tears". Other lines about Daiyu's tears are "shedding tears", "wiping tears", "tears running down", and "eyes with tears"…The lines about her crying are "keep crying", "burst into tears", "sob", "speak with tears", "cry out loud", "cry and vomit", "eyes are red with weeping", "desperately cry", "cry and quiver", "cry and faint", and "hide the face from the tears".

With a pure and clear character, Daiyu was intolerant and critical to both people and other aspects. Therefore, she was sensitive and sentimental. All her characteristics were shown to

Figure 11-16　Lin Daiyu

readers, like limpidity and purity of water. Here is the comment on Daiyu: heart of orchid, moral integrity of jade, harsh words, and she was supreme, who was matchless.

Daiyu reflected on *Peony Pavilion* "Loving you, youth passes as fleeing waves...", associating with the ancient Lines of "flowing water and falling petals," "With years passing by, things all changed", and reflection on *The Romance of the Western Chamber*, "with the falling flower, the river looks sad, too, which make people feel sorrow", heartbroken and with tears in eyes. These poems are all based on the image of falling water, lamenting the lost youth like falling water, the hopelessness like "moon in water" and "flowers in the mirror", the uncontrollable love, and the tragic ending of pure water, which is even more tragic.

Cao Xueqin devoted himself to the writing about women suffering a lot in ten years. Woman is like water, and water is like woman. The proposition that "woman is water" coincides partly with the exposition on the relationship between humans and water in *Guanzi* during the Spring and Autumn Period: "Humans are water. Spirit of men and women combines together and makes water manifold ...and this is water...to be a man after merging all the character." People are made up of water, and the "Woman is water made of flesh and blood"; The uniqueness of Cao Xueqin is that he put forward the idea that "woman" is water and man is not water. This not only literalizes the philosophical propositions in *Guanzi*, but also ascribes the patent right of "water" to women. Moreover, the spirit of "water" is concentrated in the image of Lin Daiyu, the most outstanding girl of "woman". This is like a further literary expression of the thought of "water collects in jade" in *Guanzi*.

Water is like life, and life is like water.

Chapter Twelve   Water and Art

Section I   Water and Painting

"Blue sky is waiting for the misty rain, while I'm waiting for you", "thousands of years of solitude, with pictures to learn", Chinese landscape painting is the richest accumulation of Chinese human feelings. It describes the natural landscape, originated before the Warring States Period, developed in the Eastern Jin Dynasty, established in the Southern and Northern Dynasties, and flourished in the Sui and Tang Dynasties. In Chinese landscape painting, the painting of water scenery is magnificent.

1. Unity of Form and Spirit

Let's look at some paintings. Do you know whose paintings they are? These are some of *The Twelve Paintings of Water* (Fig. 12-1) by Ma Yuan, a famous landscape painter of the Southern Song Dynasty. These paintings describe the different forms of water and the various changes brought about by the environment and climate in detail. Some of these waters are quiet, some are billowing, some are angry, some are dazzling, some are circuitous, some are circling, some are turbulent, some are surging, some are hopping, some are running, all of which are vivid and have different postures. There is no one like him who has painted 12 different water waves.

In order to show different water waves, Ma Yuan employed a variety of different painting

Figure 12-1   The Twelve Paintings of Water

techniques, some lines are as thin as hair, like flowing clouds and water, some are thick and steady, thick and majestic, with combination of thick and light ink, dry and wet ink, which is changeable. A saying about ancient painting says, it may be easy to get the brush, but difficult to get the ink; it may be easy to get the ink, but difficult to know how to show it.

He also had a very representative painting of *Fishing Alone in the Cold River* (Fig. 12 – 2) . What does it present? A boat, a fisherman, water, and a large area of blank. He only painted a boat floating on the water, a fisherman fishing alone in the boat. All the painting is blank except a few strokes of water waves, which made it a very simple painting.

Figure 12-2　*Fishing Alone in the Cold River*

It seems that the blank area is all virtual outwardly, but it is the combination of reality and void. This "reality" represents both water—the water of the river and the sky. The water seems to melt into the sky at the horizon, making the picture of boundless, empty, and desert realm, which highlights the vast and cold atmosphere of the river and the fishing scene of the fisherman alone fishing on the cold river. Ancient Chinese painters called this artistic technique of blank as "contrast of white when black", which is really a unity of both form and spirit.

Famous paintings in history are often the unity of form and spirit. Let's take *Lushan Mountain* of Shen Zhou of the Ming Dynasty as an example, which features mountains, rocks and trees of simplicity and vigor. The painting of the mountains and rocks employs the skills of Jie Suo Cun of Wang Meng and Pi Ma Cun of Dong Yuan and Ju Ran, first dying with light ink layer by layer, and then applying with thick ink layer by layer. The strokes are steady and meticulous, but not unscrupulous. The painter uses thick and light ink properly to create a clear painting of mountains and rocks, which makes it a painting of virtual reality, with spring rushing down from the peak, mountain creeks flowing gently to shape a stunning scenery.

Poetic Painting of Lin Hejing by Dong Qichang of the Ming Dynasty was created according to the poetry of Lin Hejing, a poet of the Northern Song Dynasty. The poem reads, "The mountain is not high, water not deep, and there are few fish and birds, and the dweller is reluctant to settle down. Along the lively Sanzhu stream and dainty bridge, the hermit built a cottage."This painting is also named *Painting of Sanzhu Stream.* The composition adopted the techniques of deep-reaching and far-reaching, and its colour is light crimson and green to create a mild soft atmosphere, showing the simplicity and innocence pursued by the painter in the landscape painting.

Guo Xi mentioned the technique of"three yuan (three different angles of view)"in his book *Lin Quan Gao Zhi.* To achieve the effect of "high", "deep"and "far-reaching", it is necessary to break the limitation of the focus perspective to observe the scenery, and use the cavalier perspective such as looking up, overlooking and looking horizontally to portray the scenery of the painting. A landscape of lakes and mountains, flourishing woods and tall bamboos, and waterfalls, all making a fascinating scenery. Then there are layers upon layers of mountains, followed by a sudden change of scenery of high mountain standing out and plank road along the cliff zigzagging, highlighting the magnificent spirit of China's mountains and rivers. With the end of the mountains, the river winds and gradually enters the hilly area, and the picture is gradually unfolded. Finally, there are endless misty waves and ripples. In the distance, the fishing boats are swaying on the lake, while in the near mountain village, the houses are just in order, which is a typical scenery of the south of the lower reaches of the Yangtze River. The whole volume is full of ups and downs, with clear priorities. The mountains and rocks are well merged with bamboos, and the fine strokes make the painting seem endless. The painter attaches the importance to the conception, advocating artistic image is for the internal and external communication.

Li Tang's *Painting of the Gully* and *Pine Trees*, depicts the deep ravines of high pines, the main peak towering, the rocks rising deeply, and the mountain springs running. The picture depicts a scenery of dangerously deep mountains and rocks, waterfalls and springs between the cliffs, and the white clouds floating around the mountains in the clear haze. From the foot to the top of the mountain, the pine forest is dense and lush. Stones and rocks are scattered at the foot of the mountain, among which water is flowing. The majestic atmosphere of nature is presented. The clumps of trees on the top of the mountain, the pine forest nearby and the hazy stone path highlights this painting of deep and quiet mood. The middle scene on the left consists of a waterfall gushing downward and flowing into a stream through the rocks. With the sound of the flowing water, the poem is created.

2. The Harmony of Water and Human

"Man"here refers to both the "man" in the painting and the "man" outside the painting. Landscape painting shows the relationship between man and nature and integrates them together. Painters"learn from the nature and combine the inner perception of themselves to create good works."Reading a million books and traveling a million miles, which means the painters are not supposed to be satisfied with just the objective description of the natural scenery but combines the inner perception of the scenery with the scenery itself, so as to achieve the fusion of the two. In this fusion, it shows a distinct and inspiring natural scenery that can give people inspiration and imagination and with thought-provoking meaning as well, achieving "the harmony of water and human".

As *Landscape Doctrine* by Guo Xi during the Song Dynasty states:

Why are the gentlemen fond of the beautiful scenery? Botanic gardens are a place to simplify our lifestyle; springs and rocks serve as food for impassioned cries; fishermen and woodcutters are impersonal hermits; monkeys and cranes can be seen very often. People are tired of noises, as well as fetters. The celestial life is what mortal flesh yearns for.

That is to say, the reason why gentlemen love mountains and rivers is that hills and countryside can keep their inner peace and indifference; the singing of springs and stones can make gentlemen often get the pleasure of being proud and vulgar; fishermen, woodcutters and hermits can make gentlemen feel harmonious in their daily life; the singing of apes and cranes can make gentlemen feel awfully close. Earthly life is like a rein, and a lock, which makes people generally feel disgusted. People yearn for those immortals who live in the land of haze, but it's hard to see them. "The mountains are full of clouds; the streams are flowing among trees; the spring breeze is strong, and the green is in full bloom. If possible, I will also move here to live by the river. This is Gao Xiang's painting poem who is one of the "eight talented painters of Yangzhou" in the Qing Dynasty. This poem interprets the spiritual world of Chinese literati and officials and helps to understand landscape painting. As the saying goes, "if the nation has an open-minded emperor and well governed, then people would go and help a little as official. Otherwise, people would go to live as he hermit.

There is a work regarded as the pinnacle of traditional Chinese landscape painting to win the praises and admiration of later generations. Now let me introduce an admirer of later generations: In 1965, a Taiwanese painter saw this work for the first time at the National Palace Museum in Taipei with overwhelming excitement. Subsequently, he came to appreciate the work for three days with lingering pleasures and was moved into tears, which interpreted the beauty of art. This landscape painting directly changed the way the artist defined his career, disrupting his westernized concept and turning his thoughts to the importance and necessity of national identity. The painter is Liu Guosong, the globally influential artist.

The silk scroll ink painting is the treasure of the Palace Museum in Taipei, namely, Fan Kuan's *Traveling amid Mountains and Streams* (Fig. 12-3). The work is dotted with crisscross ink marks and jagged rock texture to create a sense of magnificence, with the colossal peak almost occupying two-thirds of the space. The waterfall as thin as instrument string is extending into the infinite, with the reverberation of streams in the valley, to create a sense of majesty. Guo Xi remarked: "Mountains take the water as blood, vegetation as hair, and clouds as divine colours to grow, thrive and be sublime." The mountains and streams depicted by Fan Kuan are magnificent and secluded to showcase the traditional Chinese view of the universe. Nature is of infinite possibilities while humankind is a tiny traveller in the mountains. At the same time, we can comprehend the sublime sentiment brought by the mountains and rivers: On the journey of life, people can feel that the world is so great, and life is so tiny and short, so as to be impersonal and enjoy the natural interest.

Traveling amid Mountains and Streams enjoys an unparalleled position in the Chinese painting history in terms of its magnificence.

The utilization of water is very important for a landscape painting regarding the skilled proportion of paper water, pen water and ink water. The water colour deployment gives the artistic verve, demanding a detailed study. Ink painting is an important part of Chinese landscape painting, which conveys the "psychological harmony" of the Orient and the "external image" of introversion. The random infiltration of water and ink makes it easier for us to be introspective. The purpose of modern ink painting is the same as that of traditional ink painting, which lies at the experience and taste of our life.

Figure 12-3 *Traveling amid Mountains and Streams*

Su Shi once remarked: "Simplification is the pinnacle of splendor". As *The Analects* advocates: The artistic opinion of "Painting after Simplicity" Chinese traditional landscape painting theory also dictates: "Ink painting is best in the perfect combination of mountains and rivers". Efficient strokes combined with clean ink can render the awesome natural interest to turn the hectic mind off. Conversely, a paper predominated by disgusting black colouring is at worst.

As *Guide to Landscape Painting* by Jing Hao during the Liang Dynasty advocates:

The painting of landscape shall be in line with seasonal changes: Spring scenery features mist and fog, the half-hidden woods, azure water, and dense foliage. Summer scenery features a vast expanse of forests, tangled weeds, gushing waterfalls, travelers with a fan and secluded pavilions. Autumn scenery features the water and the sky in one colour, soughing wind in the forest, wild geese, autumnal water, dainty islands, and muddy flats. Winter scenery features a vast expanse of snow, muddy beach, frozen clouds, secluded villages, inn flags, shoreside fishing boats and a woodcutter carrying firewood.

Gazing into autumnal clouds, you are in high spirits, while enjoying the vernal breeze, you are in flights of fancy. Every stroke is the manifestation of the painter's temperament, and each ink is the portrayal of the painter's life. The painter is seemingly merging with his fantastic work.

Section II   Water and Music

Water is closely related to Chinese music. From The Book of Songs of the pre-Qin Dynasty and *Chu Ci* to *Yue Fu* of the Han Dynasty in the Wei and Jin Dynasties, then to the poems of the Tang and the Song Dynasties, operas of the Ming and Qing Dynasties, they are both classical literary works and music. They are rich movements of water in Chinese music, and modern and contemporary music also contain rich and colourful contents of water culture. In this section, we choose classical music works of different periods to analyse their water cultural implications.

1. Water and Music of Love and Friendship

Love and friendship are the themes of life and the themes are often expressed in music works. Since ancient times, water has formed an indissoluble bond with love, such as tender feelings like water, dry seas and rotten rocks, etc. . Music often uses water to express love such as passion of love, lovesickness, deception, faithfulness, and betrayal. Seeking a bosom friend in the music. The music makes friendship lasting.

From *The Book of Songs* in ancient China to modern and contemporary music, the lasting love and friendship are included. In ancient times, people lived by water, composing many poems and music about love. In ancient music of over 3000 years from ancient times to the Northern Song Dynasty, poetry and music blended perfectly, and formed a unique art form in ancient China-poetry and music. It is both "literature" and "music". The duality of literature and music is an important feature of ancient Chinese art of poetry and music.

For example, in *The Book of Songs*, the places where men and women meet are often rivers of Qinshui, Weishui, Qishui, Fenshui, Rushui, Hanshui, Sishui, Jishui, Jingshui, Weishui, Quanshui, the Yellow River, the Yangtze River and other waterfront riversides, as well as the water-related ones such as dew, current, stream, river, rain, pool and pond, and so on. According to statistics, there are about 29 water-related love chapters in *The Book of Songs*, such as *Cooing and Wooing* (Fig. 12-4), which starts with "By riverside are cooing, a pair of turtledoves" to express man's yearning for his beloved. *Notes of the Book of Songs* by Wen Yiduo said that *Cooing and Wooing*, a maiden picks nymphoides peltatum on the riverside, a gentleman is delighted to see her. "Chu Ci", which originated in the area of the south of the Yangtze River, is a love song relevant to water. Later, "Yue Fu" folk songs in the Southern Dynasty mostly depicted love songs of the southern area of the Yangtze River, such as *Midnight Song · Summer* "Green lotus covers blue water, with red lotus *flowers on it. Seeing the lotus, the man wanted to pick it when thinking about me, and I missed the cherish lotus and yearn for going back to it." Xizhou Opera*, a famous love story, also expresses the purity of love and the lingering longing of love by "missing plum blossoms of Xizhou and I want to send some to her", "Where is Xizhou, by boot getting to its bridge", "The dream is long like the deep and vast sea, and the lovesickness for both of us, as well". Li Zhiyi's "Head of Yongtze River lives me, End of it lives you. Missing you day and night without a glance, Drinking the same water in Yongtze River."The Yangtze River water is the medium for lovers, and the feeling of love is just like the Yangtze River water flowing day by day.

Figure 12-4 *Cooing and Wooing*

The singing of love in modern and contemporary music works is also inseparable from water. Yunnan folk song *Xiao He Tang Shui*: "The moon comes out, bright. Think of my lover in the deep mountains. He is like the moon in the sky. Oh, my love. The river flowing downhill is clear and endless." With the gurgling flow of water, it expresses the maiden's affection for her lover, just like the continuous flow of the river water, lingering, clear, and pure. Qiong Yao's poem *The Other Side of the River*: "There is a beautiful lady on the other side of the river, which is directly derived from the artistic conception of *The Book of Songs*, expressing the lovable but inaccessible love by"on the other side of the river". *Love of Tides* by singer Li Zongsheng, *Drizzle in March* by Xiaoxuan, and *The Wave Still as Past* by Chen Xiaoqi, and so on, convey their feelings through water.

Zhuangzi said, "A hedge between keeps friendship green. Villains turn sweet as wine". There are many chapters of water music expressing friendship. Li Bai's "Taohua Lake a thousand feet deep is shallower than the love of Wang Lun who sees me off."Wei Yingwu's "Ten years of flowing water after a farewell to floating clouds", Bao Rong's "Mountains and rivers are dwarfed, and it's more important to meet a confidant" and Chen Gangzhong's "If understanding that all the men of the world are brothers, all you meet will be your friends." The best example of expressing friendship with water is the Chinese zither song *Mountain Torrent*. Yu Boya played a piece of expressing the law of flowing water, while Zhong Ziqi said, "Goodness! It's just like a river in front of me." Zhong Ziqi perceived the law of the flowing water in the music and was regarded as a confidant by Boya. It is a really a good example of meet the confidant due to water, and the song of Mountain Torrent is used to mean the friendship through ages afterwards.

2. Water and Music of Patriotism

The theme of patriotism is expressed in water music, which is ubiquitous in music works. Artists sing in front of water mournfully, sadly, or angrily, expressing a strong sense of patriotism.

Qu Yuan lamented "With tears running down my face in front of the river, I think about my Emperor", and "The fragrance of the green weeds and orchids in Yuanshui river, but dare not express my missing, just gazing at the water flowing". Qu Yuan's thoughts of loyalty and patriotism to the monarch was expressed through his hesitation at the waterside. "To feel trepidation beside the Huangkong Beach. To sigh with loneliness by the Lingding Yang Bay" is used to show Wen Tianxiang's unyielding and patriotic spirit even after being defeated many times. Lu You's poem: "I hunted whales in the East China Sea the year before last, and the white waves were magnificent like mountains," "Rivers of 30,000 miles going east into the sea, mountains of 5,000 meters towering up into the sky". By exaggeration, Lu You expressed the magnificent momentum of the Yellow River rolling eastward into the sea, praised the magnificent mountains and rivers of the motherland, while lines of "area off 10,000 miles in front of me" (by Xi Qiji) is already a fallen area, expressing the poet's great sympathy for the people in the occupied areas and his indignation for the rulers of the Southern Song Dynasty not to recover their lost land.

In modern and contemporary water music works, a large number of water-related music works expressing patriotic themes have been composed, especially in the war period, such as Zhang Hanhui's *Songhua River*: "My home is by the Songhua River in the northeast of China, where there are forest mines, as well as the fields of soybean sorghum spread around the mountains." This music chooses the typical image of Songhua River, the hometown river, to sing about its prosperity of hometown in the past. After the "9 · 18 Incident", the Northeast was devastated. By contrasting the past with the present, people's patriotic feelings and being unwilling to be slaves and conquered were deeply expressed. *The Yellow River Chorus* (Fig. 12-5) is a patriotic song. "Not be afraid of the high waves like mountains!" "Come back to re-fight against the invading troops like the Yellow River of raging waves!" "The Yellow River is roaring; the Yellow River is roaring". The whole piece of music takes the Yellow River as the background, enthusiastically eulogizing the glorious history of the Chinese nation with a long history and the indomitable fighting spirit of the Chinese people, bitterly accusing the aggressors of their cruelty and narrating the profound disasters suffered by the people, and all of which widely displays the magnificent prospect of the War of Resistance Against Japanese Aggression, and presents the battle alarm of National Liberation to the whole world, shaping the heroic image of the Chinese nation. In Su Shuyang's *A Good River Flows Forever*: "The endless years, like the flowing torrential Yangtze River and the Yellow River, witnesses the rise and fall of the world and the sufferings of my motherland. Love is long, thought is long, the ambition of Chinese people is unpaid, the Chinese people always have their own soul, like the river flowing on". The song gives endless praise for the Yangtze River and the Yellow River, through which the long-lasting soul of Chinese nation's blood and national spirit are well expressed.

Figure 12-5　The Performance of *the Yellow River Chorus*

The water music works of the motherland hymn express deep patriotism. *Motherland Chorus* of Ma Sicong and Jinfan: "Crossing the impetuous Yellow River and the Yangtze River, heading for prosperity from now on, heading for prosperity from now on … Singing in praise of our beloved motherland", This song sings the mother rivers of the Yellow River and the Yangtze River, praising the growing strength and prosperity of the motherland. Another song of *My Motherland and I*: "My motherland and I are like the sea and the waves. Waves are the loyal son of the sea, and the sea is the support of the waves."By analogy, the song compares"individual"to"waves", "motherland" to"the sea". "Individual" is the composition of "motherland"—like infants' attachment to their mothers, and "the sea" is the dependence of "individual", like the sea supporting the waves, singing out the inseparable relationship between the two, the fate of which are blended.

Other songs like *I Love Wuzhi Mountain I Love Wanquan River*, *Frontier Springs Clear and Sweet*, *Liuyang River*, *Waters and Mountains*, *Honghu Lake*, *Overcome the Dadu River*, *Rowing on a River*, *I Love the Blue Ocean*, *Night of the Military Port*, *The Sea of My Hometown*, *Song of the Yangtze River*, *Love of Rivers and Mountains* and so on, through various forms of waters above, express people's yearning for the motherland's water and affection of motherland.

3. Water and Music of Homesickness

Water is the easiest source of worry. Facing the vast and flowing water of nature, artists express the sorrow of wandering, the suffering of serving and the pain of homesickness.

The lines of "Withered vines, old trees, and crows, small bridges, flowing water, and family house" depicts a typical image of water in the south of the Yangtze River, which is about the parting son coming back on an autumn afternoon, while the sun is heading to the west. Lines of Wang Anshi: "There is only one river in Jingkou and Guazhou, and Zhongshan Mountain is only a few mountains away. The gentle spring wind blows green the trees on the bank of the Yangtze River, but when will the bright moon in the sky shine on my way home?"; By Bai Juyi, "looking to the capital of my homeland, but the clouds cover my eyes, thinking of my hometown, eaves of rain drop into my heart,"; By Li Zhong, "spend the Cold Food Festival in a different place, feeling homesick"; By Cui Hao: "Looking at the misty river, I wonder that the sun is heading for the west but where my hometown is? The misty river even makes me sad". All the above are famous poems to express homesickness by using water.

Modern and contemporary music works, such as *The Four Stanzas of Nostalgia* by Yu Guangzhong (Fig. 12-6), known as the "nostalgic poet", "Give me a ladle of Yangtze River water, that wine-like Yangtze River water." The author associated the Yangtze River water with wine, the wine with drunkenness, and the drunkenness with homesickness, again the Yangtze River water with blood-like crabapple, resulting in the description of family affection thicker than water presented, with the image of "Yangtze River Water", parting son's heart and longing for the water of hometown were nourished. Xiao Guang's song of *That's Me* says: "I miss the rivers of my hometown and the mill singing by the riverside", slowly narrating the deep nostalgia. In the line of "Mom, if there is a spray smiling at you, that's me, that's me", the author fantasized him to be a smiling spray, throwing himself into mother's embrace. In the repeated chants, the works repose the deep feelings that the travellers cannot express literally. In the song of Lu Huabai and Zhang Fan *Hometown*, the words of "There are clear rivers there", Luobing's *Dream of Hometown by the Water*, "At dusk of spring, please accompany me to get back to my dream of hometown by the water, Looking at the water tapping the green hills", Zhang Minghe's *Two Springs Chant*, "The water of Taihu Lake is like a glass of strong wine in your life to give you courage, silent tears seeking the light", Yang Haichao's *Yueya Spring*, "Look at that Yueya Spring and miss my hometown so much, and Ye Jiaxiu's *Grandma's Penghu Bay*, "The evening breeze gently brushes the waves of Penghu Bay and the waves tapping the beach. With no slanting shadows of coconut woods and in the sunshine, only the blue of sea can be seen". By using the different forms of water above, the familiar and beautiful water in memory is presented, and so is the people's yearning, love, and praise for the homeland.

Figure 12-6　Yu Guangzhong

4. Water and Music of Philosophy

"Supreme kindness is like water", "benevolent people like mountains, wise people like water". These sentences mean that the characteristics of water contain philosophy of life. Water music also expresses the Chinese philosophy of "following nature" and "harmonious unity between man and nature".

In the poem *A Moonlit Night on The Spring River* of the Tang Dynasty, "Who first saw the moon on the riverside, and when did the moon shine on me? Life is endless from generation to generation, while the moon and the river are similar year after year. Without knowing who the moon is waiting for, but I see the water of the Yangtze River flow away." When seeing the river and the moon in front of him, the author produced a philosophy on infinite time and space and infinite life. Wang Wei, known as "Poem Buddha" in the Tang Dynasty, believed in Buddhism and was good at rhythm. Therefore, his chanting of water was often philosophical or, more precisely, Zen. The Zen Buddhism Ceremony of Shaolin adopted Wang Wei's *An Autumn Night in the Mountain* to express this kind of Zen doctrine. In his poem of *Qingxi Creek*, "Every time wandering into Huanghua River, I walk along the Qingxi Creek. With the mountain situation, rivers turn around a thousand times, but the way they pass is short. The sound of the water is noisy among the rocks in the mountains; the colour of the water is quiet and deep in the thick pine forest. The grass sway gently in the stream; the reed is clearly reflected in the clear water. My heart has always been leisurely, like the clear stream, indifferent and tranquil. I wish I could stay on the rocks by the stream and spend my life fishing." By the description of the creek, the author expressed his simple pursuit of life. The natural characteristics of the Qingxi Creek are highly consistent with Wang Wei's tranquil mind. Other poems like "eating by Panshi rock, resting by waterfalls and springs", "prefer living in the wild woods and drinking stream water", "drinking in springs, playing Chinese Zither by the pine tree", and "resting by the wood of no evils, drinking water with clear source" all express their aspirations and pure hearts of being alone and detached from the world.

Liu Xiaoxian's *Searching for the Unknown Master in Caotang Temple* says: "The moon hangs high in the sky and shines across the front of the building. It's cold at night in the deep forest, with smoke in the compound cabinet. Leaves move and the dew of flowers flow, dim springs whispering. Bamboos sway in the wind, like sounds of raining, and mountain insects sound like cicadas. Picking fruits and putting them in lotus leaves, drinking water with lotus flowers. Everything goes smoothly when you talk and drink. The image of water is composed of dew, spring, rain, and water, which expresses the Zen philosophy of being indifferent to the worldly affairs. In Han Shan's *Distant Cold Mountain Road*: "The cold mountain road is quiet, dark, and remote, with cold water around. There are often birds chirping here, but with no people around. The wind is beating against my face, and the snow keeps falling on me. I'm in the woods and don't see sunshine every day or don't know what season it is either." This poem shows the poet being aloof and detached by using "cold water" and "snow". People think that the whole poem's full of "chillness", which is all related to the coldness of water, showing the poet its indifference, calmness, and freedom of Taoism.

Tan Dun, the famous contemporary composer (Fig. 12-7), applies the element of water to modern music. He went to Sandu, Guizhou Province, the only Autonomous County of the Shui people (a nationality) of China. The Duan Festival, Shuishu (the Charao-ter and book of the Shui people) and horse tail hair embroidery were approved of the national intangible cultural heritage. He was shocked by the original music there and found many creation elements such as water, the Shui people, Shuiqiang, Shuishu, Shuiyue and so on. His water music employed "water" as an instrument. He also built the "Water Heaven" (Fig. 12-8) in Zhujiajiao, Shanghai. The saying of "architecture is mobile music, and music is mobile architecture" is well reflected here. From the perspective of architecture, the sound of water drops can be magnified by 1,000 times, which can be truly displayed, listening to the music on the water surface connecting the outdoor and indoor. The first movement is "The Sound Zen and Bach", which combines water with rock and roll to play the Compassion Mantra of Buddhism. The last movement quotes a Zen poem of Zen Master, Wumen Huikai in the Song Dynasty: "there are flowers in spring, moonlight in autumn, cool wind in summer and snow in winter. If you have nothing to worry about, it's a good time in the world." Water music shows the ancient philosophy of "harmonious

Figure 12-7　Tan Dun

unity between man and nature" and "Taoism of following nature".

Figure 12-8 The "Water Heaven"

Section III Water and Dance

Water and dance get along swimmingly with each other, they are in perfect harmony and keep growing and multiplying. Since ancient times, a lot of immortal poems concerning water and dance have been created. Next, the relationship between water and dance is analysed from two aspects of water dance tradition and water dance ethnic style.

1. Water Dance Tradition

Water dance tradition refers to the traditional culture, national symbol and spirit of water dance. Let's take a look at an ancient water dance.

Grand Xia is a very famous large-scale dance of the Han people before the Xia Dynasty. It is recorded in *Master Lv's Spring and Autumn Annals*, that "Yu the Great claimed to be the emperor and he worked indefatigably for the people and exerted himself day and night…hence, Gao Tao was ordered to create *The Panpipe of Grand Xia* to honour Yu's contribution."

The legend says that *Grand Xia* is a famous dance during the transition period from primitive society to slave society of China.

About four thousand years ago, heavy flooding attacked the Yellow River Basin. The farmland could not support farming, and people drifted from place to place. The legend went that Shun, the leader of the tribal alliance, appointed Gun to tame the flood. Gun constructed a dam to block the water, but he failed to bring the flood under control. Later, Shun assigned Yu, the son of Gun, to control the flood. Yu worked indefatigably day and night for ten years, not daring to have even a momentary lapse. During this period, he passed by his house three times without entering. Finally, he dredged the rivers and lakes, and broke Longmen (now in Luoyang city, Henan Province), resulting in the flood flowing smoothly eastward into the sea. After that, Yu personally ploughed wasteland to develop agricultural production. To celebrate the success of water control and eulogize Yu's feats, people held a grand ritual activity of singing and dancing, and the dance performed was later called *Grand Xia*.

It is said that *Grand Xia* was performed with every eight dancers standing in a line, which is called "Yi"("佾"). The dancers wore a fur hat and a white skirt, with the upper body exposed. With feathers in the right hand and the instrument of panpipe("篇") in the left, they sang and danced, appearing to be plain and straightforward. After watching the dance, Ji Zha was deeply moved by its content and performance. He said, "How beautiful it is! Who else but Yu would be so industrious and virtuous?" Overpraised as it was, it really indicated that the dance accompanied by music of *Grand Xia* did show the merits and virtues of Yu taming the flood. The ancients listed this dance as one of the "Six Dances" to worship mountains and rivers.

It is recorded in *Master Lv's Spring and Autumn Annals* that, after claiming to be the king, Yu commanded the people to tame the flood. He dredged hills and fortresses, broke Longmen, and guided the flood into the East China Sea, thereby benefiting thousands of people. Gao Tao, an expert dancer, created *Grand Xia* to record Yu's contribution. The dance movements of *Grand Xia* include "Yu Steps". It is said that, to control the flood, Yu had to get his legs soaked in the water, which hurt his legs, and he could only walk with small steps. The wizard imitated his steps to create the dance, called "Yu Steps". Yu successfully controlled the flood and benefited the people. The dance expresses the optimistic spirit of the Chinese nation fighting against the natural disaster, and praises Yu, who conquered the nature by using dance.

There is another dance called *Grand Hu*, which is recorded not only in the pre-Qin Dynasty classics, but also in the oralle bone scipt, and simply called "Hu". Its existence is beyond question, but "Hu" was denoted as "" in Oracle bone script, which means "Water" and written as "蒦" (Huo). The "Water" here is in the shape of the droplets from a cooked bird taken out from a wok. It is known that there is a widespread story in the Shang Dynasty, namely, "praying for rain in the mulberry forest by sacrificing life". According to *Master Lv's Spring and Autumn Annals*, *Shizi* and *Huainanzi*, after defeating Jie, Tang claimed to be the king of the Shang Dynasty. While people suffered a bad drought of five years, resulting in the failure of crops and the desperate situation of all people. To pray for rain, the witches must have danced the "Yu" many times, but in vain. Tang, as the head of the nation, in person went to the mulberry forest to pray for rain. With "his hair cut, his hands rubbed", and asking servants to prepare firewood, Tang would sacrifice himself to pray for rain. He kept praying: "If it is because of my sin, please do not implicate my people; if it is all the people's sin, count it all on me alone."But just as the fire was about to blaze out, a miracle appeared, "the clouds gather together, the rain pour down", Tang got wet all over and the earth was thoroughly watered. The people of the Shang Dynasty had a good harvest that year.

From this we can see that *Grand Hu* is indeed a large-scale dance created by the Shang people to worship Tang, the founder of the country. It praises Tang's magnificent feat of saving the people from the disaster at the expense of his life, and Tang's "praying for rain in the mulberry forest by sacrificing life" is precisely a very typical sorcery activity praying for rain.

In 1994, the Chinese classical dance, *The Yellow River*(Fig. 12-9) won the classic work award of "Chinese Classical Dance of 20th century". It was created according to the piano concerto *Yellow River*. In one section of the dance, with the advent of the theme melody "Dong Fang Hong", all the performers run very quickly, like the Yellow River water running straight down. By standing shoulder to shoulder and back-to-back, people encourage and support one another when rolling their bodies over repeatedly, as if struggling in the water. The primary movement of the dance is so sonorous and powerful. In the coordination of pushing aside with one hand and deep squatting step after step, the indomitable spirit of the Chinese nation in difficulties and hardships is fully manifested, which makes the dance drama reach the climax. The basic movement of the dance manifests different artistic conceptions and emotions in different contexts. It sometimes symbolizes the surging tide, sometimes symbolizes the industrious and brave Yellow River descendants, sometimes show people's roaring to the world, and sometimes presents the fearless spirit of Chinese nation.

Figure 12-9 The Chinese Classical Dance *The Yellow River*

The Chinese National Ballet *The Mermaid* is about a myth. It tells the story of the beautiful and kind mermaid living at the bottom of the sea, who fell in love with an industrious and courageous hunter in the earthly world. But the mountain demon tried hard to prevent them from getting together. With the help of the old ginseng man, the mermaid and the hunter finally broke the witchcraft of the mountain demon and became a happy couple.

In the first act, yearning for the world outside of the sea, the mermaid left the sea and came to the world. The hunter and his companions were hunting. The mermaid secretly imitated the actions of the hunters, but unexpectedly, she was dragged away by the mountain demon. Seeing a flying thing in the sky, the hunter shot it down and saved the mermaid by accident. The mermaid was grateful to him.

In the second act, the mermaid took the hunter to the mysterious underwater world, a magical world with swaying green grasses. The hunter and the mermaid were deeply attracted to each other. They got married in the earthly world, and people around came to cheer and congratulate them. The mountain demon dressed up and came too, by employing witchcraft, she made the jar broken and turned flowers black. People thought it was the mermaid's witchcraft. People then all ran away while the hunter was frightened and fainted. By taking advantage of the chaos, the mountain demon carried away the mermaid again.

"Grass Dance" is like a lyrical and beautiful woman rippling along with the waves. The arm movements and dance rhythm of the dance seem to float freely in the water, providing people with a slim and graceful image and the scene of the story shifting from the fantastic "bottom of the sea" to the "earth world" wedding with folk characteristics with the development of the story. All these show people's pursuit and yearning for beautiful things, and the struggle between justice and evil as well. They are classical works of depicting Chinese national spirit and culture by means of western dance styles.

2. Ethnic Style of Water Dance

All nationalities have their own water dance. These dances show their culture and spirit and are their treasure house as well.

In *Peacock Dance* of the Dai people (Fig. 12 - 10), with the curtain opening, a group of peacocks with turquoise blue feathers shining like gems come down, approaching. Coming to the spring and seeing their gorgeous feathers from their inflection, peacocks couldn't help dancing. When pleased, they would flutter their wings and jump into the spring one after another to wash themselves with cool and glossy spring water, after which made them more elegant and beautiful. They shake up their long tail feathers. Under the sunlight, water drops form crystal pearls on their feathers. From the early morning to the evening peacocks danced, giving the dusk in the drizzle a mythical and dreamy color. They climb up the high branches and fly high in the fresh night.

The Dai people take the peacock as the symbol of their spirit, and the peacock dance is the representative dance of the Dai people. The content of peacock dance mainly shows peacock flying down the mountain, strolling in the forest, drinking from the spring, playing in the water, chasing, and playing, dragging its wings, drying its wings, unfolding its wings, shaking its wings, showing its wings, dapping on the water, pedalling the branches, resting on the branches, spreading its tail, and flying and so on. It is a symbol of beauty, majesty, peace, and auspiciousness.

Another solo dance of the Dai people, named *Water*, manifests the beauty of Dai girls and their glorification and yearning for beautiful life. With the sun setting down, a maid comes to the riverside carrying a water pot. She puts down the pot and sees her beautiful face and graceful

Figure 12-10　*Peacock Dance*

posture from the glassy water. With a sudden joy, she unties her pitch-black and shiny hair and washes in the water. Afterwards she sits on the rock by the river and patting the water with her feet, unrestrainedly and leisurely, without sorrow or worry. Attached to the clear water, she even jumps into the water and indulges in the nature, which completely washes away her fatigue. After going ashore, she tosses her hair quickly and dries it in the afterglow of the setting sun. With the night breeze blowing, she shakes her hair, teases it skilfully, and then swiftly wears it into a bun. When the sun is setting to the other side of the mountain, the maid picks up the pot again filled with water and returns to her village leisurely in the flame of sunset.

　　The Miao dance *The Girl of Water*(Fig. 12-11) has a beauty of purity. The image of water has always been clear, transparent, soft, and continuous. The works skilfully connects water with the purity of the girl, which is in line with the Chinese tradition and culture, with high aesthetic value. By imitating the "shape" and "sound" of water and the "spirit" and "soul" of it, the dance implies the theme that water is the girl, the girl is like water, which is the perfect combination of man and nature and the praise of water and life as well.

　　The combination of the music and the dance movements of the dance is ingenious, along with "tick, tick…" the sound of water drops knocking on the ground, the group of water-like girls are dancing on the stage, like unperturbed water waves, while flowing like blue and beautiful waves from time to time.

Figure 12-11　*The Girl of Water*

　　By the riverside, girls gently lifting her long hair in the water, stirring up small sprays, with the sound of flute and drums, the girls start to dance like a group of spirits in the water. The rhythmic movements of shoulders and waist, together with the sound of the spring; the movements of arms are like flowing water; the S-shaped formation is just like the meandering flow of the spring water; girls' hands holding together and moving up and down, like rippling water…The combination of rolling movements with the girls' blue skirts is like the clear spring water on the stage, leading the audience to the spring where the "water girls" live. The sound of "Ding Dong" makes people indulge in all this intoxication. Dance depicts a beautiful and complete scenery of Huaxi Mountain, Guizhou Province and girls of Miao presents the pure and innocent love like the clear and tranquil water.

　　Water is pure and transparent, and spotless and flawless. It can purify everything. The choreographer's creative inspiration of the dance derives from the plain and simple life of the Miao people: the beautiful Huaxi River (Fig. 12-12) flows continuously, and it breeds the valiant and industrious Miao people; the trickling river bears their infinite longings for life; the beautiful girls are just like clear, pure, and cheerful water. When quiet, they seem to listen to the stories of their ancestors during the time passing by, being so pure like water flowing; when passionate, they are like flying notes and never stop their enthusiastic dancing steps, being ever so vibrant. The lyrics of *The Girl of Water* sincerely express their pursuit of the soul as clear as water.

　　You see the water, by the river.

　　You gently lift your long hair, stir up a little spoondrift.

　　Board the wooden boat, come to you silently.

　　Your sincere and lovely face, so sweet while smiling.

Chapter Twelve　Water and Art

The moon in the sky, reflected in the water.
The moon is like your face, watch and miss it, hard to sleep.
Flowers bloom on the riverside, it's spring again.
Your innocent face of that year never changed in my heart.
Water girl, I come back to you.
Now, I am more handsome than before.
You've been waiting for me, year in and year out,
From spring to winter, you are waiting by the river, by the river.
Life is like dance, and years like water.

Figure 12-12　Huaxi River, Guizhou Province

Chapter Thirteen   Water and Folkways

Section I   Water, Birth and Wedding Customs

Water is closely related to our social life since ancient time. There are water-related rituals and water-related festivals, thus creating a rich and colourful folk culture due to the worship and awe of water.

Man's life is inseparable from water. Many water-related customs have been formed at some important stages of life, such as birth, marriage, death and so on. Next let us observe the manifestation of water worship from the customs of childbirth and marriage.

1. Baby Shower

In Chinese folk culture, after the birth of the baby, midwives and family members will quickly wash the baby with warm water. On one hand, they want to clean the baby, on the other hand, they are praying to all gods to bless the baby's safety, which is called "baby shower". This custom is popular throughout the country. In the past, water used in baby shower was not just water. According to the book *Thousand Golden Prescriptions* (Qian Jin Fang) written by Sun Simiao, "It is advisable to bathe a baby with water of peach root three days of birth", because it can "eliminate the evil and make the baby free from sores all his life". In some regions, the plants including mugwort, and locust branches are also put in boiled water for a later shower. That is not only for health, but also an expression of the people's worship of water. This is a wish praying to the Gods to bless the children being healthy and safe by washing away dirt and evils.

In some regions, a bath ceremony is held on the third day after baby's birth, inviting relatives and friends to bless the baby, which is called "Xisan (it means giving the baby a shower on the third day of the birth.)". It is generally believed that this custom originated in the Tang Dynasty. At that time, absurdly, Yang Guifei treated An Lushan, who was over 40 years old, as her "son". The 22nd day of the first month in the year of 751 (lunar calender) was the exact birthday of An Lushan. Three days later, Yang Guifei regarded An Lushan as a "baby" and made a farce of

"Xisan". It was recorded that "Emperor Xuanzong (emperor of the Tang Dynasty) An summoned Lushan into the Palace. Yang Guifei used the brocade to wrap him, commanding the retinues to carry him with a colourful sedan chair", and "Emperor went there for a look and offered a big reward for them two, so as to enjoy themselves to the fullest". Liu Yuxi, a famous poet in the Tang Dynasty, said in his poem, "The family who had just given birth to a boy held a banquet and ate noodles with chopsticks to celebrate." This showed that for "Xisan", apart from a baby shower, people also had the custom of eating soup cakes or noodles. Even today, in the Central China, there is still a custom of "eating noodles" when babies are born.

When it comes to the Song Dynasty, in some places, such as Fujian Province, the family not only gave the baby the "Xi San" ceremony, but also invited guests together wearing scallions and coins. Su Shi, a great writer in the Northern Song Dynasty, said: "When the children of people in Min (short for Fujian province) were at a baby shower, their families and guests were all wearing scallions and coins. Scallions make the children wise, and coins make them rich." That is to wish their children a bright and rich future. Su Shi's fourth child was born around the same time as his friend's grandson (He Zi You Sheng Sun), both of whom experienced "Xisan". For congratulations, Su Shi wrote a poem entitled *Congratulations to the Birth of Ziyou's Grandson*. It was said in the poem "Yesterday I heard your grandson had been given a baby shower." The custom of a baby shower in the Song Dynasty was reflected in the notes of contemporary people. It was said in the fifth volume "Nurturing" of *Record on Dreams in the Capital* (Dong Jing Men Hua Lu): "Upon the delivery of a child, people around actively send corns, charcoal, vinegar and so on to the child. On the third day after birth, the child is given moxibustion. Seven days after, it is called a "la" (referring time of seven days). After the child is a month-old, a baby shower ceremony will be held, decorated with coins, jewellery, and fruits. Relatives and friends gather to make soup in a bowl, where they put fruits, coins, scallions, and garlic. And the bowl is wrapped by long coloured ribbons, which is called the Wrapping Bowl (Wei Pen); water is stirred by a hairpin, this being called the Stirring Bowl (Lang Pen); people scatter coins into the bowl, called the Adding Bowl (Tian Pen). Women compete to get and eat those dates upright in the bowl, which is regarded as a symbol of giving birth to a boy. After the shower and a haircut, the baby is brought to thank the guests and go back to the room, which is called Moving Nest Yi Chao. At that time, the etiquette of "baby shower" was very complicated and extravagant.

During the ceremony, it is indispensable to say something for best wishes. In *Xisan*, Lao She describes his own baby shower: "while showering, Grandma Bai said the auspicious message without any omission that had been said for countless times: washing head to be a prince; washing waist to excel the predecessors; washing hip (dan dan) to serve as the official; washing joints (gou gou) to serve as the magistrate."

Nowadays, with the progress of society, "baby shower" is usually carried out in hospitals, and the people who give the "shower" are mostly nurses. In the past, the ceremony was often held at homes, while today it is mainly held in the restaurant and what people usually do is also different.

2. Water Used in the Wedding Custom

"Timely raining after ages' drought, reunion with an old friend in a foreign land, enjoying the wedding night in bridal chamber, and being the very best in a national examination." These are the four great things in life mentioned by Hong Mai(Fig. 13-1), the famous writer of the Southern Song Dynasty and the author of *The Essays in Rongzhai (Rong Zhai Sui Bi)* (Fig. 13-2). Marriage is one of the most important events in one's life. Water, worshiped by people, is often used in weddings. The water-related marriage customs are manifested in various forms in different regions and nations.

Figure 13-1 Hong Mai

Figure 13-2 The Essays in Rongzhai

(1) Wedding Custom of the Han People

Record on Dreams in the Capital is an important document recording the urban life and culture of the capital Kaifeng in the Northern Song Dynasty. According to the book, at the phase of engagement, after the female received a gift from the male, "two bottles of water, three or five live fish and one pair of chopsticks" were given as gifts in return, which were called "chopsticks of returning fish (Hui Yu Zhu)". Among the gifts in return, there is water and fish. Using water is to wish early birth of a baby and a happy marriage; And fish is a symbol of fertility. Adding a pair of chopsticks is a symbol of having new family members. Chopsticks have also been given the meaning of "quick birth". Then all the meaning is to pray for more children and more blessings. Therefore, this kind of gifts in return also contains the auspicious meaning of praying for children and marriage. When Liquor came into Beijing, people took Liquor as a gift, instead of water. But the custom of giving Liquor as gifts was evolved from that of sending water.

In some places, water is splashed on the new couple. When the bride leaves her home, her father will take a bowl of clean water and sprinkle to the back of the sedan chair. This means that the married daughter is like the spilled water, never coming back (meaning having a happy life with her husband).

Those are significant rituals in weddings of the Han people to wash hands and drink Liquor wine together, from which we could see water worship. In *Origin of the Chinese Characters* by Xu Shen, it says: "盥, is for washing hands. The character 盥 is made of the characters including 臼 (mortar), 水 (water) and 皿 (vessel)." Washing hands refers to the couple washing together with clean water, which means all the filth and bad luck are washed away and predicts everything in the future is a new beginning. According to the annotation note of Duan Yucai, Yi (匜) is the instrument used in ancient times for watering. That is similar with one way of washing today, that is, people using ladle to pour out water on hands with a washbowl down there for gathering water. At that time, the usage way of washbowl is different. They do not wash hands directly in the washbowl. Instead, they wash hands with flowing water poured down. Afterwards, water used is left in the washbowl. The wedding custom in the Zhou Dynasty included the etiquette of washing, which should be carried out in the wedding. It was recorded in *Yili* that, "Servants should carry out the etiquette of washing for the new couple." That means the servants coming together with the bride should carry out the wedding duties for the couple when they get married and enter the bridal chamber.

The ancient people attached great importance to the courtesy of washing. Unexpected consequences might be caused once the rituals were not followed. In Zuo Zhuan, it is recorded that Duke Mu of the State of Qin sent five women to Chong Er, who was in exile, as concubines, including his daughter Huai Ying. Huai Ying, who had been married to Duke Huai of the State of Jin (Chong Er's nephew), remarried Chong Er. One day, Huai Ying held a washbowl and asked Chong Er to wash his hands. After washing, Chong Er waved her with wet hands. Huai Ying thought this behaviour a kind of contempt, thus blamed him angrily. At that time, Chong Er asked the State of Qin to help him seize back the power of Jin. How dare he annoy Huai Ying? So, he had to take off his clothes and lock himself up to express his apology. When it comes to the Song Dynasty and the Ming Dynasty, it evolved that men and women just washed the face.

Hejin refers to male and female sharing a bottle of drinks. In ancient times, a plant named Hu was cut into two, each of which was respectively held by husband and wife to drink wine together. That was why the etiquette was called Hejin. In the *Book of Rites*, it was recorded that Hejin has the meaning of combination. The ancient people chose the gourd cut in two to serve as drinking vessel of Hejin. First, it was because the Hu was commonly called bitter gourd that is too bitter to eat. So, the wine in the Hu was also bitter. Drinking the bitter wine warned the married couple to share weal and woe. The other reason was that in ancient times, the materials used to make musical instruments were divided into eight kinds, namely, the eight musical sounds (Bayin), including gourd, earth, leather, wood, stone, gold, silk, and bamboo. The gourd was one of the eight musical instruments, which contains the sense of harmony of a marriage life. Therefore, Heji also symbolizes the harmony between the couple after marriage. Later, it is evolved into "cross-cupped wine" (Fig. 13-3). This custom gradually evolved into drinking cross-cupped wine at the wedding, indicating that the husband and wife united after marriage, sharing weal and woe. The etiquette of Heji showed people's attention to marriage and reflected the ancestors' strong awareness of procreation worship.

Figure 13-3 Cross-Cupped Wine

(2) Wedding Customs for Minorities

Splashing water in the process of engagement and marriage is a wedding custom in the Yi people. As soon as family members of the husband enters wife's house, the wife's family would pour them with water, until they are soaked through, no matter how cold it is. The splashing of water makes people happy. Cold water is splashed over the body, but the hearts of both sides are filled with joy that could not be concealed. Because, in their opinion, water can drive away evil spirits and bring happiness. After splashing water, the girl will enjoy a happy life after marrying her husband.

The Tu people has the custom of splashing water to tease the wedding guests. On the eve of the wedding, two eloquent young men good at singing and dancing are invited to serve as distinguished wedding guests, receiving special welcome rituals. After the two guests arrive at the bride's home, they will first sing songs with friends of the bride outside the door. Then, after they enter, girls pour cool water to them, but they cannot be angry because the Tu people believe that splashing the guests is to wash away the dust and express blessings.

The She people mainly live in Fujian Province. They have a ritual of splashing the bed at the wedding. On the evening of the wedding, an elderly person holds a bowl of clear water, spraying the bed, quilt, wardrobe, and others while simultaneously singing songs. The songs are like "Spraying the bed, spraying the bedroom, men and women all celebrate in the chamber." The purpose is to hope that the couple are full of vitality like water, so that they will have more children.

It is the custom of the Miao people to ask for water which is used for washing feet during the bridal chamber pranks. On the wedding night, people involved in the pranks have a verbal battle with the bride to ask the bride to hold a bowl of water for washing their feet. If they lose the argument, they should leave the chamber and others will continue the pranks. If the bride loses, she should go to the kitchen to boil water for the winner to wash his feet. After that, the bride should also pour out the wastewater. Some brides play tricks. For example, the water the bride holds is deliberately too hot.

The wedding custom related to water, on one hand, shows the ancestors' worship of water and reproduction consciousness and people's devotion to water. On the other hand, it shows people's desire and blessing for a better life.

Section II Water and Funeral Customs

We often hear such a saying: some places have good Feng shui, while some do not have. What does Feng shui mean? In China, it mainly refers to the natural situation such as the residential base and the cemetery, such as the direction of the landscape and so on. Water and funeral customs are inextricably linked.

1. The Funeral Feng Shui

Since ancient times, people have attached great importance to the site selection of tombs. It is believed that the location of the tombs is related to the prosperity of the family, and good Feng shui can bless future generations with prosperity.

"Into the mountain to find a water source, into the cave to see the condition of water in front". In Feng shui, a Feng shui master looks for a cemetery by first looking at where the water comes from and where it goes. At the same time, more attention is paid to the water in front of the tomb. "Mountains relate to the family member and water relates to the fortune." That means the condition of water around the cemetery determines fortune of the later generations. And the condition of soil around the cemetery determines the population growth of the later generations. Therefore, the choice of cemetery, first, is the choice of water and soil. Some people think this is superstition, but in a sense, geomancy is a science, whose obvious feature is that it emphasizes harmony between human beings and the natural environment. The ancient tomb of our country is a kind of complex cultural phenomenon. So, what kind of cemetery is regarded as a good choice? It is reflected in the following four respects. Firstly, it may be near the Capital as Feng shui of the place where the emperors live is inevitably excellent. Secondly, it can be the hometown, conforming to the traditional concept of fallen leaves returning to the root like old people would also like to go back to their hometown. Thirdly, it can be the places where they ever worked during their lifetime, it can be other desirable places.

However, no matter what place is chosen, there should be "water in front and mountains behind". To make it simple, the cemetery should lean on the mountains with water flowing in front of it.

Specifically speaking, there are five principles to follow: The first is the principle of nestling under a mountain and near by a river, which is the most basic principle for a good cemetery; The second is to have things to lean on four sides. That is exactly the direction of the folk saying "it depend on that, there is a green dragon on the left, white tiger on the right, red finch in front and basalt behind", which means the cemetery should be surrounded by mountains. The third is being broad in front of the cemetery, which is beneficial to cultivate talents and develop career of the posterity. The fourth is returning to the nature, which means nature first and the unity of man and nature. The fifth is the principle of being winding, to block the head-on evil spirit. Only the mountains surrounding the land can keep out the wind, and only the slow running water and peaceful lakes can gather vitality. Originating in the Eastern Jin Dynasty (317–420 A. D.) by Guo Pu, the theory of "taking advantage of vitality" is a central theme of Feng Shui, which refers to a form of energy that flows under the earth and can bring prosperity. Thus, auspicious land is usually surrounded by mountains, rivers, and plants.

2. Corpse Bath

Cleaning the corpse is to use clear water or warm water to clean the body of the dead, which is an essential part of the funeral. This ritual has remained both in the Han and other ethnic groups. It is believed that after washing with water, the head and feet of the dead should be clean, facilitating their behaviours in the underworld.

For some ethnic groups, special water needs to be prepared for cleaning the corpse. People symbolically throw coins into a river or well and burn incense in prayer, which is regarded as the action of buying water from the God of Water. The custom of buying water for bathing corpses is more popular in regions where minorities such as Miao, Zhuang and Yao live in compact communities. Before the "corpse bath", the filial juniors take umbrellas and buckets wearing mourning clothes to the river and burn sacrificial money or throw coins into the water. Then they take water home to wash the body of the dead. In their mind, only in this way can the dead reach their ancestors, or they will not be taken in. It can be seen that "corpse bath" becomes a qualification to decide whether the soul of the dead can successfully arrive and live in the underworld. In accordance with this, these ethnic groups also have special requirements and restrictions on the water used for corpse bath, such as spring water and rainwater rather than drinking water. For example, the Yi people wash the bodies of the dead with spring water, and it is best to get water from the source of the spring, while the Miao people think it is appropriate to use "Tianshui" (rainwater). In the eyes of the people of these ethnic groups, the water bought from the god is qualitatively different from ordinary water. Such water is sacred, which can ward off evil spirits and get peace and safety.

Superficially, corpse bath is out of the need to clean the body, but in fact there is much significance neglected. Through giving a bath to the dead, the body of the dead will touch the water of life, symbolizing the injection of reproductive power into the dead, so that they can be born again. In some ethnic groups, before the burial of the dead, people use a cotton swab symbolically dipped a little water on the lips of the dead, hoping the dead can be reborn soon. Therefore, for people of all these ethnic groups, corpse bath is not just a simple matter of cleaning the body, but also an important part of life rituals and custom, which is of great significance in the culture of different ethnic groups.

3. Water Burial

Water is the source of human life, and people place infinite beautiful yearning and reverie on water. In many myths, water is associated with God, happiness, goodness and immortality. So, when burying dead relatives, water burial is a choice for the family members. Water burial is to place the dead body be taken by the rivers, lakes, and seas. It is an ancient and special burial custom, most of which is the burial custom of the ethnic groups living in the mountains and on rivers in ancient times, such as the Tibetan in Qinghai Province and Yunnan Province, the Shui Dai people in Xishuangbanna, the Shui people in Yunnan-Guizhou Plateau and the Menba people. These groups have been associated with water for generations and they regard water as the origin and destination of life. It is also believed that the emergence of water burial is closely related to the totem worship of fish by the local ancestors. People living along the waterfront regard fish as sacred objects of worship. They believe that the best choice and destination of life is to be eaten by the fish after death. This is the idea of regarding fish as Water Bodhisattva.

The choice of water burial is because that people regard water as sacred, so that life is bred in water end and in water, which is a kind of primitive water god worship. In different regions and different ethnic groups, the ways of expression are different. The Tibetans practice water burial live near all kinds of rivers and lakes. They believe that if the dead is thrown into the water and eaten by fish as food, he will become a happy person in the other life.

With the development of society, the way of water burial has changed. For example, in some cities in southern China, such as Hangzhou and Guangzhou, the "ash scattering" style of water burial has been very popular in recent years. It refers to scattering the ashes in rivers, lakes, or seas. This is a result of the funeral reform. the beloved late Premier Zhou Enlai once said that it is a revolution to change from keeping human remains to cremation. It's another revolution from keeping the ashes to not keeping them in same ways. Scattering the ashes is the best way to deal with the cremains, which requires neither a burial site nor new cremains repository and does not burden families and loved ones. With the progress of civilization of the community, this kind of funeral is becoming more common in China.

Water burial plays an important role in customs of the community, people's beliefs and life rituals, and the interpretation of water culture has its special significance. In funerals, water is called nectar and divine water. People pray for spiritual comfort with the blessing of gods, and it becomes a cultural symbol of sanctification.

Section III Praying for Water

Human beings cannot survive without water, nor can they survive with too much water. Drought and floods will also bring disaster to people. In ancient agricultural society, rain is a necessary element for the growth of crops. With enough rain and good weather, a harvest will be gained. Whereas flash floods, inundations or prolonged droughts can lead to starvation and death. To put it simply, the amount of rain is directly related to the harvest of crops and human survival.

Therefore, it also results in people's dependence on and fear of water which forms water worship and related activities. The custom of praying for rain and repressing water come into being.

1. What is the Meaning of Praying for Rain

Praying for rain is to pray for rainfall, which is a common practice in ancient times with a long history. *Shunmin · Master Lu's Spring and Autumn Annals* recorded: "The drought was severe and there was no harvest for five years. King Tang sacrificed himself to pray to the mulberry forest." It told a story about the drought in the early Shang Dynasty (about 1600 B.C.) and the failure of harvests for five consecutive years. Tang offered himself as a sacrifice to the gods and prayed for rain for the survival of his tribe (Fig. 13-4). The same sacrifice was also made by Prince Jinggong of the Song Dynasty (960-1279 A.D.). As recorded in *Taiping Yu Lan* by Li Fang of the Song Dynasty, "During the period governed by Prince Jinggong of the Song Dynasty, there was a severe drought for three years. The divination represented that there would be rainfall only by sacrificing a human. The Prince kowtowed and then said, 'I prayed for rain for my civilians. I absolutely mustn't kill people. I'll be the sacrifice myself.' Even as his voice died away, there came heavy rain in a wide area."

In ancient times, there were many ways to pray for rain, such as divination. In oracle, words related to divination of rain make up a large proportion, some of which combine the divination of rain and pray for good harvest directly, both expressing the connotation of water worship to beg for a harvest. This is one of the purposes of the initial water worship.

Figure 13-4　King Tang Praying for Rain in Shang Dynasty

Until the Han Dynasty (206 B. D. -220 A. D.), there still existed people predicting rainfall by means of divination. According to *Records of Grand History*, Sang Hongyang, a politician and financial expert during the Western Han Dynasty, encouraged the development of commerce, which hurt the interests of the bureaucrats. One year, because of a drought, the diviners said, "Kill Sang Hongyang, and it will rain." The implication was that God brought drought in order to punish Sang Hongyang who promoted the development of business since agriculture was emphasized over business in ancient times.

Some people burn mountains to pray for rain. Gan Bao, a historian of the Eastern Jin Dynasty (317-420 A. D.), said in his book *Search for the Spirit*: "There is a mountain at the east of Fandong. If there is a drought, the mountain will be set on fire, which will lead to heavy rain immediately." How can it happen? It's a small artificial rainfall. After the fire starts, the hot air rises, and there are many small ashes in the hot air. When rising, the water condenses on the ashes. As the water drops get bigger and bigger, they will fall.

2. The Object of the Prayer for Rain

Well, to whom do they pray for rain? There are many objects of the pray which wore, mainly divided into three categories: The Dragon King, Guanyin Buddha, and deified people.

(1) The Dragon King

One is the Dragon King. The dragon is a kind of totem symbol which integrates various animal images and is the most characteristic worship object of the Chinese nation. *Origin of Chinese Characters* said: "The dragon is as long as lindworm. The dragon can live in the dark and it can also live in the light. It can be thick and it can also be thin. It can be long, and it can also be short. While in the autumn equinox, the dragon dives into the abyss." Since long time ago people have associated dragons with water. In *Twenty-Ninth Year of Zhaogong · Tradition of Zuo*, it was said "Dragon is the creature relevant to water." *Xici · I-Ging* recorded that "The cloud complies with the dragon. Those who can summon the cloud are dragons." The dragon can summon the clouds, equivalent to calling for rainfall. Thus, the ancient people imagined the dragon as the god in charge of rainfall. Among the civilians, it was the most common way of praying for rain to the Dragon King. According to *Anthology of Stone Sculptures of the Han Dynasty in Shandong* Province compiled by Shandong Provincial Museum, a stone sculpture of the Han Dynasty was unearthed in Hanjiaqu, Yishui County, Shandong Province in 1972. The upper part of the stone is a double-headed dragon, whose mouths spray water. Under the two heads there is a person with Han-clothing and hair-down kneeling with a bowl on top to gather water. There is also a record of asking for rain from the dragon in the *Book of monks* · *Book of Jin*: "Fu Jian, a man of the Western Region lived in Chang 'an, and was able to cast a magic spell on the dragon. Once there was a drought, Jian often made a curse on the dragon for rain. After the dragon was put into a bowl, it would rain heavily."

Figure 13-5　Temple of the Dragon King

This is reflected in literature. In *Journey to the West*, there is a plot in which the Tang monk and his disciples come to Che Chi Country and find that the king is enthusiastic about Taoism and says monks are useless. The reason is that the monks here can't ask for rain in a drought, but the three Taoists who are actually demons can ask for rain. Tang monk and his disciples then fight with the three Taoist priests. Monkey King asks his master, Tang monk, to pray for rain on the altar, while he secretly helps him. When Monkey King sees his master finish reading a verse, he pulls out the golden staff from his ear and points it toward the sky. Then the gods of heaven cast spells together, the wind god making wind, the thunder god making thunder, the lightening god making lightening and the Dragon Kings making rainfall. In the legendary novel *Liu Yi Biography* of the Tang Dynasty (618-907 A. D.), the Dragon Kings Dongtingjun and Qiantangjun are brothers. The water god of Dongting Lake was originally Ehuang and Nuying, two concubines of Emperor Shun, and Wu Zixu was the water god of Qiantang River. However, in the Tang Dynasty, the Dragon Kings became the water gods of Dongting Lake and Qiantang River.

Among the people, we can also see the record of the Dragon King as the rain god. After the Tang Dynasty, the status of the Dragon God was constantly improved, and he was respected as the Dragon King. People believed that the Dragon King live in rivers, lakes, seas, wells and everywhere there was water. In the Yellow River valley, there is still a popular saying that "on the second day of the second lunar month, the dragon raises its head". It is said that during the reign of Empress Wu Zetian in the Tang Dynasty because she had offended the Jade Emperor, she was so punished that there was no rain for three years in her kingdom. The Dragon King, who oversaw the Heaven River, could not bear to see such case. He secretly sent rain to the world on the second day of the second lunar month, for which he was punished by the Jade Emperor. Therefore, every year on this day, people would offer corn flowers and fried beans to the Dragon King, to express their gratitude for saving their lives.

Although the dragon god has magical power, there is no clear and specific image of it. Thus, in the past, fish, frogs, snakes, scorpions, and other aquatic animals are regarded as the symbol of the dragon god in some regions. *Taiping Guangji* cited Duan Chengshi's *Youyang Zazu Story*: In the summer of the second year when Wang Yanwei guarded Kaifeng, a severe drought took place. At that time, Li Qi, the master of the King, passed by Kaifeng and a banquet was given. When Wang Yanwei talked about his worries about the drought, Li Qi said, "It's easy to pray for rain. You can find four salamanders and two large urns that can hold ten stones of water. Each urn is filled with water. Let two salamanders float on the water, covering the urn with a lid, sealing it with mud, and putting them in a lively place. Put a feast in front of the urn and burn incense. Choose a dozen children under ten years old and ask them to hold textilis in their hands, whipping the two urns regardless of day and night without pauses. " Wang Yanwei experimented according to his words, and it really rained twice a day, covering an area of hundreds of square miles. It is said that the dragon and the snake are relatives by marriage. Because lizards are often used as medicine, they are also called snake doctors or snake masters. In the 12th year of Shenzong in the Northern Song Dynasty (1077 A. D.), the royal court promulgated the *Lizard Praying for Rain Act*, asking each block to capture ten lizards and put them in water urn, and put in some mixed leaves. They should select 28 10–13-year-old boys and divide them into two groups, who wore green clothes. The boys were asked to splash water with willow branches in day and night and shout around the water urn: "Lizard lizard, enliven the cloud. Give us heavy rain, and let you go back home." In June of the same year, Su Shi, a famous poet of the Song Dynasty wrote the poem *Gecko*: "This year's drought calls for lizards. Bustling children run, dance and sing. Lizards can make hail and look for clouds and rain from dragons. Gecko, please try to fight files. Next year we may beg you if drought." The poem says, this year they utilize lizards for rain, and next year they may have to turn to the gecko. Although the poem satirizes the predicament of the imperial court, it is not hard to see that the lizard serves as a substitute for the dragon accepted by the authorities at that time. Sometimes, because lizards are rare, geckos are used instead. Li E of the Qing Dynasty said in his poem, "In the middle year of Xining, there was a long drought in the capital. According to the ancient method, each block had a big urn storing water with willow branches and lizards. Children in green clothes would surround the urn and shouted. Kaifeng government cannot get all the lizards, so they use the gecko instead. As the gecko will die in water, children change their words they shouted." At first children sing the song named Lizard Praying for Rain, and their song will change to "How bitter the geckos are as they are not lizards. How can someone who is foolish be given a good rain by the heavens! "

In the past, the Dragon King temples were found even in most of rural areas. In the long history of the Chinese nation, the dragon has been inextricably linked with many aspects, so that some sayings and customs today still have various relations with the dragon. As the saying goes, "The flood destroyed the Dragon King Temple. Therefore, member of family did not get along well with each other." and "On February 2nd, the dragon raised its head, and every family use cattle to farm." It is said that the Fu Xi "emphasized farming". On February 2nd every year, "the emperor's mother sent rice to him and the Emperor plough the land in person." In people's minds, dragons can control clouds and rain, which made it a common custom to pray to the dragon for safety and peace. In addition, there are activities of bringing water into the house in many regions. Xiong Mengxiang, living in the Yuan Dynasty, described local customs in his *Records on the Jin District*: "The day of February 2nd is called the dragon raising its head. Before dawn, the families sprinkle lime around the wells and create a white line straight into the house. Men and women do not need to sweep the floor for fear of frightening dragon eyes."*Wan Shu Za Ji* records that people call the day of February 2nd as dragon raising head. They scatter plant ash along the river and wells all the way to the water tanks in their homes to obtain good weather.

Taking the Dragon King as the god in charge of rain is one of the religious beliefs of the dragon totem in the primitive society of the Chinese nation. Belief in and sacrifice to the dragon reflect the ancient people's expectation for good weather and a happy life. With the development of history, the dragon gradually stepped down from the altar and became a symbol of auspiciousness instead of the god of rain. The various folk customs gradually evolved from the dragon worship and rain praying activities, bringing not only infinite joy to people, but also hope to people's future life.

(2) Guanyin Buddha

In addition to the Dragon King, Guanyin Buddha (Fig. 13-6) is also a popular god praying for rain in China.

The belief of Guanyin Buddha originates from the belief of Indian Buddhism. After being introduced into China, the image of Guanyin Bodhisattva soon became not only the main representative of saving the suffering, but also one of the most important rain gods. After the Sui and Tang Dynasties, the image of Guanyin Buddha gradually changed from the vigorous and rich

Figure 13-6 Guanyin Baddha

male image to the female image holding a willow branch and a clean bottle with a kind face. As a Bodhisattva of "great compassion to save the suffering", Guanyin Buddha has boundless magical power to save all living beings, and the pure water from willow branches is an important instrument for her to exert her magic power. In the Song Dynasty, willow branches began to be used to purify water in the ceremony of praying for rain. When drawing dragons to pray for rain, people would "use willow branches to sprinkle water on dragons". In the Ming Dynasty, there is a famous travel book named *Tour Records of West Lake*. It is recorded that during the reign of Xianping in the Northern Song Dynasty, there was a severe drought in western Zhejiang. Zhang Quhua, the governor of the county, led his subordinates to greet the statue of Guanyin Buddha to pray for rain. Since then, "there is a prayer response", which is very effective.

The religious belief of Guanyin Buddha extended to Guanyin's prayer for rain, which was the further deification of Guanyin's divine power.

The practice of praying to Guanyin Buddha for rain was very popular throughout the late Qing Dynasty. Lu Gongming, an American missionary, said in his book *Social Life of the Chinese* that in Fuzhou, "almost every year when the government prayed for rain", some people would be sent out of the city to "borrow a famous statue of Guanyin Bodhisattva". One summer they "took eight men to bring back the statue of the Bodhisattva". After the arrival of the Bodhisattva, "senior officials burned incense twice a day, and a group of monks prayed for rain from time to time. 'After' a heavy rain fell as they wished, 'they' provided a large table of vegetable dishes, burned incense, candles and burial money, and burned a symbol to announce that it had rained." After that, he "joyfully returned the Bodhisattva to the temple". From Lu Gongming's description, we can see that

Americans are still relatively new and curious about Chinese people asking Bodhisattva for rain.

(3) Deified Persons

Some of these deified people were rulers of the state, such as Shang Tang. In ancient times, he was treated respectively as a god of rain in many regions of the north China. Deified persons also include prominent pesonages, or officials who have inade great contributions to their local areas. There are also some ordinary people, who have had a successful career in life. After they died, they will be appointed as God, each in charge of one aspect. The people's respect for them turned into a kind of worship over time, so it became a common practice to pray for rain to these people. For example, Guan Yu, a famous figure in the Three Kingdoms Period (220-280 A. D.), was originally a military general. But with the widespread recognition of the people and the authorities, he gradually became the "omnipotent god" who dominated war, wealth, rainfall, and higher education. After the late Ming Dynasty, belief in Guan Yu became increasingly popular. Xie Zhaozhi of the Ming dynasty wrote in *Wu Za Zu*: "Today there is no temple more popular in incense than Guan Yu." According to *Shandong Folklore* by Shan Man and others, when praying for rain in some villages in Shandong in the past, people would carry the portraits of the Dragon King, Guan Yin Buddha, and Guan Yu out on a tour. And those praying for rain would wear willow branch hats, hold willow branches, and chant Buddha's name. Carry the statue of Guan Yu to turn a few laps, they would put the master's portrait into the sun for a few days if there was still no rain.

As a matter of fact, in the early period of Chinese civilization, people worshiped all kinds of rain gods and bred various behaviours of water worship. Dong Zhongshu in the Western Han Dynasty (206 B. C-25 A. D) recorded in *The Spring and Autumn Flowery Dews (Chun Qiu Fan Lu)* that every time there was a spring drought, people offered sacrifices to Gong Gong (God of Water) to pray for rain. "They offered sacrifices to the God of Water to pray for rain, including eight raw fish, Xuan wine, sake and dried meat. Every summer when Here was drought, people sacrificed to the God Chi You with seven red roosters, Xuan wine, sake, and dried meat. Every autumn drought, people sacrificed to the God Shao Hao with nine fish made of tung wood, Xuan wine, sake, and dried meat. Every winter drought, people sacrifice to the God Xuan Ming for rainfall with six black dogs, Xuan wine, sake, and dried meat. At that time, it was also the ritual to pray for rain from the God Hou Ji: "At the end of summer, they prayed to the mountain for help. The county was asked to be relocated outside the south gate in ten days. Men were forbidden to enter the city for five days. Near Wu City, people are gathered to construct the alter for sacrifice. They sacrificed to the God Hou Ji with five treasures, Xuan wine, sake, and dried meat. Let the chief priests fast for three days and wear yellow clothes, all like spring sacrifices. On the day of Wuji, they made a huge fifteen-meter dragon and put it in the centre. And another four small dragons measuring roughly nine meters were made and put in the south being five feet apart. They assigned five men to fast for three days and dance in yellow clothes. And five elders also are arranged to fast for three days and stand there in yellow clothes. The ditch through the city was dug. The toad pool was five feet in radius and one foot deep. Everything else is the same as before."

Figure 13-7 Jiaying Taoist Temple in Wuzhi County

Located in Wuzhi County, Henan Province, Jiaying Taoist Temple (Fig. 13-7) is the only temple that records the history of the Yellow River in China. It is not only a place to commemorate the Yellow River God, but also a place to commend the outstanding officials of river control through the ages, such as Dayu, Wang Jing, Jia Lu, Pan Jixun and Lin Zexu, all of whom were outstanding officials of the past dynasties in river control. Some of them have been deified, like Da Yu.

This shows that people hope that the people they believe in can bring good fortune and remove evil, and their divine power can still play a role after the death.

3. Ceremony of Praying for Rain

It is the most basic material needs of human beings to have ample food and clothing, so the ceremony of praying for rain is a common cultural phenomenon in the world. James George Fraser, a British anthropologist, wrote in his book *Golden Bough* that "among the Mara tribes of northern Australia, the rain-prayer would come to a pool and sing a witch song, then he would take some water in his hand, drawing it in, and spray it all around. Then he sprinkled the water all over himself, shook it all around, and quietly returned to the tent. People thought the rain would come."

Specific stipulation was settled in the Han Dynasty by the authority that people should set a soil dragon praying for rain. Dong Zhongshu of the Western Han Dynasty had a special chapter in

Water and the Chinese Culture

The Spring and Autumn Flowery Dews, which described in detail the sacrificial ceremony of setting a soil dragon to pray for rain. Take the spring drought as an example: "Outside the east gate of the city is a four-way altar measuring eight feet. They sacrifice God of Water with eight raw fish, Xuan wine, sake, and dried meat. The clean and host persons are chosen to fast for three days in yellow clothes…On the day of Jiayi, a huge twenty-four-meter dragon is made and put in the centre. Seven smaller twelve-meter dragons are made and put in the east, being eight feet apart. Eight children are chosen to fast for three days and dance wearing green clothes. There is also the elder fasting for three days and standing there in yellow…Sake and dried meat are prepared for the fast. A three-year-old rooster and a three-year-old boar are cooked near the alter. People are asked to close the south gate of the city and put some water outside. They should also open the north gate and put a boar outside. Inside the city there should also put a boar. Upon the drum, they shall burn the pigtail…If fortunately, it rains, they will in turn reward a pig, wine, salt and money." During the ceremony of praying for rain with soil dragon, a few selected children fast in green and perform "Yu" dance, which is a way praying for rain that appeared in the Shang (1300–1046 B. C.) and Zhou (1046–256 B. C.) Dynasties to worship and amuse the god to get rainfall.

To cope with the increasingly frequent arid weather, in April of the tenth year of Xining in the Northern Song Dynasty (1077 A. D.), the imperial court issued the *Law of Lizard Prayer (Xi Yi Qi Yu Fa) for Rain* for the whole country, making clear stipulations on the time, place and method of praying for rain.

In the traditional ceremony of praying for rain, it is necessary to recite the poetry whose theme is about praying for rain. Therefore, many famous statesmen and litterateurs in Chinese history have written poems praying for rain. Su Zhe used to be an official in many regions. Every time there was a meteorological disaster, he would write articles to present to the gods praying for rainfall, snow, or sunshine, such as *Prayer for Rain and Snow in Qizhou*, *Prayer for Rain in Qizhou*, *Prayer for Rain in Nanjing*, *Prayer for Rain in Yunzhou* and so on. If the prayer for rain is successful, thanks must be given to the gods. For instance, in the fifth year of Yuan You, Su Zhe wrote the *Prayer for Rain from Five Mountains and Four Rivers*, "We sincerely pray for rainfall to obtain a harvest. The god will not ignore the unified wish of all." Then it rained that day, Su Zhe wrote *Message on Thanks to the Rain*: "The God replied to our beg and gave us bounties. The land is saved from severe drought, leading to a harvest in autumn." Most of these poems are written to tell various water gods about the severe drought and the difficulties of people's livelihood. They hope the gods can have mercy on the people and bring rain in time, etc. From this, we can see that in the event of praying for rain, men and women, old, and young gathered together for a parade. People surrounded the god of water and marched towards the venue of worship, during which the beating of gongs and drums resounded to the skies. As they walked, the wizard dipped a willow branch in water, brushed it along the way, and muttered some words. The spectacle was huge and spectacular. Sometimes people replace dragon images with portrait of dragons. In the Song Dynasty, when setting alter for rain, people would post a portrait of a dragon, and then throw the portrait into the water to pray for rain.

In addition to sacrificial activities, the ceremony of praying for rain in traditional times was often accompanied by music and dance to please the god of water. Sacrifice is to let the gods get material satisfaction, while music and dance are to let the gods get spiritual enjoyment. The "Yu Sacrifice" ceremony held by the ancient people for praying for rain was mainly organized in the form of dance. During the ceremony, the maidens formed a dance team, dancing, shouting, and offering sacrificial jade and silk. Dance was accompanied by song and music. "To pray for rain and pray for mercy, beat the drum and play lyre." "Yu" is a rain prayer ritual accompanied by singing and dancing. "Yu Sacrifice" aims to satisfy the gods to bring rainfall with sacrifice, music, and dance.

Section IV Suppression of Water Monsters

Due to the limited knowledge about nature, the ancient Chinese people believed that the water was inhabited by demons and monsters, who sometimes made waves and caused floods. To suppress flood was to suppress the monster that made trouble in the water. Because of people's fear of water and self-protection consciousness, they began to adopt the method of "Yan Sheng Tactic" to prevent flooding very early. "Yan" here refers to "pressure", which means restraint and suppression. The custom of water suppression is the reflection of the thought of "Yan Sheng" in water control activities. The custom of water suppression is relatively easy to understand, and the key lies in what is used to suppress water. According to the concept of water suppression culture in ancient China, gods, animals, towers, temples, steles, and deified persons all could suppress flood. Therefore, in the rivers, lakes, and seas in China, there are a lot of mythical sacred objects left behind.

1. Rhino and Iron Ox

The earliest custom of water suppression in ancient times can be traced back to the time of Yu. According to the legend, when coping with the floods, Yu cast an iron ox and sank it into the water to control the water monster wherever he was controlling the flood. It was said that the Flood Dragon is afraid of iron. In the traditional Yin and Yang Five Elements (Yin Yang Wu Xing), "Ox embodies the nature of earth, and earth can resist water", thus possessing the magical power of avoiding floods. Therefore, in many places of China, the iron ox was chosen for water suppression, praying for the peace of rivers and the well-being of the people.

The iron rhino cast by Yu Qian in the Ming Dynasty after controlling the Yellow River floods can still be seen outside Kaifeng, Henan today (Fig. 13-8).

Kaifeng City, located in the lower reaches of the Yellow River, is prone to floods. In the fifth year of the Ming Zhengtong (1440 A. C.), the river rose, forcing the embankment, and Yu Qian personally organized the people to fight the flood. He threw the embroidered robe granted by the

Figure 13-8 Water Suppression Iron Rhino in Kaifeng

Emperor, expressing the determination to overcome the flood. He led his men to repair the dikes in the east, north and west, which were destroyed by the flood. Together with the dikes in the south, they stretched for more than 20 kilometres, forming a barrier to guard the city. In the year of 1446, Yu Qian ordered people to build the iron rhino and put it on the city embankment. At that time, the iron rhino was placed in the newly built Huilong Temple on the banks of the Yellow River. In the year of 1642, the Yellow River burst, and the Huilong Temple was flattened by the water, the iron rhino sank in mud. During the reign of Emperor Shunzhi of the Qing Dynasty, the iron rhino was dug up again. In the 30th year of Kangxi (1691 A. D.), the temple was rebuilt and renamed the Huilong Temple to the Temple of Iron Rhino Suppressing River. In the 21st year of Daoguang (1841 A. D.), the Iron Rhino Temple was destroyed by floods, but the iron rhino inside has been preserved ever since.

In Chengdu, a deep-buried stone beast resembling a rhinoceros was excavated in 2013 which was carved out of a single block of red sandstone (Fig. 13-9). It is a stone beast with stubby legs, a strong back, a slightly pointed head, hooves, and a round body. In the Western Han Dynasty (206 B. C. -25 A. D.), Yang Xiong, a man of the State of Shu, wrote in *The Chronicles of the King of Shu (Shu Wang Ben Ji)*: "The river was a nuisance. Li Bing made five stone, rhinos, placing two in the house, one under the bridge in the city, and two in the water, to suppress water." Thus, it can be proved that the stone rhinoceros excavated should be an object used for water suppression.

The theory of yin-yang and five elements is an expression of simple materialism and dialectics thought of ancient people in China. People believed that gold, wood, water, fire, and earth were the five most basic materials in the world, and they interacted with each other. Cows can plow the

Figure 13-9　Stone Rhino Kept in Chengdu Museum

field, belonging to the "Kun" beast. "Kun" in the five elements correspond to earth, which can restrain water. In ancient times, rhinoceros and oxen were not separated, belonging to the same species. It was said that when digging the Dujiangyan Dam, Li Bing became an ox to conquer the river god. So later generations chose rhinoceros or iron ox as the god beast for water suppression.

2. Mythical Creatures

In the traditional custom of water suppression in China, there are many kinds of animals serving as mythical creatures.

In Cangzhou, Hebei Province, there is an iron lion, which is called "Sea Suppression Roar" by the local people. This iron lion carries a huge lotus basin. Its limbs outstretched, its head held high, and its mouth stretched wide to the sky. On its head and neck, the words "Lion King" are engraved. According to the legend, Cangzhou faced the Bohai Sea to the east, and the sea frequently flooded. Local people collected money and cast lions to prevent the flood. The ancients created many deities through myths and legends, including many water deities. On one hand, people offered sacrifices to the God of Water, and on the other hand, they used sacred objects to suppress the God of Water, hoping that the god would not harm the people. The lion is the king of all animals. In traditional Chinese culture, it is believed that the lion has the divinity of suppressing evil spirits. At the same time, in Buddhism, the lion is the mount of Manjusri Bodhisattva, which has the symbolic significance of fearlessness and power.

In Kunming, Yunnan Province, there is a mythical creature suppressing water named Tong Han. According to the Chinese traditional culture, Tong Han was the incarnation of southern Jing Star, which was one of the Twenty-eighth Star Mansion. In the five elements, Han belonged to wood responsible for water affairs, for which it was called Jing Wood Han (Jing Mu Han). The water god beasts of China are all kinds of strange things. They are the places for the ancient people to entrust their hope for flood suppression, water disaster prevention and good luck.

Ba Xia, also known as water swallowing beast or water absorbing beast, was one of the nine sons of the dragon in legend in charge of water suppression. It was said that its image seemed like a dragon and a shrimp, but it was not a dragon or shrimp. There were a pair of horns on the top of the head and dragon scales on the whole body. Ba Xia liked water the most in its whole life, thus it lived near water. It loved to play with waves and play in the river for years. It was often decorated on the vaults, pillars, wings, and railings of stone bridges for decoration as well as water monster suppression. In 2000, the Houmen Bridge in Beijing was repaired. During the process, six statues of Ba Xia carved with bluestone were excavated lying down in the river silt, which were the same as the carved stones of Ba Xia for bank protection. They were the relics of the Yuan Dynasty and the Ming Dynasty.

3. Weapons

On the beach below Yueyang Tower by the shore of Dongting Lake in Hunan Province, there are three huge iron objects, whose overall shape resembles the cangue of ancient prisoners. Fan Zhiming, a famous historical geographer of the late Northern Song Dynasty, speculated that these iron objects were used by ancient people to keep down the goblin in Dongting Lake. In ancient times, people believed that objects such as iron could drive away the flood dragon and suppress water. Therefore, there are legends of locking flood dragons ancient in China. The earliest myth was that Yu locking the dragon. In Sichuan, there is the legend of Li Bing chaining a dragon, and in Jiangxi, there is the legend of Xu Xun, a Taoist master, chaining a dragon with a diamond iron chain. In Yanzhou, Shandong Province, there is the legend using swords to suppress water. It was said that the local people saw dragons making waves in the water. After the flood receded, people made swords and put them in the water, to daunt flood dragons.

The existing huge "water suppression sword" in Yanzhou City of Shandong Province is a kind of water control weapon with a high artistic level. In the spring of 1988, the Sishui River in the south of Yanzhou City was in the dry season and there was no water. Many people dug sand at the bottom of the dry river, and some unexpectedly dug a big ancient iron sword that was sank at the bottom. Cultural relics workers rushed to the scene upon hearing the news. They dug out the huge iron sword and transported it to Yanzhou Museum for preservation. The 7.5 m-long iron sword had characters and designs cast on its hilt. The swallow mouth of the sword was shaped like a monster's head, and it was called "Ya Zi". According to the legend, it was the second son of the Dragon King's nine sons. It was so fierce that people adorned it on the sword. This iron sword was specially forged for protection against water disaster.

This shows the weapons such as iron cangue, iron chain, and sword are all divine objects for water suppression.

4. Tower Buildings

When travelling, we can often see tall tower buildings. Why did the ancients build these towers? Many people may have heard the saying: "The King of Heaven excels the tiger which is the King of Land, and the pagoda town suppresses the river demon." A very important reason is that towers is believed to suppress the so-called "water demon" and "water monster". *The Legend of White Snake* is widely known. In our mind, Lady White is beautiful, kind, wise and loyal to love, but in a sense, she is just a snake demon making troubles. When fighting against Fahai, she made waves and flooded the Jinshan Temple, hurting innocent people. Finally, she was suppressed by Fahai and held under Leifeng Pagoda.

In the past, it was believed that the pagoda could prevent floods, so many people would pray to the pagoda for safety and peace. In the poem *Seng Jia Pagoda in Sizhou*, Su Shi mentioned the success of praying to the tower for water suppression: "I went to the south by boat, and the wind with sand blew my face for three days. The boatman persuaded us to pray to the pagoda. Before the incense was collected, the direction of wind has changed." Seng Jia was the first-class scholar in the country during the period of the Tang Dynasty. It was said that he was the incarnation of Guanyin Bodhisattva. After death, he was placed in the Linhuai Pagoda. People then called the pagoda "Seng Jia Pagoda" to suppress the water monster. When Su Shi and his brother Su Zhe passed through this place, the water flow was too rapid to drive the boat. Under the persuasion of the boatman, they climbed the tower to pray. As a result, before the two brothers finished their worship, the wind turned its direction which is helpful for sail. The incident impressed Su Shi so much that he later recalled it in a poem.

In the ancients' opinions, wherever there was water, no matter in rivers, lakes or seas, there was the Dragon King stationed. The Dragon King can produce wind, rain, thunder and lightning. Therefore, on one hand, people build the Dragon King Temple for worship, on the other hand, they use various measures to get it restrained. So that the Dragon King can benefit people by promoting the good and avoiding the bad.

Other methods used to suppress water include building pavilions, temples, or erecting monuments. For example, Zhenghuai Lou in Huai'an, Jiangsu Province, used to tell the time and alarm the police. In the Qing Dynasty, due to so many floods, the building was renamed Zhenghuai Lou, which took the meaning of suppressing floods. In the Song Dynasty, when Su Shi was controlling the breach of the Yellow River in Xuzhou, he built the Yellow Tower to suppress the water. In the year of 1077, Su Shi and his younger brother Su Zhe went to Xuzhou and served for more than 100 days. He then led the army and the people to fight floods and protect the city. He was awarded by the emperor for his contribution. In the process of restoration and reconstruction of Xuzhou City, Su Shi, at the request of his officials and people, built a tall building above the east gate of Xuzhou City. He decorated it with yellow colour to commemorate the flood fighting. The building was 33 meters high, adding one more scenic spot for Xuzhou.

The ancients believed that the power of Buddha's Dharma was boundless, and the Buddha could not only subdue demons and remove demons, but also prevent flood and disasters. So, they carved Buddha statues to suppress the water. The Leshan Giant Buddha (Fig. 13 - 10) in Sichuan Province is a statue of Buddha used to keep water down. At the foot of Leshan Mount, Minjiang River, Qingyi River and Dadu River converge. The water is fierce, for which tragedies often occur as boats are destroyed and people die when they travel here. During the reign of Emperor Xuanzong of the Tang Dynasty, Monk Haitong carved a large statue of Maitreya Buddha on the cliff, hoping to calm the turbulent waters of the Three Rivers with the help of the giant Buddha.

Figure 13-10   Leshan Giant Buddha

In ancient times, there was the phenomenon of building tablets to suppress the water, and there were tablets in Dujiangyan of Sichuan Province. The water suppression stone tablets here were composed of three parts, respectively, the "Shenyu Tablet", the "Taoist Character Tablet" and the "Buddhist Character Tablet", which were intended to draw support from the divine power of Confucianism, Buddhism and Tao to suppress water. According to the legend, there was an evil dragon pressed beneath these tablets. If there was no pressure on the evil dragon, there would be a flood. That's why this kind of tablet is known as the "Water Suppression Tablet".

5. Deified People

In the Chinese history, it is common for famous historical figures to be honored as the god of water after their death. Because they had made great contributions to society and the local people, especially in water conservancy and disaster prevention. Thus, people built temples and other buildings to worship them.

In Fulong Temple of Dujiangyan, there is a stone statue of Li Bing (Fig. 13-11). This stone statue of Li Bing not only accepts people's worship, but also has an important task, which is to suppress water monsters. People believed that Li Bing had the magical power to control water, so it was hoped that his power could still work after his death to suppress water monsters. Guan Yu, a fierce general during the Three Kingdoms period, later also became an omnipotent god, and was seen as a water god in some places. For instance, the statue of Guan Yu in the Jing River embankment and the Guan Di Temple in Xiajiang River both have functions as the water god. There is also a folk proverb that the drought will not last until May 13 (the birthday of Guan Gong or the day of sharpening the knife). Moreover, in the festival of the year, May 13 of the lunar calendar is designated as the Rain Festival, and it is believed that there will be rain on that day. All these phenomena reflect people's belief that Guan Gong can master the rain. This psychology highlights the belief characteristics of the agricultural areas.

Figure 13-11　The Statue of Li Bing

　　Whether it is praying for rain or suppressing the water, these water-related beliefs and practices are rooted in farming culture. In the face of the flood, people made sacrifices to the gods on the one hand, and on the other hand, they made artifacts against the gods to avoid the flood. It can be seen that in the worship of water, people pray for harvest and further pray for auspiciousness. It also shows a rich and colourful water culture, reflecting people's strong desire to overcome nature, and the spirit of resistance in the face of natural disasters.

Section V　Water and Festival Activities of the Han People

　　China has the very important traditional festivals such as Spring Festival, March 3rd, Dragon Boat Festival and Qixi Festival, all of which are closely related to water.

Water and the Chinese Culture

1. The Shangsi Festival

(1) Fuxi

As we all know, March is the time when vegetation just sprouts, and people are attracted by the prosperity of nature of the countryside. It is the time for people to having an outing in spring in ancient times. The third day of March of lunatic calendar was called "Shangsi Festival" in ancient times. It's a festival of sacrificial rites held every spring by the water. Fuxi means remove dirt and bad luck with water. *The Book of Songs* says: "Qin Shui River and Wei Shui River, flowing endlessly. The young people going out to the countryside, holding the orchids hoping to eliminate disasters and evils through sacrificial activities. The custom of Fuxi (Fig. 13-12) by the riverside existed for a long time."

Figure 13-12　Fuxi Ritual

Liang Jing Xin Ji of the Tang Dynasty says: "In Chang'an (capital city) of the Tang Dynasty, Princess Taiping goes to the pavilion of the Leyouyuan mountain, enjoying the spring scenery… During Shangsi Festival and Double Ninth Festival, Princess Taiping holds a banquet by the Qujiang pool, the maidservants going to the pool to get rid of the dirt and bad luck and the poets enjoying singing and composing poetry."

After the Wei and Jin Dynasties, people's custom of eliminating bad luck in Shangsi Festival gradually declined. Later, it evolved into a grand gathering of outings and banquets. Du Fu said in his poem *Journey of Beauties* that "it is a great day on March 3rd, and many young and beautiful ladies go out to the countryside lake to have a good time."

(2) Qu Shui Liu Shang

People may know *Lantingxi Xu*, which is known as the best running script(a kind of Chinese calligraphy) of the world, and a unique cultural landscape. It is also related to water activities, one of which is called Qu Shui Liu Shang (Fig. 13-13).

What is Qu Shui Liu Shang? The Shang is a kind of wine cup. *Jing Chu Sui Shi Ji* is a collection of notes recording the folk customs of the Chu Dynasty in ancient China. It recorded that: "on March 3rd, the poets and the civilian people came out to the pool, putting the cup with wine into the upstream of the curved water. People would wait at the different places of the stream for the cup to stop and drink it, composing a poem as well."

Figure 13-13　Ruins of Qu Shui Liu Shang

It is said that this drinking way of "Qu Shui Liu Shang" can be traced back to the Western Zhou Dynasty (1046-771 B. C.). During the Northern and Southern Dynasties (420-589 A. D.), Wu Jun recorded in *Xuqixieji* that "the emperor of the West Zhou Dynasty (1046-256 B. C.) moved to the city of Luoyi (now Luoyan city) and composed a poem saying 'Yushangsuiboliu' due to the cup with wine floating on the flowing water." This way of drinking and entertaining used to be popular only among the civilian people, but later literati as well.

The reason why Qu Shui Liu Shang in *Lantingji Xu* is so well known is that the people who participated in this activity are very famous. The participants are Wang Xizhi, the great calligrapher and Xie An, the great military strategist who commanded the famous Battle of Feishui.

On March 3rd of in the ninth year of Yonghe of the Eastern Jin Dynasty (353 A. D.), a group of famous literati and the descendants of the official families, including Wang Xizhi and Xie An, 42 persons altogether, held the first literati gathering at Lan Pavilion of the north Kuaiji Mountain

(Shaoxing City, Zhejiang Province today). All the people present enjoy drinking wine and composing poetry, with a collection of 37 poems. *Lantingji Xu* by Wang Xizhi was just written for those poems. And this gathering is the most famous one in Chinese history.

Qu Shui Liu Shang is even widely accepted by some other East Asian countries. In ancient times, Japan and Korea built the garden and pavilion to the Lan Pavilion of China. On March 3rd, people there had a gathering and composed poetry. As time went by, Qu Shui Liu Shang declined, but the connotation of the literati gathering has been preserved evolved and with new content.

2. The Dragon Boat Festival

The fifth day of the fifth lunar month is a traditional Chinese festival——the Dragon Boat Festival. When it comes to the Dragon Boat Festival, there are many different theories in history. Some people think it is to commemorate Qu Yuan, Wu Zixu, filial daughter Cao E, Jie Zitui, and others think it comes from the evil taboo, hanging Zhong Kui's portrait, sending the God of Plague, and so on. But for thousands of years, the memory of Qu Yuan has had a wider impact. Today, when it comes to the Dragon Boat Festival, we all think of Qu Yuan, zongzi and dragon boats. Eating zongzi and racing dragon boats are two of the customs that mark the festival.

(1) Zongzi

About the origin of the Dragon Boat Festival, the most popular is to commemorate Qu Yuan, the statesman and great poet of Warring States Period. During the Warring States Period, Qu Yuan carried out the political reforms in the Chu State , while being opposed, squeezed, exiled by Chu Huai Wang(the 37th emperor of the Chu State) and the old tribes, and finally he committed suicide by drowning himself in the Miluo River.

Tai Ping Yu Lan written in the early years of the Northern Song Dynasty records that: "Qu Yuan died in Miluo on May 5th, and Chu people mourned. On this day, people threw the bamboo pipes stuffed with rice into water to worship him", which gradually evolved into the custom of eating zongzi (rice dumpling wrapped in leaves) to mourn Qu Yuan.

Zongzi of the early time did not have a certain shape. Nowadays, most of them are of triangle shape, like women's bound feet, which is said to be related to the story of Meng Jiangnv. Meng Jiangnv's husband, Fan Xiliang, was sent by the first Emperor of the Qin Dynasty to build the Great Wall. But three years later, Meng Jiangnv still didn't have a single word about her husband. She missed him so much, that she took good care of her parents in law before leaving for her husband alone. She wondered what to bring to her husband. Thinking of the strong wind of the northern frontier fortress, she decided to make zongzi with glutinous rice and three dates inside, meaning parting for three years. She made the zongzi of triangle shape thinking of the shape of her bound feet to let her husband know that she came to see him after covering a long difficult trip. Since then, zongzi has been of triangle shape. People will think of the story of Meng Jiangnv looking for her husband.

According to the different tools, there were two kinds of zongzi in ancient times: one was "Jiaoshu" and the other was "Tongzong" or "Yuntongzong". It is said that as early as the Spring and Autumn Period, "Tongzong" has existed. *Shi Xu Bu* 16 · *May 5th*, the volume 31st of *Tai Ping Yu Lan*, by quoting *Xu Qi Xie Ji* of Wu Jun of the Liang Dynasty (502-557 A. D.), says: "Qu Yuan died in Miluo on May 5th, and Chu people mourned. On this day, people threw bamboo pipes stuffed with rice into water to worship him." In late Eastern Han Dynasty, people made Jianshuizong (alkali water soaked zongzi) of square shape with alkali water-soaked rice and wrapped with Gu (Zizania aquatica) leaves. In the Jin Dynasty (265–420 A. D.), zongzi was officially designated as the food of the Dragon Boat Festival. *Shi Yin Bu Jiu · Zong*,

Figure 13-14　Qu Yuan

the volume 851st, by quoting *Feng Tu Ji* of the West Jin Dynasty, says: the tradition is that people wrap the millet with wild Gu leaves, cooking it with thick soup, and eating it on May 5th and the summer solstice. It is called zongzi or Jiaoshu. In addition to the main ingredients such as glutinous rice, traditional Chinese medicine is also added to zongzi. The combination of traditional Chinese medicine and traditional Chinese food is fully reflected in zongzi. During the Northern and Southern Dynasties (420-589 A. D.), zongzi began to exist. In addition to rice, meat, chestnut, jujube, red bean, and other ingredients are mixed. There are more and more kinds of zongzi, with more and more complicated making process, and better taste. During the Song Dynasty, there were some unique varieties of zongzi, such as Guozong, Mizong and Yangmeizong. Du fan's lines such as "delicious food gathering the neighbours, Guozong of Luodoudeng", "it's easy for old people to eat honey zongzi, but it's hard for the gods to eat cattail root even when they are sick" by Xiang Shi'an and "even having the finest Ge (a kind of plant used to weave cloth) grated, but never seen Yangmeizong" all reflect the diversification of people making zongzi at that time. At the same time, zongzi was mentioned in many poems, which also means that it has become the most representative food of the Dragon Boat Festival.

Today, with the rapid development of the society, zongzi, as a traditional food, is still very popular in many places. There are many kinds of zongzi, such as meat zongzi in Jiangsu, Zhejiang and Shanghai, beans zongzi in Guangdong and Guangxi, and zongzi of seafoods in coastal areas, etc. Among them, zongzi of Jiaxing, Zhejiang Province has a long history and is very famous. It is rectangular, with fresh meat, bean paste, Babao (different cereals), or chicken etc. inside. Zongzi of "Wufangzhai" is said to be the best in Jiaxing, which is regards as " Zongzi King of Jiangnan". It is unique in material selection, production, and cooking, such as good white glutinous rice and well-chosen meat of pig hind legs. Putting some fat oil into it after it is thoroughly cooked, which tastes delicious, but not greasy.

(2) Dragon Boat Race

During the Dragon Boat Festival, a grand dragon boat race will be held. Dragon boat race is a typical activity of the Dragon Boat Festival. It is said that people hated to part with Qu Yuan and then rowed to rescue him, but there was still no trace of him until they got to Dongting Lake. Since then, on the fifth day of May every year, people have this dragon boat race to drive away the fish and prevent Qu Yuan's remains from being eating by them. The custom of dragon boat race has been handed down from generation to generation.

Dragon boat race has an exceptionally long history. A bronze of Yue unearthed in Zhejiang Province in the Spring and Autumn Period was engraved with the design of a dragon boat race (Fig. 13-15). In ancient times, dragon boat racing was a both religious and recreational activity. Before the dragon boat race, various sacrificial and commemorative events would be held. People usually light incense candles, burn paper money, and take rice, meat and zongzi as offerings at the ceremony to pray for a good harvest, elimination of disasters and peace of next year.

Figure 13-15 The Yue Bronze of Yu People's Boat Race

Dragon boat race has been always very popular in Hunan Province. Li Dongyang of the Ming Dynasty described it in detail in his *Ballad of Dragon Boat Race*: "People in Hunan attach great importance to the Dragon Boat Festival, and many boats compete in the race during the festival. During the race, people row the boats decorated with colourful flags and drum, singing and crossing the river, so quickly and like flying, with clothes splashed wet by the water. People enjoy this activity with cheer and try hard for the championship. They are surprised at and jealous of those who win the race continuously. Participants of the two sides work together and compete fiercely, all of them buying a boat and hoping to drive the plague away by rowing hard in the competition. After Qu Yuan's death, this dragon boat race has been taken as a traditional activity, while all people enjoy the race except me, but just do not let Peng Xian (the literati of Yin Dynasty, who also killed himself by drowning in the river) know it." From this poem, people can see that the purpose of Hunan people's race at that time was to eliminate the plague they enjoyed it very much. The boat race of the Dragon Boat Festival is also a popular recreational activity in the loyal palace. It is recorded in *The Jiu Tang Shu (The Old History of the Tang Dynasty)* that the Emperor Mu Zong of the Tang Dynasty, "in the year of Xinchou, a party was held and watched the boat race in Yuzao Palace", and Emperor Wenzong of the Tang Dynasty, "in year of Wuyin, a party was held and watched the boat race in Yuzao Palace". *History of the Song Dynasty* recorded that: "Every Lantern Festival, Shangsi, and Dragon Boat Festival, people enjoyed the beautiful lanterns, watching boat races and other activities."

The custom of dragon boat race is popular not only among Han people, but also the ethnic groups. The ethnic Miao people Dragon Boat Festival is the most representative one. It is said that a long time ago, there was a man named Gou Ya who lived on fishing. One day, he went to the lake of the Rongshan Mountain to fish with his son. He cast the net at the head of the boat but getting nothing. Turning the boat about, he planned to go somewhere else to try his luck, but he just couldn't find his son who had been at the stern of the boat. With great shock, he jumped down into the lake to look for him. He went down to the bottom of the lake, while he found nothing but a dragon cave. Going into the cave, he saw an evil dragon sleeping with his son as a pillow. The dragon's nest was full of hay. Gou Ya came closer and saw that his son was dead. Gou Ya wanted to avenge his son's death, but he had nothing on hand, so he went home to get prepared and went back to the dragon's nest again. The dragon was still sleeping. Gou Ya lit the hay in the dragon's nest and went up to the bank of the lake, watching the big fire which lasted three days. The dragon was burned to death and finally floated to the top of the water. From then on, all villages cut down trees to build dragon boats looking like dragons to commemorate Gou Ya's eliminating the dragon. Every May, they row dragon boats on the Qingshui River and Bala River, symbolizing to subdue the dragon and play with it, hoping that the dragon would never dare to do evil again and people have good harvests each year.

Today, people combine the dragon boat race with sports events, the local economic construction and mass entertainment culture, which has an increasingly widespread influence all over the world.

(3) The Wushi Water (Water at Noon)

In the south of Fujian Province and Taiwan, the Dragon Boat Festival has its own local features. For example, people attach great importance to the water at noon. Wen Ge of the Song

Dynasty wrote in *Suo Sui Lu*: "People take the well water at noon on May 5th to bathe to drive away the plague for a year. It is also common for people to bathe with wormwood strips and the leaves of peach trees." In Taiwan, there is a legend saying that when Zheng Chenggong(a general living at the end of the Ming Dynasty and early the Qing Dynasty) entered Taiwan with his troops, they couldn't find any water sources. Zheng Chenggong inserted his sword into the ground. As a result, when the sword was pulled out, the water gushed out. It was noon of the Dragon Boat Festival at that time and the water was called Wushi Water (Fig. 13-16). From 11:00 a. m. to 1: 00 p. m. on the day of Dragon Boat Festival every year, local people rush to the old well of the village to fetch water with different containers, believing Wushi Water can exorcise the evil. People use the water for cleaning the house, bathing, and drinking, etc. People believe that Wushi Water can ward off evil spirits, hot summer and the plague. The well where Zheng Chengong inserted his sword and the spring water gushed out is said to be in Tiezhen Mountian of Dajia District and named as "the well of sword". The custom of the Dragon Boat Festival and the legend of Zheng Chenggong make the "the well of sword" the first choice for people to get Wushi Water. Thousands of people go up the mountain to get water every year on the Dragon Boat Festival.

Figure 13-16　The Well of Wushi Water

3. The Qixi Festival

(1) Story of the Cowboy and the Girl Weaver

When it comes to Qixi Festival, people will think of the story of the Cowboy and the Girl Weaver.

The origin of Qixi Festival is related to the ancient people's belief in Vega and Altair. *Xia Xiaozheng* says: "In July, at the beginning of dusk, Vega is heading east." *The Book of the Songs* says: "Looking up high into the splendid Milky Way, the Girl Weaver is busy with weaving day and night but making no beautiful clothes. And the Cowboy just couldn't pull the carriage like the real cattle." By taking the personalized weather of July, the lines above satirize that the Zhou Dynasty only focused on how to plunder property and enslave the people. At high position as they are, they could not relieve people's suffering. This provided a clue for the later fairy tales of the Cowboy and the Girl Weaver. In the Southern Dynasties, there were complete myths about the Cowboy and the Girl Weaver. *Jing Chu Sui Shi Ji* records: "In the east of the Milky Way, there was a girl weaver, the grandchild of the Emperor of Heaven, who every year worked hard with a loom to weave splendid clothes of brocade. The Emperor of Heaven pitied her for her solitude and allowed her to marry a cowboy in the west of the river. But the girl weaver stopped weaving after the marriage. Being angry with her, the Emperor ordered her to return to the east of the river and meet the cowboy once a year." Since then, their simple and sincere love stories have had a great impact on the people and produced various customs of Qixi Festival.

Collection of Nineteen Ancient Poems and many other documents witness the beautiful love passing down ages between mankind and God: "The Cowboy and the Girl Weaver, separated by just a river, the Milky Way, couldn't listen to each other." The love story of the Cowboy and the Girl Weaver has long been deeply rooted in the hearts of the people. Even the famous emperor Xuanzong of the Tang Dynasty (618–907 A.D.) and Yang Guifei, one of the empoisons concubine, chose to reveal their innermost feelings on that night. A few lines of *Chang hege* by Bai Juyi are about the emperor Xuanzong's reminiscence of their vows on the night of Qixi Festival after Yang Guifei's death: "On the quiet late night of July 7th, in the Changshen Palace, in heaven let us be two birds flying ever together, and on earth two trees with branches interlocked forever."

Praised by people, the seventh day of July has gradually become China's Valentine's Day and has been handed down till now.

(2) Diu Qiao Zhen

In traditional Chinese culture, people have a high demand of women's hand skilfulness ("Qiao" in Chinese) in employing needles ("Zhen" in Chinese). Therefore, on Qixi Festival, girls always try to ask for some handy skills.

In ancient times, people had the custom of Diu Qiao Zhen (Fig. 13-17), meaning throwing needles into the bowl full of water, on Qixi Festival. In the traditional agricultural society of China, "men farming and women weaving" was the main mode of production. The main social labour that women undertake was weaving, sewing and so on, which were called Nv Gong (needlework) and was attached great importance by them. It was recorded in *Di Jing Jing Wu Lue*, a culture book of the Ming Dynasty's that: "People have the activity of Diu Qiao Zhen at noon of July 7th, look at the needle shadows under the water. If the shadows are of shape of clouds, flowers, birds and animals, shoes, scissors and Shuiqie (a kind of solanum plant), which are called Qiqiao, while if that of only too thick, too thin or no shape, then bad ones." This custom was very popular in the Ming and Qing Dynasties.

Figure 13-17　Diu Qiao Zhen

(3) Qixi Water

In Guangzhou City and other places, people have the custom of taking "Qixi water". In the late Ming and early Qing Dynasties, Qu Dajun recorded in *Guangdong Xin Yu*: "at the time of first crow on the morning of Qixi Festival, the people of Guangzhou went to collect Qixi water (Xi water) from the rivers or wells. People collected and stored a lot of Xi water which had the same taste, even tasting sweeter to cure febrile disease and could be kept fresh through years. People called it holy water or Tian Sun Sheng. At the time of the second crow, the water then wouldn't be that good."

If two chickens sing, people think that taking spring water and river water on Tanabata Day, just like taking Silver River water, has the holy power of cleanliness. Therefore, every year when the rooster crows for the first time, people go to the riverside or well to collect water for storage. At this time, the weight of water is heavier than that of other times, the pureness and taste remains unchanged over the years, and the sweeter it is put, so it is called "holy water". This kind of water can treat febrile diseases, which are characterized by fever. When the chicken crows for the second time, water should not have such effect.

(4) Paoqiao and Huasheng

In the past, the practice of "Paoqiao" and "Huasheng" were popular somewhere in southern China. In "Paoqiao", bean sprouts were called "Spout of Qiao" or "Qiaoya". People ever threw "Qiaoya" instead of needles, onto the water surface for Qiqiao. In other regions, women bought wax baby puppets and float them on the water surface, believing it was good for bearing babies, calling it "Huasheng".

The connotation of water culture in these traditional festivals ranges from praying for a good harvest to more rich significance, which endows water with the auspicious meaning of health, happiness, wealth, wisdom, and diligence, and so on.

Section VI Water-related Festivals and the Ethnic Groups

When it comes to water-related festivals of ethnic groups, many people may immediately think of the Water Splashing Festival. In fact, many nationalities have their own water-related festivals. This section will introduce the water-related festival and its customs of three different nationalities.

1. The Dai People and Water Splashing Festival

The Dai people mostly live around water. They believe that water is the material that existed earliest, and it is water that breed all living things. *Ba Ta Ma Ga Peng Shang Luo*, the dialect of the Dai people, meaning the God creates the world. The Epic of Dai says that "in ancient times, the whole world was just chaos, without clear boundaries of heaven and earth, but only water and air. Later, water and air kept rolling and stirring with the blow of the cold wind, and finally Ying Ba, the ancestor of Dai was created, who created heaven and earth and all living things afterwards."

Most of the Dai people of China live in the southwest of China, where features tropical or subtropical climate, with rivers crisscrossed, lush vegetation, abundant rainfall, and rich natural resources. The main local crop is rice and the Dai people have their own unique rice farming habits. While water is indispensable in the growing process of rice, which means the life of the Dai people is greatly dependent on water. In *Yunan Annal* by Li Jing of the Yuan Dynasty, it says, "the local climate is hot and humid, and the typical buildings are bamboo huts. Living by the river, people must take ten baths a day." The 30th volume of *The Annal of Dian* (Dian means Yunan Province) says, "The Shui Bai Yi people (Dai people), both men and women, live by the river and bathe every day." Due to living by the river, the Dai people are called the nationality of water. With abundant water resources, rivers, and lakes to provide natural sports fields for the Dai people's sports of "swimming" and "diving". In the hot summer, drinking water or soaking in water can help people cool down. "Ten baths a day" is exaggerated, but clearly shows how important the water is to the Dai people.

The Dai people have many water-related festivals, among which the most popular and grandest is the Water Splashing Festival (Fig. 13-18).

Water and the Chinese Culture

Figure 13-18 Water Splashing Festival of Dai People

In the middle of April of each year is the new year of the Dai People, which usually lasts three or four days. The first day is called "Wan Duo Shang Han", which means "Songjiu", like Chinese New Year's Eve, to send off the old year; the second day is called "Wan Nao", or "Kongri zi", which means this day does not belong to the old year or the new year. On this day, all work stops. What do people do today? Splash water; the third day is called "Mai Pa Ya Wan Ma", or "the coming of Kongri zi", which is the beginning of the near year of the Dai calendar. On this day, people will hold important activities such as parade, dragon boat racing, Fang Gao Sheng (sending Kongming Lanterns or arrows with fire into the sky) and so on. People splash water at each other to express their best wishes.

Many people are not familiar with such activities as Fang Gao Sheng or Kongming lanterns. Gao Sheng is a kind of firework made by the Dai people, which is often set off at night. The bottom of the bamboo tube is filled with sulphur, nitric acid, and other gunpowder ingredients, which is placed on a frame. Igniting the fuse, the bamboo tube will go up high into the sky with a sharp whistling and blazing. What an enjoyable scene! Flying Kongming Lantern is also very popular there. When night falls, people light the candle inside the lantern and the lantern will slowly go up in the sky, like shining stars, with people's hope to be blessed by Buddha.

(1) Seven Women Killing the Devil

There is a best-known legend about the seven women killing the devil among the Dai people. Long ago, there was a cruel devil, who had powerful witchcraft. People just couldn't kill him with knives, halberds, water or fire. The devil was ferocious and stopped at nothing. He forced seven beautiful maidens to marry him, the last of which was a princess named Nan Zongbu, who was beautiful, kind-hearted, smart, and brave. In one new year of Dai, Nan Zongbu got to know the devil's secret blurted by himself when he was drunk: his weakness was that he could only be strangled to death by his own hair! When the devil was falling asleep, Nan Zongbu cut a single strand of his hair and strangled him. The devil's head fell apart from his body, while his head burst into a big fire, rolling around catching everything on fire. To get the fire under control, Nan Zongbu and the other six wives of the devil held the head until it rotted. To help the seven women with getting rid of the ash, people splashed water at them. From then on, people have this Water Splashing Festival to remember them when new year comes.

The Water Splashing Festival is also related to praying for rain. An old ballad called *December* is popular in the Dai region. When mentioning the origin of the Water Splashing Festival, the ballad depicts rain after a bad drought: "It was May and the big fire was burning everywhere, all the dry branches and thick bushes were falling down. When June came, there was a sudden rain, bringing back the vitality..." There is drought very often in the Dai region, so people often pray for rain. Water splashing is originally an activity of praying for rain, and people splash water at one another to imitate the witchcraft.

(2) Mild Splashing and Impetuous Splashing

Water splashing is divided into "Mild Splashing" and "Impetuous Splashing". The former is usually the blessing to the elders and people you respect. People will just sprinkle gently at the rear of others' neck by using branches, leaves, or flowers and send their best wishes before doing so.

As for the latter, impetuous splashing, it is to splash a bowl, a basin, or a bucket of water whether completely in the square or on the road, and the person who is splashed will immediately get soaked. When splashing water, people can chase and splash others, or even give others a sudden splash, and the persons who are splashed can run away but can't get angry. People take it as water of good luck, which can protect them from disasters and diseases, so they will enjoy it very much on this day. On this day, people will feel relaxed splashing water and cheerful laughter makes the festival a carnival. Nowadays, the Water Splashing Festival of Xishuangbanna, in Yunan Province attracts many tourists all over the world every year. People will enjoy splashing water of good luck at one another, no matter who you are or where you are from.

2. Tibetans and the Bathing Festival

The Bathing Festival, "Ga Ma Ri Ji" in Tibetan, meaning "bath". The Bathing Festival (Fig. 13-19) is a traditional festival of Tibetan people. It is said that seven or eight hundred years ago, there was a woman who was suffering from illness for a long time. One night, she had a dream. In the dream, a doctor named Yu Tuo said, "tomorrow night, when a bright star appears in the southeast of the sky, you can take a bath in the Jiqu river, and you will recover." This woman did so and recovered soon. Jiqu River is now Lhasa River. Since then, people believe that this magic star is reincarnation of Dr. Yu Tuo and go to bathe in the river, hoping to realize their wish of physical fitness and removing disease.

The Bathing Festival takes place in the first ten days of July of the Tibetan calendar. During the festival, all the families will come to the river to celebrate, bringing tents, and food and drink like beef and mutton, butter tea, highland barley wine, Zanba, tea, chatting and enjoying themselves, which usually lasts for one week. During this time, all members of the family, whether young or old, will take a bath in the river. The old usually take a bath, the young swim, and the children play in the water. All of them have a picnic by the water at noon. People are singing, dancing, and having a great time. It is said that bathing at this time can get rid of diseases, just like medical bath. Therefore, this festival is also called "Medical Bath Festival", which has its scientific basis. The water on the plateau is mainly the snow water melting from high mountains where many precious herbs such as "snow Letus" grow, involving the ingredients of the rare herbs in the crystal-clear water, which produces this natural bathing water with healthcare function. Nowadays, great changes have taken place and all kinds of modern bathrooms can be seen everywhere in the city, but some people still enjoy this tradition of bathing in the river.

Figure 13-19 The Bathing Festival

3. The De'ang People and the Jiaohua Festival

The De'ang Nationality is one of the 56 ethnic minorities of China. Its Jiaohua Festival is a romantic festival with a long history. It is seven days after Tomb-Sweeping Day. The festival combines the three dates of Buddha's birth, enlightenment, and nirvana. This three-day Jiaohua Festival is both the most important festival of the De'ang people of the year and an event that best embodies the traditional culture of this nationality. Same as its sense is with Water Splashing Festival of the Dai people, the activities of Jiaohua Festival are quite different.

There are different legends about the origin of this festival. Some people say that a disobedient son worked in the mountains on the seventh day after the Tomb-Sweeping Day when he saw the chicks feeding back the mother hen. It dawned on him, and he decided to serve his mother well. One day, his mother came to deliver food for him, but slipped and fell over. The son came up to help her, while his mother thought he was going to hit her, so she ran into a tree and died. The son regretted so much that he cut down the tree and carved it into a statue of his mother. Every year on the seventh day after the Tomb-Sweeping Day, he would wash the statue in warm water sprinkled with petals. Since then, it became a custom.

Some people say that Sakyamuni cared about the Benglong people (referring to the De'ang people) who were suffering from the bad drought and told them to carry water to splash on the Buddha statue every Duisha Festival (referring to Jiaohua Festival) to pray for rain, so that they would be blessed and have a good harvest.

During the festival, people clean the Buddha statues with water to show their memory and respect for their ancestors and benefactors with costumes. On the first day of the festival ceremony, people have activities such as picking flowers, inviting Buddha and bathing Buddha statues, carrying water and guarding Buddha statues. At dawn, the men and women followers of the village gather under the big trees at the village gate heading to the mountain to pick flowers. Young men lead the way by beating elephant foot drums and gongs. People sing and dance while picking flowers. The flowers are used to decorate the Longting (the pavilion temporarily built with bamboo strips and wood to bath the Buddha statues) outside the Zangfang (the Buddhist temple). After the decoration, presided over by Buddhists (the old who are responsible for chanting sutras), villagers start to pray and invite the Buddha statues. After inviting (means, moving) over ten statues, villagers get together in front the of the pavilion to listen to the Buddhists chanting and sprinkling water during the time, which is called "Sprinkle Ceremony". After chanting, villagers begin to bathe the Buddha statues, and the young people of the village will go to the puddles nearby and carry the water to bath the Buddha statues as well in the following days, two or three times a day. In the evening, the old people would sleep in the shed outside the Zangfang to guard the Buddha, and chant in the Longting to repent for offending gods of mountain and water when carrying water during the day.

Villagers will also present appreciation and best wish for the old people over sixty years by treating them to a dinner and celebrating their birthdays. There are norms in the way of sprinkling water. When sprinkling the old man, people will use the clear spring water in the bamboo pipe with flowers inside, with the water dripping down the flowers into the hands of the old people, but not onto his body. The respected elders will hold flowers, with fingers dipping into the water and gently sprinkling at the surrounding people to bless everyone and celebrate the advent of the new year. When young people pour water on each other, they also use bamboo pipes to gently sprinkle water from the shoulders, not on the heads. After that, people will head to the spring and riverside in lines, singing and dancing to celebrate the festival.

The end of the Jiaohua Festival signifies the start of the new year, and the village people should start working in the new year.

The celebration of Jiaohua Festival of the De'ang Nationality, involving music, dance, and painting, is widely welcomed. It reflects the virtue of society in respecting the old and caring about the young and getting along well with each other, and it is also a opportunity for young men and women to communicate or express their love as well.